THE
IDAHO
BIRD
GUIDE

what, where, when

THE
IDAHO
BIRD
GUIDE

what, where, when

edited by
Dan Svingen and Kas Dumroese

BACKEDDY
BOOKS

ISBN Number: 0-9710813-1-X
Second Edition
1   2   3   4
Printed in the United States of America

Publisher
Dan Svingen and Kas Dumroese

First Edition published by: American Birding Association, Inc.
First Edition Series Editor: Paul J. Baicich
First Edition Associate Editors: Cindy Lippincott and Bob Berman
First Edition Copy Editor: Hugh Willoughby

Layout and Typography
Bob Berman; using CorelVENTURA, Windows version 8.0

Maps
Cindy Lippincott; using CorelDRAW version 8.0

Cover Photography
front cover: *Red-breasted Nuthatch* by Stan Tekiela (© StanTekiela.com)
back cover: *Varied Thrush* by Alison Meyer, *Route 1, Box 62, Worley, ID 83876*

Illustrations
Mike Denny, *323 Scenic View Drive, College Place, WA 99324*

Publisher and Distributor:
Backeddy Books

For Idaho's Birders:
past, present, and future

ACKNOWLEDGEMENTS

Sitting on a couple of comfortable patio chairs in 1995, we discussed the need for an Idaho birdfinding guide. The more we chatted, the more apparent it was that no one person—or even one pair of persons—knew the state well enough to write such a guide. So we contacted everyone we knew (and several whom we didn't), and the result is what you hold in your hand, a truly collaborative effort. We thank the fifty-four authors who wrote about their favorite birding spots, provided data on "Idaho Rarities," and field-checked site descriptions. (Their individual names can be found at the beginning of their site descriptions.) We are grateful that they are a patient bunch, since this collaborative process was long and involved. We are thankful for additional field-checking performed by Tom Besser, Lucretia Chew, Philip Chu, Margaret Gorski, Geoff Hill, Elissa Landre, Jan and Neil Martin, Dan Taylor, Clare and Sharon Wiser, and managers of the parks, preserves, reserves, refuges, recreation areas, and wildlife management areas described in this book. Supplemental information provided by John Liller is also appreciated.

Our friend and fellow birder, Mike Denny, created the book's line-drawings, for which we are most thankful. Alison Meyer kindly donated the bird photograph on the back cover; the front cover photo is by Stan Tekiela.

This guide was originally published by the American Birding Association in their ABA/Lane Birdfinding Guide series. Their support and advice is gratefully acknowledged. Paul Baicich, as series editor, and Cindy Lippincott, as associate editor and meticulous mapmaker, were instrumental in this guide's completion. Bob Berman, another associate editor, helped bring text and tables to life; Hugh Willoughby, with exacting standards, served as copy editor. We also gratefully acknowledge the financial assistance provided by the Idaho Department of Fish and Game's Nongame Program.

A special thanks goes to our respective wives, Ila and Debbie, for patience, support, and understanding.

We are delighted, on behalf of all the authors, to donate royalties from this guide to the Idaho Rare Bird Committee in order to advance an awareness and appreciation for Idaho's birdlife.

Dan Svingen and Kas Dumroese

TABLE OF CONTENTS

AMERICAN BIRDING ASSOCIATION
PRINCIPLES OF BIRDING ETHICS

Everyone who enjoys birds and birding must always respect wildlife, its environment, and the rights of others. In any conflict of interest between birds and birders, the welfare of the birds and their environment comes first.

CODE OF BIRDING ETHICS

1. Promote the welfare of birds and their environment.

1(a) Support the protection of important bird habitat.

1(b) To avoid stressing birds or exposing them to danger, exercise restraint and caution during observation, photography, sound recording, or filming.

Limit the use of recordings and other methods of attracting birds, and never use such methods in heavily birded areas or for attracting any species that is Threatened, Endangered, or of Special Concern, or is rare in your local area.

Keep well back from nests and nesting colonies, roosts, display areas, and important feeding sites. In such sensitive areas, if there is a need for extended observation, photography, filming, or recording, try to use a blind or hide, and take advantage of natural cover.

Use artificial light sparingly for filming or photography, especially for close-ups.

1(c) Before advertising the presence of a rare bird, evaluate the potential for disturbance to the bird, its surroundings, and other people in the area, and proceed only if access can be controlled, disturbance can be minimized, and permission has been obtained from private land-owners. The sites of rare nesting birds should be divulged only to the proper conservation authorities.

1(d) Stay on roads, trails, and paths where they exist; otherwise keep habitat disturbance to a minimum.

2. Respect the law and the rights of others.

2(a) Do not enter private property without the owner's explicit permission.

2(b) Follow all laws, rules, and regulations governing use of roads and public areas, both at home and abroad.

2(c) Practice common courtesy in contacts with other people. Your exemplary behavior will generate goodwill with birders and non-birders alike.

3. Ensure that feeders, nest structures, and other artificial bird environments are safe.

3(a) Keep dispensers, water, and food clean and free of decay or disease. It is important to feed birds continually during harsh weather.

3(b) Maintain and clean nest structures regularly.

3(c) If you are attracting birds to an area, ensure the birds are not exposed to predation from cats and other domestic animals, or dangers posed by artificial hazards.

4. Group birding, whether organized or impromptu, requires special care.

Each individual in the group, in addition to the obligations spelled out in Items #1 and #2, has responsibilities as a Group Member.

4(a) Respect the interests, rights, and skills of fellow birders, as well as those of people participating in other legitimate outdoor activities. Freely share your knowledge and experience, except where code 1(c) applies. Be especially helpful to beginning birders.

4(b) If you witness unethical birding behavior, assess the situation and intervene if you think it prudent. When interceding, inform the person(s) of the inappropriate action and attempt, within reason, to have it stopped. If the behavior continues, document it and notify appropriate individuals or organizations.

Group Leader Responsibilities [amateur and professional trips and tours].

4(c) Be an exemplary ethical role model for the group. Teach through word and example.

4(d) Keep groups to a size that limits impact on the environment and does not interfere with others using the same area.

4(e) Ensure everyone in the group knows of and practices this code.

4(f) Learn and inform the group of any special circumstances applicable to the areas being visited (e.g., no tape recorders allowed).

4(g) Acknowledge that professional tour companies bear a special responsibility to place the welfare of birds and the benefits of public knowledge ahead of the company's commercial interests. Ideally, leaders should keep track of tour sightings, document unusual occurrences, and submit records to appropriate organizations.

PLEASE FOLLOW THIS CODE— DISTRIBUTE IT AND TEACH IT TO OTHERS.

Additional copies of the Code of Birding Ethics can be obtained from:

ABA, PO Box 6599, Colorado Springs, CO 80934-6599.
Phone 800/850-2473 or 719/578-1614; fax 800/247-3329 or 719/578-1480; e-mail:
member@aba.org

This ABA Code of Birding Ethics may be reprinted, reproduced, and distributed without restriction. Please acknowledge the role of ABA in developing and promoting this code.

7/1/96

INTRODUCTION

Idaho is justifiably famous for its incredible recreational opportunities, such as downhill and cross-country skiing, snowmobiling, fly-fishing, rock-climbing, white-water rafting, kayaking, backpacking, and hunting. There's plenty of room for these activities, since an astounding two-thirds of the state is publicly owned. Few people however, put Idaho on their list of top birding destinations. That's unfortunate, since the state has much to offer to birders.

Idaho is blessed with a fascinating mix of Rocky Mountain and Great Basin birds, incredible scenery, and great habitat diversity. In many places, you can drive from low-elevation sagebrush to high-elevation alpine tundra in a couple of hours.

Especially alluring is the opportunity for *real* exploration. An ever-present theme in Idaho birding is "nobody knows." The simple fact is that Idaho birders are spread thin (*real thin*), with about one dedicated birder for every one *million* acres. That fact means that, regardless of your level of expertise, *you* can make a significant contribution to Idaho ornithology. Our motivation for compiling this guide is to encourage more birding, so that more can be learned about Idaho's avifauna.

When Lewis and Clark passed through Idaho they recorded a mere two dozen species. At the time that was real "discovery." Today other discoveries await; this book will help you to make them a reality.

Please, come to Idaho. Enjoy the scenery. Have fun. Explore the hinterlands. Find great birds—then tell *us* about them!

ABOUT IDAHO

Idaho's geology, climate, and vegetation are extreme. A short synopsis of Idaho's geology would include tales of ocean shores, a collision with Pacific islands, belching volcanoes, a huge meteorite, mighty glaciers, and catastrophic floods. The wonderfully varied topography created by these forces allows one end of state to be dominated by wet, maritime-influenced climate, while the other end is high desert. Vegetation varies from moisture-loving Western Hemlock to drought-resistant Creosote-bush. Even Idaho's shape is extreme: 50 miles wide at the north end, 300 miles wide at the south, and a full 500 miles long. Idahoans are extreme, too, ranging from rugged, individualist fourth-generation loggers and ranchers to recent urban refugees intent on developing microchips.

To understand Idaho, you must understand its two halves: the mountains and the Snake River Plain. This division pervades many aspects of Idaho culture, including both pre- and post-European settlement history, current land use, land-ownership patterns, religion, politics, and transportation systems.

Mountains dominate northern and central Idaho. Depending on who does the counting, there are about 39 mountain ranges. Major chains include the Selkirks, Bitterroots, Clearwaters, Salmon Rivers, and Boises. Valleys between these ranges are natural migration corridors which support the greatest bird diversity, especially in conjunction with large lakes and reservoirs. The mountains themselves are covered with coniferous forest and are largely administered by the United States Department of Agriculture's Forest Service.

The Snake River Plain begins near Yellowstone National Park and extends in a sweeping curve to the southwest. This is Idaho's agricultural heartland, supporting the bulk of the human population. Fourteen of Idaho's 15 largest communities are within 25 miles of the river. The Snake River is the state's economic catalyst, providing hydro-power and precious irrigation water. Historically, most of this area was shrub-steppe, but vast tracts have been replaced by towns and farm fields. Most remaining shrub-steppe habitat is administered by the United States Department of the Interior's Bureau of Land Management.

ECOLOGICAL OVERVIEW

An appreciation of Idaho's major ecological divisions can help to focus your birding efforts. The problem is that Idaho can be divided up in any of a dozen or more ways. Although the division between the mountains and the Snake River Plain is an important one, a more refined system is necessary for our purposes. We use the "ecoregion" system[1]. There are five ecoregions in Idaho: Northern Rocky Mountain, Palouse Prairie, Middle Rocky Mountain, Intermountain Semidesert, and Southern Rocky Mountain (see map inside front cover). All of these ecoregions are generally coldest in December (20-35°F) and hottest in July and August (80-95°F). Most precipitation occurs from fall through spring; summers are dry with extremely low humidity.

[1]Idaho's main ecoregion provinces were defined by Bailey, divided into sections by McNab and Avers, and mapped by Nesser and Ford:

Bailey, R.G. 1995. *Description of the Ecoregions of the United States* (with separate map at 1:7,500,000). 2nd Edition. Washington, DC: USDA Forest Service Misc. Pub. 1391. 108 pp.

McNab, W.H., and P.E. Avers. 1994. *Ecological Subregions of the United States: Section Descriptions.* Washington, DC: USDA Forest Service Ecosystem Management Administrative Publication WO-WSA-5. 267 pp.

Nesser, J., and G. Ford. 1995. A 1:2,000,000 map entitled: *Subsections: Interior Columbia Basin Ecosystem Management Project, Version 2.0.* Missoula, MT: USDA Forest Service Intermountain Fire Sciences Lab.

Bird species common to all ecoregions include Cinnamon Teal, Osprey, Gray Partridge, Northern Saw-whet Owl, Calliope Hummingbird, Red-naped Sapsucker, Western Wood-Pewee, Dusky Flycatcher, Violet-green Swallow, Steller's Jay, Clark's Nutcracker, Black-billed Magpie, Mountain Chickadee, American Dipper, Golden-crowned Kinglet, Mountain Bluebird, Townsend's Solitaire, Warbling Vireo, MacGillivray's Warbler, Western Tanager, Black-headed Grosbeak, Lazuli Bunting, Spotted Towhee, Yellow-headed Blackbird, Bullock's Oriole, Cassin's Finch, and Red Crossbill.

Ecological differences between ecoregions are detailed below, along with lists of typical and specialty birds (i.e., species that are easiest to find in that ecoregion). Of course, every bird is also associated with its preferred habitat. To help you to further focus your birding, we have listed the habitats found at each birding site (see pp. 13-15 for more details).

Northern Rocky Mountain

The mountainous and conifer-dominated Northern Rocky Mountain Ecoregion extends from Canada to the Middle Fork Clearwater River. Mountain ranges, including the Selkirks, Cabinets, and Bitterroots, vary from 1,200 to 10,000 feet high with treeline at around 8,000 feet. Three large, glacier-scoured lakes punctuate the forest: Priest Lake, Coeur d'Alene Lake, and Lake Pend Oreille, one of the world's deepest at 1,150 feet.

Most of this ecoregion is influenced by maritime climate. At lower elevations, annual precipitation averages 20 to 40 inches, with most of it arriving as 30 to 80 inches of wet snow during winter. Douglas-fir and Grand Fir are the most abundant conifers, although Lodgepole, Ponderosa, and Western White Pines, Western Larch, and Western Redcedar are also common. Western and Mountain Hemlocks and Engelmann Spruce are present in lesser amounts. At the highest elevations Whitebark Pine, Subalpine Fir, and Subalpine Larch add to the conifer diversity.

The combination of maritime-influenced climate and highly productive soils makes this ecoregion one of the Inland Northwest's most productive forest lands, as well as one of the most beautiful. Logging and recreation are primary land uses. Typical species include Ruffed Grouse, Vaux's Swift, Rufous Hummingbird, Hammond's Flycatcher, Gray Jay, Chestnut-backed Chickadee, Winter Wren, Varied Thrush, Bohemian Waxwing (winter), Red-eyed Vireo, Townsend's Warbler, and Red Crossbill. Specialties include Red-necked Grebe, Harlequin Duck, Black Swift, American Three-toed and Black-backed Woodpeckers, Boreal Chickadee, Pygmy Nuthatch, American Redstart, Northern Waterthrush, Pine Grosbeak, White-winged Crossbill, and Common Redpoll (winter).

Palouse Prairie

The Palouse Prairie Ecoregion extends into Idaho from Washington, diminishing along a jagged line from Moscow to Grangeville as prairie gives way to mountains. The Palouse is characterized by rolling loess dunes over basalt bedrock, providing some of the world's most productive dryland farming areas. Elevations range from 700 to 3,500 feet, with annual precipitation between 15 and 25 inches. Farming, mainly for wheat, peas, and lentils, is the primary land use.

The Palouse Prairie is Idaho's most transformed ecoregion. Only scattered fragments of native prairie have escaped both plow and housing developments. Where present, the native flora is characterized by rich stands of grass, especially Idaho Fescue and Bluebunch Wheatgrass, with a hardy mix of herbaceous plants. Along riparian strips or on north-facing slopes, there are scattered Ponderosa Pines, a few Quaking Aspens, and an understory of deciduous shrubs (hawthorn, Common Snowberry, Serviceberry, Chokecherry). In some areas, such as east of Moscow and west of Grangeville, flat, wet meadows are still covered with expanses of Common Camas, whose starchy, bulbous root was once an important food staple of the Nez Perce Indians.

Bird diversity is relatively low here, consisting mostly of common, widespread species. Examples of prominent birds are Mallard, Ring-necked Pheasant, Gray Partridge, American Kestrel, Rough-legged (winter) and Red-tailed Hawks, Great Horned Owl, Bohemian Waxwing (winter, in towns), Savannah Sparrow, Lazuli Bunting, Bullock's Oriole, and Western Meadowlark. This ecoregion is Idaho's best locale for Bewick's Wren, especially where deep, brush-covered ravines descend dramatically from the prairie to the Clearwater River.

Middle Rocky Mountain

From Grangeville and the Middle Fork Clearwater River on the north, this ecoregion extends southward through most of central Idaho. Its southern boundary is basically a line from Weiser to Mountain Home to Arco to Dubois.

Many of Idaho's highest peaks are in the Middle Rocky Mountain region, but typical elevations range from 3,000 to 7,000 feet. The climate is semiarid; heavy winter snows account for most of the 10 to 30 inches of annual precipitation. The resort town of McCall receives about 28 inches of annual precipitation, much of it occurring as 150 inches of dry snow.

Conifer forest covers much of the Middle Rocky Mountain Ecoregion. The most common tree species is Douglas-fir, with large amounts of Grand Fir, Lodgepole Pine, and Ponderosa Pine (northwestern half) also present. High-elevation forests include Engelmann Spruce, Subalpine Fir, and small stands of Whitebark Pine. Other conifer species found in the Northern Rocky Mountain Ecoregion are uncommon to absent here. In the lowest and driest elevations, sagebrush and grasses are the dominant vegetation. As in most of Idaho, this region's economy is centered on natural resources, with logging, ranching, mining, and tourism being important.

Typical bird species include Blue Grouse, Vaux's Swift, Rufous Hummingbird, Lewis's and Pileated Woodpeckers, Gray Jay, Winter Wren, Varied Thrush, Townsend's Warbler, and Cassin's Finch. Specialty species are Gambel's and Mountain Quail, Spruce Grouse, Flammulated Owl, Williamson's Sapsucker, White-headed and American Three-toed Woodpeckers, and Black Rosy-Finch.

Intermountain Semidesert

The Intermountain Semidesert encompasses most of southern Idaho, with three distinct subdivisions: 1) heavily farmed Snake River Plain; 2) expansive, rolling grass/sagebrush deserts; and 3) isolated, dry mountain ranges covered with juniper and Quaking Aspen. Elevations range from 3,000 to 8,000 feet. Precipitation is scant (8 to 20 inches per year) and arrives mainly as winter snow and rain. Several large wetlands protected as National Wildlife Refuges or Wildlife Management Areas provide the best birding. The main land uses are ranching and irrigated farming. Most of Idaho's famous potatoes are produced in the southeast portion of this ecoregion.

Typical species of the Intermountain Semidesert Ecoregion are Snowy Egret, White-faced Ibis, Swainson's and Ferruginous Hawks, Golden Eagle, Greater Sage-Grouse, California Quail, Virginia Rail, American Avocet, Long-billed Curlew, Franklin's Gull, Forster's Tern, Western Screech-Owl, Common Nighthawk, Western Kingbird, Horned Lark, Say's Phoebe, Canyon Wren, Sage Thrasher, Loggerhead Shrike, Yellow-breasted Chat, Green-tailed Towhee, Brewer's, Vesper, Lark, and Sage Sparrows, and Bullock's Oriole. Specialties include Clark's Grebe, Great and Cattle Egrets, Sharp-tailed Grouse, Barn and Burrowing Owls, Gray and Ash-throated Flycatchers, Pinyon Jay, Western Scrub-Jay, Juniper Titmouse, Blue-gray Gnatcatcher, Virginia's and Black-throated Gray Warblers, Black-throated Sparrow, Great-tailed Grackle, Scott's Oriole, and Lesser Goldfinch.

Southern Rocky Mountain

This ecoregion is restricted to Idaho's eastern boundary, encompassing only 5% of the state. It is characterized by glaciated volcanic calderas and dramatic mountain ranges separated by narrow river valleys. Coniferous forest is dominated by Douglas-fir and Lodgepole Pine, with some Subalpine Fir and Whitebark Pine at high elevations. Low elevations are covered with grasses (especially *Agropyron* and *Stipa*) and sagebrush. Elevations range from 5,000 to 12,000 feet. Average annual precipitation ranges from 16 to 40 inches. Logging, mining, and grazing are all important land uses.

Species regularly seen include Trumpeter Swan, Sandhill Crane, Willet, Long-billed Curlew, Broad-tailed Hummingbird, Green-tailed Towhee, and Fox Sparrow. Among the specialties are Red-necked Grebe, Great Gray and Boreal Owls, Northern Goshawk, American Pipit, and Pine Grosbeak.

BIRDING IDAHO

When to Come and Where to Go

In much of Idaho, spring migration is generally over before it is even noticed. There are only a few spots where migrants stack up, mostly along the Snake River Plain. Peak numbers and diversity occur in mid-May. If you are interested in seeing breeding species, plan on visiting from late May through early July. Remember that late May and early June is still the rainy season, particularly in the northern Panhandle. A few species, such as raptors and grouse, nest much earlier, mostly in February through April.

Fall shorebird migration peaks in late July/early August. The rest of fall migration is even more diffuse (both temporally and spatially) than spring migration. It is during fall migration (especially October to January), however, when most of the locally rare species are found. Large lakes and reservoirs are prime birding locations during this time of year, especially for vagrant waterfowl, shorebirds, and gulls. Late winter (February) and early spring (March) are usually slow, bird-wise.

As for locations, Sandpoint/Bonners Ferry is recommended for boreal species, while the southeast region has almost everything else packed into one small area. If you can explore only one region, stage out of Idaho Falls or Pocatello and take day trips into the wide variety of habitats within a few hours drive.

Critter and Plant Hazards

Idaho has ticks, Poison-Ivy, Western Rattlesnakes, scorpions, Black Bears, Grizzly Bears (just a few), and Mountain Lions. The easiest to encounter are ticks and Poison-Ivy. Even seeing one of the others is a rare event. Idaho ticks are generally large, brown, and a nuisance from early spring into early summer. Tuck your pants into your socks and your shirt into your pants. You'll likely feel 'em tickling your neck before they have a chance to burrow in. Do a check often, since ticks can be found in *any* vegetation (sagebrush can be particularly bad)—seemingly even in parking lots. Both Lyme Disease and Rocky Mountain Spotted Fever are carried by ticks in Idaho. Poison-Ivy is generally encountered in riparian zones. Remember the old adage, "Leaflets three, let it be." Common sense will go a long way toward avoiding problems with the larger creatures. For example, use proper camping etiquette to discourage bears.

There are other critters to be aware of. Most places have mosquitoes in season (i.e., spring and early summer), but they're particularly thick in the southeast mountains. Remember, too, that Moose aren't as stupid (or as slow) as they look. And, finally, keep your valuables locked up and out of sight to discourage thieves.

Driving Hazards

Expect some "interesting" motoring anywhere off of the Snake River Plain interstates. The major north/south highway (US 95) is only two lanes wide for most of its length, snaking up and down narrow canyons. One former governor calls it "the old goat trail," a description which may actually be giving it more credit than it deserves. Speed limits change every few miles (most of it is 55 or 65 m.p.h.), depending on whether you're on a straight stretch or on yet another curve. Many of the two-lane highways, including US 95, have had sections closed in the last few years because of floods, mudslides, or avalanches.

Beware of ice from late fall through late spring. Black ice is a real challenge to detect, and it often goes unnoticed until you're spinning into the ditch. If you are out in winter, carry a survival kit (extra clothes, supplemental heat, food, and water). You can get stuck in snow or mud without even trying hard. Think twice before leaving downtown without spare tire (and necessary equipment), extra food and water, tow rope, tire chains, and shovel. A listing of telephone numbers for the statewide and regional road-condition hotlines is given on p. 17.

In mountains, slow down (*way down*) on blind corners. A Citizens Band (CB) radio can improve safety near active logging areas. If you have one (not necessary but helpful), watch for signs at the start of any mountain road. The local CB channel should be posted (often abbreviated as, for example, "Ch 4" or "CB 4"). Switch to that channel, and say something like "car starting up the so-and-so creek road." Every time you pass a milemarker (which may simply be a number spray-painted on a roadside rock or tree), re-announce your presence with "car headed up so-and-so creek road, milemarker 3 to 4." If you get a response to the effect of "headed down so-and-so creek road, milemarker 4 to 3, loaded," *find a good pull-over and wait.* Once the logging truck passes, continue your journey. At any rate, be careful and remember that not everyone has a CB radio.

Two other common driving hazards in the mountains are driving too close to the outside road shoulder (don't assume that a road shoulder is stable), and sly pokes, which are small trees which have fallen and now jut out into the roadway. More than one vehicle has been skewered because its driver took a corner too close and too fast.

Time Zones

Idaho has two time zones: Pacific in the northern portion and Mountain in the south. You'll change time zones when you cross the Salmon River near Riggins.

Ethics and Local Attitudes

Please follow the American Birding Association's code of birding ethics (see pp. xi-xii), and be courteous, honest, respectful, and non-confrontational with locals. As pointed out earlier, birders are still a rarity in Idaho. You might meet folks who will assume that you are trying to find an endangered species so that you can shut down whatever land use they're most interested in.

Ask permission to enter private land. Fence posts and gates painted orange or red are thereby posted "no trespassing" even if no other signs are evident. All cultivated land is posted *de facto.* Entry into private, industry-owned timberland is usually allowed. Private, non-industrial timberland should be entered only after obtaining permission. Make sure that you wave at people whom you drive by, say "hello" to folks whom you walk past, and if you run into natives whose land-use ethic is different from yours, politely agree to disagree and get back to looking at birds.

Other Information

We strongly encourage Idaho birders to buy a copy of the *DeLorme Idaho Atlas and Gazetteer*. The DeLorme atlas covers the entire state, showing back roads and geographical place-names. It can be a very useful navigational aid. Although the current edition (1992) is somewhat outdated, it does a good job of depicting road locations, with the southeast corner of the state seeming to have the majority of the mapping errors. A bigger problem is that many road names shown in the DeLorme atlas are different from those on other maps, as well as from on-the-ground signs. DeLorme atlases are available from ABA Sales (see p. 326), and from most Idaho gas stations and grocery, book, and sporting-goods stores.

Idaho has two Rare Bird Alerts: Northern updated on Mondays (208/882.6195; transcripts available at http://www.palouseaudubon.org); and Southwest (208/368-6096), updated as warranted.

To gain a better understanding of the seasonal and geographic distribution of Idaho birds, refer to *Idaho Bird Distribution* by Daniel Stephens and Shirley Sturts, of which the second edition is due out shortly. This book plots species presence/absence by "latilongs," which is the area encompassed by one degree of latitude and one degree of longitude. Bird status at a more local scale is summarized in the excellent *Birds of East Central Idaho* by Hadley Roberts. Birders visiting northern Idaho will find *Birds and Birding Routes of the Idaho Panhandle*, by Shirley Sturts, helpful. These books, ordering information, and titles of other helpful books on Idaho are listed on pp. 322-323 and 325.

About 66% of Idaho is owned by the federal government, making the federal land-management agencies major sources of information. The USDA Forest Service and USDI Bureau of Land Management have offices scattered throughout the state, and they can provide guidance on camping, hiking, and local road conditions. Some agency biologists are birders and can provide additional tips.

Consider buying Forest Service or Bureau of Land Management maps (see pp. 17-18) to supplement the DeLorme atlas. United States Geological Survey maps can be obtained by writing USGS, Box 25286, Denver Federal Center, Denver, CO 80225 (telephone 888/ASK-USGS).

If you're looking for a place to stay, try renting one of the rustic recreational cabins or look-outs available from the USDA Forest Service. For further information, contact any of the National Forest Headquarters listed on p. 17. *Idaho Handbook* and *Idaho* (see p. 322) both list restaurants, motels, and tourist attractions, so they can be very useful for trip planning.

An Idaho highway map, more tourist information, and listings of all Idaho campgrounds and RV parks are available by telephoning 800/VISIT-ID.

Reporting Your Sightings

One motivation to compile this book was to increase birding activity and thus increase our knowledge of Idaho's avifauna. Please help by reporting your trip lists, specifying the date, the exact location, and the particulars of your sightings. Your data may be incorporated into the seasonal report for *North American Birds* and used to update latilong distributions. Rare birds should be thoroughly documented for evaluation by the Idaho Rare Bird Committee. To make sure that your information is used in a timely fashion, send it to the Regional Editor for *North American Birds* (the editor's address is updated in every issue; currently Dave Trochlell, 1931 Tallwood Lane, Boise, ID 83706-4040) or the Idaho Rare Bird Committee (address updated biannually in ABA Sales catalog). The current address for the Rare Bird Committee is Dr. Chuck Trost, Idaho Rare Bird Committee, 225 North Lincoln Avenue, Pocatello, ID 83204. Deadlines for submitting records for use in *North American Birds* are June 15 (March to May sightings), August 15 (June and July sightings), December 15 (August to November sightings), and March 15 (December to February sightings).

Idaho's Nongame Wildlife Program

The Idaho Department of Fish and Game (IDFG), responsible for preserving, protecting, and managing all Idaho wildlife, manages over 200,000 acres, including more than two dozen Wildlife Management Areas. IDFG's Nongame Wildlife Program (includes threatened *and* endangered species and Watchable Wildlife programs), in existence since 1982, is of particular interest to birders. The program helped produce the *Idaho Wildlife Viewing Guide* (see p. 322), describing 94 of the best and most easily accessible general wildlife viewing sites in the state. The guide has helped to popularize the "binocular logo" placed at the viewing sites. The IDFG has developed a series of nongame leaflets, several of which are on Idaho birdlife, and also has made available *Idaho Bird Distribution* by Daniel Stephens and Shirley Sturts (see p. 322). The Nongame Program has other projects of interest to birders, including backyard habitat improvements for wildlife, wildlife rehabilitation, placing bird feeders at nursing homes, and avian monitoring. For more information on the IDFG Nongame Wildlife Program (IDFG, Nongame Program, PO Box 25, Boise, ID 83707) see the end of the book (pp. 324-325).

Idaho Partners in Flight

Formed in 1992, Idaho's Partners in Flight (PIF) has over 100 cooperating members from government agencies and non-governmental organizations. This broad bird conservation network is striving to develop the best management practices for vital habitats in the state, such as riparian and shrub-steppe. Idaho PIF will also develop a statewide plan to monitor bird populations, production of young, and survival. Another plan will recommend research needed to answer the bird-related questions from private and public land managers. Idaho PIF not only focuses on broad avian management issues, but also the popularization of bird appreciation, such as through the promotion of International Migratory Bird Day (IMBD) in May. You can currently reach Idaho PIF through the IDFG Nongame Wildlife Program.

ABOUT THIS GUIDE

Our objective was "to produce a concise, informative, user-friendly guide to finding birds in Idaho." Each one of this guide's features was chosen because we believe that it makes trip planning easier and/or field use more efficient. The site descriptions are long on details and short on observations of Idaho's geology, ecology, and history. That weighting was chosen not because these subjects aren't interesting—just the opposite! Space limitations prevent us from treating those subjects properly. Instead, we suggest that you use one of the references listed on pp. 322-323.

Bird and Other Names in this Book

Bird names and taxonomic order follow the *Birds of Idaho Field Checklist*, 2003 and the *ABA Checklist* (6th edition, 2002) with a few exceptions. Two subspecies of Solitary Vireo, "Cassin's" and "Plumbeous," both of which nest in Idaho, were elevated to species status (in the *Forty-First Supplement to the AOU Check-List of North American Birds*, July 1997). Where we knew (or strongly suspected) the identity of either species by locale, we noted it; otherwise, the form was indicated as simply "Solitary" Vireo.

All the specific names of plants and animals are capitalized, while general names are not. For example, when we refer to sagebrush (of any species), the word is not capitalized, while Big Sagebrush is. See p. 327 for the common and scientific names of plants and animals other than birds that are mentioned in this book.

Regions in this Book

We've divided Idaho into four regions: Panhandle, Central, Southwest, and Southeast. A map introduces each region, showing the birding sites and major highways and towns. Regional boundaries follow county lines, and approximate those used by the *Birds of Idaho Field Checklist*.

The **Panhandle** region includes Benewah, Bonner, Boundary, Clearwater, Kootenai, Latah, Lewis, Nez Perce, and Shoshone Counties. **Central** Idaho includes Adams, Custer, Idaho, Lemhi, Valley, and Washington Counties. The **Southwest** region includes Ada, Blaine, Boise, Camas, Canyon, Elmore, Gem, Gooding, Jerome, Lincoln, Owyhee, Payette, and Twin Falls Counties. **Southeast** Idaho includes Bannock, Bear Lake, Bingham, Bonneville, Butte, Caribou, Cassia, Clark, Franklin, Fremont, Jefferson, Madison, Minidoka, Oneida, Power, and Teton Counties. Corresponding latilongs, for cross-referencing *Idaho Bird Distribution*, are shown on the *Birds of Idaho Field Checklist*.

We describe three types of "sites" in this guide. "Routes" are sites for which driving from one spot to another to another, with no one specific end-point in mind, is the whole idea. Routes involve a lot of birding from the car. "Areas" are sites where several good birding spots are located in close proximity, or within a single town or city. Sites not designated as either routes or areas are simply destinations to which you make a specific trip to a specific spot to view birds.

Site Headings

At the beginning of each site description are several headings, including Author(s), Highlights, Major Habitats, Location, and quality ratings. Highlights are bird species particularly easy to find at that site, or rare species for which the site is a relatively good bet. The listing of major habitats (defined below) should give you an idea of what to expect at a given site. Habitat categories are not meant to be technically precise.

The primary county and nearest town (miles as the corvid flies—not driving distance) are included so that sites are easier to find on a state highway map. We're also hoping to encourage county listing so that more fine-scale bird distribution data is collected.

The seasons referred to follow those used by *Field Notes*: Spring (March 1–May 31), Summer (June 1–July 31), Fall (August 1–November 30), and Winter (December 1–February 28). We have subjectively rated each site for the quality of spring, summer, fall, and winter birding that it normally provides. Ratings were defined as: * a nice place to spend some time; ** somewhere that you can find several "good" species; *** the best birding spot in these-here parts; and **** one of the best birding spots in Idaho. A "N/A" means that you can't bird the site during that season, usually because access is denied by snow or mud, or in a few instances, because the area is seasonally-closed to protect wildlife.

You will find a chart at the end of the book listing the "Best Sites." These are all the three-star and four-star sites. The chart, which can help you to plan your birding trip by location and season, begins on page 320.

Habitat Definitions

Cliff. Steep rocky things. Cliffs are often used by nesting Canada Geese, Red-tailed Hawks, Golden Eagles, Prairie Falcons, Cliff Swallows, Common Ravens, Rock and Canyon Wrens, and American Dippers. In winter, abandoned Cliff Swallow nests are used by roosting Black and Gray-crowned Rosy-Finches.

Deciduous Forest. This habitat is dominated by deciduous trees (most often Quaking Aspen or cottonwoods) or tree/shrubs (hawthorn, alder, willow, etc.), and includes everything from narrow willow strips along a brook, to isolated patches of Russian-olive. Deciduous Forest is one of Idaho's birdiest habitats. Look there for Sharp-shinned, Cooper's, Swainson's, and Red-tailed Hawks, American Kestrels, Ruffed Grouse, Wild Turkeys, California Quail, Mourning Doves, Western Screech-Owls, Great Horned and Long-eared Owls, Northern Saw-whet Owls, Calliope Hummingbirds, Red-naped Sapsuckers, Lewis's, Downy, Hairy, and Pileated Woodpeckers, Northern Flickers, Western Wood-Pewees, Willow and Cordilleran Flycatchers, Western and Eastern Kingbirds, Tree Swallows, Black-billed Magpies, American Crows, Black-capped Chickadees, House Wrens, Swainson's Thrushes, Veeries, American Robins, Gray Catbirds, Cedar Waxwings, Plumbeous and Warbling Vireos, Orange-crowned, Nashville, Yellow, and Wilson's Warblers, Black-headed Grosbeaks, Lazuli Buntings, Spotted Towhees, Fox Sparrows, Bullock's Orioles, and American Goldfinches.

Dry Conifer Forest. We have referred to Ponderosa Pine, Douglas-fir, and Lodgepole Pine forests as Dry Conifer Forest. These habitats usually have open understories of grass (often Bluebunch Wheatgrass or Idaho Fescue) and small shrubs (Oceanspray, Mallow Ninebark, Common Snowberry, etc.). Birds to watch for include Northern Goshawks, Blue and Spruce Grouse, Wild Turkeys, Flammulated Owls, Western Screech-Owls, Great Horned Owls, Common Nighthawks, Williamson's Sapsuckers, Lewis's, White-headed, and Pileated Woodpeckers, Northern Flickers, Dusky and Cordilleran Flycatchers, Steller's Jays, Clark's Nutcrackers, Mountain Chickadees, White-breasted and Pygmy Nuthatches, Brown Creepers, Mountain Bluebirds, Townsend's Solitaires, Cassin's Vireos, Orange-crowned, Nashville, and Yellow-rumped Warblers, Western Tanagers, Chipping Sparrows, Dark-eyed Juncos, Cassin's Finches, and Red Crossbills.

Farmland. Plowed land used to raise cereal grains and row-crops. Expect Canada Geese, Mallards, Red-tailed Hawks, Swainson's Hawks, American Kestrels, Gray Partridges, Ring-necked Pheasants, California Quail, Killdeer, Ring-billed and California Gulls, Rock Pigeon, Mourning Dove, Barn and Great Horned Owls, Northern Flickers, Western and Eastern Kingbirds, Barn Swallows, Black-billed Magpies, American Crows, Common Ravens, European Starlings, Yellow Warblers, Savannah and Song Sparrows, Red-winged and Yellow-headed Blackbirds, Western Meadowlarks, Brewer's Blackbirds, Brown-headed Cowbirds, House Finches, and House Sparrows.

Grassland. As defined here, grasslands are areas dominated by grasses (what a stretch, huh?). In general, grassland habitats have not been plowed, but do include hay-land and Conservation Reserve Program (CRP) land. Dominant vegetation includes Bluebunch Wheatgrass and Idaho Fescue (natives) and/or Cheatgrass and Medusahead Wildrye (aliens). Swainson's, Ferruginous, and Rough-legged (winter) Hawks, Sharp-tailed Grouse, Burrowing and Short-eared Owls, Western Kingbirds, Horned Larks, Say's Phoebes, Western Meadowlarks, and Grasshopper, Vesper, Lark, and Savannah Sparrows are often seen in grassland habitats.

Juniper. These very dry forests, found in southern Idaho, are dominated by Utah, Western, and Rocky Mountain Junipers, Pinyon (local) and Limber Pines, and Curl-leaf Mountain Mahogany. There is typically an understory of grasses, forbs, and small shrubs (bitterbrush, sagebrush, rabbitbrush). Mourning Doves, Common Poorwills, Broad-tailed Hummingbirds, Gray and Ash-throated Flycatchers, Western Scrub-Jays, Pinyon Jays, Black-billed Magpies, Juniper Titmice, Bushtits, Loggerhead Shrikes, Virginia's and Black-throated Gray Warblers, Green-tailed Towhees, Dark-eyed Juncos, Chipping Sparrows, and Scott's Orioles breed in such areas.

Meadow. This habitat is similar to grasslands, but is wetter and is typified by thick expanses of grasses, sedges, and rushes. Meadows are often covered by surface water into the early growing season. Killdeer, Wilson's Snipe, Willow Flycatchers, Violet-green and Tree Swallows, Brewer's Blackbirds, and Lincoln's and Savannah Sparrows can often be found in meadows.

Mixed Conifer Forest. All conifer forests not classified as dry or juniper forest fit this category. Mixed Conifer Forest is primary habitat for Cooper's and Sharp-shinned Hawks, Ruffed Grouse, Northern Saw-whet Owls, Vaux's Swifts, Hairy and Pileated Woodpeckers, Hammond's Flycatchers, Gray and Steller's Jays, Common Ravens, Mountain and Chestnut-backed Chickadees,

Red-breasted Nuthatches, Winter Wrens, Varied and Swainson's Thrushes, Golden-crowned Kinglets, Yellow-rumped and Townsend's Warblers, Western Tanagers, Cassin's Finches, Pine Siskins, and Red Crossbills.

Shrub-steppe. Dry grasslands intermixed with extensive stands of sagebrush and/or bitterbrush are classified as Shrub-steppe. This habitat is most common in southern Idaho. Typical shrub-steppe birds include Turkey Vultures, Rough-legged (winter) and Ferruginous Hawks, Golden Eagles, Prairie Falcons, Gray Partridges, Sharp-tailed and Greater Sage-Grouse, Chukars, Burrowing Owls, Common Nighthawks, Common Ravens, Horned Larks, Rock Wrens, Sage Thrashers, Loggerhead Shrikes, Vesper, Lark, Sage, and Brewer's Sparrows, Western Meadowlarks, and Brewer's Blackbirds.

Wetland. As used here, "wetland" encompasses mostly lakes, ponds, rivers, and reservoirs, and is, arguably, Idaho's birdiest habitat. Common Loons, Pied-billed, Horned, Red-necked, Eared, Western, and Clark's Grebes, American White Pelicans, Double-crested Cormorants, Great Blue Herons, Snowy and Cattle Egrets, Black-crowned Night-Herons, White-faced Ibises, waterfowl, Ospreys, Bald Eagles, Virginia Rails, Soras, American Coots, shorebirds, gulls, terns, Marsh Wrens, Common Yellowthroats, Song Sparrows, and Red-winged and Yellow-headed Blackbirds use wetlands regularly.

Urban. Habitat found in cities and towns, with utility-pole overstories and asphalt understories. Look for Great Blue Herons, Wood Ducks, Mallards, California Quail, Killdeer, Ring-billed and California Gulls, Rock Pigeon, Mourning Dove, Western Screech-Owls, Great Horned Owls, Belted Kingfishers, Downy and Hairy Woodpeckers, Northern Flickers, Western and Eastern Kingbirds, Violet-green Swallows, American Crows, White-breasted Nuthatches, House Wrens, Golden-crowned and Ruby-crowned Kinglets, American Robins, Bohemian (winter) and Cedar Waxwings, European Starlings, Yellow and Yellow-rumped Warblers, Chipping and Song Sparrows, Dark-eyed Juncos, Red-winged and Brewer's Blackbirds, Cassin's and House Finches, Pine Siskins, American Goldfinches, and Evening Grosbeaks (winter).

Maps, Directions, Site Text, and Other

Starting directions for each site are included in a distinct section for easy reference. We have indicated what direction a given turn is, particularly important if you happen to be running a route backwards. (It helps to carry a compass.)

For many sites an additional, detailed map is provided. Numbers in black or gray boxes correspond to the mileage figures given in the text. Milepost numbers are also highlighted in boxes, but have the word "milepost" across the top. We've used mileposts whenever possible, since mileposts are more permanent landmarks than many other features. Mileposts are given to the nearest tenth-mile when known, but be aware that odometers vary. Don't be surprised if you're off a tenth or two. The farther you go, the more cumulative the error may be. It helps to remember that milepost numbers on even-numbered highways and on interstates increase from west to east. Odd-numbered highways run south and north, so their milepost numbers increase heading north. Be aware that other types of roadways do not necessarily follow the same protocol.

As noted above, we encourage all Idaho birders to pick up a *DeLorme Idaho Atlas and Gazetteer*, as well as local USDA Forest Service and USDI Bureau of Land Management maps. Be aware that road names are often different between various maps. Where we knew of such discrepancies, we listed alternative road names, using the initials "a.k.a." for "also known as." Because of Idaho's complex mix of public, private, and corporate land ownership, we have identified public versus private land when known. At the end of each site description, the "Other" section provides a few notes focusing mostly on where more information can be obtained, and where the closest services (fuel, food, lodging) are located.

Commonly used words, phrases, and organizations have been abbreviated as follows:

BLM—USDI Bureau of Land Management
BOR—USDI Bureau of Reclamation
FR—Forest Road (USDA Forest Service)
FS—USDA Forest Service
I—Interstate highway
ID—Idaho state highway
IDFG—Idaho Department of Fish and Game
NF—National Forest (USDA Forest Service)
NWR—National Wildlife Refuge (USDI Fish and Wildlife Service)
SP—Idaho State Park
US—United States highway
WMA—Wildlife Management Area (State of Idaho)

USEFUL TELEPHONE NUMBERS AND ADDRESSES

Idaho Travel Council, 700 West SW State Street, PO Box 83720, Boise, ID 83720-0093. (800/VISIT-ID [800/847-4843] or 800/635-7820).

Idaho Department of Transportation (24-hour Road Condition Hotlines)
IDT Statewide: 888/IDA-ROAD [888/432-7623]
Treasure Valley (Boise Region): 208/336-6600

Idaho Department of Fish and Game
Headquarters, Box 25, Boise, ID 83707 (208/334-3700).
Panhandle Region, 2750 Kathleen Avenue, Coeur d'Alene, ID 83814 (208/769-1414).
Clearwater Region, 1540 Warner Avenue, Lewiston, ID 83501 (208/799-5010).
Southwest Region, 3101 South Powerline Road, Nampa, ID 83686 (208/465-8465).
   McCall Subregion, 555 Deinhard Lane, McCall, ID 83638 (208/634-8137).
Magic Valley Region, PO Box 425, Jerome, ID 83338 (208/324-4350).
Southeast Region, 1345 Barton Road, Pocatello, ID 83204 (208/232-4703).
Upper Snake Region, 1515 Lincoln Road, Idaho Falls, ID 83401 (208/525-7290).
Salmon Region, PO Box 1336, Salmon, ID 83467 (208/756-2271).

USDA Forest Service
Boise National Forest, 1249 S. Vinnell Way, Suite 200, Boise, ID 83709 (208/373-4100).
Caribou-Targhee National Forest, 1405 Hollipark Drive, Idaho Falls, ID 83401 (208/524-7500)
Clearwater National Forest, 12730 Highway 12, Orofino, ID 83544 (208/476-4541).
Hells Canyon National Recreation Area, PO Box 832, Riggins, ID 83549 (208/628-3916).
Idaho Panhandle National Forests, 3815 Schrieber Way, Coeur d'Alene, ID 83814 (208/765-7223).
Nez Perce National Forest, Route 2, Box 475, Grangeville, ID 83530 (208/983-1950).
Payette National Forest, PO Box 1026, McCall, ID 83638 (208/634-0700).
Salmon-Challis National Forest, 50 Hwy 93 South, Salmon, ID 83467 (208/756-5100)
Sawtooth National Recreation Area, HC 64, Box 8291, Ketchum, ID 83340 (208/727-5000)
Sawtooth National Recreation Area Headquarters Office, Star Route, Ketchum, ID 83340 (208/726-8291).

USDI Bureau of Land Management
Four Rivers Field Office and Owyhee Field Office, 3948 Development Avenue, Boise, ID 83705 (208/384-3300).
Burley Field Office, 15 East 200 South, Burley, ID 83318-9501 (208/677-6641).
Challis Field Office, 801 Blue Mountain Road, Challis, ID 83226 (208/879-6200).
Coeur d'Alene Field Office, 1808 North Third Street, Coeur d'Alene, ID 83814-3407 (208/769-5000).
Cottonwood Field Office, House 1, Butte Drive Route 3, Box 181, Cottonwood, ID 83522-9498 (208/962-3245).
Idaho Falls Field Office, 1405 Hollipark Drive, Idaho Falls, ID 83401 (208/524-7500).
Jarbidge Resource Area Office, 2620 Kimberly Road, Twin Falls, ID 83301-7975 (208/736-2350).
Pocatello Field Office, 1111 North 8th Avenue, Pocatello, ID 83201-5789 (208/478-6340).
Salmon Field Office, 50 Hwy 93 South, Salmon, ID 83467 (208/756-5400).
Shoshone Field Office, 400 West F Street, PO Box 2-B, Shoshone, ID 83352 (208/732-7200).

USDI Fish and Wildlife Service (National Wildlife Refuges)
Bear Lake National Wildlife Refuge, 370 Webster Street, PO Box 9, Montpelier, ID 83254 (208/847-1757).
Camas National Wildlife Refuge, 2150 East 250 North, Hamer, ID 83425 (208/662-5243).
Deer Flat National Wildlife Refuge, 13751 Upper Embankment Road, Nampa, ID 83686 (208/467-9278).
Grays Lake National Wildlife Refuge, 74 Grays Lake Road, Wayan, ID 83285. (208/574-2755).
Kootenai National Wildlife Refuge, HCR 60, Box 283, Bonners Ferry, ID 83805 (208/267-3888).
Minidoka National Wildlife Refuge, 961 East Minidoka Dam, Rupert, ID 83350 (208/436-3589).
Southeast Idaho Refuge Complex, 4425 Burley Drive, Suite A, Chubbuck, ID 83202 (208/237-6615).

(See p. 9 for Idaho Rare Bird Alerts.)

Errors and Corrections

After an author submitted a write-up for a particular site, we reformatted and word-smithed it. Because that process may have introduced errors, we rechecked the revised site descriptions on the ground, as did the authors. In addition, revised site descriptions were also field-checked by as many as four independent birding parties. After we entered corrections, both we and the original authors proofed the final maps and text for clarity and accuracy. Even with all this care, however, errors are certain to have escaped notice. Conditions on the ground also change quickly. It is not unusual—especially in logging country—for entire road systems to change within a year or two. It helps to remember this fact when you're lost (i.e., for what it's worth, it may be this guide which is mistaken, not you.) If so, it's our responsibility, not that of the individual site authors.

Corrections, deletions, updates, or suggestions for improving this book are welcome. Please send comments to: Kas Dumroese, 1096 Eid Road, Moscow, ID 83843.

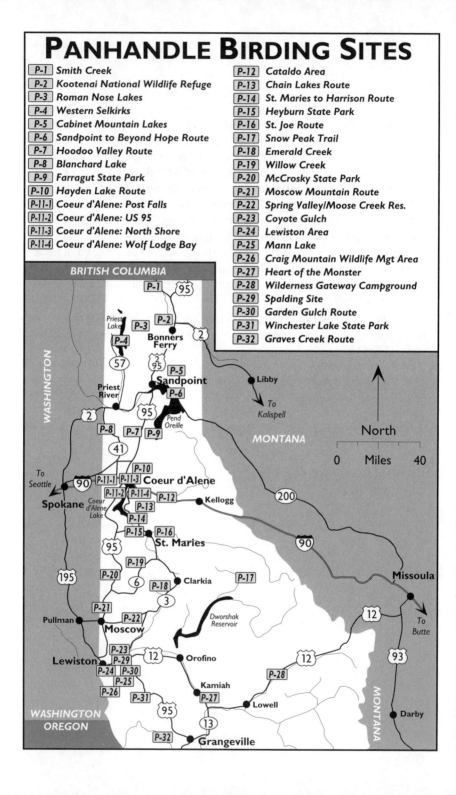

PANHANDLE BIRDING SITES

- P-1 Smith Creek
- P-2 Kootenai National Wildlife Refuge
- P-3 Roman Nose Lakes
- P-4 Western Selkirks
- P-5 Cabinet Mountain Lakes
- P-6 Sandpoint to Beyond Hope Route
- P-7 Hoodoo Valley Route
- P-8 Blanchard Lake
- P-9 Farragut State Park
- P-10 Hayden Lake Route
- P-11-1 Coeur d'Alene: Post Falls
- P-11-2 Coeur d'Alene: US 95
- P-11-3 Coeur d'Alene: North Shore
- P-11-4 Coeur d'Alene: Wolf Lodge Bay

- P-12 Cataldo Area
- P-13 Chain Lakes Route
- P-14 St. Maries to Harrison Route
- P-15 Heyburn State Park
- P-16 St. Joe Route
- P-17 Snow Peak Trail
- P-18 Emerald Creek
- P-19 Willow Creek
- P-20 McCrosky State Park
- P-21 Moscow Mountain Route
- P-22 Spring Valley/Moose Creek Res.
- P-23 Coyote Gulch
- P-24 Lewiston Area
- P-25 Mann Lake
- P-26 Craig Mountain Wildlife Mgt Area
- P-27 Heart of the Monster
- P-28 Wilderness Gateway Campground
- P-29 Spalding Site
- P-30 Garden Gulch Route
- P-31 Winchester Lake State Park
- P-32 Graves Creek Route

IDAHO PANHANDLE

Idaho's Panhandle stretches from Canada to the Clearwater River, encompassing the Northern Rocky Mountain and Palouse Prairie Ecoregions. Coeur d'Alene and Sandpoint, two of Idaho's fastest growing communities, are found here. In farmland areas, numerous small communities provide services, but gas stations, motels, and restaurants are scarce in the backwoods.

Most of the Panhandle is covered with dense, wet, mixed conifer forest. This is the most boreal of Idaho's regions, and resembles habitats in western Washington and southern British Columbia. Several large, deep-water lakes provide additional diversity.

The best summer birding is in the coniferous forest. Vaux's Swift, Hammond's Flycatcher, Chestnut-backed Chickadee, and Townsend's Warbler are all common, and Spruce Grouse, Black Swift, American Three-toed and Black-backed Woodpeckers, Boreal Chickadee, and White-winged Crossbill can be found with diligent searching. High-elevation habitats are particularly interesting, although bird numbers and diversity are often low due to the naturally low productivity. From fall to spring, most local birders concentrate on the large lakes, such as Pend Oreille, Coeur d'Alene, and Chatcolet. All are heavily used by waterfowl and other migrants. Winter birding is restricted to mid- and low elevations, as heavy, wet snows exclude all but the hardiest adventurers from the high country. Fighting Creek Landfill and downtown Coeur d'Alene host the state's best gull watching, with Mew, Herring, Thayer's, Glaucous-winged, and Glaucous Gulls now regular.

Red-necked Grebe
Mike Denny

21

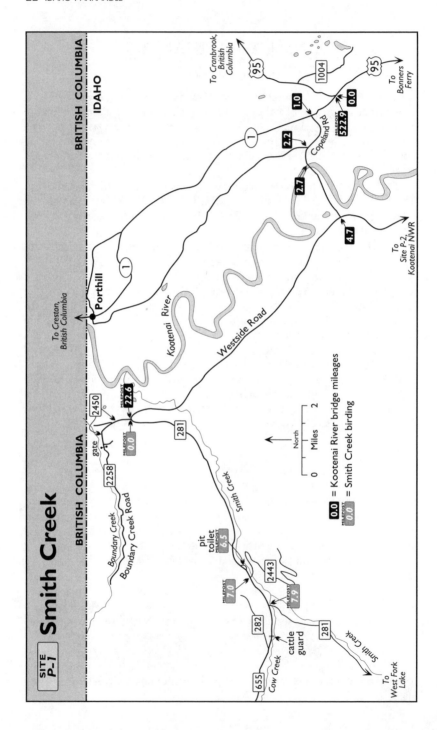

SMITH CREEK

Author: Earl Chapin

Site P-1 — Map P-1

Highlights: Black Swift, Boreal Chickadee, White-winged Crossbill
Major Habitats: Mixed Conifer Forest
Location: Boundary Co., 24 miles northwest of Bonners Ferry
Spring: N/A   **Summer:** * * *   **Fall:** * *   **Winter:** N/A

Just six miles from Canada, this 30-mile-long route will take you to Idaho's northern-most birding spot. All of Idaho's boreal bird species can be found here.

DIRECTIONS:

From Bonners Ferry follow US 95 north 14 miles. At milepost 522.9, turn left (north) on ID 1 (toward Porthill) and zero your mileage. At mile 1.0 turn left (west) on Copeland Road (toward Sportsman Access). At the Y at mile 2.2, continue straight (west) and cross the Kootenai River at mile 2.7. Stop to bird the bridge area, which can be very productive. Continue west to mile 4.7 and the T intersection. Turn right (north) onto Westside Road and follow it about 9 miles. (Mileposts here are marked with small white square signs.) At milepost 22.6 (mile 13.7), follow Westside Road as it makes a sweeping left curve and becomes FR 281 heading up Smith Creek. This is all public land (FS). (Mileposts here are the regular brown-and-white rectangular signs used by the FS.) FR 281 is paved for 6 miles, then turns to gravel. There's a pit toilet at milepost 6.5. Stay right at the Y at milepost 7. At milepost 7.9, FR 281 turns left (south; toward Westfork Lake), while FR 655 continues west (toward Shorty Peak) along Cow Creek.

BIRDING:

As you ascend FR 281, watch for Spruce Grouse along the road. The entire area by the FR 655/281 junction is excellent birding. Look in any forest opening (creeks, clearcuts, meadows) for flying Black Swifts. This is Idaho's most dependable spot for this elusive, enigmatic species. In forest areas, watch and listen for American Three-toed and Black-backed Woodpeckers, Boreal Chickadees, and White-winged Crossbills, as well as for a variety of more typical mixed conifer forest species.

The best place to look for Boreal Chickadees is along the first 3 miles of FR 655 west of the FR 655/281 junction. You'll cross a cattle-guard 1.2 miles west of this junction. Boreals are usually found within a few hundred feet either up or down the road from here. They are typically mixed in with other chickadees, nuthatches, and warblers, so look at every flock carefully.

A nice side trip is to backtrack all the way down FR 281 to where milepost 0 would be, and turn left (north) onto graveled Boundary Creek Road (a.k.a. FR 2450). In 0.4 mile stay left at the Y, and in about another mile you'll reach

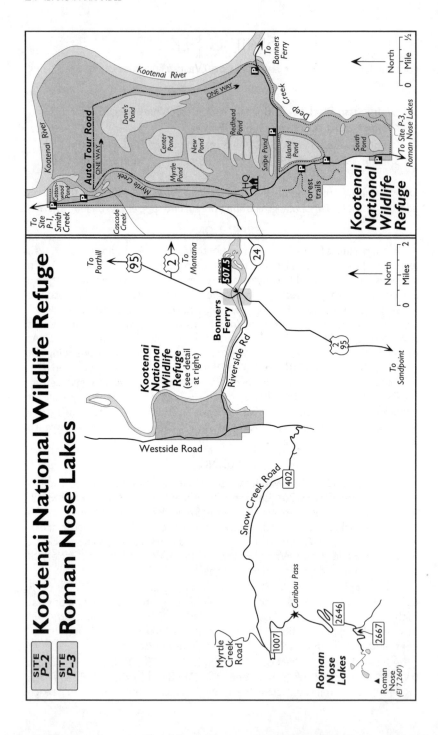

SITE P-2 **Kootenai National Wildlife Refuge**

SITE P-3 **Roman Nose Lakes**

the junction of FR 2450 and FR 2258. FR 2258 continues upstream along Boundary Creek. If the road is gated, walk. The first 3 to 4 miles are very good birding. At times as many as 25 to 30 Varied Thrushes can be seen along the road.

OTHER:

Bonners Ferry is a full-service community. A FS map can be very useful. Maps may be purchased at the FS station (208/267-5561) in Bonners Ferry (at US 95 milepost 505.2). It's possible that a Grizzly Bear could be somewhere in this general area, so remain alert.

KOOTENAI NATIONAL WILDLIFE REFUGE
Author: Earl Chapin
Site P-2 — Map P-2/P-3

Highlights: Waterfowl
Major Habitats: Wetland, Meadow
Location: Boundary Co., 5 miles west of Bonners Ferry
Spring: * * *   **Summer:** * * *   **Fall:** * * *   **Winter:** *

Large expanses of cattail marsh are rare in the Idaho Panhandle, making 2,774-acre Kootenai NWR a unique birding spot. Over 200 bird species have been recorded here. The refuge's location at the south end of the Purcell Trench increases the probability of finding vagrants.

DIRECTIONS:

Just south of the Kootenai River bridge at the north end of downtown Bonners Ferry, turn west at US 95 milepost 507.5 toward Kootenai NWR. Immediately bear right onto paved Riverside Road and follow it and the Kootenai River toward Kootenai NWR. Stay on pavement, and after about 5.5 miles you'll reach headquarters. Stop for a map and a checklist.

BIRDING:

The best way to bird the refuge is to drive the graveled 4.5-mile-long auto tour road that begins at headquarters, then hike along the 5 miles of trail. The 1.5-mile-long Island Pond Wildlife Trail has interpretive stops around a cattail marsh. Be aware that the auto tour is closed on Tuesdays, Thursdays, and weekends during the fall waterfowl hunting season.

Kootenai NWR can be a great spot for both waterfowl and shorebirds. In spring and fall Greater White-fronted Geese sometimes rest here, while Tundra Swans, Canada Geese, Barrow's Goldeneyes, and tens of thousands of Mallards stop by every year. Red-necked Grebe, American Bittern, Bald Eagle, Gray Partridge, and Black Tern are a few of the more interesting local breeding species. Watch for American Redstarts, too.

Rare species recorded at the refuge include White-winged and Surf Scoters, Great and Cattle Egrets, White-faced Ibis, Black-necked Stilt, Stilt Sandpiper, and Barn Owl. In winter, this is the best place in Idaho to find Common Redpoll flocks (check for Hoaries) feeding on seed plants surrounding the marsh. Deer and Coyotes are common, and there is usually a Moose or two living in the swamps.

OTHER:

Bonners Ferry is a full-service community. Kootenai NWR headquarters (208/267-3888) is open weekdays 8 am to 4:30 pm. See also Roman Nose Lakes, the next site.

ROMAN NOSE LAKES

Author: Earl Chapin

Site P-3 — Map P-2/P-3

Highlights: American Three-toed and Black-backed Woodpeckers
Major Habitats: Mixed Conifer Forest
Location: Boundary Co., 12 miles west of Bonners Ferry
Spring: N/A   **Summer:** * *   **Fall:** *   **Winter:** N/A

The Selkirk Mountains extend south from British Columbia, forming a long narrow peninsula. This is the most "boreal flavored" of Idaho's mountain ranges. It's here that the state's Woodland Caribous and Grizzly Bears precariously hang on to existence.

DIRECTIONS:

In Bonners Ferry turn west at US 95 milepost 507.5 (just south of the Kootenai River bridge) toward Kootenai NWR. Immediately bear right onto paved Riverside Road and follow it and the Kootenai River toward Kootenai NWR. After about 5 miles (inside Kootenai NWR) you'll come to a Y. Go left (south) onto the gravel road (Westside Road; unmarked). In another 3 miles, turn right (west) onto graveled FR 402 (a.k.a. Snow Creek Road) and head up Snow Creek. On the 20-mile-long trip to Roman Nose Lakes, both the road and the trails are well-marked. Stay on the well-traveled, well-maintained road. There are only two ungated roads. The first is about ten miles up FR 402; there, stay left (south), crossing Snow Creek, rather than dropping down Myrtle Creek Road. After crossing Snow Creek, the main road changes from FR 1007 to FR 2646 and finally to FR 2667. At mile 18, turn right toward Roman Nose Lakes. The road ends at Roman Nose Lake #3. From the trailhead here, it's an easy 3-mile round-trip to Roman Nose #1 and #2.

BIRDING:

Sharp-shinned and Cooper's Hawks, Downy, Hairy, American Three-toed, and Black-backed Woodpeckers, Clark's Nutcrackers, both kinglets, Swainson's and Hermit Thrushes, and Pine Grosbeaks frequent this area. This is a beautiful hike, and huckleberries are abundant in July and August.

OTHER:

A FS map can be very useful. Maps can be purchased at the FS station (208/267-5561) in Bonners Ferry (US 95 milepost 505.2). Bonners Ferry is a full-service community. See also Kootenai NWR (p. 25) and Smith Creek (p. 23).

WESTERN SELKIRKS
Author: Earl Chapin
Site P-4 — Map P-4

Highlights: Spruce Grouse, American Three-toed Woodpecker
Major Habitats: Mixed Conifer Forest
Location: Bonner Co., 30 miles north of Priest River
Spring: N/A   **Summer:** * * *   **Fall:** * *   **Winter:** N/A

The Priest Lake area is very popular with fishermen, but it's largely unexplored by birders. What exciting finds occur on or around Priest Lake is anyone's guess. For finding boreal species, however, your best bet is to leave the lake behind and head up the western slope of the Selkirk Mountains.

DIRECTIONS:

From the junction of US 2 and ID 57 in Priest River (US 2 milepost 5.9), follow ID 57 (a.k.a. Westside Road) north. At milepost 22.5, turn right (east) on Coolin Road. The junction of ID 57 and Coolin Road is commonly called Dickensheet Junction on maps, although nothing on the ground identifies it that way. Follow Coolin Road northeast to Coolin in 5.4 miles.

In Coolin turn right (east) onto Eastshore Road (a.k.a. Road 1), zero your mileage, and follow the sign for "Priest Lake State Park" and "Cavanaugh Bay." At mile 3.3 turn left (north) and follow the paved road about one mile to the Idaho Department of Lands (IDL) Priest Lake Area Office. Stop and buy a $3 map and check on recent road closures and conditions. Continue straight to the stop-sign and turn left (north) onto Eastshore Road. Follow it as it parallels the east shore of Priest Lake for about 20 miles. Eastshore Road is paved to milepost 17.5.

There are several roads that head east from Eastshore Road into the Selkirks. All of these roads cross public land (IDL). Roads are maintained for logging, not for recreation. They are numbered but without detail. Road numbers increase heading both north and east. An IDL map and an orienteer-

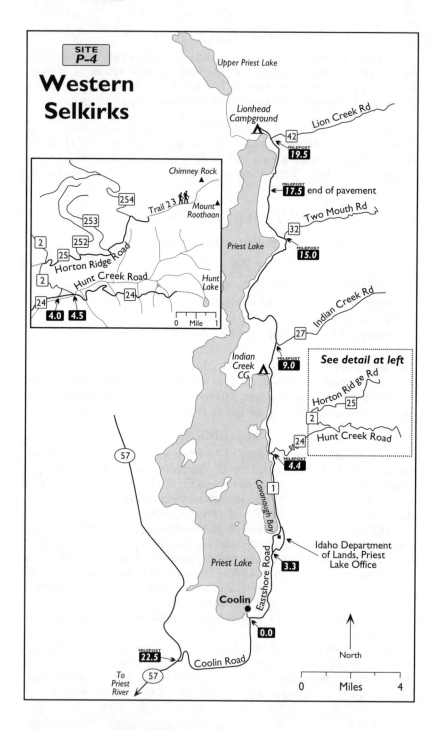

SITE
P-4

Western
Selkirks

Upper Priest Lake

Lionhead
Campground

Lion Creek Rd

42

MILEPOST
19.5

MILEPOST
17.5 end of pavement

Two Mouth Rd

32

MILEPOST
15.0

Priest Lake

Chimney Rock

254

Trail 23

Mount
Roothaan

253

252

25

2

Horton Ridge Road

2

Hunt Creek Road

24

Hunt
Lake

24

24

4.0 **4.5**

0   Mile   1

Indian Creek Rd

27

Indian
Creek
CG

MILEPOST
9.0

See detail at left

Horton Ridge Rd

25

2

24

Hunt Creek Road

MILEPOST
4.4

1

57

Cavanaugh Bay

Idaho Department
of Lands, Priest
Lake Office

Priest Lake

Eastshore Road

3.3

Coolin

0.0

North

MILEPOST
22.5

Coolin Road

57

To
Priest
River

0   Miles   4

ing compass can be helpful. A high-clearance vehicle is a must, and except for the drier portions of August and September, 4-wheel-drive is warranted. The best roads for birding are Hunt Creek (Road 24) at milepost 4.4, Horton Ridge (Road 25) accessed from Hunt Creek, Indian Creek (Road 27) at milepost 9, Two Mouth Road (Road 32) at milepost 15, and Lion Creek Road (Road 42) at milepost 19.5.

An explorer's attitude can be vital for birding this area. There is no one place to investigate, and even if there were, logging, road-building, and bird movements constantly change the situation, anyway.

BIRDING:

All roads mentioned above are good for Spruce and Blue Grouse, American Three-toed and Black-backed Woodpeckers, and Clark's Nutcrackers, as well as for the more common mixed conifer forest species such as Swainson's, Hermit, and Varied Thrushes, Black-headed Grosbeaks, and Fox Sparrows. Other interesting species possible include Northern Goshawk, Barred Owl, Boreal Chickadee, Pine Grosbeak, and White-winged Crossbill.

My favorite route is Hunt Creek Road (a.k.a. Road 24). From milepost 4.4 on Eastshore Road, zero your mileage and head uphill. Stay right at the Ys at miles 2.1 and 4.0. There's another Y at mile 4.5 marked with a sign discussing reforestation of burned land. Go left (east) along the north bank, rather than take the rough, rocky road along the south bank. Hunt Creek Road ends at a trailhead in another 4 miles.

Another great spot is Mt. Roothaan, which is at the end of the Horton Ridge Road (a.k.a. Road 25). Access to Horton Ridge Road from Eastshore Road is now blocked, so start by heading up Hunt Creek Road, staying right at all Ys. If you happen to see Road 2 veering off to the left at about mile 4, go for it (see map). Otherwise, continue to the aforementioned Y at mile 4.5 marked with the reforestation sign. Make a U-turn and backtrack 100 feet across the culvert (Hunt Creek) and head up the gravel road to the right (Road 2). In a mile this brings you to Horton Ridge Road. Turn right (east) onto Horton Ridge; almost immediately Road 2 heads off to the left. As of this writing, there are three roads (252, 253, 254) heading off from Horton Ridge Road, each about a mile apart and each heading off to the left. Horton Ridge Road is the most reliable spot for Spruce Grouse in this entire area. The last 0.5 mile of road is very rough. From the trailhead at road's end, it's about a 3-mile hike to Chimney Rock. This beautiful alpine area is the only place in the Idaho Panhandle where American Pipits are known to nest. White-tailed Ptarmigans have been reported in the meadows on the east side of Chimney Rock. To get to this area you must go between Roothaan and Chimney Rock. Stay just to the north base of Roothaan and go east over the saddle, which requires rock scrambling, but not technical rock climbing.

OTHER:

Developed campgrounds (pit toilets, water, picnic tables, boat launch) are available at Indian Creek and Lionhead along the east shore of Priest Lake. Both parks are open during winter for snow camping. Indian Creek also has a trailer dump and a park store open in season (weekends in May and full-time June to September). Priest Lake SP Headquarters (208/443-2200) are at Indian Creek. Camping reservations are recommended.

Fuel, food, and lodging are available in Priest River. Other services are available in Sandpoint, Idaho, or Spokane, Washington. The IDL Priest Lake Area Office is open 8 am to 5 pm weekdays (208/443-2516). *100 Hikes in the Inland Northwest* (see p. 321) can be very useful.

Blue Grouse
Mike Denny

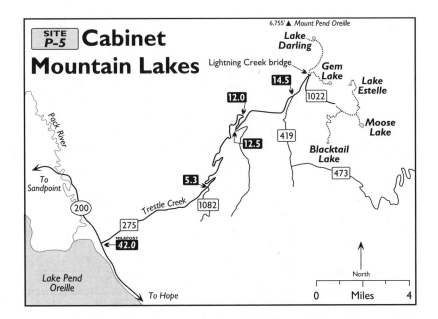

SITE
P-5 **Cabinet**

Mountain Lakes

6,755' ▲ Mount Pend Oreille

Lake Darling

Lightning Creek bridge

Gem Lake

14.5

12.0

1022

Lake Estelle

Moose Lake

419

Blacktail Lake

12.5

5.3

To Sandpoint

200

Trestle Creek

1082

275

MILEPOST
42.0

Lake Pend Oreille

To Hope

473

North

0   Miles   4

CABINET MOUNTAIN LAKES

Author: Earl Chapin

Site P-5 — Map P-5

Highlights: Pine Grosbeak, White-winged Crossbill
Major Habitats: Mixed Conifer Forest, Wetland
Location: Bonner Co., 20 miles northeast of Sandpoint
Spring: N/A   **Summer:** * *   **Fall:** * *   **Winter:** N/A

The Cabinet Mountains mark the boundary between Idaho and Montana. The rugged, remote wilderness guarded by these peaks has low bird diversity and density, but it is one of Idaho's best places to look for "boreal" species. The most enjoyable aspect however, is the opportunity to take long hikes through beautiful high-elevation forest and alpine tundra on your way to crystal-clear mountain lakes.

DIRECTIONS:

From downtown Sandpoint take US 95/US 2 north about 2 miles to the junction with ID 200. Continue straight (east) on ID 200 about 13 miles. At milepost 42, turn left (northeast), zero your mileage, and follow graveled FR 275 up Trestle Creek for 16 miles. (At mile 4.7 there is a pit toilet.) Stay left at the Y at mile 5.3. At mile 12 is a T; go right (south; not toward Lunch Peak). At about mile 12.5 stay left at the Y. You'll reach the junction of FR 275 and FR 419 near mile 14.5. Turn left (north; not Clark Fork), and go up the Lightning

Creek drainage toward "end of road." You'll reach the trailhead area by Lightning Creek Bridge at mile 15.5. All land here is public (FS).

Just before the bridge is the 2-mile-long, "easy" Trail 52 to Lake Darling. On the north side of the creek, about 200 yards beyond the bridge, is the 1-mile-long "moderate" Trail 554 to Gem Lake. You can drive about 2 miles farther along FR 1022 to the trailhead for Moose Creek Trail 237, Lake Estelle Trail 36, and Blacktail Lake Trail 24. The trails for Lake Estelle and Blacktail Lake branch off Trail 237. It's an "easy" 3-mile hike to Lake Estelle, an "easy" 1.5-mile hike to Moose Lake, and a "moderate" 3-mile hike to Blacktail Lake.

BIRDING:

On your drive up Trestle Creek, watch the roadsides for Spruce Grouse, and keep an eye out for American Three-toed or Black-backed Woodpeckers flying across the road. The best birding, however, is along the lakes themselves. Regular summer species include Red-tailed Hawk, Vaux's and Black (rare) Swifts, Red-naped Sapsucker, Downy, Hairy, American Three-toed, Black-backed, and Pileated Woodpeckers, Olive-sided and Hammond's Fly-catchers, Gray and Steller's Jays, Clark's Nutcracker, Common Raven, Black-capped, Mountain, and Chestnut-backed Chickadees, Golden-crowned and Ruby-crowned King-lets, Mountain Bluebird, Swainson's, Hermit, and Varied Thrushes, Cassin's and Warbling Vireos, Townsend's, Yellow-rumped, MacGillivray's, and Wilson's Warblers, Western Tanager, Pine Grosbeak, Cassin's Finch, Red and White-winged Crossbills, and Pine Siskin. In fall, American Pipits and Lapland Longspurs have been found in the short grass around the lakes. Expect to see Moose on nearly every trip to Gem, Moose, Darling, and Blacktail Lakes.

OTHER:

There is good trout fishing at all the lakes. A FS map can be very helpful, and can be purchased at the FS office (208/263-5111) in Sandpoint. The book *100 Hikes in the Inland Northwest* (see p. 321) can be useful, as well. See also Sandpoint to Beyond Hope Route, the next site.

SANDPOINT TO BEYOND HOPE ROUTE

Authors: Earl Chapin, Kas Dumroese

Site P-6 — Map P-6

Highlights: Waterfowl, Shorebirds, Bobolinks
Major Habitats: Wetland, Meadow
Location: Bonner Co., Sandpoint
Spring: **** **Summer:** *** **Fall:** **** **Winter:** ****

Sandpoint's city beach is one of Idaho's most dependable birding hotspots. The beach's sand is a precious commodity, since the rest of Lake Pend Oreille's (pond-o-RAY) long shoreline is mostly mud or rock. Many Idahoans believe that Pend Oreille is the prettiest lake in the entire state. Its huge size and bountiful fishes attract hundreds of diving birds, particularly loons, grebes, and bay ducks. Although beautiful vistas are found around the entire lake, the best birding is usually along the northeast shore. This 35-mile-long route starts in Sandpoint and ends near Clark Fork.

DIRECTIONS:

This route begins in Sandpoint, at the intersection of US 95 North and US 2 East. From here, go north about 1 block, then turn right (east) on Bridge Street and follow it 0.1 mile to the city beach (go through the underpass).

BIRDING:

The city beach is always worth a visit. Check the jetty to the north of the beach, as well. In winter and spring large rafts of diving ducks, including Greater Scaup, can be seen. Rare species have included Pacific Loon, Little Blue Heron, Black, Surf, and White-winged Scoters, Long-tailed Duck, American Golden-Plover, Snowy Plover, Whimbrel, Marbled Godwit, Ruddy Turnstone, Short-billed Dowitcher, Little, Mew, Iceland, Slaty-backed, Glaucous, and Sabine's Gulls, and Common, Arctic, and Least Terns. Many of these were first state records, which emphasizes the importance of this tiny, productive vagrant trap. A few Lapland Longspurs and Snow Buntings are seen every October to November.

Backtrack to US 95/US 2 and turn right (north), following it through downtown Sandpoint, then turn right (north) following US 95 toward Canada. In about 1.5 miles, continue straight (east) on ID 200 toward Hope.

At milepost 35, ID 200 reaches Oden Bay. Turn right (south) at the Sportsman Access and go under the railroad bridge, then turn left (east) onto Sunnyside Road, zero your mileage, and follow Sunnyside as it parallels the water. The wet fields along the first three miles of Sunnyside attract Franklin's, Bonaparte's, and Ring-billed Gulls in spring. In summer, this is a good place to find a variety of seedeaters, especially finches and sparrows. In winter, look for Snowy Owls (rare), Northern Pygmy-Owls, Northern Shrikes,

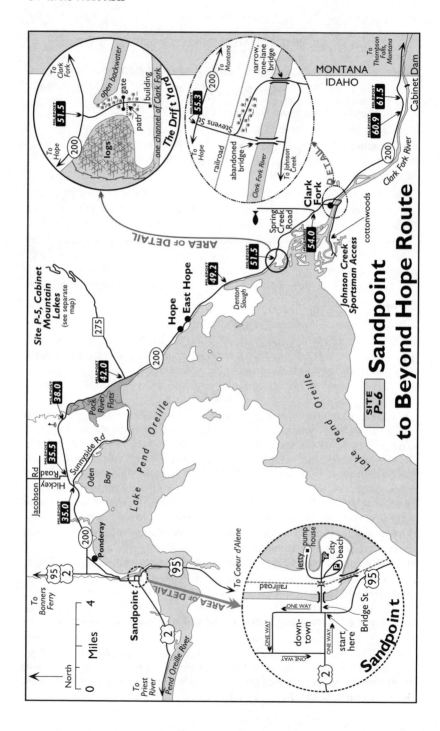

SITE P-6

Sandpoint to Beyond Hope Route

To Thompson Falls, Montana

Cabinet Dam

MONTANA
IDAHO

Clark Fork River

MILEPOST 60.9
MILEPOST 61.5

200

MILEPOST 54.0

Johnson Creek Sportsman Access

cottonwoods

Spring Creek Road

Clark Fork

AREA OF DETAIL

MILEPOST 51.5

MILEPOST 49.2

Denton Slough

East Hope

Hope

Lake Pend Oreille

200

275

Site P-5, Cabinet Mountain Lakes (see separate map)

MILEPOST 42.0

MILEPOST 38.0

Pack River Flats

MILEPOST 35.5

Jacobson Rd

Hickey Road

Sunnyside Rd

Oden Bay

MILEPOST 35.0

Ponderay

200

95
2

To Bonners Ferry

95
2

Sandpoint

AREA OF DETAIL

95

To Coeur d'Alene

2

To Priest River

Pend Oreille River

North

0   Miles   4

The Drift Yard

To Clark Fork

open backwater

building

gate

path

200

To Hope

logs

MILEPOST 51.5

one channel of Clark Fork

narrow, one-lane bridge

To Montana

200

MILEPOST 55.3

Stevens St

To Hope

railroad

abandoned bridge

Clark Fork River

To Johnson Creek

DETAIL

Sandpoint

jetty

pump house

city beach

railroad

ONE WAY

ONE WAY

downtown

ONE WAY

ONE WAY

start here

Bridge St

95

2

Pine Grosbeaks, and, on the lakeshore, Glaucous Gulls. Stop frequently to scan for migrating loons and waterfowl, especially Red-necked Grebes, Ross's Geese, and Barrow's Goldeneyes. Although most of the loons will be Commons, both Pacific and Red-throateds have been found here several times. Yellow-billed Loons are becoming almost regular, being found in three of the last four winters. Red-breasted Mergansers are usually present in April and May and again in October to December. Sunnyside Road ends at a primitive campground at mile 9.5. In spring or summer, you may see one of the Bald Eagles nesting on the small islands in this area. Clark's Nutcrackers, Townsend's Solitaires, and Red Crossbills winter on the timbered slopes above Sunnyside Road.

Backtrack to ID 200 and turn right (east). If you're looking for Bobolinks, turn left (north) at milepost 35.5 onto Hickey Road. This dirt road goes straight 0.25 mile, turns left (west) for another 0.1 mile, and then goes right (north) for 1 mile. Check both sides of the road for Bobolinks. At the stop-sign at Jacobson Road, turn around, backtrack to ID 200, and turn left, continuing east.

You'll pass Hidden Lakes Golf Course and Resort at milepost 38. Watch for Moose on the right (south). In another 0.5 mile you'll encounter the flats of the Pack River. This expansive shallow floodplain extends 3 miles southeast along US 200. The bridge at milepost 38.5 offers a good vantage point. A variety of migrant waterfowl, including Eurasian Wigeons, might be found here.

Additional viewpoints overlooking Lake Pend Oreille are found all the way to Hope. In fall and winter scope the huge rafts of ducks for Eurasian Wigeons and maybe scoters or Long-tailed Ducks. South of Hope, at milepost 49.2, you'll see a large turn-out on the right (west) side of the highway with a small sign for Denton Slough. For the next mile, ID 200 parallels the narrow confines of Denton Slough, and you can scope from several turn-outs (mileposts 49.3, 49.7, and 50.4). During May and early June this is a great place to watch dancing Western Grebes. Look for migrant waterfowl, Bonaparte's Gulls, and Caspian Terns. Summer birds include Double-crested Cormorants, Great Blue Herons, Canada Geese, and Black Terns. The deciduous trees opposite the turn-out hold vireos, Yellow Warblers, and Bullock's Orioles.

At milepost 51.5 a small gravel road heads south into the Drift Yard. The slack water and boom system intercepts logs flowing down the Clark Fork River. Virginia Rails and Soras, along with shorebirds, teal, American Pipits, and Common Yellowthroats, use the marshy area on the left (east) side of the gravel road in spring. You may walk this road all the way to the Clark Fork River, but after 0.3 mile it's closed from March 1 to June 15. From June to August, scan the tall grass and cattails to the south and west of the gate for displaying Bobolinks.

Continue east toward Clark Fork. At milepost 54, just before the Lightning Creek Bridge, turn left (north) onto graveled Spring Creek Road toward the fish hatchery. In June the first quarter-mile of river is good for Harlequin Ducks. Return to ID 200 and turn left (east).

At milepost 55.3 in "downtown" Clark Fork you may take a 4-mile-long side trip to Johnson Creek Sportsman Access. To do so, turn right (south) onto Stevens Street. In a quarter-mile you'll cross the railroad tracks and stay left (east). Watch for Lewis's Woodpeckers (May and June) for the next half-mile until you cross the one-lane bridge. (There is an Osprey nest on top.) Just across the bridge, turn right (west) onto the gravel road. From here to Johnson Creek, watch for Cordilleran Flycatchers, American Redstarts, and Northern Waterthrushes, especially in the brushy areas and near cottonwoods. About 1.8 miles from the bridge you'll enter a cottonwood stand. *The land is all private, so stay on the road.* Stop and listen for Western Wood-Pewees, Eastern Kingbirds, vireos, Lazuli Buntings, and Bullock's Orioles. Continue another 0.75 mile to a Y and stay right toward Sportsman Access, watching for Black Swifts (rare) mixed with Vaux's during August and September. The parking lot and pit toilet are another 0.2 mile past the Y. Look for Barred Owls, Belted Kingfishers, Red-naped Sapsuckers, Swainson's Thrushes, Cassin's, Warbling, and Red-eyed Vireos, and Gray Catbirds. You may wish to backtrack to the Y and take the other fork (FR 278) about 100 feet to the bridge. Check underneath for nesting American Dippers.

Backtrack to ID 200. If you're visiting in August or September and want to try for Black Swifts, turn right (east). At milepost 60.9 is a pull-off on the north side of the road. This is just below Cabinet Dam, and Blacks often fly with Vaux's Swifts above the river. Another vantage is from the VFW Campground at milepost 61.5. The road in is steep and rutted. *Permission is required for entry.* As of this writing, permission could be obtained at Nate's Gun Repair (208/266-1252; best luck after 4 pm).

OTHER:

Fuel and food are available in Hope and Clark Fork. Sandpoint is a full-service community. See also Cabinet Mountain Lakes (p. 31).

HOODOO VALLEY ROUTE

Author: Earl Chapin

Site P-7 — Map P-7/P-8/P-9

Highlights: American Bittern, American Redstart
Major Habitats: Mixed Conifer Forest, Wetland
Location: Bonner Co., 20 miles south of Sandpoint
Spring: * * *　　**Summer:** * * *　**Fall:** *　　**Winter:** N/A

A short, 8-mile-long drive up the Hoodoo Valley can produce more than 100 bird species. Although late May to late June is the best time to visit, Hoodoo Valley is worth investigating all spring and summer.

DIRECTIONS:

From Athol follow US 95 north 4 miles to milepost 453, then turn left (northwest) onto graveled Granite (a.k.a. Granite Lake) Road. Follow it about a mile to the T at Kelso Lake Road. Zero your mileage and turn left (southwest) on Kelso Lake Road. There is good birding all along this route. Stop and investigate wherever you see a birdy-looking area, but remember that *most land here is private.*

BIRDING:

At mile 0.5 is a small, primitive campground on the right (north) side of the road (at the western end of Granite Lake). Look in the rock slide behind the campground for Rock Wrens, and check the marshy area for Willow Flycatchers, Common Yellowthroats, Lazuli Buntings, Fox and Song Sparrows, and Red-winged Blackbirds.

Continuing west on Kelso Lake Road, you'll reach Kelso Lake and a good parking area at mile 1.6. Red-necked and Pied-billed Grebes nest here, as do a variety of ducks, including Common Goldeneyes. Continuing to about mile 4, investigate marshy areas on the left (south) side of the road for American Bitterns, Virginia Rails, Soras, Marsh Wrens, and Yellow-headed Blackbirds. Pay particular attention to the larger stands of Quaking Aspen lining the roads, since this is one of the best places in Idaho to find Red-eyed Vireos and American Redstarts. In conifer areas, you may find Red-naped Sapsuckers, Downy and Hairy Woodpeckers, Olive-sided Flycatchers, Western Wood-Pewees, Hammond's and Dusky Flycatchers, Chestnut-backed Chickadees, House and Winter Wrens, Townsend's Solitaires, Swainson's and Varied Thrushes, Cassin's Vireos, Yellow, Yellow-rumped, Townsend's, MacGillivray's, and Wilson's Warblers, Western Tanagers, Evening Grosbeaks, Cassin's Finches, and Red Crossbills.

At about mile 5 marsh and forest habitat are replaced by broad open meadows on both sides of the road. Nest boxes along the fence-line attract Tree and Violet-green Swallows, as well as Western and Mountain Bluebirds.

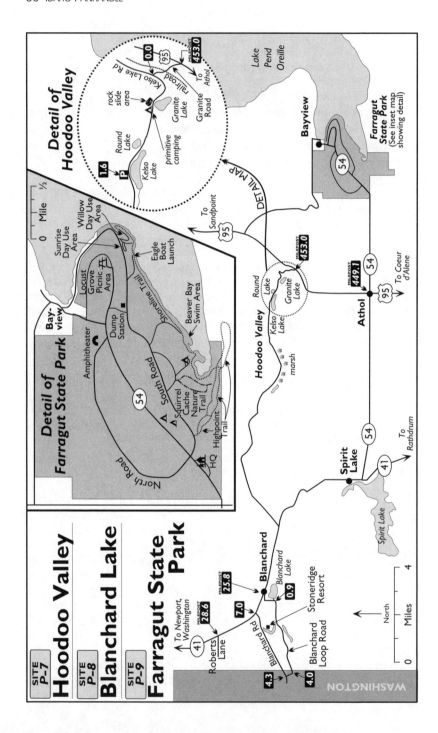

SITE P-7 **Hoodoo Valley**

SITE P-8 **Blanchard Lake**

SITE P-9 **Farragut State Park**

Other species likely to be seen here include Red-tailed Hawk, American Kestrel, Northern Harrier, Eastern Kingbird, and Savannah and Vesper Sparrows. Short-eared Owls and Bobolinks are possible but rare. Forest returns to the roadside at about mile 7. Although you can continue driving west to bird additional mixed conifer forest habitat, it's usually best to turn around and backtrack to US 95 since the rest of this forest is not particularly productive.

OTHER:

Sandpoint is a full-service community. Both Granite and Kelso Lakes feature good fishing for trout, bass, perch, Pumpkinseed, and Bluegill. Fuel and convenience stores are to be found at Athol.

BLANCHARD LAKE

Author: John Roberson

Site P-8 — Map P-7/P-8/P-9

Highlights: Osprey, Shorebirds
Major Habitats: Wetland, Farmland
Location: Bonner Co., Blanchard
Spring: * *   **Summer:** * *   **Fall:** * *   **Winter:** *

Blanchard Lake is a private reservoir, but the current owners, Mr. and Mrs. Poirier (POY-er), welcome birders. Check in with them before birding the lake. Scanning from the road is always okay. The 100-acre lake attracts many spring migrants, and Wood Ducks, Mallards, and Ospreys regularly nest here. During late summer, exposed mudflats are a haven for shorebirds.

DIRECTIONS:

From the junction of ID 54 and US 95 in Athol, head west on ID 54 about 8 miles. ID 54 ends at ID 41; turn right (north) on ID 41, and follow it through Spirit Lake to Blanchard, another 6 miles. At ID 41 milepost 25.8, turn left (west) onto a dirt road (Rusho Lane; unmarked) at the green "Entering Blanchard" sign. Zero your mileage, then follow this road 0.2 mile to a Y intersection (stay left), at which point you can view Blanchard Lake to the south.

BIRDING:

In late March and April, scope the lake for Common Loons, Horned and Red-necked Grebes, and waterfowl. Nearby flooded pastures are used by Tundra Swans (rare), geese, and ducks. Check large cottonwood trees for Bald Eagles.

Continue straight to mile 0.4 and the intersection of Poirier Ranch Road and Rusho Lane. Turn left (south) onto Poirier Ranch Road, and as you drive check the trees and brush for Western Wood-Pewees, Eastern Kingbirds, swallows, nuthatches, Western Bluebirds, and Evening Grosbeaks. At mile 0.9 the main road curves right (west) and becomes Blanchard Loop Road. Southeast of the curve is a "Poirier Tree Farm" sign and the Poirier residence. A dirt access road leads down to the lake. After asking permission to walk the dirt road, scan the northwest corner of the lake (best done with a scope from the southwest corner) for grebes and, from July on, for Lesser Yellowlegs, Semipalmated, Western, and Least Sandpipers, and Long-billed Dowitchers. An Upland Sandpiper was spotted here in August 1994. In summer check willow trees along the western edge of the lake for Western Wood-Pewees, Eastern Kingbirds, swallows, Gray Catbirds, and Cedar Waxwings.

To bird Blanchard Loop Road, continue driving west. At mile 1.3 is the Stone Ridge Golf Course. Check power-lines and trees on your right (north) for Western Bluebirds. From mile 2.0 to 2.3, look for Great Blue Herons and waterfowl on the reservoir to the left (south). At about mile 4.0 you drive into Washington state. At mile 4.3, turn right (northeast) onto Blanchard Road, which leads back into Idaho at about mile 4.5 (watch for stray Bobolinks in June) and Blanchard at mile 7.

If you want to do more birding from Blanchard, turn left (north) onto ID 41 and travel northwest 1.8 miles to milepost 28.6, then turn left (west) on Roberts Lane. Check the grassy fields along the road for Northern Harriers, Red-tailed Hawks, swallows, Western Bluebirds, Bobolinks, and sparrows.

OTHER:

In fall, hunting occurs at Blanchard Lake, so fewer waterfowl are seen then. Stoneridge Timeshare Resort (208/437-2451) is located one mile southwest of Blanchard on Blanchard Road. The resort has a gymnasium, heated Olympic-size swimming pool, sauna, golf course, and a restaurant for evening meals (closed Mondays and Tuesdays). Rooms with cooking facilities are often available.

There is a convenience store, gas station, and several dining options in Blanchard. Groceries are available in Spirit Lake. See also Farragut SP, the next site.

FARRAGUT STATE PARK

Authors: Kris Buchler, Cynthia Langlitz, Shirley Sturts

Site P-9 — Map P-7/P-8/P-9

Highlights: Western Bluebird, Cassin's Vireo
Major Habitats: Dry Conifer Forest and Mixed Conifer Forest
Location: Kootenai Co., 20 miles north of Coeur d'Alene
Spring: * * *   **Summer:** * * *   **Fall:** * *   **Winter:** * *

Farragut SP is situated on Idaho's largest lake, Pend Oreille. The park covers about 6 square miles and offers good birding, great views, and a chance to see Mountain Goats. In winter, only ID 54 is plowed; all side roads become favored destinations for cross-country skiers and snowmobilers. There is an entrance fee.

DIRECTIONS:

From Coeur d'Alene travel north on US 95 about 20 miles to Athol. At milepost 449.1, turn right (east) on ID 54 and go about 4 miles to the park entrance. Stop at park headquarters, located on the right (south) just after entering the park, and pick up a bird checklist and a park map.

BIRDING:

Walk around park headquarters and look and listen for Black-capped Chickadees, Red-breasted Nuthatches, Swainson's Thrushes, and Cassin's Vireos. In winter look for Northern Pygmy-Owls. When you're done birding here, continue driving northeast on ID 54, and take the next right (east) onto paved South Road. Watch for American Kestrels and Western and Mountain Bluebirds on the wires, and Wild Turkeys and Coyotes in the meadow. After South Road curves left, your first birding stop could be to hike Highpoint Trail. It takes about 2½ to 3 hours to hike the entire trail, which offers three loops through various habitats, starting with open meadows, then conifer forest, and a final difficult loop that climbs through forest and up steep rocky slopes. Species seen might include Pileated Woodpecker, Mountain Chickadee, Cassin's Vireo, and Townsend's and MacGillivray's Warblers.

From Highpoint Trail, continue along South Road, passing Kestrel/Nighthawk Campground (on the left) along the way. Take the first right past the campground, onto an unmarked, somewhat paved road which leads you to Squirrel Cache Trailhead in about 0.1 mile. (You may also access this spot from the paved road to Button Hook Campground.) This trail through conifer forest can be easily walked in an hour; it is home to Ruffed Grouse, Swainson's Thrushes, and Townsend's and MacGillivray's Warblers.

Return to South Road and turn right (northeast). Turn right (south) for the Beaver Bay Swim Area. From the parking area you can walk in either direction (southwest or northeast) along Shoreline Trail, watching for Belted Kingfishers, Brown Creepers, and Yellow and MacGillivray's Warblers. (If the gate to Beaver Bay is closed, you can access Shoreline Trail from Eagle Boat Launch, which is farther along South Road.)

From Beaver Bay return to South Road and turn right, continuing northeast past the RV dump station. Turn right (south) onto Eagle Boat Launch Road. Check the habitat surrounding the boat launch for Cedar Waxwings, Western Tanagers, and Black-headed Grosbeaks. Here you can access Shoreline Trail again. Follow it southwest toward Beaver Bay or northeast toward Sunrise and Willow Day Use Areas. Check the lake for loons, grebes, and ducks. Red-necked Grebes, Barrow's Goldeneyes, and Bald Eagles have been seen during winter. Willow and Sunrise Day Use Areas are the best places from which to view Mountain Goats residing on cliffs across the lake. You can also drive to Willow and Sunrise Day Use Areas by returning to South Road, turning right, and driving about 0.5 mile.

Your next stop is Locust Grove Picnic Area. From either Eagle Boat Launch or Willow Day Use Area, backtrack on South Road past the RV dump station, and turn right (north) at the sign that says "Bayview." Go about 0.2 mile to the stop-sign and turn right (east) and follow the road about 0.3 mile. Watch carefully—the sign for Locust Grove is on the right, but the picnic area is on the left and up a little hill. Start birding at the far end of the picnic area's parking lot, where there are several unmarked paths to explore. Species that frequent the area include Cordilleran Flycatcher, Red-eyed Vireo, Western Tanager, Black-headed Grosbeak, and Spotted Towhee. Near the restrooms you can walk a short loop road to access other forest habitat and meadows where Yellow and Yellow-rumped Warblers are frequently seen.

From Locust Grove Picnic Area, turn right (west) and continue straight about 0.5 mile back to ID 54. At ID 54, turn right (north) and go about 0.1 mile to a large pull-out on the left (west). A short path from this pull-out leads to a large amphitheater where a pair of Sharp-shinned Hawks is regularly seen.

Backtrack south on ID 54; it turns sharply to the right (west). In about 0.1 mile turn right (north) onto somewhat-paved North Road, marked by two concrete pillars. As you travel along North Road, there are several pull-outs where you can look for woodpeckers, chickadees, nuthatches, and kinglets. This area has nesting Red-tailed Hawks, American Kestrels, and a large concentration of Western and Mountain Bluebirds. In winter you may see Rough-legged Hawks, Northern Goshawks (rare), and Great Gray Owls (rare).

North Road terminates at ID 54, just opposite from where you initially turned onto South Road. Turn right (west) to exit the park. The park nature interpreter would welcome a list of your sightings for park records. Someone at headquarters will photocopy your checklist before you leave.

OTHER:

Farragut SP offers full-service campgrounds, museum, boat launch, swimming beach, and hiking trails. Cross-country skiing is popular in the winter season. Reservations are highly recommended during summer. Headquarters (13400 East Ranger Road, Athol, ID 83801; 208/683-2425) is open from about 7:30 am until 9:30 pm, Memorial Day through Labor Day (depending on weather). During winter, headquarters is open only on weekends, 9 am to 4 pm. See also Blanchard Lake (p. 39).

HAYDEN LAKE ROUTE

Author: Shirley Sturts

Site P-10 — Map P-10

Highlights: Red-necked Grebe, Osprey, Red-eyed Vireo
Major Habitats: Wetland, Mixed Conifer Forest
Location: Kootenai Co., 5 miles north of Coeur d'Alene
Spring: * * **Summer:** * * **Fall:** * * **Winter:** * *

This 30-mile-long drive around Hayden Lake will take you through a variety of habitats. Much of the lakeshore is privately owned and difficult to access, but there are several good viewing-areas as well. Be aware that the center portion of this route follows a steep, curvy, gravel road that can be very snowy in winter and very muddy during spring.

DIRECTIONS:

From I-90 Exit 12 in Coeur d'Alene, go north on US 95 for 3.6 miles. At milepost 434.3, turn right (east) on Honeysuckle Avenue. At the intersection in 0.7 mile, turn left (east), staying on Honeysuckle Avenue, and go one mile to Honeysuckle Beach. *All land is private except where noted.*

BIRDING:

If you have a scope, Honeysuckle Beach is a good place to check for grebes, ducks, and gulls from late fall to spring. It is also a popular swimming area and boat launch, so you may want to avoid it on busy summer days.

From the beach parking area backtrack on Honeysuckle Avenue about 100 feet and take the very first road to your left (south). This 0.4-mile-long, unmarked, seldom-used dirt road is sometimes called Dike Road; it is excellent for seeing waterfowl close by. Look for songbirds in cottonwoods and fields to the right (west), and waterfowl in the lake to your left (east).

At the end of Dike Road turn left (east) onto Lower Hayden Lake Road (narrow, busy, few pull-outs) and follow it one mile to Tobler Marina. Since 1981, there have been 7 fall or winter sightings of Long-tailed Duck along this

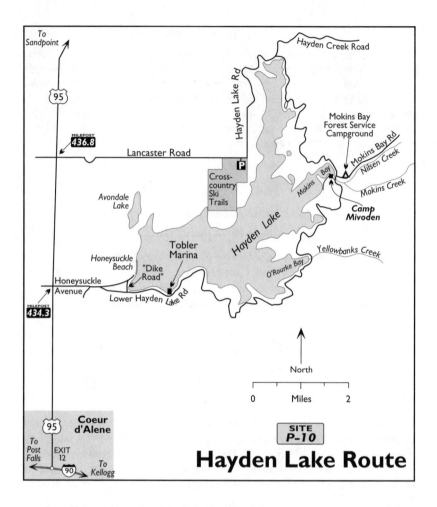

To
Sandpoint

Hayden Creek Road

95

MILEPOST
436.8

Hayden Lake Rd

Lancaster Road

Mokins Bay
Forest Service
Campground

Mokins Bay Rd

Nilsen Creek

P

Cross-country
Ski
Trails

Mokins Bay

Mokins Creek

Avondale
Lake

Camp
Mivoden

Hayden Lake

Tobler
Marina

Yellowbanks Creek

Honeysuckle
Beach

"Dike
Road"

O'Rourke Bay

Honeysuckle
Avenue

Lower Hayden Lake Rd

MILEPOST
434.3

North

0   Miles   2

95

Coeur
d'Alene

SITE
P-10

To
Post
Falls

EXIT
12

To
Kellogg

90

Hayden Lake Route

section of lake. Horned and Red-necked Grebes are common from late fall to freeze-up.

After leaving Tobler Marina, continue east. Lower Hayden Road winds away from the lake, rejoins Upper Hayden Road, becomes gravel, and enters conifer forest. Stop when you find available pull-outs to check for Hairy Woodpeckers, Cordilleran Flycatchers, Cassin's Vireos, Yellow Warblers, Black-headed Grosbeaks, and Cassin's Finches. In winter check tree-tops for Northern Pygmy-Owls and watch for Common Redpolls in birch trees or weedy patches. Along the way you'll drive past three creeks flowing through Western Redcedar and Western Hemlock forests. The creeks have unofficial trails that you can follow for short hikes.

After you wind downhill 6.1 miles from Tobler Marina, Yellowbanks Creek flows into O'Rourke Bay, and there you'll find a small two-track trail to the left (southwest) where you can get down to the lake. In cottonwood trees and along the creek look for Red-naped Sapsuckers and Red-eyed Vireos.

From Yellowbanks Creek it's another 3.4 miles to Mokins Bay, the best birding-spot on this route. At Mokins Bay, you'll see a road on your left (west) that goes to Camp Mivoden and a good parking spot just opposite it. Park and walk along Hayden Lake Road (paved again) and check the marsh on both sides of the road for nesting Red-necked Grebes, Wood Ducks, and Cinnamon Teal, and listen for Willow Flycatchers, Red-eyed Vireos, Yellow Warblers, and Black-headed Grosbeaks. You can also walk up graveled Mokins Bay Road (on the right [east] 0.1 mile beyond the Camp Mivoden turn-off) 0.1 mile to Mokins Bay FS Campground. Look here for Mountain Chickadees and Cassin's Vireos.

Continue on Hayden Lake Road, stopping at various pull-outs to look for Red-naped Sapsuckers, Pileated Woodpeckers, Olive-sided, Hammond's, and Dusky Flycatchers, Mountain Chickadees, Cassin's Vireos, MacGillivray's Warblers, Western Tanagers, and Black-headed Grosbeaks.

Hayden Creek Road (gravel) heads right (north) 4.7 miles past Mokins Bay. A drive up Hayden Creek Road for a mile or two may yield Red-eyed Vireos and Nashville Warblers singing along Hayden Creek. Logging trucks sometimes use this road, so stop only when you can completely pull off the road. Backtrack to Hayden Lake Road and turn right (west) to continue the loop.

From Hayden Creek continue south on Hayden Lake Road. In 3.1 miles Hayden Lake Road becomes Lancaster Road (a.k.a. Sportsman Park Road). Go another 0.1 mile to the cross-country ski course at English Point Road. Turn left (south) and you'll see a public (FS) parking area and restrooms. The ski course is groomed when there's enough snow, but at other times of year you can hike the trails as they wind their way through Ponderosa Pines and Douglas-firs. Watch and listen for woodpeckers and Pygmy Nuthatches.

To finish the loop, continue west on Lancaster Road another 3.8 miles to US 95 (milepost 436.8). Turning left (south) will return you to Coeur d'Alene and I-90 in about 6.5 miles.

OTHER:

Coeur d'Alene is a full-service community. Most amenities can also be found in Hayden Lake and in the sprawling urban landscape between Coeur d'Alene and Hayden Lake. See also the Coeur d'Alene Area, the next site.

COEUR D'ALENE AREA

Authors: Shirley Sturts, Gertie Hanson, Roger Young

Site P-11— Maps P-11 (1-4)

Highlights: Gulls, Pygmy Nuthatch
Major Habitats: Mixed Conifer Forest, Wetland
Location: Kootenai Co., Coeur d'Alene
Spring: * *   **Summer:** *   **Fall:** * *   **Winter:** * * *

The Coeur d'Alene Area can pack in some great birding. This is one of the easiest spots to find Pygmy Nuthatches and rare waterfowl in Idaho, and it's also the single best place to look for uncommon gulls.

DIRECTIONS:

The Coeur d'Alene Area can be divided into four sections: Post Falls, US 95, North Shore, and Wolf Lodge Bay. The starting point for all four sections is the intersection of US 95 and I-90 (Exit 12), in Coeur d'Alene. *Unless specified otherwise, all land is private, and roads are paved.*

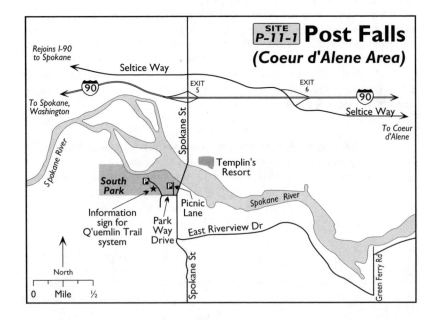

BIRDING:

POST FALLS

From the starting point follow I-90 west 7 miles to Post Falls. At Exit 5 turn left (south) on Spokane Street (toward tourist info) and follow it 0.5 mile to the Spokane River. Immediately after crossing the bridge, turn right (west) onto Park Way Drive. Go 100 feet and take the next right (north) on Picnic Lane to the parking lot of South Park. Except for summer, South Park is generally little used. Scope here for wintering waterfowl, including Ring-necked Ducks, Common and Barrow's Goldeneyes, Buffleheads, and Hooded, Common, and Red-breasted (rare) Mergansers. Vagrants have included a Pacific Loon (October) and a Double-crested Cormorant (January). Backtrack to Park Way Drive and turn right (west). In 0.1 mile you'll come to the Q'uemlin Trail sign and parking area on the right (north). Turn into the parking area. In 0.1 mile, on the left (west) you'll find a large map of the 13 trails, with a combined total distance in excess of 4 miles. Trail signs have disappeared over the years so it's easy to get lost, but if you're adventurous, exploring the area on foot is well worth your time (maps available; see below). Species include Downy and Pileated (rare) Woodpeckers, Cliff Swallow, Townsend's Solitaire, Cassin's Vireo, MacGillivray's Warbler, Spotted Towhee, and Red Crossbill.

For another good winter waterfowl spot or to see summer Ospreys, backtrack to Spokane Street and turn right (south). Go about 0.3 mile and turn left (east) on East Riverview Drive. Go 1.9 miles and take a left (north) on Green Ferry Road. In 0.2 mile, where Green Ferry Road veers right, continue straight on a dirt road 0.1 mile to the river. This spot is good for close views of Horned Grebes, Tundra Swans, Canada Geese, Ring-necked Ducks, Common Goldeneyes, and Hooded Mergansers during late fall and winter. Look for Bald Eagles as well. There are three Osprey nests here.

US 95

A 10-mile drive south of Coeur d'Alene takes you to several good birding spots. From the starting point follow US 95 south 1.4 miles. At milepost 429.2, turn right (west) into the parking area for Blackwell Island. The BLM manages 22 acres of river and riparian habitat at the mouth of the Spokane River. If the road is gated, park alongside and walk in. This area is currently undeveloped. To bird, just wander along the unimproved road and trails, investigating the deciduous and coniferous forest for Northern Flickers, Black-capped Chickadees, and Pygmy Nuthatches. In summer, also look for Red-naped Sapsuckers, Swainson's Thrushes, and Yellow and MacGillivray's Warblers. Ring-necked Pheasants and Ruffed Grouse are seen year round in hawthorns along the canal.

Return to US 95 and continue south about 2 miles to milepost 427. Then turn right (west) onto Cougar Gulch Road and park. You may bird the marshy area directly to your left (south) from the road and, using extreme caution, walk across the highway to view the more-expansive wetland on the east side of US 95. Unfortunately, the highway can be very noisy. Red-necked Grebe, Cin-

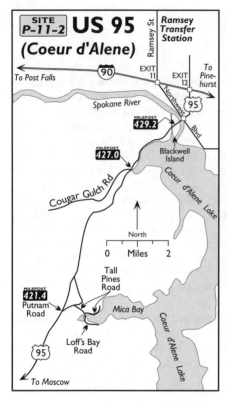

SITE P-11-2 US 95 (Coeur d'Alene)

Ramsey Transfer Station

Ramsey St

To Post Falls

90

EXIT 11

EXIT 12

To Pine-hurst

Northwest Blvd

95

Spokane River

MILEPOST 429.2

MILEPOST 427.0

Blackwell Island

Cougar Gulch Rd

Coeur d'Alene Lake

North

0   Miles   2

Tall Pines Road

MILEPOST 421.4

Putnam Road

Mica Bay

Loff's Bay Road

95

To Moscow

Coeur d'Alene Lake

namon Teal, Osprey, Sora, and Red-winged Blackbird are some of the nesting species. During migration large numbers of Tundra Swans, Canada Geese, Mallards, American Wigeons, and Northern Pintails can be seen, as well as smaller numbers of Green-winged and Blue-winged Teals, Northern Shovelers, and Eurasian Wigeons (rare, winter/spring). Other interesting migrants include Double-crested Cormorant, Great Egret (vagrant), American Avocet, Greater and Lesser Yellowlegs, Western Sandpiper, Long-billed Dowitcher, and Wilson's Phalarope. If the water is unfrozen, look for wintering Ring-necked Ducks, Buffleheads, Hooded Mergansers, and Bald Eagles.

About another 5.5 miles south along US 95, turn left (east) onto paved Tall Pines (a.k.a. Putnam) Road at milepost 421.4 toward Mica Bay. Go 0.6 mile to the Y and bear right (south) onto Tall Pines Road. After another 0.7 mile, turn left (east), staying on Tall Pines Road. After 0.1 mile stop at the large "Adopt a Wetland" sign on the right (south) and look for Belted Kingfishers, Eastern Kingbirds, and Winter Wrens. You may drive another 0.1 mile to the public boat ramp, a good place to look for migrant and wintering waterfowl, Bald Eagles, Herring and Glaucous Gulls, Caspian Terns, Northern Pygmy-Owls, and Northern Shrikes.

Backtrack on Tall Pine Road, and go left (south) along graveled Loff's Bay Road. In the first 100 feet you'll cross Mica Creek bridge, which supports nesting Barn Swallows. As you continue south, look for Pied-billed and Red-necked Grebes, Canada Geese, Wood Ducks, Mallards, Cinnamon and Blue-winged Teals, and Virginia Rails on both sides of the road. In spring and summer, watch for Willow Flycatchers, Eastern Kingbirds, Red-eyed Vireos, Yellow and MacGillivray's Warblers, and Song Sparrows in the roadside willows, alders, and cottonwoods. In 0.6 mile you'll reach the Mica Bay Boater Park (BLM campground), which is always worth a visit. A short, closed road provides walk-in access, passing through habitat for woodpeckers, Black-capped, Mountain, and Chestnut-backed Chickadees, Brown Creepers, and Golden-crowned Kinglets. Once you reach the campground, scope the bay for waterfowl.

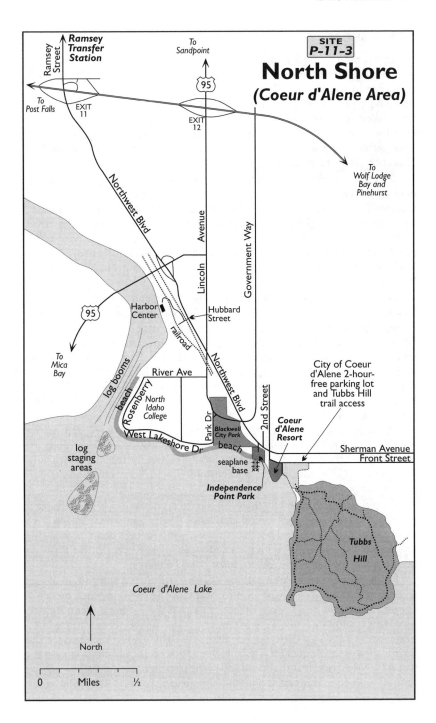

SITE
P-11-3

North Shore
(Coeur d'Alene Area)

Ramsey
Transfer
Station

Ramsey Street

To Sandpoint

95

To Post Falls

EXIT 11

EXIT 12

To Wolf Lodge Bay and Pinehurst

Northwest Blvd

Avenue

Lincoln

Government Way

95

To Mica Bay

Harbor Center

Hubbard Street

railroad

River Ave

Northwest Blvd

log booms

beach

Rosenberry

North Idaho College

Park Dr

Blackwell City Park

2nd Street

City of Coeur d'Alene 2-hour-free parking lot and Tubbs Hill trail access

Coeur d'Alene Resort

West Lakeshore Dr

beach

log staging areas

seaplane base

Sherman Avenue
Front Street

Independence Point Park

Tubbs Hill

Coeur d'Alene Lake

North

0   Miles   ½

NORTH SHORE

This is the section for Pygmy Nuthatches and rare wintering gulls. From the starting point head west on I-90 to Exit 11 (Northwest Boulevard). Turn right (north) onto Ramsey Street and go 0.9 mile to the Ramsey Transfer Station where garbage is collected. The station's entrance is on the right (east) side. Ask if you may look at gulls, and you'll probably be directed to drive behind the transfer building where you can park and get close-up views from your car of Ring-billed, California, Herring, and Thayer's Gulls, and maybe a Glaucous-winged and/or Glaucous.

To continue birding, backtrack over the interstate and go another 1.3 miles southeast on Northwest Boulevard, and turn right (south) at the wooden "Harbor Center" sign (Hubbard Street). Cross the railroad tracks and take the first right (west), following the road for 0.3 mile to the lower parking lot and office building. The wooden boardwalk along the river offers good opportunities for examining gulls (same species as at Ramsey Transfer Station) roosting on floating log booms. Listen for Pygmy Nuthatches in the Ponderosa Pines.

Return to Northwest Boulevard, turn right (east) and continue 0.2 mile before turning right (south) onto Lincoln Way for one block, where you turn right (west) onto River Avenue. Drive west for 0.3 mile until River Avenue ends on Rosenberry Drive. Rosenberry Drive (a one-way drive) follows the dike which separates North Idaho College from the Spokane River. Look for vagrant gulls on log booms in the river. Wintering duck species include Ring-necked Duck, Common Goldeneye, Bufflehead, and Common Merganser. The dike is shaded by large Ponderosa Pines which often contain Pygmy Nuthatches, Red Crossbills, and occasionally Pileated Woodpeckers. Beware of vehicle and pedestrian congestion along the dike when college is in session. Follow Rosenberry Drive along the dike for 1.1 miles (Rosenberry Drive turns into Lakeshore Drive along the way) to where the dike ends. Turn left onto Park Drive for 0.2 mile before turning right onto Government Way, which returns you to Northwest Boulevard after one block.

Turn right (east) onto Northwest Boulevard, go one block, and turn right (south) into the parking lot for Independence Point Park. The seaplane dock on the west end of the sand beach provides a good vantage point for scanning the lake and the river for both gulls and waterfowl. Recently, this park has been a good spot for Mew Gulls (January and February).

From Independence Point parking lot, turn right (east) and go two blocks to Second Street. Turn right (south) onto Second for one block before it curves left and becomes Front Street. Just past the Coeur d'Alene Resort, turn right (south) into the "City of Coeur d'Alene 2 Hour Free Parking Lot." You'll have to get a validation ticket, then stay right heading back toward the boat launch area. Access for Tubbs Hill, a 135-acre, largely undeveloped urban wilderness park, is at the south end of the parking area. Accessible only by foot, a 2-mile-loop trail begins near the large map of Tubbs Hill and follows the shoreline, providing picturesque views of Coeur d'Alene Lake along the west, south, and east sides of the hill. Secondary trails lead you to the top of the hill. Look for grebes, ducks, and gulls out on the water. Ospreys may be seen flying overhead during spring and summer. During winter, Bald Eagles are often seen flying over the lake. Along the western side of the hill are several dead and dying trees that attract Hairy Woodpeckers, Northern Flickers, Black-capped, Mountain, and Chestnut-backed Chickadees, Red-breasted and Pygmy Nuthatches, and Brown Creepers. Vagrants have included Lewis's and Pileated Woodpeckers and Northern Shrikes. Fall is a good time to look for Golden-crowned Kinglets, Red Crossbills, Pine Siskins, Evening Grosbeaks, and migrating warblers. In spring and summer, enjoy the many wildflowers while looking for nesting Cassin's Vireos and Yellow and Yellow-rumped Warblers.

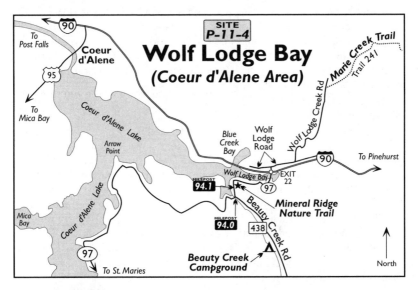

WOLF LODGE BAY

From the starting point follow I-90 east 10 miles to Exit 22. Turn right (south) on ID 97, zero your mileage, and cross over Wolf Lodge Creek. Scan the bay wherever there is a pull-out. Two of the best are at miles 0.2 and 0.8 (Mineral Ridge Public Boat Launch at milepost 95.4).

From late November to mid-March, migrant Bald Eagles come to Wolf Lodge Bay to feed on spawned-out Kokanee Salmon. Most eagles (40 to 70) and eagle-watchers are present mid-December to mid-January. There's also a good population of wintering waterfowl, such as Horned, Red-necked, and Western Grebes, Common and Barrow's Goldeneyes, Buffleheads, and Hooded Mergansers. The bay is also popular with gulls, which are best viewed at the east end of the bay. Rarities include Mew, Herring, Glaucous-winged, and Glaucous. Watch for Clark's Grebes in migration.

Ospreys arrive in late March, as do Common Loons, Tundra Swans, and Northern Pintails. If you're lucky enough to have a canoe, meander up Wolf Lodge Creek in the warmer months, and look for Wood Ducks, Cinnamon Teal, Vaux's Swifts, Eastern Kingbirds, Red-eyed Vireos, MacGillivray's Warblers, and Red-winged Blackbirds. American Dippers may be seen during winter.

The Mineral Ridge Nature Trail (pit toilets and picnic tables available) is on the left (east), at ID 97 milepost 94.1. The 3.3-mile-long, moderate-to-difficult nature trail leads to the top of Mineral Ridge. Along the way, look for Northern Pygmy-Owls (winter), Red-naped Sapsuckers, Mountain and Chestnut-backed Chickadees, Swainson's and Varied Thrushes, Cassin's Vireos, and Black-headed Grosbeaks.

At ID 97 milepost 94, turn left (east) on Beauty Creek Road (a.k.a. FR 438). Stay right at both Y intersections. In 0.6 mile you'll come to Beauty Creek Campground. Hike the well-marked Caribou Ridge Trail 79 to viewpoints in 1.8 and 4.6 miles, watching for Warbling Vireos, Hammond's Flycatchers, and Western Tanagers. Locally rare Pine Grosbeaks and American Tree Sparrows may be found in winter.

For good riparian birding, backtrack on ID 97 all the way to the north side of I-90, and turn right (east) on Wolf Lodge Road. Go one mile and turn left (north) on Marie Creek (a.k.a. Wolf Lodge Creek) Road (gravel/dirt). Follow it 1.2 miles and look for a road on the right (east), marked by a sign with two hikers, which is the trailhead. Marie Creek Trail 241 (moderate) goes over a ridge and down to Marie Creek in a mile, and then goes another five miles to its end. The first 0.5 mile can be very wet and muddy, especially before early June. The best birding is mid-June through July. Listen for Red-naped Sapsuckers, Pileated Woodpeckers, Olive-sided, Hammond's, and Dusky Flycatchers, Mountain and Chestnut-backed Chickadees, American Dippers, Veeries, Varied Thrushes, Cassin's, Warbling, and Red-eyed Vireos, Nashville, Townsend's, and MacGillivray's Warblers, Western Tanagers, and Black-headed Grosbeaks.

OTHER:

Additional fall/winter gull viewing might be available at the Fighting Creek Landfill, 14 miles south of Coeur d'Alene on the west side of US 95 (milepost 415.4). Call before visiting (Kootenai County Solid Waste Department, 208/769-4402), to receive permission and to find out if gulls are present. Past birding here has been wonderful, but a recent hazing program has reduced gull numbers.

Post Falls and Coeur d'Alene are full-service communities.

A map for Q'uemlin Trail can be picked up at the Post Falls Recreation Department, which is located next to City Hall on Spokane Street immediately south of I-90 (office hours, weekdays from 8 am to 5 pm; 208/773-0539). Coeur d'Alene Lake attractions include swimming, boating, tennis, playground equipment, boat cruises, picnic tables, parasailing, and airplane (pontoon) tours. You may obtain a pamphlet (with historical information about Tubbs Hill, a map of the trails, and a self-guided walk) from the Parks Department (221 South Fifth Street [three blocks east of the Tubbs Hill parking lot]; office hours: weekdays from 8 am to 5 pm; 208/769-2252). The BLM Mica Bay Boater Park (fee campground) includes boat docks, swimming beach, picnic tables, picnic shelters, a playground, a horseshoe pit, and vault toilets. A camp host is present during summer.

There's a KOA Campground at Wolf Lodge Bay, while the Wolf Lodge Campground and RV Park and the Wolf Lodge Bed and Breakfast are both on the north side of the interstate along Wolf Lodge Road. See also Hayden Lake Route (p. 43).

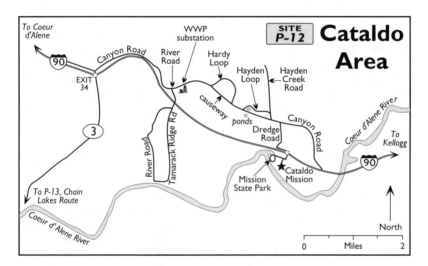

CATALDO AREA

Authors: Susan Weller, Marie Jordan

Site P-12 — Map P-12

Highlights: Black Tern, Wild Turkey
Major Habitats: Wetland, Mixed Conifer Forest
Location: Kootenai Co., 3 miles northeast of Rose Lake
Spring: * * *   **Summer:** * * *   **Fall:** * * *   **Winter:** * *

This 10-mile drive will circle you around Cataldo and various wetlands fed by the Coeur d'Alene River. Although the river system appears healthy at first glance, it has been contaminated by tons of mine tailings. This area is now considered one of the most contaminated in the country, but it is mending.

DIRECTIONS:

From I-90 Exit 34 (Rose Lake), head north to the T intersection, zero your mileage, then turn right (east) onto paved Canyon Road. *All land here is private.*

BIRDING:

At mile 1.0 begin looking for American Kestrels and Mourning Doves on power-lines on the left (north) side of the road. At mile 1.9 turn right (south) onto River Road. After crossing over I-90, continue straight ahead on Tamarack Ridge Road and look for Bobolinks in the hayfields, in May and June. Tamarack Ridge Road turns to gravel in about 1.0 mile, loops right (west) back into River Road, and passes through flooded hayfields (April to June) where thousands of waterfowl congregate, before rejoining Tamarack Ridge Road just south of I-90. Turn left (north) onto River Road and return to Canyon Road. Turn right (east) onto Canyon Road, and in 0.1 mile you'll see a Washington Water Power (WWP) substation on the right (south). You may park here, but don't block the gates leading to the transformers. Watch and listen for Killdeer, Mountain Bluebirds, and Western Meadowlarks in fields behind the substation. The current (1997) homeowner across the road welcomes birders, and you need only follow the din of bird songs up the circular driveway to locate the front door. A tour of the property reveals Red-naped Sapsuckers, Tree Swallows, Black-capped, Mountain, and Chestnut-backed Chickadees, Veeries, Swainson's Thrushes, Cassin's and Warbling Vireos, Western Tanagers, Lazuli Buntings, and Spotted Towhees. Pileated Woodpeckers, White-breasted Nuthatches, Brown Creepers, and American Tree Sparrows are uncommon winter visitors.

Continue east on Canyon Road 0.4 mile, where a pull-out on the right (south) allows an opportunity to glass the meadow for Northern Harriers and enjoy the carpet of Common Camas in June. White-crowned Sparrows feed along the roadside in fall. Northern Pygmy-Owls are commonly seen in bushes and on power-lines in winter. Wild Turkeys are abundant year round. After another 0.2 mile east on Canyon Road you'll see some Kootenai County garbage dumpsters. Here you may park and walk along Canyon Road over the causeway into Cataldo Slough. (*Please don't park on the causeway.*) In late winter look for Buffleheads, Hooded and Common Mergansers, and Ring-billed Gulls. In late spring Great Egrets have been seen flying over the mudflats. In summer Wilson's Snipe are abundant on both sides of the road, as are Pied-billed Grebes, Wood Ducks, Green-winged and Cinnamon Teal, and numerous other waterfowl species. A resident Bald Eagle helps to keep the ducks on their webbed toes. Black Terns grace the sky between nesting Ospreys on the wooden transmission towers on the right (south).

The graveled Hardy Loop Road heads left (north) just opposite the dumpsters and offers a nice one-mile-long diversion before connecting back to Canyon Road. In fall exposed mudflats offer a diversity of migrating shorebirds, including Semipalmated Plovers, Solitary and Spotted Sandpipers, Marbled Godwits, Semipalmated, Western, and Pectoral Sandpipers, and

Long-billed Dowitchers. Turkey Vultures might be seen lurking in trees, and Snow Buntings were seen here in the fall of 1995.

From where Hardy Loop Road rejoins Canyon Road, drive 0.3 mile to the base of a hill and two small ponds. The shoulder isn't very wide, and you may find it safer to turn left (north) onto graveled Hayden Loop Road to park. You can walk back to Canyon Road and glass the two small ponds just to the east. Red-winged Blackbirds may be found in the pond on the right (south) side of Canyon Road while Yellow-headed Blackbirds usually stay in the pond on the left (north). River Otters may be spied in either pond. Wood Ducks, Hooded Mergansers, Soras, Belted Kingfishers, House Wrens, and several species of warbler inhabit either side. Look for Vaux's Swifts mixed with the swallows, and for Western Wood-Pewees, and Eastern Kingbirds in the vicinity. Looking west, you can see the great expanse of Common Reed Grass planted by the Mine Operator's Association to help keep down tailings dust. Reed Grass offers cover and nesting sites for American Bitterns and Northern Harriers. Shrubs interspersed in the grass host Common Yellowthroats. Northern Shrikes are uncommon, but one or two might be seen hunting along the road during fall and winter.

If you parked on Hayden Loop Road, follow it 0.8 mile for a different perspective of the north pond—bear right as it becomes Hayden Creek Road. Turn left (east) onto Canyon Road.

From the junction of Hayden Creek Road and Canyon Road go another 0.2 mile east to Dredge Road and turn right (south), keeping a wary look-out for logging trucks. Wild rice has been planted on the left (east) side of Dredge Road (private). Pied-billed Grebes, Wood Ducks, American Wigeons, and Ruddy Ducks may all be found here. Tundra Swans and Canada Geese feed here in spring, but this is a dangerous place for deep-feeders. Every year a few birds die from feeding in the contaminated muck. Dredge Road continues across Cataldo Flats, where one might be momentarily fooled by the Washington Water Power owls perched upon the power poles. After Dredge Road curves left (east) at the interstate, a series of long ponds is visible on the left. Few waterfowl are seen here, but in fall Solitary Sandpipers and American Pipits may be found. Follow Dredge Road until it curves right and passes over the freeway (1.3 miles from Canyon Road). On-ramps allow for easy access to Coeur d'Alene (westbound) or Kellogg (eastbound). Continuing on the road will lead you to the Cataldo Mission in 0.3 mile and Old Mission SP in 0.4 mile.

OTHER:

Cataldo Mission (208/682-3814) was built in 1853 by Jesuit missionaries and Coeur d'Alene Indians, and is Idaho's oldest building. The mission and parish house have been lovingly restored, and tours are offered year round. The visitors center boasts an outstanding interpretive display on the history of the missionaries and Coeur d'Alene Indians. A nominal fee is charged. Plenty of songbirds may be found on the mission grounds. August 15 is the Feast of the Assumption Pilgrimage. The public is welcome to join in the religious observance, including the feast on venison, corn, fry bread, and melon. The dancing is not to be missed.

A cafe, gas stations, and the Rose Lake General Store are all located just south of the interstate at Exit 34. Look there for Steller's Jay year round and for Violet-green Swallows and Orange-crowned Warblers during summer. See also Chain Lakes Route, the next site.

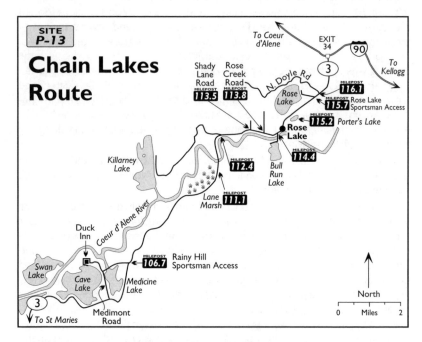

CHAIN LAKES ROUTE

Author: Susan Weller

Site P-13 — Map P-13

Highlights: American Bittern, Least Flycatcher
Major Habitats: Wetland, Mixed Conifer Forest
Location: Kootenai Co., 3 miles northeast of Rose Lake
Spring: * *   **Summer:** * *   **Fall:** * *   **Winter:** *

This 30-mile-long route follows the Coeur d'Alene River, visiting several lakes along the way. The main attractions are waterfowl and riparian birds. Except for ID 3, all roads are gravel of various quality. Unless otherwise specified, all land is private.

DIRECTIONS:

About 20 miles east of Coeur d'Alene, take I-90 Exit 34 and head south on ID 3 toward Rose Lake.

BIRDING:

In the first 0.3 mile, Elk may be seen grazing in enclosures on both sides of ID 3. Birders hoping to see Wild Turkeys and Varied Thrushes should turn right (west) at milepost 116.1 onto North Doyle Road—zero your mileage here. Flanked by private property and few pull-outs, this 2.8-mile-long road takes the traveler around the back of Rose Lake, and through habitat used by Wild Turkeys and Varied Thrushes. A pull-out at mile 0.8 offers an opportunity to view the lake. Set up your spotting scope to look for American Bitterns, Soras, and Wilson's Snipe in the cattail marsh. Western Grebes may be seen plying the open water, along with Ring-necked Ducks and Hooded Mergansers. There is another pull-out at mile 1.6. Yellow-rumped and Townsend's Warblers may be seen and heard in the woods along the road, along with Cordilleran Flycatchers and Brown Creepers. In open meadows look for Wilson's Snipe, Orange-crowned Warblers, and Western Meadowlarks. At mile 2.8 the road ends at a meadow with distant views of the backwaters of Rose Lake on the left. Check for Northern Harriers, Black Terns, and Mountain Bluebirds.

Returning to ID 3, continue south and look carefully for the easily-missed Rose Lake Sportsman Access, which is on the right (west) at milepost 115.7. Follow the graveled access road less than 0.5 mile to the restrooms, picnic tables, and public boat dock. Pied-billed, Horned, and Western Grebes are often seen here, and even a White-winged Scoter showed up once.

Farther south on ID 3, Porter's Lake is at milepost 115.2. A generous pull-out on the left (east) makes for safe and easy viewing of American Bitterns, waterfowl, and Black Terns.

Entering Rose Lake, turn right (west) at milepost 114.5 onto King Street. After one block stop at the intersection with Queen Street. The lucky birder may be able to hear the Blue Jays that visit this neighborhood almost every spring. Go around the block to return to ID 3. Turn right and continue south on ID 3.

At milepost 114.4 you'll see the sign for Bull Run Lake. Turn left (south) and cross the bridge over the Coeur d'Alene River. Just across the bridge bear right (west), pull over, and listen for Veeries on the left (south) side of the road. Continue driving west, cross the railroad tracks, and turn right (west), following the tracks along the western end of Bull Run Lake. Hiking down any of the roads here may reveal Ospreys, Tree and Violet-green Swallows, Wilson's Warblers, and Black-headed Grosbeaks.

Backtrack to ID 3 and turn left (southwest). A portion of the Coeur d'Alene WMA begins on the right (west) at Rose Creek Road (milepost 113.8). Pull in and park. Between Rose Creek Road and Shady Lane Road (unmarked at milepost 113.5) is a cottonwood/Quaking Aspen grove that extends north about 0.25 mile. This piece of public property is your best chance for finding Least Flycatchers in Idaho, and is also good for species such as Veery, Red-eyed Vireo, and American Redstart.

Farther south on ID 3, the entrance road for Killarney Lake is on the right (west) at milepost 112.4. A boat launch and a picnic area will be found after driving the entrance road for 3.5 and 4 miles, respectively. Flooded hayfields on the left (south) side of the entrance road may hold a vagrant Great Egret in spring. The woods and meadow edges on the right (north) promise Lewis's (rare) and Pileated Woodpeckers. Vegetation along the lake is home to Cordilleran Flycatchers, Eastern Kingbirds, Gray Catbirds, Townsend's and MacGillivray's Warblers, and Western Tanagers. Barred Owls may be heard calling from across the lake on a summer's eve.

After returning to ID 3, turn right (south). The road soon crosses the Coeur d'Alene River. A large pull-out on the right (west) at milepost 111.1 affords an opportunity to glass Lane Marsh and view Ospreys nesting on power poles. American Bitterns and Soras (abundant) reside here. MacGillivray's Warblers and Common Yellowthroats may be found in the bushes. Look for nesting Bald Eagles across the railroad grade.

The next 4.5 miles of ID 3 offer great birding, but they have few safe pull-outs. Look for Bald Eagles, Rough-legged Hawks, Northern Pygmy-Owls, Chestnut-backed Chickadees, Northern Shrikes, and American Tree Sparrows in fall and winter, and for waterfowl in spring and summer.

At milepost 106.7 is the Rainy Hill Sportsman Access to Medimont and Rainy Hill. Zero your mileage and turn right (west). Stop at mile 0.4 and check for American Bitterns, then continue to mile 1.1 and the picnic tables and restrooms at Rainy Hill Boat Launch on Medicine Lake. Rainy Hill (across the road from the picnic area) boasts nesting Gray Catbirds and Bullock's Orioles. Common Loons may be found testing their voices on Medicine Lake in spring and early summer. At mile 1.4 Rainy Hill Road ends at a T intersection with Medimont Road. This is a great place to set up the spotting scope to view waterfowl. During winter, Cave and Medicine Lakes are host to thousands of clamoring waterfowl, including Barrow's Goldeneyes, Eurasian Wigeons, and perhaps a Red-throated Loon. Turn right (north) on Medimont Road, driving between Cave Lake and backwaters of the Coeur d'Alene River. Be sure to look for American Goldfinch flocks as you pass by the farms. At mile 1.8 stay left after crossing the railroad bridge and enjoy fields of blooming Common Camas on your right during May and June.

At mile 2.5 you'll reach Duck Inn, which provides a nice view of the river delta. Make a loop around Duck Inn by turning right and then making three left turns. Immediately after the last left turn, turn right and proceed downhill to the railroad tracks. Park the car and walk west along the railroad grade. This walk is not advisable during nesting season, but it yields a number of migratory species during spring and fall, including American Pipit and Lincoln's and White-crowned Sparrows. Watch for Pectoral Sandpipers and vagrant Short-billed Dowitchers.

Backtrack to the T intersection of Rainy Hill Road and Medimont Road and continue straight 0.9 mile on Medimont Road to ID 3, and the end of this route.

OTHER:

Coeur d'Alene and St. Maries are both full-service communities. Fishing for bass, bullhead, perch, and Northern Pike makes the Chain Lakes popular with both humans and waterfowl. All the lakes are great for canoeing. Bait, lures, flies, and local fishing news may be obtained at the Rose Lake Store in Rose Lake. See also Cataldo Route, the previous site, and St. Maries to Harrison Route, below.

ST. MARIES TO HARRISON ROUTE

Authors: Dan Svingen, Kas Dumroese

Site P-14 — Map P-14

Highlights: Loons, Rusty Blackbird
Major Habitats: Wetland, Dry Conifer Forest, Farmland
Location: Benewah Co., St. Maries
Spring: * * *   **Summer:** * * *   **Fall:** * * * * **Winter:** * * * *

This 20-mile-long route offers some of Idaho's best birding, especially during fall and winter. Spectacular views of the St. Joe River and Coeur d'Alene Lake make the trip even more worthwhile. All land along this route is private, except at the WMA.

DIRECTIONS:

Start at the intersection of ID 3 and ID 5 in St. Maries, adjacent to the Exxon Station. Take ID 3 north across the St. Joe River.

BIRDING:

The St. Maries sewage lagoons are alongside ID 3 at milepost 86, about 1 mile northwest of the starting point. Good viewing is provided at pull-outs at each end. During summer look for breeding species such as Wood Duck, Northern Shoveler, Bufflehead, and Common Goldeneye. The lagoons have attracted vagrants such as Harlequin Ducks in May and Long-tailed Ducks and Surf Scoters in November. Barrow's Goldeneyes are regular from October to freeze-up. Bonaparte's and Franklin's Gulls (both rare) can be present at any time from April to December. Cottonwoods lining the highway host breeding Gray Catbirds, Warbling Vireos, Northern Waterthrushes, Bullock's Orioles, and Black-headed Grosbeaks.

Approximately 3.5 miles northwest of St. Maries (milepost 87.9), a gravel road goes northeast into the Cassandra Hills Housing Development, an area

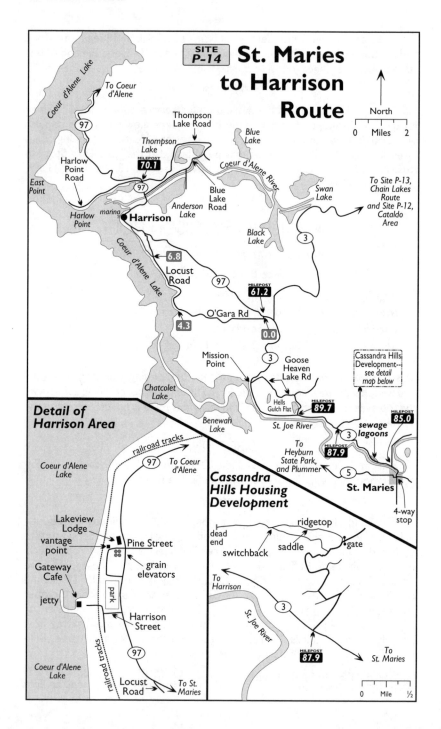

SITE
P-14
St. Maries to Harrison Route

North

0 Miles 2

To Coeur d'Alene

97

Coeur d'Alene Lake

Thompson Lake Road

Blue Lake

Thompson Lake

MILEPOST 70.1

Harlow Point Road

97

Coeur d'Alene River

Swan Lake

East Point

Blue Lake Road

Anderson Lake

To Site P-13, Chain Lakes Route and Site P-12, Cataldo Area

Harlow Point

marina ● **Harrison**

Black Lake

3

Coeur d'Alene Lake

6.8

Locust Road

97

MILEPOST 61.2

O'Gara Rd

4.3

0.0

Mission Point

3

Goose Heaven Lake Rd

Cassandra Hills Development-- see detail map below

Chatcolet Lake

Hells Gulch Flat

MILEPOST 89.7

MILEPOST 85.0

Benewah Lake

St. Joe River

3 sewage lagoons

To Heyburn State Park, and Plummer

MILEPOST 87.9

5

St. Maries

4-way stop

Detail of Harrison Area

railroad tracks

97 To Coeur d'Alene

Coeur d'Alene Lake

Lakeview Lodge

vantage point

Pine Street

Gateway Cafe

grain elevators

park

jetty

Harrison Street

Coeur d'Alene Lake

97

railroad tracks

Locust Road

To St. Maries

Cassandra Hills Housing Development

ridgetop

dead end

switchback

saddle

gate

To Harrison

3

St. Joe River

MILEPOST 87.9

To St. Maries

0 Mile ½

of dry Ponderosa Pine habitat. It's the haunt of Dusky Flycatchers, Pygmy Nuthatches, Western Tanagers, Spotted Towhees, and Cassin's Finches. The best habitat is reached by driving 2 miles uphill to the ridgetop. The main road is the widest one; it's always headed up. Caution should be used whenever this steep road is wet or snow-covered, for it can be very slick. After 1.7 miles the main road is closed by a green metal gate. Turn left (northwest) onto the narrower road to reach the ridgetop in 0.2 mile. At the ridgetop you'll enter a small topographic saddle, where you can decide whether to walk or to brave further driving. Driving requires vehicles which can make sharp turns. Whether you walk or drive, go left (northwest) from the saddle on the graveled 2-track road. You'll have great views of the St. Joe River Valley and pass through the best birding area. After 1.3 miles, the 2-track trail enters a sharp switchback where you can go straight, through more Ponderosa Pine (that road dead-ends in 0.5 mile), or turn left (southeast) and return to the main road in 0.7 mile. When you reach the main road, turn right (southwest) and go downhill 1.6 miles to where you turned off ID 3, then continue right (northwest) on the highway. Future plans are to build a confusing road maze within the housing development area, but don't despair; you're welcome to drive any of the open roads, and good birding is available throughout the hillside.

At ID 3 milepost 89.7, graveled Hells Gulch Road begins on the right (north) and circles Hells Gulch Flat, a productive migrant trap. The three square miles of the flat support wheat, cattle, and sheep. After autumn harvest, the exposed rodent population attracts up to 30 raptors (mostly Rough-legged and Red-tailed Hawks). From October to April accipiters hunt brushy slopes ringing the flat. Brushy slopes may also hold Bewick's Wrens and Cordilleran Flycatchers in summer, and Pine Grosbeaks in winter.

To find the best birding sites around Hells Gulch Flat, zero out your mileage at the junction of Hells Gulch Road and ID 3. At mile 0.5 the road swings west past a small stockyard where Rusty Blackbirds wintered in 1992, 1993, and 1994. At mile 0.9 stay left at the Y intersection, and proceed onto Goose Heaven Lake Road (unmarked). A small pull-out at 1.7 miles (just north of the two barns) allows scoping of Goose Heaven Lake, a 25-acre wetland which attracts large swallow flocks in August and assorted waterfowl in migration. Idaho's first documented female Eurasian Wigeon was seen here in February 1995.

A second stockyard at 2.3 miles has been dependable for wintering blackbirds. Scan the large cottonwood tree and sheep feeders in the feedlot, but please don't park in front of the farmer's home. A pump-house is located below the road at mile 2.5, between two pole barns. Killdeer, Mourning Doves, blackbirds, and Northern Shrikes should be looked for in late fall. At mile 2.6, another stockyard should also be scoped for wintering blackbirds. If operating, the pump-house at mile 3.0 often attracts Winter Wrens. At mile 3.2 the road rejoins ID 3 at "Mission Point." Turn right onto ID 3 and continue north.

About 3 miles north of Mission Point, ID 3 intersects ID 97. Take the left fork onto ID 97 toward Harrison. At milepost 61.2 turn left onto O'Gara Road and zero out your odometer. O'Gara Road passes by Kootenai High

School before running through open grassland that attracts wintering Rough-legged Hawks, Northern Pygmy-Owls, and Northern Shrikes, as well as an occasional "Harlan's" Red-tailed Hawk. Once through the grasslands (about 1 mile), the road descends into a wooded canyon where Ruffed Grouse, Barred Owls, Pileated Woodpeckers, and Wild Turkeys are resident. Black-capped, Mountain, and Chestnut-backed Chickadees, Red-naped Sapsuckers, and Varied and Swainson's Thrushes are common summer residents. After 4.3 miles, the road passes by a small riparian area stocked with cottonwoods containing breeding American Redstarts. At mile 6.8, turn left (northwest) onto graveled and oooh-so-narrow Locust Road, which allows good views of Coeur d'Alene Lake. After passing through 0.5 mile of broken forest where Orange-crowned and Nashville Warblers can be found and through 0.6 mile of broken suburbia where Idahoans can be found, Locust Road rejoins ID 97.

From the junction of ID 97 and Locust Road, take a left (northwest) and proceed 0.3 mile to the intersection of ID 97 and Harrison Street within the city of Harrison. You can go left here, cross the railroad, and drive to the Gateway Cafe, which marks the Harrison Marina. The rock jetty and docks allow vantage points from which to scan the lake.

An even better place to scope the marina is behind the grain elevators. Continue north on ID 97 for two blocks, then turn left (west) on Pine Street (by Lakeview Lodge) and park at road's end. This overlook provides good viewing of the marina and Coeur d'Alene River delta, but it requires a spotting scope. The marina and delta are worth looking over at any time of year, but they are especially productive from October to March. Yellow-billed Loons wintered here in 1991, 1993, and 1994. One or two Pacific Loons are regular October to November. Red-throated Loons and Red-breasted Mergansers (both rare) have been reported during the period of October to January.

The Coeur d'Alene WMA is located 1.4 miles northeast of Harrison on ID 97. Take the first right onto Blue Lake Road after crossing the Coeur d'Alene River bridge (see map). Follow Blue Lake Road east, watching for Tundra Swans, Golden Eagles, and Eurasian Wigeons amongst the large flocks of migrating waterfowl. Wintering Swamp Sparrows, American Tree Sparrows, and Northern Shrikes have been found near the junction of Blue Lake Road and ID 97. Canada Geese, Black Terns, Violet-green Swallows, and Yellow Warblers are common during summer.

Ospreys are abundant at this WMA, much to the annoyance of the local utility company. Repeated attempts at discouraging birds from nesting atop utility poles have failed. The birds quickly dealt with one past effort (twisting rebar over the pole crossarms), by incorporating the exclusion devices into their nests as a sort of "living-room chair"! The latest offerings, "guardian owls" (*Bubo virginianus plasticus*), have also been incorporated into nests.

To see all the WMA, continue east 2 miles along paved Blue Lake Road (which turns into graveled Thompson Lake Road along the way). Where Blue Lake and Thompson Lake Roads split (see map), go left (west) on Thompson

Lake Road through the farmyard, where up to 80 Wild Turkeys winter. Follow the road as it turns back to the west and rejoins ID 97 in 3.9 miles. Keep an eye out for Pied-billed, Horned, and Red-necked Grebes, Trumpeter Swans (rare migrant), Willow Flycatchers, Eastern Kingbirds, and Cedar Waxwings along the way.

The last stop on this route is Harlow Point Road (ID 97 milepost 70.1). It begins at the junction of Thompson Lake Road and ID 97 and proceeds west along the lake. This 3-mile-long, paved/graveled road allows good viewing of the entire Coeur d'Alene River delta and is a good place to check for various loon, waterfowl, and gull species. The dry, open Ponderosa Pine forest above the road attracts wintering Bald Eagles, Clark's Nutcrackers, and an occasional vagrant Blue Jay.

OTHER:

St. Maries is a full-service community. Food and lodging are available in Harrison.

HEYBURN STATE PARK

Authors: Dan Svingen, Kas Dumroese

Site P-15 — Map P-15

Highlights: Eurasian Wigeon, Northern Waterthrush
Major Habitats: Wetland, Dry Conifer Forest, Mixed Conifer Forest
Location: Benewah Co., 10 miles west of St. Maries
Spring: * * *   **Summer:** * *   **Fall:** * * * * **Winter:** * * * *

Heyburn SP surrounds Chatcolet and Benewah Lakes, which border the southern end of Coeur d'Alene Lake. All this water divides the park into two main divisions: the west shore of Chatcolet Lake and the east shore of Benewah Lake. The 20-mile-long route described below will take you along the border of this wetland complex, from St. Maries to Plummer.

DIRECTIONS:

This route's starting point is downtown St. Maries at the junction of ID 3 and ID 5 (the 4-way stop by the Exxon Station). Follow ID 5 west 7.4 miles, then turn right (north) at milepost 11.7 onto paved Benewah Resort Road.

BIRDING:

After 0.1 mile the resort road passes by a cottonwood and aspen stand (private), where Red-naped Sapsuckers, Veeries, American Redstarts, and Northern Waterthrushes breed. When you reach the resort (in about 1 mile), walk down to the dock. A spotting scope can be of great help in finding

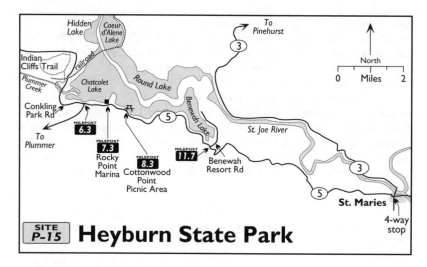

SITE P-15 Heyburn State Park

Red-necked Grebes, usually present from April to November. Benewah Lake is one of this species' Idaho strongholds.

Backtrack to ID 5. Other views of Benewah Lake are possible at pull-outs along ID 5, at mileposts 10.7 and 10.6. Red-necked Grebes, Wood Ducks, and Ospreys can be seen here during summer, while large waterfowl flocks are present during migration and winter. Common Terns are possible during fall.

Cottonwood Point Picnic Area is at milepost 8.3 along ID 5. Watch for the sign pointing out this tiny public picnic ground on the right (north). Western Wood-Pewees, Winter Wrens, Northern Waterthrushes, and Fox Sparrows nest here. Interesting migrants have included Bewick's Wrens, Brown Creepers, and White-throated Sparrows. During migration and winter, Bald Eagles and waterfowl congregate at this spot, and it is usually possible to find a Eurasian Wigeon or two and a few Greater Scaup.

The best place from which to scope Chatcolet Lake is Rocky Point Marina (milepost 7.3). Scan the lake from docks at either end of the marina. Although productive during migration and winter, Chatcolet Lake supports few summer birds because of its heavy recreational boat traffic.

After leaving Rocky Point Marina, continue west on ID 5 about one mile to milepost 6.3. Turn right (north) on Conkling Park Road (a.k.a. Chatcolet Road), and go 0.9 mile to Plummer Creek bridge. Plummer Creek marsh, which borders the bridge, is used by breeding Red-necked Grebes, Ospreys, Soras, and Marsh Wrens, and attracted vagrant Swamp Sparrows in the winters of 1992 and 1994. The flat, 0.6-mile-long Plummer Creek Trail shadows Plummer Creek upstream from the bridge. Its terminus is on Conkling Park Road, 0.2 mile north of Plummer Creek bridge. Olive-sided, Willow, and Cordilleran Flycatchers, Chestnut-backed Chickadees, Golden-crowned Kinglets, Swainson's and Varied Thrushes, and Townsend's Warblers are common breeders. Barred Owls are often heard hooting. Bewick's Wrens,

American Dippers, and American Tree Sparrows are among the more unusual winter birds occasionally found along the trail. The gated Fire Control Road next to the trailhead can also be walked, but its twisty path may get you lost!

Continuing north on Conkling Park Road, you'll cross railroad tracks 0.3 mile north of Plummer Creek bridge. On the left (west) side of the road, is Indian Cliffs Trailhead. This 3-mile-long hiking trail is classified as moderate-to-steep; it accesses open Ponderosa Pine habitat, which attracts Pileated Woodpeckers, Pygmy Nuthatches, Townsend's Solitaires, Pine Grosbeaks (winter), and Red Crossbills. Watch for Hammond's Flycatchers and MacGillivray's and Yellow-rumped Warblers along the trail's lower portion.

OTHER:

For more information, stop in at park headquarters, located 0.1 mile north of Indian Cliffs Trailhead. St. Maries is a full-service community. Heyburn SP (208/686-1308) has a full-service campground. See also St. Maries to Harrison Route, the previous site, and St. Joe Route, below.

ST. JOE ROUTE

Authors: Dan Svingen, Kas Dumroese

Site P-16 — Map P-16

Highlights: Tundra Swan, Northern Pygmy-Owl
Major Habitats: Deciduous Forest, Wetland
Location: Benewah Co., St. Maries
Spring: * * *   **Summer:** * * *   **Fall:** * *   **Winter:** * *

This 40-mile-long drive will take you up the Shadowy St. Joe, the highest navigable river in the world. Tugboats work the river weekly, pulling huge "brails" of timber down to sawmills in Post Falls, 80 miles away. This route's unique birding opportunities center around the deep, waterlily-filled wetlands and cottonwood forest associated with this historic river.

DIRECTIONS:

The route begins in St. Maries, at the junction of ID 3 and ID 5 (the 4-way stop adjacent to the Exxon Station). From here, take ID 3 north across the St. Joe River and follow it as it curves west. At milepost 85, turn right (north) toward Avery on Forest Highway (FH) 50 (a.k.a. St. Joe Road).

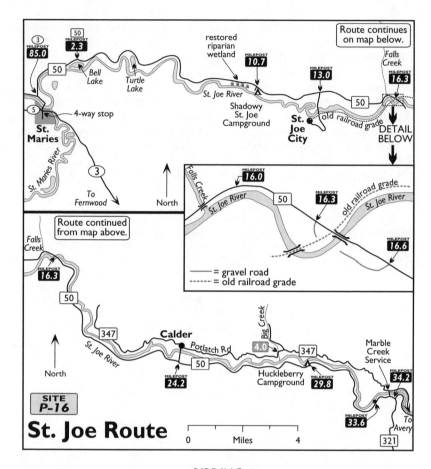

SITE
P-16

St. Joe Route

0   Miles   4

BIRDING:

At FH 50 milepost 2.3 you'll pass St. Maries Concrete. Pull over and quickly scan Bell Lake. Although often unproductive birdwise, Bell Lake has attracted American Bitterns and Great Egrets (rare) during summer.

St. Maries Wild Rice is a highly praised culinary delight available in local grocery stores. Part of the crop is raised in the flooded field at milepost 3.4. Pull-outs are available at milepost 3.6 (north side of road) and 4.0 (south side of road). During spring, these fields host large waterfowl flocks, including hundreds of Tundra Swans, Cinnamon Teal, Barrow's Goldeneyes, and usually a Eurasian Wigeon or two.

At milepost 5 you may want to stop and quickly scan Turtle Lake, which is similar to Bell Lake. Better birding, however, is available just down the road at milepost 8. The second flooded rice field here can be scanned from the pull-out on the right (south) side of the road.

The FS, Washington Water Power, and Federal Highway Administration have restored a riparian wetland on the south side of the road at milepost 10.5. You can access this area by parking at Shadowy St. Joe Campground (see below) and walking in. The wetland should be checked for American Bitterns, Wood Ducks, Hooded Mergansers, Soras, and Marsh Wrens.

At milepost 10.7, turn right (south) into Shadowy St. Joe Campground. A quick walk around this small site will usually reveal common summer residents: Western Wood-Pewees, Violet-green Swallows, Red-eyed Vireos, and Cedar Waxwings.

All along this route, but especially between mileposts 11 and 13, scan small trees and utility poles for Northern Pygmy-Owls. Your best bet for finding these tiny raptors is very early in the morning or at dusk, November to March. This is one of the most dependable spots for the species in Idaho. During irruption years, up to five owls can be seen along this short stretch of road.

The richest habitat along this route is the riparian cottonwood forest, best accessed along the abandoned railroad grade paralleling the St. Joe River. The rail line was decommissioned years ago, but the grade has been used as a road ever since, with portions incorporated into the highway. Most of the grade is open in summer. To detour along the railroad grade, turn right (south) at milepost 13, toward St. Joe City. After 0.7 mile, you'll cross the St. Joe River. Turn left (east) onto the gravel road along the river's south bank. This road passes by several stands of riparian forest, hosting a variety of birds. Regular species include Wild Turkey, Western Screech-Owl, Barred Owl, Western Wood-Pewee, Eastern Kingbird, Mountain Bluebird, Veery, Gray Catbird, Warbling Vireo, Townsend's Warbler, American Redstart, Northern Waterthrush, MacGillivray's Warbler, Black-headed Grosbeak, and Fox Sparrow. Watch for Bewick's Wren, too.

If you don't detour through St. Joe City, and instead continue east on FH 50, you'll pass over Falls Creek at milepost 15.8. Just east of Falls Creek, at milepost 16.3, a gravel road leaves on the right (south) side and descends to the St. Joe River. If the gate is open, you can access the railroad grade here. Turning right (southwest) will take you over a narrow bridge and then to St. Joe City in 3 miles. Turning left (northeast) will take you upstream one mile, where the railroad grade is typically blocked-off at a turn-around. You can also access a 40-acre tract of riparian forest by staying on FH 50 until milepost 16.6, then turning right (south) as soon as you cross the large concrete bridge. The 0.1-mile gravel road descends to the river and the riparian forest.

Big Eddy Cafe at milepost 19.2 is a useful landmark. During early morning and late evening, scattered herds of White-tailed Deer and Wapiti (American Elk) feed on grassy hillsides across the river.

At milepost 24.2 is the turn-off to Calder. By going left (north), you can again access the railroad grade along the St. Joe River. To get to the railroad grade, drive 0.4 mile toward Calder. As soon as you cross the bridge, turn right (east) onto the grade (Potlatch Road) and continue toward Big Creek. This road passes through a short rock tunnel (watch for Rock Wrens), before taking you back across the river and rejoining FH 50 at Marble Creek Service in 9.5 miles (see below). Examples of good riparian habitat can be found at mileposts 1 and 8. On the dry brushy hillsides above, watch and listen for Wild Turkeys, Dusky Flycatchers, Orange-crowned Warblers, Lazuli Buntings, Black-headed Grosbeaks, and Chipping Sparrows. At Potlatch Road milepost 4, you'll cross Big Creek, where Spotted Sandpipers and American Dippers are regular.

If you didn't take the Calder turn-off, continue east along FH 50 toward Avery. Huckleberry Campground at milepost 29.8 offers primitive camping and access to the St. Joe River. Common Mergansers, Spotted Sandpipers, Belted Kingfishers, Willow Flycatchers, and American Dippers are usually present along this river stretch, especially from May to August.

The St. Joe Lodge and Resort at milepost 33.6 provides meals, gas, camping, and rental cabins. Hummingbird feeders on the back porch attract Black-chinned, Calliope, Rufous, and, occasionally, Broad-tailed Hummingbirds. Western Screech-Owls nest in the large Western Redcedars and Black Cottonwoods.

If you drove the railroad grade east of Calder, you rejoin FH 50 at Marble Creek Service, a small cafe at milepost 34.2. Continue east 0.2 mile to the mouth of Marble Creek and the start of FR 321. An interpretative building explains the historic logging that occurred in the area. American Dippers are usually present along Marble Creek, and shy Harlequin Ducks may be seen occasionally, May through August.

OTHER:

St. Maries is a full-service community. See also St. Maries to Harrison Route (p. 59) and Heyburn SP, the previous site.

SNOW PEAK TRAIL

Author: Dan Svingen

Site P-17 — Map P-17

Highlights: Accipiters, Pine Grosbeak
Major Habitats: Mixed Conifer Forest
Location: Shoshone Co., 48 miles southeast of St. Maries
Spring: N/A   **Summer:** * * *   **Fall:** * *   **Winter:** N/A

Snow Peak is one of those spots that you really have to want to get to. Access is not a minor consideration. From St. Maries, it takes 6 hours to arrive; 3 by car and another 3 by foot. The rewards, however, are great views and neat birds. From the look-out atop the 6,700-foot crest, you can admire the Mallard-Larkins Pioneer Area, watch for birds flying along the ridgetop, and observe Mountain Goats at close quarters.

DIRECTIONS:

From Avery follow FH 50 east 19.2 miles. Turn right (south) onto graveled FR 509, cross the St. Joe River, and proceed up West Fork Bluff Creek. If you have a CB radio, now is the time to use it, since a loaded logging truck might come around the corner at any time. After 9 miles you'll come to a 4-way intersection. Turn left (south) onto FR Road 201 and drive 4.2 miles to the Snow Peak Trailhead in Bathtub Meadows. On the way you'll pass Dismal Lake (0.8 mile south of the FR Road 509/FR Road 201 intersection) and primitive Mammoth Springs Campground (1.1 miles south of Dismal Lake).

From Bathtub Meadows trailhead, follow the well-marked path (Trail 55) southwest for 5 miles to the look-out. The trail, rated as "moderately difficult," is relatively flat for the first 4 miles, before climbing over 1,000 feet to the look-out.

BIRDING:

The trail and the look-out itself offer the best birding. Blue Grouse, Gray Jays, and Pine Grosbeaks breed in the Subalpine Fir and Engelmann Spruce forest lining the trail, and they can be found by careful listening. Boreal Owls are much harder to find. Try calling for them at night in October.

Four miles from the parking area, the trail enters a small meadow complete with rock slides and boggy lakes. This meadow is a good place to camp, and it allows scoping the cliffs below the look-out before you begin your ascent; recommended if you're searching for resident Mountain Goats. From the look-out, watch for accipiters, August until snowfall. The ridge system seems to be a favored thermal-producer, evident by mid-morning appearances of several Sharp-shinneds, a few Cooper's, and an occasional Northern Goshawk circling back and forth.

OTHER:

The road and trail are typically snow-free from mid-June to mid-October, but it's always wise to check with the FS station (208/245-4517), six miles west of Avery along FH 50, for the latest information. Because of the maze of roads and trails in this area, a recent FS map is highly recommended. St. Maries is the closest full-service community.

EMERALD CREEK

Author: Dan Svingen

Site P-18 — Map P-18

Highlights: Northern Goshawk, Barred Owl, Northern Pygmy-Owl
Major Habitats: Mixed Conifer Forest, Wetland
Location: Shoshone Co., 18 miles southeast of St. Maries
Spring: * *   **Summer:** * *   **Fall:** *   **Winter:** N/A

Scores of rockhounds visit Emerald Creek each year. Emerald Creek and India are the only places in the world where you can excavate your own Star Garnet; Idaho's State Gem. With patience, you may also see a Northern Goshawk or a Barred Owl.

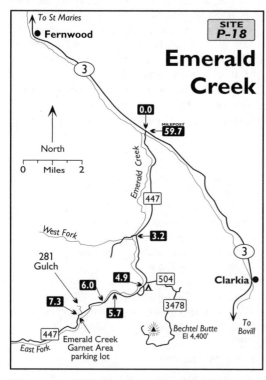

DIRECTIONS:

From Fernwood follow ID 3 southeast about 4 miles. At milepost 59.7 turn right (south) onto FR 447. (Look for the large brown sign for Emerald Creek.) Zero your mileage and go straight over the railroad tracks, cattle-guard, and bridge. Watch for Ruffed Grouse, American Dippers, Mountain Bluebirds, and American Pipits (September–October), but *please bird from the road only since this is private land.* Pavement ends at mile 0.3.

At mile 3.2 is a confusing junction. Take the second left, staying on FR 447 (signed for "Campground"). Garnet sand is processed at this road junction, so it may appear that you're driving into a gravel-crushing operation. Don't despair, since the road snakes through the congestion for only 0.2 mile before entering the forest canopy and running up East Fork Emerald Creek. From here on up is public land (FS), all open for birding.

BIRDING:

At mile 4.9, pull over and bird Emerald Creek Campground (FS), on the left (south). Barred Owls are often found at night in or around the campground. During the day, you are likely to find Common Ravens, Willow and Cordilleran Flycatchers, Eastern Kingbirds, and Townsend's Warblers.

Continue west on FR 447. At mile 5.7, park in the small pull-out on the right (north) and cross the creek. Currently, there's an old dilapidated bridge here, but it may be safer to wade the creek. If you use the bridge, be very careful of your footing. Future plans call for a foot bridge to be put in at mile 5.5. Once you're on the north side of East Fork Emerald Creek, cross the electric fence and enter the small (20 acre) meadow. This site was strip-mined for decades but has been reclaimed as a wildlife area. Look for Willow Flycatchers, Cedar Waxwings, MacGillivray's Warblers, and Song Sparrows along the creek, and Canada Geese, Mallards, Hooded Mergansers, Soras, and Vaux's Swifts by the 1.5-acre pond. Also investigate the little potholes in the meadow for Spotted Sandpipers, and hordes of Spotted Frog, Western Toad, and Long-toed Salamander young'ns. Mountains form an amphitheater around the meadow, echoing calls of Northern Pygmy-Owls (August and September) and of Pileated Woodpeckers (year round).

Continuing west on FR 447, you'll cross East Fork Emerald Creek at mile 6.0. Look for Willow Flycatchers, Cassin's Vireos, Wilson's Warblers, and Fox Sparrows.

If you're looking for Northern Goshawks, ask FS rangers at the garnet-digging site. To reach the site, continue up East Fork Emerald Creek to mile 7.3. Pull over at the large parking lot on the left (south) and leave your car. Backtrack east on FS 447 (i.e., downstream) about 100 yards, where a gated road goes up a side draw ("281 Gulch"), to the northwest. The ranger shack (and garnet-digging areas) are up the road about 0.3 mile. The shack sits in a small meadow hosting a lively colony of Columbian Ground Squirrels. At least one pair of Northern Goshawks dines heavily on these large rodents.

For an interesting side trip, return to Emerald Creek Campground and head north on FR 447 for 0.2 mile, then go right (east) on FR 504 for 2.5 miles. At the T intersection, go right (south) and follow the main road as it winds to the top of Bechtel Butte. A high-clearance vehicle is necessary for the last 0.2 mile. (Be aware that there is a tight turn-around at road's end.) From Bechtel Butte, scan the wide swaths of conifer forest for soaring Northern Goshawks. At least three pairs nest in the drainage, but you'll have to be lucky to see one. Northern Pygmy-Owls often hunt here also, perching on snag tops or bushes. Although resident all year, pygmy-owls are most often seen in late fall.

OTHER:

Fuel, food, and some supplies are available in Fernwood. Additional services are available in St. Maries or Moscow. Primitive camping is available at the FS Emerald Creek Campground for most of the non-snow season.

You can dig garnets from Memorial Day to Labor Day, but fee permits are required. This popular adult/children activity requires getting very muddy. For more information, call the FS (208/245-2531) in St. Maries.

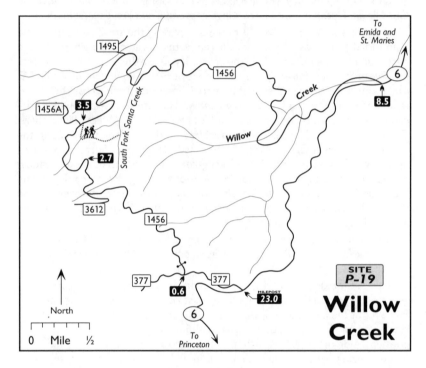

WILLOW CREEK

Author: Dan Svingen

Site P-19 — Map P-19

Highlights: Olive-sided Flycatcher, Fox Sparrow
Major Habitats: Mixed Conifer Forest
Location: Shoshone Co., 30 miles southwest of St. Maries
Spring: N/A   **Summer:** * *   **Fall:** *   **Winter:** N/A

Willow Creek is a 3,700-acre chunk of NF land, about 6 miles southwest of Emida. Although over 100 bird species have been found here, Willow Creek is unlikely to be a prime birding destination. This area does, however, provide a welcome respite from the highway. The ease of birding Willow Creek will improve once current plans for an auto tour and interpretive trails are activated. Because of the uncertainty of these improvements, you may want to telephone the St. Joe Ranger District (208/245-2531) regarding the status of timber harvest, road closures, and interpretive improvements before venturing forth.

Both clearcuts and partial cuts are obvious in Willow Creek. Edges of these timber units are favored by Moose; keep an eye out, and provoke neither bull nor cow.

DIRECTIONS:

To explore Willow Creek, follow ID 6 southwest of Emida to the crest of the Palouse Divide. At milepost 23 turn right (northwest) into a large pull-out and zero your mileage. Follow graveled FR 377, which climbs up the cutbank from the back of the pull-out. FR 377 soon enters the forest and then winds along the ridgetop. At mile 0.6, turn right (north) onto FR 1456 and drive into Willow Creek drainage.

BIRDING:

At mile 0.7 you'll reach a gate at the edge of a large clearcut. Stop and look for House and Rock Wrens, Mountain and Western Bluebirds, Townsend's Solitaires, Western Tanagers, Gray-crowned Rosy-Finches (occasional, September to April), and Pine Grosbeaks (uncommon). Drive through the gate (open during the summer but closed during the rest of the year). You enter forest at mile 1, where you are likely to hear multitudes of Red-breasted Nuthatches, Winter Wrens, Golden-crowned and Ruby-crowned Kinglets, Swainson's and Varied Thrushes, Townsend's and Yellow-rumped Warblers, Cassin's Finches, and Red Crossbills. Keep watch for Barred Owls, too. Be sure to stop and scan clearcuts along this route as well. At mile 1.9 you'll pass a young conifer plantation on the right (north) where Yellow and MacGillivray's Warblers and Dark-eyed Juncos are common. At mile 2.3 go straight (i.e., stay right). At mile 2.7 stop to see if the planned "Root Rot" trail on the right has been brushed-out yet. American Three-toed, Black-backed, and Pileated Woodpeckers are occasionally seen here. At mile 2.9 you reach a 20-year-old clearcut, covered with vigorous young conifers and plentiful MacGillivray's Warblers. At mile 3.5 is a road junction. Park and walk the old logging-road to the right (southeast) for 0.5 mile. In the mixed brush/forest habitat at the end of this road, listen for Dusky Flycatchers, Orange-crowned Warblers, and Black-headed Grosbeaks.

The most diverse birding along this route is in partially-cut forest between miles 5.9 and 7.4. A variety of species occur, including Cassin's and Warbling Vireos, Western Tanager, and Black-headed Grosbeak. Olive-sided Flycatchers and Fox Sparrows should be looked for in the older plantations around mile 7.5. You'll rejoin ID 6 at mile 8.5, 3 miles southwest of Emida.

OTHER:

A restaurant in Emida is usually open. For all other services, try St. Maries, Potlatch, or Moscow. See also Moscow Mountain Route (p. 76).

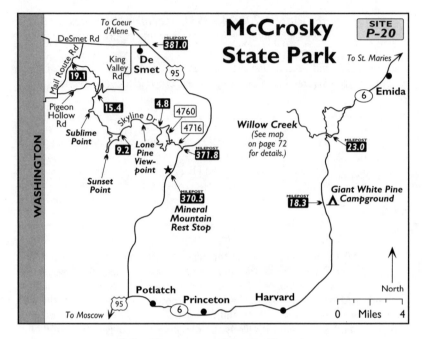

MCCROSKY STATE PARK

Authors: John and Marty Hirth, Carole Vande Voorde, Kas Dumroese

Site P-20 — Map P-20

Highlights: Ruffed Grouse, Western Bluebird
Major Habitats: Mixed Conifer Forest
Location: Latah Co., 25 miles north of Moscow
Spring: * *   **Summer:** * *   **Fall:** *   **Winter:** *

The 4,500-acre Mary Minerva McCrosky SP is a strictly low-budget spot. There's no map, maybe one toilet and about eight picnic tables, and the place accommodates only primitive camping—but it's worth visiting for the spectacular views alone. This 20-mile drive takes you through forest along ridgetops, and provides access to several dirt spurs and trails in a mish-mash of federal, state, tribal, and industrial forest land. Snow closes the road, late October until well into April.

DIRECTIONS:

From Moscow follow US 95 north for 25 miles. At milepost 371.8 (on the Latah and Benewah County line), turn left (west) onto Skyline Drive (a.k.a. FR 4716) and zero your mileage. *Beware of on-coming traffic.* At mile 0.5 is an information sign on the right (north). Stop and note the "Skyline Drive" markers; these are about the only road signs that you'll see.

BIRDING:

Along this route Ruffed Grouse are abundant, Black-capped and Mountain Chickadees and Townsend's Solitaires are common, and Pileated Wood-peckers and Evening Grosbeaks are uncommon. At mile 1.1, you can park and hike FR 4760 toward Mineral Mountain. (If you don't want to hike, vehicular access is possible farther along the route.) Look for Red-eyed Vireos, MacGillivray's and Wilson's Warblers, and White-crowned Sparrows during migration, Western Wood-Pewees and Cordilleran Flycatchers in summer, and at all seasons Blue Grouse (rare and declining) and Clark's Nutcrackers.

Back on the route, you'll pass through Western Redcedars in wet draws; listen for Winter Wrens and Varied Thrushes and watch for Barred Owls (un-common). On the dry, shrubby slopes above the road listen for Or-ange-crowned and Nashville Warblers.

At mile 4.8, FR 4760 is reached by a sharp turn to the right (east). With a high-clearance vehicle, you can drive 2 miles up this narrow dirt road to the old look-out on top of Mineral Mountain (4,128 feet) for a panoramic view of the Palouse/Hoodoo Range.

At mile 5.7 is a short turn-off (left; south) to Lone Pine Viewpoint, a good spot for Western Bluebirds. The vista should be scanned for Swainson's Hawks in summer, Rough-legged Hawks in migration, and Sharp-shinned and Cooper's Hawks year round. A trail originates here and meanders down the ridge side for a mile to a picnic area. Dusky Flycatchers and Gray Jays can be found along Skyline Drive in this vicinity.

The dirt road reached by a right turn at mile 8.7 leads 0.7 mile to Mission Mountain (4,324 feet), ending at a picnic area. This road is particularly good for Swainson's (nesting) and Hermit (migrating) Thrushes. Northern Gos-hawks nest nearby. At the Y at mile 9.2, go left on "old" Skyline Drive. The "old" road is good, and at mile 10.3 you reach Sunset Point and another fine view of the Palouse Prairie. Hawks seen here are the same as those at Lone Pine. At this point the ridge projects into the Palouse, suggesting that it might be a good spot for hawks and falcons during fall migration. Stay right (north) at the point and follow the road as it winds along the forest edge, where Cassin's and Warbling Vireos and Townsend's Warblers again are prevalent. You'll re-join "new" Skyline Drive at mile 11.7.

Skyline Drive continues at somewhat lower altitude with another fine viewpoint of the Palouse and conical Steptoe Butte at Sublime Point (mile 14). Late October may host Gray-crowned Rosy-Finches along the rock cutbanks for the next mile. Skyline Drive becomes muddier as you continue, especially in spring and late fall. (At mile 15.4 you can take King Valley Road, which veers right (east) for a shortcut back to civilization.) Skyline Drive continues straight, and in 0.1 mile Pigeon Hollow Road heads left (west) toward Farmington, Washington. If you stay on Skyline, stay left at the Y at mile 16.5. At mile 19.1 you intersect Mail Route Road; turn right (northeast) and follow it to a T intersection at mile 21.1. The forest is somewhat more open in this sec-tion and features Western Bluebirds and Western Tanagers. At the T turn

right (east) onto poorly marked DeSmet Road and follow it to mile 25.1 and
US 95 at milepost 381.

OTHER:

Fuel, groceries, and a restaurant can be found in Tensed, one mile north of
where DeSmet Road meets US 95. Unfortunately, the Idaho DeLorme Atlas
(1992 edition) has most of the roads in and around McCrosky erroneously
named. Moscow is the nearest full-service community.

The Mineral Mountain Rest Stop at US 95 milepost 370.5 has a nice nature
trail where you might find House Wrens, both kinglet species, Cassin's, Warbling, and Red-eyed Vireos, and Cassin's Finches.

MOSCOW MOUNTAIN ROUTE

Authors: John and Marty Hirth, Kas Dumroese

Site P-21 — Map P-21

Highlights: Barred Owl, Varied Thrush
Major Habitats: Mixed Conifer Forest, Deciduous Forest
Location: Latah Co., 8 miles north of Moscow
Spring: * * **Summer:** * * **Fall:** * **Winter:** *

*This 50-mile route leads you up the north slope of Moscow Mountain (4,983
feet) and ends near the Palouse Divide, where much turn-of-the-century gold
mining occurred.*

DIRECTIONS:

From Moscow drive north on US 95 about 8 miles to Viola. At milepost
353.6, zero your mileage and turn right (east) on Four Mile Road. Stay left at
the Y at mile 0.1 and right at the Ys at mile 0.6 and 4.1, as Four Mile Road becomes Flanagan Creek Road at the latter spot. Stay left at the Y at mile 4.8. At
mile 6.1 turn right (southeast) on Davis Road (gravel). Follow Davis Road,
checking the stream edge from the road, especially between miles 6.1 and 6.6,
for warblers and Red-eyed Vireos. You'll reach a T intersection with Rock
Creek Road at mile 10.6. Turn right (southeast) and ascend Moscow Mountain. This road is gravel for 3 miles and is usually plowed in winter, and then it
becomes dirt which is not maintained in winter (reopening about mid-May).

BIRDING:

Throughout this route, near the forest edge one may find Great Horned,
Northern Pygmy-, Barred (uncommon) and Northern Saw-whet Owls.
These species are permanent residents but are more vocal and visible from
February to April and again in September. Other birds visible from along the
edge include migrating Vaux's Swifts, Hermit Thrushes, Nashville,

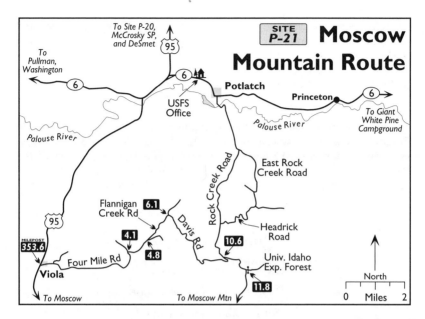

To Site P-20,
McCrosky SP,
and DeSmet
To
Pullman,
Washington

SITE P-21 MOSCOW
Mountain Route

Potlatch

Princeton

USFS
Office

Palouse River

To Giant
White Pine
Campground

Palouse River

East Rock
Creek Road

Flannigan **6.1**
Creek Rd

Rock Creek Road

Davis Rd

Headrick
Road

4.1
10.6

HILEPOST
353.6

Four Mile Rd **4.8**
Viola

Univ. Idaho
Exp. Forest

North

11.8

To Moscow

To Moscow Mtn

0   Miles   2

MacGillivray's, and Wilson's Warblers, and Fox, White-throated (rare), and Golden-crowned (rare) Sparrows. Local breeders include Cordilleran Flycatchers, Western Bluebirds, Swainson's Thrushes, Yellow Warblers, Black-headed Grosbeaks, and Lazuli Buntings. Winter species to look for are Northern Goshawk (uncommon), Bohemian Waxwing, Northern Shrike, Pine Grosbeak (occasional), Cassin's Finch, and Common Redpoll.

A gated road on the left (north) side of the road at mile 11.8 leads into the University of Idaho Experimental Forest (public). Besides this road, there are numerous old, unused logging roads where one can hike into the forest. Birds here include nesting American Three-toed and Pileated Woodpeckers, Clark's Nutcrackers, Mountain and Chestnut-backed Chickadees, and Townsend's Warblers. There's also the possibility of Olive-sided Flycatchers (rare, summer) and White-winged Crossbills (very rare, winter).

Return to the T and follow Rock Creek Road (go straight) 1.3 miles north; then turn right (east) on Headrick Road. This 2-mile-long gravel road passes through forest and then brushy slopes and is very good in spring for migrating warblers and in summer for Hammond's, Dusky, and Cordilleran Flycatchers, Cassin's and Warbling Vireos, Western Tanagers, and Black-headed Grosbeaks. In winter this road is not snowplowed, but one can by-pass it by continuing to Potlatch via Rock Creek Road. Just past "Lucy Lane," Headrick Road curves left (north) and goes up a slight hill, becoming East Rock Creek Road. In 0.4 mile stay right at the Y and you'll rejoin the paved Rock Creek Road in 2 miles. It's another 2 miles to ID 6 in Potlatch. Along the way you'll cross the Palouse River. In willows and shrubs along Rock Creek and the Palouse River are nesting Willow Flycatchers and Gray Catbirds.

Another fun birding spot is at Giant White Pine Campground, located north of Princeton and Harvard along ID 6 at milepost 18.3. Swainson's and Varied Thrushes are abundant, although better heard at dawn and dusk than seen in underbrush. Often Great Horned and/or Barred Owls nest nearby and can be heard hooting at night.

OTHER:

Moscow is a full service community. Food, fuel, and lodging are available in Potlatch. Maps are available from the FS (1221 S. Main; 208/882-3557) in Moscow, or Potlatch (ID 6, 1.2 miles east of US 95; 208/875-1131). Maps for the University of Idaho Experimental Forest are available from the College of Forestry (Experimental Forest, University of Idaho, Moscow, ID 83844-1133; 208/885-7016) in Moscow.

SPRING VALLEY
AND MOOSE CREEK RESERVOIRS
Authors: Dave Holick, Carole Vande Voorde
Site P-22 — Map P-22

Highlights: Sora, Virginia Rail, Western Bluebird
Habitat: Wetland, Mixed Conifer Forest
Location: Latah Co., 5 miles north of Troy
Spring: * *   **Summer:** * *   **Fall:** *   **Winter:** *

These two reservoirs offer fun birding close to Moscow. IDFG manages the 50-acre Spring Valley Reservoir and surrounding land. Each year the reservoir is stocked with Rainbow Trout, Smallmouth Bass, and perch, making this a popular family recreation area. Moose Creek Reservoir is maintained by Latah County Parks and Recreation. It's one of the best local sites for Virginia Rails and Soras.

DIRECTIONS:

Both reservoirs are along ID 8 between Troy and Bovill. From Moscow follow ID 8 east about 12.3 miles. At milepost 17, turn left (north) onto Spring Valley Road. Go 2.7 miles to the reservoir, bearing left at all three forks. The first half of Spring Valley Road is paved, but the second half is gravel.

BIRDING:

Birding Spring Valley Reservoir is best done from a boat along the south and west sides of the reservoir or from the trail leading from the northwestern-most parking area around the lake to the dam. Many trails crisscross the northwest corner of the area bordering the reservoir. The mix of lake, cattail marsh, conifers, and deciduous brush at the trailhead is an excellent place to start, with everything from Pied-billed and Western Grebes, Great Blue

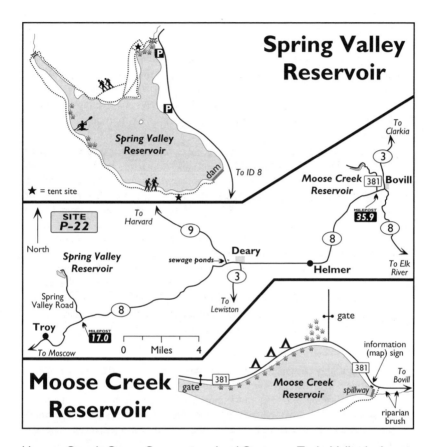

Herons, Canada Geese, Green-winged and Cinnamon Teals, Mallards, American Wigeons, Ring-necked Ducks, Common Goldeneyes, Buffleheads, Common Mergansers, Ruddy Ducks, and American Coots on the water, to Orange-crowned, Yellow, Yellow-rumped, and MacGillivray's Warblers in the brush. Ospreys have been present through the summer. Cooper's Hawks have nested on the west side of the reservoir. The reservoir also attracts many migrants but on a seemingly random basis. Spring sightings of Bald Eagles, Killdeer, Wilson's Snipe, Ring-billed and Bonaparte's Gulls, Caspian, Forster's, and Black Terns, Northern Shrikes, and Red Crossbills have all been recorded.

To reach Moose Creek Reservoir, backtrack to ID 8 and turn left (northeast). As you drive along, watch for Western and Mountain Bluebirds, common along the highway in spring and summer. In winter, look for Rough-legged Hawks and Pine Grosbeaks. Also watch the top of conifers for Northern Pygmy-Owls. You may wish to check the Deary sewage ponds on the north side of the junction of ID 8 and ID 9. From Deary, continue (east) on ID 8 for about 8 miles. At milepost 35.9, turn left (north) onto FR 381.

There's a sign for the reservoir and Sportsman Access on the highway. Follow the gravel road 1.8 miles to the reservoir.

Along FR 381, the riparian brush just below the spillway is busy in spring and summer with Black-chinned Hummingbirds, Dusky Flycatchers, House Wrens, and Orange-crowned, Yellow, Townsend's, and MacGillivray's Warblers. In winter, Black-capped Chickadees, Winter Wrens, Golden-crowned Kinglets, Cassin's and House Finches, Pine Siskins, and American Goldfinches are present.

Just 0.1 mile beyond the spillway is a reservoir map for you to get your bearings. Late May is the best time for rails and waterfowl. Both Virginia Rails and Soras can be lured out with judicious use of tapes. Green-winged, Blue-winged, and Cinnamon Teals, Barrow's Goldeneyes, Osprey, Greater and Lesser Yellowlegs, Wilson's Snipe, Wilson's Phalaropes, and Marsh Wrens can be seen along the lake's north side. Wood Ducks are common. Conifers in the campground host Red-naped Sapsuckers, Downy and Hairy Woodpeckers, Black-capped, Mountain, and Chestnut-backed Chickadees, Red-breasted and White-breasted Nuthatches, and Varied Thrushes. The gate at the west end is closed, but it's an easy walk to the end of the lake.

You may also drive or hike to the south side of the lake. Access is just below the spillway. There is no bridge, so access depends on stream depth. There are a couple of campsites and trails for hiking on the south side.

OTHER:

At Spring Valley overnight parking for RVs and camper trailers is available (no hook-ups). There are a few picnic tables near the parking areas and a few tent sites. A number of docks and fishing-platforms have been built to make access easy. Fishing (year round), boating (electric motors and oars only), camping, picnicking, and swimming are the most common activities. There is no entry fee.

At Moose Creek there are 16 campsites, two of them drive-throughs, and three tent sites. Drinking-water, fire rings, picnic tables, and pit toilets are available. The lake is stocked with trout and is open to fishing year round with excellent ice-fishing in winter and waterfowl hunting in season. Electric motors are permitted.

Moscow is the nearest full-service community.

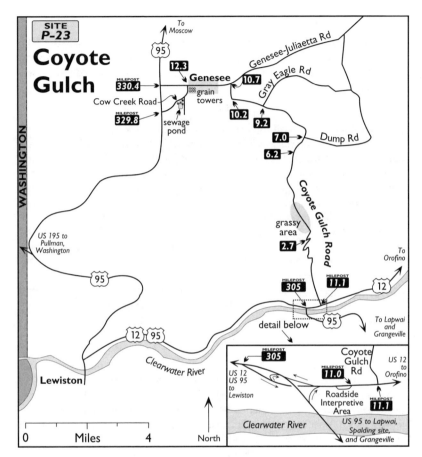

COYOTE GULCH

Author: Kas Dumroese

Site P-23 — Map P-23

Highlights: Bewick's Wren, Snowy Owl
Major Habitats: Shrub-steppe, Farmland
Location: Nez Perce Co., 8 miles east of Lewiston
Spring: ✳✳✳   **Summer:** ✳✳   **Fall:** ✳✳✳   **Winter:** ✳

Coyote Gulch (a.k.a. Coyote Grade) is situated on the breaks of the Clearwater River. From the top of the grade to the river is an elevational change of about 2,000 feet, occurring quite drastically along a gravel road that is steep and narrow with a few switch-backs. Long motor-homes should avoid this road. All land here is private.

DIRECTIONS:

From Lewiston head east on US 12/US 95 for 7.5 miles to milepost 305. Take the US 12 exit toward Orofino. At US 12 milepost 11.1, turn left (north) onto graveled Coyote Gulch Road (a.k.a. Nez Perce County Road 170), and zero your mileage.

BIRDING:

As soon as you turn off the highway, check for Chukars on the rocky hill-sides. As you drive up the grade, stop periodically to listen for Chukars (year round) and Grasshopper Sparrows (May and June). Check the road cutbank at mile 2.7 for a Bank Swallow colony. Grassy fields and fence-rows from about mile 3 to 3.8 are good during spring migration (April to June) for Say's Phoebes, Western Kingbirds, Western and Mountain Bluebirds, and Vesper, Savannah, and White-crowned Sparrows. The best birding begins at mile 5.8, where the brush starts, and continues to mile 6.6. Park here and walk along the brushy hillsides. This is Idaho's most reliable spot for Bewick's Wrens. Lately, birds have been found year round and are probably breeding here. Migration up this canyon is poorly understood, but this site looks like a great spot to find vagrants. Usual spring and summer species include California Quail, Western Screech-Owl, Black-capped Chickadee, Lazuli Bunting, Spotted Towhee, MacGillivray's Warbler, and, occasionally, Wild Turkey.

During May migrating Cordilleran Flycatchers, Western Tanagers, and Black-headed Grosbeaks are common. During fall (especially September), Lincoln's Sparrows are regular, as are large flocks of White-crowned Sparrows. (There must be a Golden-crowned or a White-throated Sparrow in there, as well.) In winter check for owls, Downy Woodpeckers, Black-capped Chickadees, Bewick's Wrens, Golden-crowned Kinglets, and Northern Shrikes. The unmarked graveled road at mile 6.2 that heads right (east) from this birdy spot is private, although it's not posted.

You may retrace the route back to Lewiston or continue north to Moscow. If you continue north, the intersection of Coyote Grade and Dump Road is at mile 7.0. Stay left (west) on Coyote Grade Road; at mile 9.2 it intersects with Gray Eagle Road. Stay left (west) on Coyote Grade Road (paved) and follow it to mile 10.2 and Central Grade Road. Stay right (north) on paved Central Grade Road until you reach the T intersection at the Genesee-Juliaetta Road at mile 10.7. Turn left (west) and continue straight west through the small community of Genesee to mile 13.0 at US 95 milepost 330.4. Along the route back to US 95, watch for Northern Harriers (year round), American Kestrels, other falcons, and Short-eared and Snowy Owls (November–February). The stretch between Coyote Grade and Genesee is one of Idaho's most reliable areas for Snowy Owls. Watch out: farmers have placed white plastic bottles on fence-posts which at first glance give enthusiastic birders the false impression of an owl.

If you're visiting in the April-to-June period, you may wish to take a quick peek at the Genesee sewage pond. Instead of driving through Genesee, turn left (south) at mile 12.3 on Jackson Street (becomes Cow Creek Road), which is just past the grain towers, and follow it to an unmarked road on the left (south) at mile 12.7. You may drive 0.1 mile down this road to scan the pond (and the marsh to the north). Look for Green-winged, Blue-winged, and Cinnamon Teals, Black-necked Stilts, American Avocets, Wilson's Snipe, and Wilson's and Red-necked Phalaropes. This is also a good spot for migrating Swainson's Hawks (April and May). There's a fairly decent turn-around spot for cars just south of the sewage pond across the bridge. Backtrack to Cow Creek Road and turn left (west) and continue 0.6 mile to rejoin US 95, at milepost 329.8.

OTHER:

Both Moscow and Lewiston are full-service communities. Groceries are available in Genesee. See also Spalding Site (p. 95) and Lewiston Area, the next site.

LEWISTON AREA

Authors: Merlene Koliner, Carole Vande Voorde, Kas Dumroese

Site P-24 — Map P-24/P-25

Highlights: Eurasian Wigeon, Chukar, Barn Owl
Habitat: Urban, Cliff, Wetland
Location: Nez Perce Co., Lewiston
Spring: * * *   **Summer:** *   **Fall:** * * *   **Winter:** * * * *

Although a few Idaho locales claim to be the state's "Banana Belt," we think that Lewiston is really the reigning king, with hot summers and mild winters. Only about 710 feet above sea level, Lewiston is located at Idaho's lowest elevation. Levee ponds along the river are usually ice-free all winter, so lots of waterfowl congregate here. This is one of the best spots for finding wintering Eurasian Wigeons.

DIRECTIONS:

When entering Lewiston from the north or east, follow US 12 West into town. This route starts at the junction of US 12 and 3rd Avenue North (the first traffic light and next to the tourist information booth).

BIRDING:

The first stop is the sewage treatment plant located behind the port district, which can be extremely noisy and busy during the week. After zeroing your mileage at the junction of US 12 and 3rd Avenue North, turn right (west) onto 3rd Avenue North and follow it 0.7 mile (past the Lewis-Clark Grain Terminal) to 6th Avenue North. Be sure to check any wintering Canada

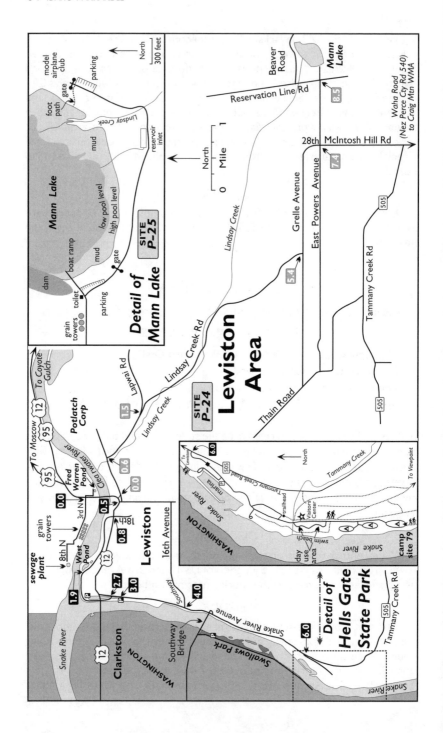

Detail of Mann Lake

SITE P-25

Lewiston Area

SITE P-24

Detail of Hells Gate State Park

Geese flocks that you pass for Greater White-fronted Geese or a Brant (vagrant). *Watch out for large forklifts and other heavy equipment.* At 6th Avenue turn left (west) and go one block to 12th Street North. Turn right (north) and follow 12th Street as it curves left (becoming unmarked 8th Avenue North) to the dead-end at the Lewiston sewage treatment plant at mile 1.1. Park before the gate in the gravel pull-out on the left. Check the cattail marsh outside the fence for Wood Ducks, California Quail, accipiters, Marsh Wrens, sparrows, and American Goldfinches year-round, and Virginia Rails and Soras in all but the coldest months.

Backtrack to the intersection of US 12 and 3rd Avenue North and continue straight (east) across US 12, and then immediately turn right (south) onto East 22nd Street North. Follow it 0.1 mile to 1st Avenue North and to the Fred Warren Memorial Fish Pond in Clearwater Park. In late fall through March, this is one of three Lewiston hotspots for Eurasian Wigeon. Check the wigeon flock grazing on the baseball diamond or next to the fishing pond. You can also access the levee here. A walk east on the levee's paved path may reward you with Horned, Eared, or Western Grebes; they seem to prefer this section of the river. Backtrack to the intersection of US 12 and 3rd Avenue North.

Zero your mileage, turn left (south) on US 12, and cross the Clearwater River, staying in the right lane. At mile 0.5, follow US 12 West, skirting around Locomotive Park and the first traffic light. At mile 0.8 is the next traffic light (18th Street); turn right (northwest) following the US 12 levee bypass toward Clarkston. Stop in the levee parking lot at mile 1.1. Hike to the top of the levee and scan across the river toward the grain terminal. In winter, several thousand Barrow's Goldeneyes may feed here, along with Mallards, Ring-necked Ducks, Greater (rare) and Lesser Scaup, Common Goldeneyes, and Buffleheads.

West Pond, the largest pond of the levee system, is at mile 1.9. Wood Ducks are common and reside year round. From late October through March, this is a great spot for waterfowl, with up to 15 species possible. A paved walking/fitness trail encompasses the pond. Species to look for include Northern Pintail, Eurasian and American Wigeons, Canvasback, Redhead, both scaup, both goldeneyes, Hooded Merganser, and an assortment of exotics. The flocks thin in spring, leaving Wood Ducks to raise their broods in solitude. Usually a Belted Kingfisher is present. Lately, Cattle Egrets have been present in late fall, and an occasional Say's Phoebe overwinters.

From the West Pond parking lot, turn right and continue west to mile 2.5. Turn left (east) on US 12 West (a.k.a. D Street) toward Clarkston and go 100 feet to the entrance of "Lewis and Clark Center" parking lot (left turn, north side). Take the pedestrian bridge across the highway for views of the confluence of the Snake and Clearwater Rivers. In fall and winter check waterfowl flocks for vagrants such as Brant, scoters, or an odd gull, like the Iceland Gull that wintered in 1994-1995. There's also a restroom here. Turn right (west) out of the parking lot and then immediately left (south) toward Hells Gate SP.

Snake River Avenue is at mile 2.7. Turn right (south) and at mile 3.0 is the parking lot for Kiwanis Park and its pond. Waterfowl here are extremely tame and allow a close approach. Mallards, American Wigeons, and American Coots make up most of the flock, but occasionally a wintering Eurasian Wigeon joins them. Check for weird gulls, too.

From Kiwanis Park continue south on Snake River Avenue (a.k.a. Nez Perce County Road 505; a.k.a. Tammany Creek Road), through the traffic light at Southway (mile 4.0), to the entrance of Hells Gate SP (right turn; west side) at mile 6.0.

From the fee station just inside Hells Gate SP, go 0.3 mile to the road on your right (west; marina access) for an excellent view of waterfowl at the marina. Pied-billed, Horned, Eared, and Western Grebes are seen in winter and spring. Just past the marina are two rock jetties that form coves in the river; check for shorebirds and waterfowl. Trees around the marina have Western Wood-Pewees, Say's Phoebes, and Western and Eastern Kingbirds in summer, and House Finches and American Goldfinches in fall and winter.

Backtrack to the main road and continue south into the park. In 0.5 mile you'll cross the bridge over Tammany Creek. Park in the day-use area to your immediate right (west). From here it's a leisurely one-mile walk south to the end of the campground, and this is the best way to bird the area. Start by walking along Tammany Creek and check the brush for Western Bluebirds, Yellow, Yellow-rumped, and Wilson's Warblers, Western Tanagers, Black-headed Grosbeak, Chipping, Savannah, Song, and White-crowned Sparrows, and Bullock's Orioles. At the mouth of the creek is a sandbar where Black-crowned Night-Herons and American Avocets have been seen. Spotted Sandpipers and Belted Kingfishers are common along the Snake River. Check the swimming beach for gulls. Keep walking south toward the campground. There are three camp loops in the park with more trees and brushy spots. A dirt trail along the river provides access to good riparian habitat which attracts Sharp-shinned and Cooper's Hawks, Willow Flycatchers, and Say's Phoebes. Marsh Wrens, Townsend's Warblers, and Lincoln's Sparrows are seen in fall. Species in the camping area include California Quail, Willow Flycatcher, Western and Eastern Kingbirds, and Black-capped Chickadee. At the south end of campground loop C, the park continues for another 2 miles. A dirt path, originating at camp-site 79, follows the river. It can be overgrown with thistles in summer, but it ends at spectacular cliffs of columnar basalt. Poison-Ivy is common here. The cliffs are home to Rock and Canyon Wrens. Five species of swallows and an occasional White-throated Swift can be seen flying over the water and banks of the river. Red-tailed Hawks and Northern Harriers fly over the hills used by Brewer's, Vesper, Lark, Savannah, and Grasshopper Sparrows. The dry hills are criss-crossed with equestrian trails and park vehicle roads that you may roam, checking the gullies for Chukars and watching the flats for Horned Larks.

If you're not particular that you find an *Idaho* Eurasian Wigeon, another great spot for this species is across the Snake River in Clarkston, Washington.

From Hells Gate SP, backtrack north on Snake River Avenue 1.3 miles and take Southway Bridge over the river to Clarkston. Take the second exit right toward Asotin via Washington Highway 129, curving back under the bridge (tricky; watch the signs). Continue south on Washington Highway 129 about 0.5 mile to the first entrance to Swallow's Park (US Army Corps of Engineers). Look for the big flocks of American Wigeon grazing on turf between the parking lot and the marina, which is a 0.3-mile walk to the south (upstream). Restrooms are available. Sometimes a Bewick's Wren can be heard from the island at the swimming area, and wintering gulls, including Mew, often congregate here.

OTHER:

Lewiston/Clarkston are full-service communities.

The Nez Perce called this area "Tse-me-na-kem" (si-MIN-i-kum), meaning "Meeting-of-the-Waters." Situated at the confluence of the Snake and Clearwater Rivers, Lewiston, Idaho, and Clarkston, Washington, are named for the famous duo who explored the area in 1805.

Lower Monumental Dam in southeastern Washington has allowed Lewiston to become the most inland seaport in the Pacific Northwest. The US Army Corps of Engineers has built a system of levees to restrain the rivers, and has further developed the area into a parkway, with 16 miles of paved, wheelchair-accessible paths for walking, biking, roller-blading, etc. The Corps has a Clarkston office (509/751-0240).

Hells Gate is the premier, full-service campground in Nez Perce County. Informative programs are held on summer evenings while Barn Owls fly through the campground. A swimming area is maintained on the Snake River. The park is open all year. Day-use areas are open 8 am to sunset (entrance fee). For more information, call the park office (208/799-5015).

MANN LAKE

Author: Kas Dumroese

Site P-25 — Map P-24/P-25

Highlights: Ross's Goose, Shorebirds
Major Habitats: Wetland
Location: Nez Perce Co., 3 miles east of Lewiston
Spring: * * *   **Summer:** * *   **Fall:** * * * * **Winter:** *

Mann Lake is a 35-acre reservoir operated by the Lewiston Orchards Irrigation District (LOID). IDFG cooperates with LOID in managing the reservoir for wildlife and sportfishing. Fortunately for shorebirds and shorebirders, LOID spends considerable time and money removing water-side vegetation. This activity, along with an irrigation season of July to September, generally results in fresh mud being exposed weekly, and therefore provides unobstructed views of shorebirds.

DIRECTIONS:

From the north end of Lewiston follow US 12 West south into town, cross the Clearwater River on Memorial Bridge, and immediately take the first left (east) toward East Lewiston. At the stop-sign zero your mileage and turn left (east) onto East Main Street and go to the T intersection with flashing yellow lights at mile 0.6. Turn right (south) onto Lapwai (a.k.a. Lindsay Creek) Road. At mile 1.5 the road forks; stay right on Lindsay Creek Road (Nez Perce County Road 460) and follow it to its terminus at Grelle Avenue at mile 5.4. Turn left (east) onto Grelle Avenue. At mile 7.1, Grelle Avenue makes a sharp right curve, where it becomes 28th Street (poorly marked). At mile 7.4, turn left (east) onto East Powers Avenue (a.k.a. Lapwai Road). The reservoir entrance is at mile 8.5. Continue straight (east) on gravel past the grain towers to the main parking lot. All roads are paved except those at the reservoir.

BIRDING:

Mann Lake is a popular fishing-hole, and weekend crowds can sometimes be annoying. Fortunately, the best shorebird area is the worst fishing area. Best birding is generally in early morning along the eastern shore. (Park by the model-airplane club and follow the footpath down to the water.) From this vantage point, you can easily scan most of the reservoir with the sun at your back. From mid-day to early evening, good viewing can also be achieved from the main parking area.

In spring, April is the peak month for observing migrating birds. American Avocets, maybe some Black-necked Stilts, and a smattering of shorebirds pass through, along with 21 waterfowl species, including Tundra Swan, Greater White-fronted and Snow Geese, all three of our regular teal, Gadwall, and Canvasback. Watch for Ross's Geese mixed in with any Snow Goose flock that may be present. During April or May look for a few Common Loons, Horned and Red-necked Grebes on the lake, and Say's Phoebes nesting in out-houses. Spring vagrants have included an April Willet and a May Snowy Plover.

The real excitement begins in July when fall shorebirds start moving through. Early flocks are mostly Western Sandpipers, with a few Semipalmateds and Leasts mixed in. The greatest diversity and density of shorebirds usually occurs in mid-August, when Semipalmated Plovers, Killdeer, American Avocets, Greater and Lesser Yellowlegs, Spotted Sandpipers, Semipalmated, Western, Least, Baird's, and Stilt Sandpipers, Long-billed Dowitchers, and Wilson's and Red-necked Phalaropes are possible. Most dowitchers are Long-billeds, but a few Short-billeds turn up each season. September is also good as plover numbers increase. Black-bellied Plovers are often present in low numbers, and one or two American Golden-Plovers usually make an appearance. A Sanderling or two are expected as well. Other species possible include Solitary Sandpiper, Willet, Long-billed Curlew, Marbled Godwit, and Dunlin, the latter sometimes persisting into late December.

Six species of swallows are possible during July and August, while fall is the time to check the Western Grebe flocks for Clark's, which is rare in the Idaho Panhandle. Besides these two species, Pied-billed, Horned, Red-necked, and Eared Grebes are fall visitors. Immature Black-crowned Night-Herons often roost in the willow trees along the creek by the model-airplane club. Caspian, Common, and Forster's Terns are possible from July into September. In September, Vaux's Swifts and American Pipits numbers usually peak, moving through in flocks of more than 200 birds each.

Check the brushy willow area on the east side of the lake for fall migrating Yellow, Yellow-rumped, Townsend's, MacGillivray's, and Wilson's Warblers, Western Tanagers, and Black-headed Grosbeaks, as well as White-throated (rare) and White-crowned Sparrows.

OTHER:

The reservoir is open year round. The main gate opens 30 minutes after sunrise and closes 30 minutes before sunset. Occasionally during summer, and often during winter and early spring, a second gate precludes driving to the model-airplane club, but walking is permitted. See also the Lewiston Area (p. 83).

CRAIG MOUNTAIN
WILDLIFE MANAGEMENT AREA

Author: Frances Cassirer

Site P-26 — Map P-26

Highlights: Chukar, Williamson's Sapsucker, Western Bluebird
Major Habitats: Dry Conifer Forest, Mixed Conifer Forest, Grassland
Location: Nez Perce Co., 20 miles southeast of Lewiston
Spring: * *　　**Summer:** * *　　**Fall:** * *　　**Winter:** N/A

Craig Mountain is a rolling forested plateau perched between the steep breaklands of the Snake and Salmon Rivers. The 40-mile-long route described below will take you along graveled and dirt roads, some of which require a high-clearance vehicle. A 4-wheel-drive vehicle is needed to see the entire area. Be aware that WMA roads are usually snow-covered from November into April.

DIRECTIONS:

From the north side of Lewiston follow US 12 West into town. After crossing Memorial Bridge, turn left (south) at the confusing 5-way intersection, and head uphill on 21st Street. Follow 21st Street (which becomes Thain Road) through Lewiston and Lewiston Orchards 4.0 miles, then follow it as it curves south, becoming 14th Street. After 2 blocks follow the main road left (east) onto Ripon Avenue (a.k.a. P2) for 3.5 blocks, then follow the right curve onto Barr Street. At the bottom of the hill, follow the curve left (east) onto Tammany Creek Road (a.k.a. Nez Perce County Road 505) toward Waha. In another 4 miles, take Nez Perce County Road 540 (a.k.a. Waha Road) to the right (south), and drive to the top of Craig Mountain in another 15 miles.

You'll reach the junction of Nez Perce County Roads 540 and 575 about 20 miles from Lewiston Orchards. Zero your mileage here, then turn right (south), following Road 540 into the WMA. As you enter, watch for Great Gray Owls, since they sometimes perch in this general area. Most of Craig Mountain is public land (IDFG, BLM, FS). Some private inholdings do occur, however, so be aware of posted signs.

BIRDING:

At mile 0.9 (just past the old corral), park at the yellow gate on the left (east) and walk down the road about 0.5 mile, staying to the right on Snowmachine Trail 2 (marked with small orange triangles). You'll pass between Kruze Meadow and a heavily logged forest. In summer, you're likely to find Wilson's Snipe, Olive-sided Flycatchers, Red-naped Sapsuckers, Red-breasted and White-breasted Nuthatches, Western and Mountain Bluebirds, and Red-winged Blackbirds. In spring you'll also be treated to a chorus of Pacific Treefrogs.

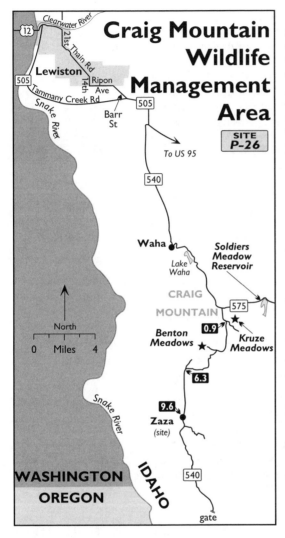

Craig Mountain Wildlife Management Area

SITE P-26

Clearwater River

12

Lewiston

21st

Thain Rd

505

Ripon

4th Ave

Tammany Creek Rd

Barr St

505

Snake River

To US 95

540

Waha

Lake Waha

Soldiers Meadow Reservoir

CRAIG MOUNTAIN

575

Benton Meadows

0.9

Kruze Meadows

North

0 Miles 4

6.3

Snake River

9.6

Zaza (site)

WASHINGTON

OREGON

IDAHO

540

gate

Farther south, at mile 2.3 (just before the gravel pit), park where the side road takes off to your right (west). This road leads to two gated roads. Follow the left "Snowmachine Road 2" past Benton Meadows to a cattle pond in about 0.75 mile. Look in this general area for Northern Goshawks, Red-tailed Hawks, Wilson's Snipe, various woodpeckers, Mountain and Western Bluebirds, and Cassin's Finches.

From about mile 3.5 on, Road 540 is often snowblocked until May. You'll pass the junction with Eagle Creek Road at mile 5.2. Eagle Creek road offers additional birding opportunities, but it's basically a jeep trail; *don't try driving it without a high-clearance 4x4.*

Continuing south on 540, park in the pull-out on the right (northwest) near the blue gate at mile 6.3. Walk down this gated road for 0.5 mile, then cut up to the ridgetop for a beautiful view of the Snake River Canyon. Birding in this area is best in spring and summer. Regular species include Northern Goshawk, Red-naped and Williamson's Sapsuckers, Mountain Chickadee, Brown Creeper, Ruby-crowned Kinglet, and Townsend's Warbler.

The ghost "town" of Zaza is along Road 540 at mile 9.6. Nez Perce County doesn't maintain Road 540 beyond this point, though it's usually passable in summer and fall.

In the next few miles you'll pass gated roads leading off to the left (east). A walk through the Grand Fir forest bordering these roads may yield Barred Owls, Pileated Woodpeckers, Varied Thrushes, and Cassin's Vireos.

At mile 12.4 Road 540 climbs to the top of a hill, allowing another spectacular view of the Snake River Canyon's grassland habitat. As you continue south on Road 540, you'll have even more awesome views when you enter bunchgrass habitat within Hells Canyon. Species here include American Kestrel, Blue Grouse, Chukar, Lewis's Woodpecker, Horned Lark, Western Bluebird, and Western Tanager. At night you may find Flammulated Owls or Common Poorwills. Continue to explore this area by vehicle or on foot. There is no one single place to bird here—it's all good!

OTHER:

The only designated campground near Craig Mountain WMA is at Soldiers Meadow Reservoir. A WMA map is available from the IDFG (208/799-5010) in Lewiston. Lewiston is a full service community. There are no other services along this route itself.

HEART OF THE MONSTER

Author: Dan Svingen

Site P-27 — See Panhandle map, page 20

Highlights: Gray Catbird, Bewick's Wren, Red-eyed Vireo
Major Habitats: Deciduous Forest, Meadow
Location: Idaho Co., 2 miles south of Kamiah
Spring: *   **Summer:** * *   **Fall:** *   **Winter:** N/A

With guile and intelligence, Coyote slew a great monster at this very site, giving rise to Nee-Mee-Poo (the Nez Perce people)—so goes the tale told at this small (100-acre) National Historic Site. You can hear a recording of the story in both English and Nez Perce.

DIRECTIONS:

Heart of the Monster National Historic Site is on the west side of US 12, 1.6 miles south of Kamiah, at milepost 68.5.

BIRDING:

The best birding is along the Clearwater River. From the parking lot, go west 60 yards to a small maintenance shed hidden behind bushes. Listen for Veeries singing in cottonwoods upstream (on private land). In May and June look for showy Common Camas growing in the meadow just south of the shed. (The meadow is public land until you reach the barbed-wire fence.) A mowed grass trail starts at the shed and goes north along an oxbow. Take the trail, watching for Wood Ducks, Osprey, Gray Catbirds (which seem to be in every other bush), Yellow Warblers (which *are* in every other bush), and Cedar Waxwings. Bewick's Wrens recently colonized this area. The grass trail continues about 600 yards until it ducks under some mature cottonwoods where Western Wood-Pewees and Warbling and Red-eyed Vireos are common. The 500-yard-long paved trail begins at the parking lot and passes by several brush patches, where migrating passerines often gorge on ripened berries.

OTHER:

The closest lodging, food, and fuel are in Kamiah. Picnic tables and pit toilets are available at the historic site.

WILDERNESS GATEWAY CAMPGROUND

Author: Winifred Hepburn

Site P-28 — See Panhandle map, page 20

Highlights: Harlequin Duck, Red-eyed Vireo, American Redstart
Major Habitats: Mixed Conifer Forest, Deciduous Forest
Location: Idaho Co., 40 miles east of Kooskia
Spring: * *   **Summer:** * * *   **Fall:** * * *   **Winter:** N/A

Wilderness Gateway Campground borders the Lochsa River and is the best place in Idaho to see Harlequin Ducks. Because the campground is also a trailhead for the Selway-Bitterroot Wilderness, there are endless birding opportunities on the miles and miles of paths which begin here. After birding this diverse spot has worn your legs to the nubbins, dip your feet in the river, pick a comfortable chair and your favorite beverage, and let the birds come to you!

DIRECTIONS:

From Kooskia, take US 12 northeast 49 miles, following the Middle Fork Clearwater and Lochsa Rivers upstream. The entrance to Wilderness Gateway Campground is on the right (south) side of the road at milepost 122.6. The campground is comprised of 4 camp loops (A, B, C, and D).

BIRDING:

Just before you cross the bridge to enter the campground, look for the information board on the right (west) side of the road. Opposite the information board (on the east side of the road), is a fishing trail leading to the Lochsa River. Spotted Sandpipers nest in the rocks there. This is a good spot to check the river for Harlequin Ducks and American Dippers. From the bridge itself, watch for Tree Swallows overhead, and keep an eye out for Vaux's and Black Swifts, the latter being a rare migrant.

There are two riverside hiking trails on the south bank: the 0.5-mile Downriver Trail (which begins between campsites C22 and C23) and the 0.5-mile Upriver Trail. Rumor has it that the Upriver Trail begins by campsite A14, but you may have difficulty finding the entrance. If so, walk the service road near the dump station and watch for the trail to cut across. The Downriver Trail is better-maintained, but it's not as birdy. Keep an ear open for Cordilleran Flycatchers near the end. At the lower end of the Upriver Trail, listen for Pileated Woodpeckers and Ruffed Grouse. The open areas along this trail are excellent for hummingbirds, which can often be seen courting in May. Be sure to watch for vireos and warblers chasing through the tree tops, as well. Be especially alert for American Redstarts, which are local and often hard to find in Idaho.

In early morning walk the main campground roadway and scan brush and trees for vireos and warblers. Search the open hillsides for Elk. The trail from Camp A to the amphitheater can be good birding. The entrance to Camp C is good for Hammond's Flycatchers and Gray Catbirds. Camp D is best for Ruffed Grouse, Black-chinned, Calliope, and Rufous Hummingbirds, Golden-crowned Kinglets, Black-capped and Chestnut-backed Chickadees, and Western Tanagers. Swainson's Thrushes and Red-eyed Vireos are everywhere.

To look for Harlequin Ducks, drive US 12, watching for males (mid-April to early June) or females with broods (July and August). Keep an eye on exposed rocks and logs, in or adjacent to shallow, swift water. Some of the best spots are the islands by US 12 mileposts 120, 142, 151, and 158. Although the Lochsa River Harlequin Duck population is the largest in Idaho, it still numbers fewer than 50 birds. Don't be surprised if you miss 'em!

OTHER:

Wilderness Gateway Campground has 88 campsites, water, playground, pit toilets (flush toilets in Camps A and B), picnic tables, group shelter, dump station, and horse facilities. A camp host is available from Memorial Day to Labor Day. In summer there may be evening programs at the amphitheater. Flyfishing, horseback riding, hiking, rafting, and kayaking are all popular activities here—at times it can be down-right crowded!

The Historical Lochsa Ranger Station is located across the road from the campground. For more information, contact the Kooskia Ranger Station (208/926-4274). The nearest town is Lowell, 21 miles southwest, where Three Rivers Resort (208/926-4430) has cabins, pool, and a restaurant. Fuel (and other necessities) can be hard to find east of Kooskia, so plan accordingly.

Harlequin Duck
Mike Denny

SPALDING SITE

Author: Dan Svingen

Site P-29 — Map P-29/P-30

Highlights: California Quail
Major Habitats: Deciduous Forest
Location: Nez Perce Co., 9 miles east of Lewiston
Spring: * *   **Summer:** * *   **Fall:** * *   **Winter:** * *

The Nez Perce Interpretive Center at Spalding Site provides insight into this area's rich history, including the operation of Spalding Mission. The best birding is in the picnic area along the Clearwater River. Because this spot offers a rare bit of shade, it can be crowded on summer weekends.

DIRECTIONS:

If the visitors center is open, you can reach the picnic area from the visitors center entrance road, which is on the north side of US 95 at milepost 303. As soon as you drive through the visitors center entrance gate, turn right (east) and go downhill 0.5 mile to the T intersection. Turn left (north), crossing the railroad tracks. Keep right to the picnic area in 0.2 mile.

If the visitors center is closed, the picnic area may still be open; try coming in the back way. At US 95 milepost 302.8, turn north onto the paved road that descends 0.5 mile along Lapwai Creek to the picnic area. You may still find a closed gate, but you can walk in.

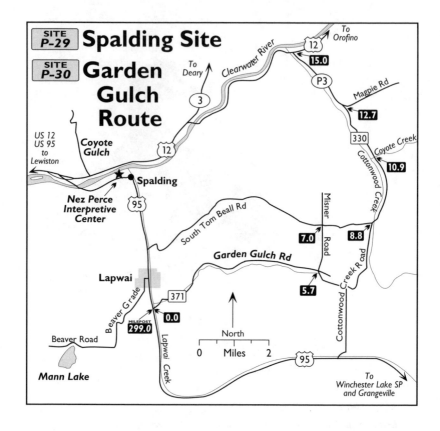

BIRDING:

Approximately 150 species have been recorded at the picnic ground, with one of the most prominent being California Quail. Quail are most often found hiding in the trees and shrubs at the picnic area's eastern boundary (by the barbed-wire fence). During late evening, it's not uncommon to see a Cooper's Hawk fly stealthily into the area. The best place to stake-out for the Cooper's (and Black-headed Grosbeaks and Bullock's Orioles) is among the shrubs and trees lining the railroad tracks. Listen for Cordilleran Flycatchers. A pair of Great Horned Owls usually nests somewhere in the park, occasionally under the old bridge.

In winter Spalding Site marks the upper-limit of major waterfowl activity along the Clearwater River, while the trees often act as a vagrant trap, collecting such interesting visitors as Barn, Long-eared, and Northern Saw-whet Owls, Brown Creepers, Townsend's Solitaires, and Bohemian Waxwings.

OTHER:

The visitors center is open 9 am to 5 pm from September to May, and 8 am to 5 pm during summer. The closest services are at Lapwai and Lewiston. Bigfoot was reportedly sighted here in 1992, just above US 95—keep an eye out. See also Coyote Gulch (p. 81), Lewiston Area (p. 83), and Mann Lake (p. 88).

GARDEN GULCH ROUTE

Author: Winifred Hepburn

Site P-30 — Map P-29/P-30

Highlights: Wild Turkey, Yellow-breasted Chat
Major Habitats: Farmland, Deciduous Forest
Location: Nez Perce Co., Lapwai
Spring: * *   **Summer:** * * *   **Fall:** * *   **Winter:** * * *

This 15-mile-long drive will take you through the southern edge of the Palouse Prairie. There is good birding here any time of year, but it's best during summer.

DIRECTIONS:

The route begins at the south end of Lapwai. At US 95 milepost 299, turn east onto graveled Garden Gulch Road (a.k.a. Road 371), zero your mileage, cross the creek, pull over, and start birding. *All land along this route is private.*

BIRDING:

The tall trees and brush in this area are good for nesting Warbling Vireos and Black-headed Grosbeaks, and they also attract migrating warblers, such as Orange-crowned, Nashville, Yellow-rumped, and MacGillivray's. You may see a Golden Eagle or a Red-tailed Hawk flying along the canyon rim. As you drive farther down Garden Gulch Road, start scanning the rocky hillside near mile 0.2 for Chukars and Rock Wrens. The large storage barn at mile 2.5 is surrounded by Black Locust trees, which host Western Kingbirds and Bullock's Orioles in summer. Teasel weeds and berry brambles are good for California Quail, House Wrens, House Finches, and House Sparrows. Walk up the road to hear Willow Flycatchers, Western Wood-Pewees, and Yellow-breasted Chats.

At mile 5.4 stop at the old homestead for Great Horned Owls, House Wrens, and Spotted Towhees. Turn left (north) at mile 5.7, where Garden Gulch Road joins Misner Road. In fall and winter, watch in this area for swirling flocks of White-crowned Sparrows, Dark-eyed Juncos, and American Goldfinches. Keep an eye out for Northern Shrikes, American Tree Sparrows, and Common Redpolls, as well.

At mile 7 turn right (east) on South Tom Beall Road. At the stop-sign at mile 8.8, go straight, onto Cottonwood Creek Road (a.k.a Road 330) and follow the pavement northwest. Pull over at mile 10.9 after crossing the creek, and check the hillsides for Wild Turkeys. In the early morning, turkeys may even be seen on the road. Red-breasted Nuthatches, Black-capped Chicka-dees, Ruby-crowned and Golden-crowned Kinglets, Dusky Flycatchers, Spotted Towhees, and Black-headed Grosbeaks may be present along the creek, and both Cooper's and Sharp-shinned Hawks should be watched for.

Cottonwood Creek Road joins Ruebens-Gifford Road (a.k.a. Nez Perce County Road P3) at mile 12.7. Turn left (northwest) here to access US 12 at mile 15.

OTHER:

Food and fuel are available in Lapwai. All services are available in Lewiston.

WINCHESTER LAKE STATE PARK

Authors: Dan Svingen, Winifred Hepburn

Site P-31 — Map P-31

Highlights: Common Loon, Solitary Sandpiper
Major Habitats: Wetland, Dry Conifer Forest, Mixed Conifer Forest
Location: Lewis Co., 22 miles southeast of Lewiston
Spring: *   **Summer:** * *   **Fall:** * *   **Winter:** *

Annual stocking of Rainbow Trout makes Winchester Lake SP a popular location for humans, Great Blue Herons, and Double-crested Cormorants. A few Common Loons use the 100-acre lake each spring and fall, and occasionally one will even summer here.

DIRECTIONS:

To reach the park's main entrance, turn west onto US 95A at US 95 mile-post 278. Follow the road southwest to Winchester Lake at US 95A milepost 2.1.

BIRDING:

At milepost 2.1 you cross Winchester Lake's overflow channel. There's a small parking lot and a short (0.1 to 0.2 mile) access road on each side of the overflow. Use these to get various views of the lake, scanning for Common Loons, Pied-billed and Western Grebes, Double-crested Cormorants, and waterfowl.

Continue west/southwest on US 95A as it swings north into the town of Winchester. At milepost 2.4 turn left (west) onto Forest Road and go 0.2 mile to Ponderosa Point Picnic Area on the left (southeast). The picnic area con-tains a small stand of old-growth Ponderosa Pines which attracts Dusky Fly-catchers, Pygmy Nuthatches, Western Tanagers, and Red Crossbills. The

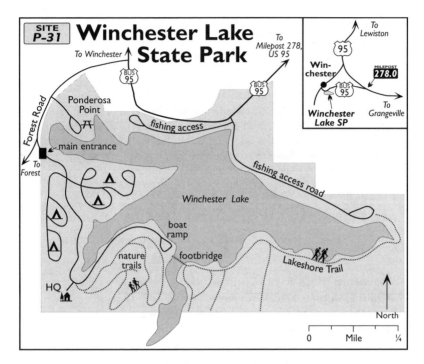

SITE P-31 | **Winchester Lake State Park**

To Winchester

To Milepost 278, US 95

To Lewiston

Winchester

MILEPOST 278.0

Winchester Lake SP

To Grangeville

BUS 95

Forest Road

Ponderosa Point

fishing access

main entrance

To Forest

Winchester Lake

fishing access road

boat ramp

nature trails

footbridge

Lakeshore Trail

HQ

North

0   Mile   ¼

lake's northwest arm can be scanned from here as well. This seems to be the favored spot for Wood Ducks, Green-winged Teal, Mallards, and assorted diving ducks.

The park's main entrance is another 0.2 mile to the southwest on Forest Road. At the entrance sign, turn left (southeast) and pull up to the entrance station. From here continue straight, following the road as it weaves around the lake to the boat ramp at the end of the road in another 0.7 mile. Lakeshore Trail begins by the boat launch and follows the southeast edge of the lake, providing the best birding opportunities. Look for Solitary Sandpipers along lake margins in May, and again in July and August. This is one of the most reliable spot in northern Idaho for this uncommon migrant. Because it's wetter on this side of the lake, the forest shifts to mixed conifers. Local nesters include Sharp-shinned Hawks, Ruffed Grouse, Barred Owls, Calliope Hummingbirds, Red-naped Sapsuckers, Hammond's Flycatchers, Steller's Jays, Swainson's and Varied Thrushes, Cassin's and Warbling Vireos, and Orange-crowned, Nashville, Townsend's, and MacGillivray's Warblers. Year-round residents include Steller's Jays, Mountain, Black-capped, and Chestnut-backed Chickadees, Brown Creepers, Winter Wrens, Golden-crowned Kinglets, Cassin's Finches, and Red Crossbills.

You can also access a couple other trails from the boat ramp parking lot. Wandering any of these trails (especially the one which follows the southern lake arm) can produce good birding for common mixed conifer bird species.

For additional birding, return to the main entrance and turn left (southwest) on Forest Road, and follow it 8 miles to the town of Forest. Watch for Northern Goshawks, Great Gray Owls, Gray Jays, and Western and Mountain Bluebirds along the way, especially near Forest.

OTHER:

Winchester has fuel, food, and lodging. The closest full-service communities are Grangeville and Lewiston. Winchester Lake SP (208/924-7563) offers a full-service campground, the only such public facility between Lewiston and McCall. Several docks have been built around the lake, making fishing access easy. Cross-country skiing is popular during winter.

GRAVES CREEK ROUTE

Author: Winifred Hepburn

Site P-32 — Map P-32

Highlights: Cordilleran Flycatcher, Veery, Yellow-breasted Chat
Major Habitats: Deciduous Forest, Dry Conifer Forest
Location: Idaho Co., 2 miles east of Cottonwood
Spring: * * *   **Summer:** * * *   **Fall:** * *   **Winter:** *

Graves Creek descends 11 miles from the Camas Prairie to the Salmon River. Along the way this beautiful, lush riparian area passes by moss-covered walls and miniature waterfalls. May and June are the best times to bird here.

DIRECTIONS:

From Cottonwood go southeast on US 95 to milepost 252.4, then turn right (west) onto paved Twin House Road (signed for "Weis Rock Shelter 7 miles", and zero your mileage.

At mile 1.4 turn left (south) onto Graves Creek Road. Except for the last 3 miles, all property is private, so please bird exclusively from the road. The route's lower portion is good gravel.

BIRDING:

Birding is good along this entire trip. The best strategy is simply to use whatever pull-outs are available and walk along the road. A few suggested stops are listed below.

At mile 1.9 check the two small farm ponds on the left (east) for migrating Greater and Lesser Yellowlegs and Solitary Sandpipers—but be careful, since parking is limited. At mile 2.6 is an old orchard on the right (west); you never know what will turn up here.

At mile 3.5 you'll descend through a big curve. Just past the curve you'll see a large pull-out on the left (north). Stop here to look for Cordilleran, Willow, and Dusky Flycatchers, Veeries, Cassin's Vireos, MacGillivray's Warblers, Western Tanagers, Lazuli Buntings, and Spotted Towhees. At mile 3.8 are some tiny marsh areas surrounded by brush, where you should listen for Orange-crowned, Nashville, Yellow, and MacGillivray's Warblers and Black-headed Grosbeaks. At mile 5.0 look for nesting swallows and Cordilleran Flycatchers by the large pull-out on the right (west). The Weis Rock Shelter at mile 7.2 is good for Yellow-breasted Chats. The junction of Rock Creek and Graves Creek at mile 7.9 is often birdy. Watch for Lewis's Woodpeckers, Red-eyed Vireos, and Yellow-breasted Chats for the next 3 miles. At mile 11.5 follow the road past the information signs and dumpster, staying to the left. Graves Creek empties into the Salmon River at mile 11.7, where numerous Lazuli Buntings are usually seen.

The road now parallels the Salmon River upstream, ending at mile 14.7 and Pine Bar Recreation Area. Watch for Common Mergansers, Chukars, Lewis's Woodpeckers, and Canyon Wrens along this last 3 miles.

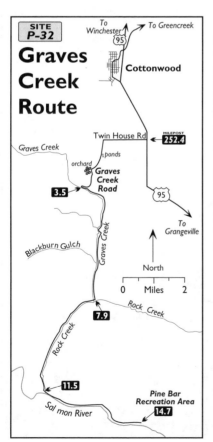

OTHER:

Food, fuel, and lodging are available in Cottonwood. For other services, try Grangeville. Local attractions include the St. Gertrude Museum (please call ahead at: 208/962-7123), and the Weis Rock Shelter, a shallow indentation in the canyon wall once inhabited by people of the Clovis culture.

Pine Bar Recreation Area offers primitive camping (pit toilets, water) and a boat ramp. Additional maps and information can be obtained from the BLM (208/962-3245) in Cottonwood, or the FS (208/983-1950) in Grangeville.

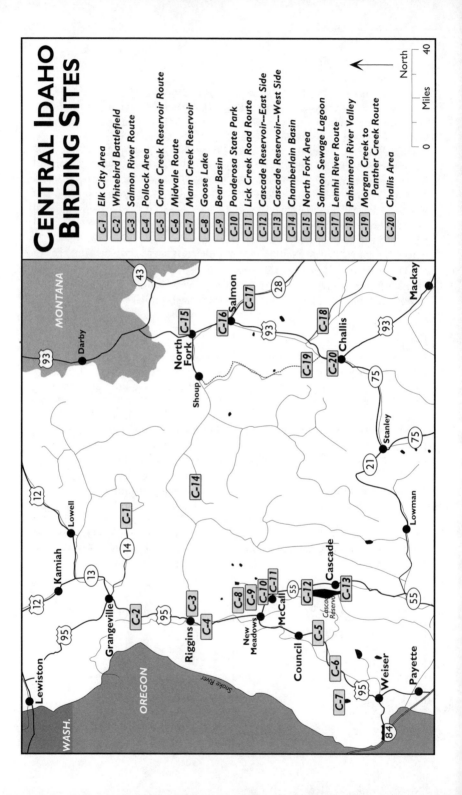

CENTRAL IDAHO BIRDING SITES

C-1 Elk City Area
C-2 Whitebird Battlefield
C-3 Salmon River Route
C-4 Pollock Area
C-5 Crane Creek Reservoir Route
C-6 Midvale Route
C-7 Mann Creek Reservoir
C-8 Goose Lake
C-9 Bear Basin
C-10 Ponderosa State Park
C-11 Lick Creek Road Route
C-12 Cascade Reservoir—East Side
C-13 Cascade Reservoir—West Side
C-14 Chamberlain Basin
C-15 North Fork Area
C-16 Salmon Sewage Lagoon
C-17 Lemhi River Route
C-18 Pahsimeroi River Valley
C-19 Morgan Creek to
      Panther Creek Route
C-20 Challis Area

CENTRAL IDAHO

This is Idaho's widest, wildest, and most sparsely settled region. Vast acreages are recognized for their incredible scenic, conservation, and recreational values and are designated as wilderness areas, recreation areas, research natural areas, and state parks. The massive sweep of the Selway-Bitterroot, Gospel-Hump, and Frank Church River of No Return Wildernesses is particularly awe-inspiring. This was the site for the successful reintroduction of Gray Wolves in 1995.

Because of the juxtaposition of the wilderness areas, long detours are required to drive from Central Idaho's western to eastern boundary, making the phrase "you can't get there from here," particularly apt. The remote, unspoiled beauty makes this region the state's favorite playground. Hiking, white-water rafting, kayaking, and downhill skiing are all very popular.

Central Idaho is dominated by the Middle Rocky Mountain Ecoregion. Coniferous forests are drier than those found in the Panhandle. At low elevations the forests are bordered by sagebrush. The gamebird community is particularly diverse, with all of Idaho's 14 species possible. Birds to especially watch for include Blue Grouse, Williamson's Sapsuckers, and Clark's Nutcrackers, as well as Flammulated, Great Gray, and Boreal Owls. Small populations of Gambel's and Mountain Quail and White-headed Woodpeckers add further spice to the avifauna.

Townsend's Warbler
Mike Denny

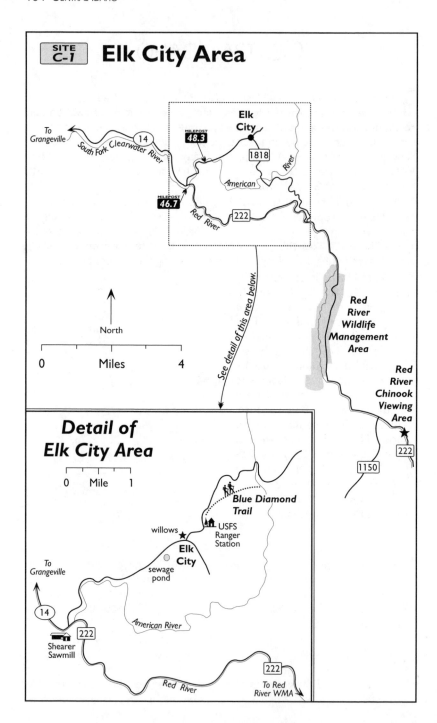

SITE C-1 **Elk City Area**

To
Grangeville

South Fork Clearwater River

14

MILEPOST **48.3**

Elk City

1818

American River

MILEPOST **46.7**

Red River

222

North

0 Miles 4

See detail of this area below.

Red River Wildlife Management Area

Red River Chinook Viewing Area

222

1150

Detail of Elk City Area

0 Mile 1

Blue Diamond Trail

willows

USFS Ranger Station

Elk City

sewage pond

To Grangeville

14

222

Shearer Sawmill

American River

222

To Red River WMA

Red River

ELK CITY AREA

Authors: Mindy Wiebush, Steve Blair

Site C 1 — Map C-1

Highlights: American Three-toed Woodpecker, Bobolink, Pine Grosbeak
Major Habitats: Wetland, Meadow, Mixed Conifer Forest
Location: Idaho Co., 50 miles east of Grangeville
Spring: * *   **Summer:** * *   **Fall:** * *   **Winter:** * *

Two small rivers, the American and the Red, join to form the South Fork Clearwater River near Elk City. Birding spots along both of these remote watercourses are described below. Additional birding can be had while you are getting here. Stop often in the scenic South Fork Clearwater River canyon to hear Winter Wrens in wet draws, Canyon and Rock Wrens near huge rock slabs, and American Dippers along the river. You may also see Mountain Goats scrambling on the rocks high above the river's south bank between mileposts 22 and 23.

DIRECTIONS:

This tour's starting point is the junction of ID 14 and FR 222 at ID 14 milepost 46.7 (just past the sawmill). The roads throughout this area are narrow and twisty; *please drive safely.*

BIRDING:

AMERICAN RIVER

From the starting point go left (northeast) on ID 14, following the American River upstream toward Elk City. Watch for Belted Kingfishers and American Dippers along the way. River Otters are often visible along here during winter.

At milepost 48.3 the narrow canyon opens into a broad, privately-owned meadow. In April and May the meadow's wetlands attract Tundra and Trumpeter Swans (the latter being rare), Snow Geese, various ducks, Soras, Greater and Lesser Yellowlegs, and Wilson's and Red-necked Phalaropes.

At milepost 48.8, scan the sewage pond on the right (south) for Wood Ducks and the occasional Moose. In downtown Elk City (milepost 49.4) park at the historical marker by the rodeo grounds. From April through June, the surrounding willows and wetlands support Soras, Wilson's Snipe, Willow Flycatchers, and Yellow Warblers. Bobolinks and Savannah Sparrows are often seen on fence-posts in the background.

For a little variety, consider hiking "Blue Diamond" trail, which starts 0.1 mile beyond the Elk City Ranger Station. To find the ranger station, turn left (north) at "The Store" in downtown Elk City and follow American River Road for 0.4 mile. The trailhead is marked with a green-and-white "Snowmobile Route" sign. The trail itself is flagged with small orange and blue diamonds. Be aware that recent timber harvest has obscured portions of the trail. During spring and summer, Pileated and American Three-toed Woodpeckers are fairly common, and Williamson's Sapsuckers are possible. In fact, a day without a woodpecker here is like a day without orange juice—it just doesn't happen! Also keep your eyes and ears ready for Varied Thrushes, Townsend's and MacGillivray's Warblers, Western Tanagers, and Pine Grosbeaks. In winter this trail is packed down by snowmobiles and provides a good walking surface to look for Hairy Woodpeckers, Black-capped, Mountain, and Chestnut-backed Chickadees, Brown Creepers, and Golden-crowned Kinglets.

RED RIVER

Back at the starting point, zero your odometer and follow FR 222 (a.k.a. Red River Road) southeast toward Red River and Dixie. About 9.7 miles from the starting point (there are no mileposts), you'll see the sign and driveway for the Red River WMA on the right (west). This complex, consisting of two small houses, a corral, and a 300-acre meadow, is managed by the IDFG and is open to the public from June 16 to February 28. Elk are often thick here in early morning or late evening. To bird, walk behind the headquarters (the tan house) into the meadow, wandering on the various trails and roads. Spotted Sandpiper, Violet-green Swallow, Willow Flycatcher, and Savannah Sparrow are common summer species. Future plans call for a nature trail somewhere in this area.

Approximately 4.3 miles upstream from the Red River WMA is the Red River Chinook Viewing Area on the right (east), with interpretive signs and a short trail. The focus is on the nearby fish-rearing facility, but you might also look for Vaux's Swifts, various swallows, and American Dippers. You may also find these species 0.3 mile upstream, by the Red River Ranger Station.

The best way to locate Spruce Grouse in this area is to walk the semi-open Engelmann Spruce/Lodgepole Pine forest surrounding wet mountain meadows. Although the grouse can be found in these habitats throughout the snowfree period, they are most likely from July to October. A particularly good place is Trail 505, between FR 468 and Soda Creek Point. You'll need a Nez Perce NF map to find this area (see below).

OTHER:

Area maps and more information can be obtained from FS offices in Grangeville (208/983-1950) or Elk City (208/842-2245). Primitive campgrounds and additional trails are abundant (see FS map). Elk City has fuel, food, and lodging. For other services, try Grangeville. Snowmobiling, history-touring, and hunting are all popular here. Be sure to bring warm clothing and wet-weather foot-gear whenever you visit.

WHITEBIRD BATTLEFIELD
Author: Dan Svingen
Site C-2 — See Central map, page 102

Highlights: Yellow-breasted Chat, Lazuli Bunting
Major Habitats: Grassland, Deciduous Forest, Wetland
Location: Idaho Co., 10 miles south of Grangeville
Spring: * *   **Summer:** * *   **Fall:** *   **Winter:** *

Whitebird Battlefield, managed by the National Park Service, is where the infamous Nez Perce Indian War started in 1877. You can follow the battle's course along an auto tour and intrepretive trail. The best birding is during May and June.

DIRECTIONS:

From Grangeville follow US 95 south for 9.8 miles. Turn left (east) at mile-post 230 (signed for "Whitebird Battlefield Auto Tour"). Zero your odometer and pick-up a brochure at Autotour stop #1, then follow Old Highway 95 down Whitebird Hill to the town of Whitebird. *Think twice about taking this twisty, narrow road if you're driving an extra-long or extra-wide vehicle.*

BIRDING:

As you descend Whitebird Hill, watch the rock outcrops for Rock Wrens, especially from May to August. Between miles 1 and 3.6, the road snakes through a series of switchbacks where you might spot American Kestrels, Gray Partridge, Chukars (April to November; uncommon), or Northern Shrikes (October to April; common). After the switchbacks, the road parallels Magpie Gulch, which hosts its namesake Black-billed Magpies, as well as Cooper's Hawks, Yellow-breasted Chats, Lazuli Buntings, and Spotted Towhees. Watch overhead for Prairie Falcons.

At mile 5.0 is a pull-off which accesses a walk-through gate on the right (northwest). You can scan 2-acre Swartz Pond from here, then go through the gate for a closer look. You can also wander up the draw, following the tiny creek to its origin, a quarter-mile north of Swartz Pond. On the way you'll pass two more ponds and several tree/shrub clumps. Birds to watch for include various waterfowl (including Cinnamon Teal, Greater Scaup, and Barrow's Goldeneye), Red-tailed Hawks, Golden Eagles, California Quail, Soras, Black-headed Grosbeaks, and Yellow-headed Blackbirds. In winter search the cattails and rose bushes for gamebirds, Northern Saw-whet Owls, Marsh Wrens, and sparrows.

Spend some time birding near Autotour stop #5 (mile 7.6). A walk along the grassland trail west of stop #5 may produce Grasshopper Sparrows (June through August; uncommon). You can also explore the newly acquired riparian area east of the road, accessed by driving to mile 7.9 and walking through the green metal gateway on the left (east). Follow the dirt road through the old farmyard, which contains several outbuildings, a barn, and a corral. The best birding is in the tall grass, shrubs, and cottonwood trees along Whitebird Creek, behind (i.e., 100 yards northeast of) the old barn. *Make sure that you stay on National Park Service land, and do not enter the neighboring private stuff. Public land is enclosed by a fence with rectangular, white signs reading "BOUNDARY LINE, NATIONAL PARK SERVICE."* Beware of the over-friendly horse and donkey often pastured here. If you pet 'em, they'll follow you around like puppies! Birds along Whitebird Creek include Western Screech-Owls, Great Horned Owls, Lewis's Woodpeckers, Western Wood-Pewees, Say's Phoebes, Warbling Vireos, and Bullock's Orioles.

To return to US 95, continue south on Old Highway 95, passing through Whitebird at mile 9.6. Birding can be good right in town. Just park and take a short walk. Calliope and Rufous Hummingbirds are often easy to find. At the T intersection at the south end of Whitebird, you can turn left and follow the signs up the hill to US 95 in 0.1 mile, or turn right and follow Whitebird Creek down to the Salmon River (mile 10.9). Then follow the Salmon upstream to where the road rejoins US 95 at mile 12.3. Along the way you'll pass more riparian habitat containing many of the species found on the Battlefield, as well as having an opportunity to view wintering waterfowl, Bald Eagles, Chukars, Canyon Wrens, and Townsend's Solitaires.

OTHER:

Grangeville is a full-service community. Fuel, food, and lodging are available in Whitebird, also.

SALMON RIVER ROUTE

Author: Sharon Ritter

Site C-3 — See Central map, page 102

Highlights: Chukar, Lewis's Woodpecker, Canyon Wren
Major Habitats: Dry Conifer Forest, Wetland, Cliffs
Location: Idaho Co., Riggins
Spring: * * **Summer:** * * **Fall:** * * **Winter:** * *

This 19-mile route takes you from Riggins to French Creek. If you're looking for Lewis's Woodpeckers, this place is for you! Between April and August, one or two of these beautiful and entertaining tree excavators can be seen in riverside Ponderosa Pine snags every quarter-mile. Your only problem will be finding a safe place to pull over to look at them!

DIRECTIONS:

From downtown Riggins follow US 95 south about 1 mile. At milepost 194.6 turn left (east) on Big Salmon River Road and follow it upstream. This narrow road is paved to Partridge Creek Bridge (milepost 12.6), with fairly good gravel to French Creek (milepost 18.6), then rough gravel to road's end (milepost 26.5). In winter, be especially careful upstream of Manning Bridge (milepost 13.5), since the road there can get rutted and muddy.

Big Salmon River Road passes through private land for about 7 miles until it crosses the river at Rough Creek. Because of scattered parcels of private land from Rough Creek to French Creek, however, you shouldn't wander far off the road without checking a FS map for land-ownership data.

BIRDING:

Stringers of deciduous trees and shrubs occur wherever a side stream enters the river. Allison Creek (milepost 9.7) and Spring Bar Campground (milepost 10.4) are particularly good spots for riparian birds, and they both have nearby Ponderosa Pine stands for additional exploring. Also check Van Creek (milepost 11.2), Elkhorn Creek (milepost 14.7), and Carey Creek (milepost 23.2). These are all good for American Kestrels, Northern Flickers, Mountain Chickadees, Cedar Waxwings, Red-eyed Vireos, MacGillivray's Warblers, Yellow-breasted Chats, Song Sparrows, and Lazuli Buntings in spring and summer. In winter you can find Bald Eagles, Northern Flickers, Hairy Woodpeckers, Golden-crowned Kinglets, and Black-capped Chickadees in these same areas.

Continue straight at Partridge Creek Bridge (milepost 12.6). From here to Manning Bridge (milepost 13.5) you'll find big rock slabs and narrow canyon walls. Listen and watch for White-throated Swifts and Canyon Wrens. Additional species might include Belted Kingfisher, Violet-green Swallow, Rock Wren, Nashville Warbler, MacGillivray's Warbler, Lazuli Bunting, Spotted Towhee, and American Goldfinch.

Look for Chukars by milepost 17 and at other rocky areas along the river. Cassin's Vireo can often be heard near mileposts 17 and 18. American Dippers and Spotted Sandpipers forage along the entire length of the river.

There are also several places where you can take a short hike. At milepost 15.3 there is an open stand of Ponderosa Pine between two sandy beaches. Investigate this area, then walk up the jeep road along the canyon's south side to look for White-headed and Pileated Woodpeckers, Canyon and Rock Wrens, Pygmy Nuthatches, MacGillivray's Warblers, Spotted Towhees, and Western Tanagers.

Most birders turn around at French Creek. If you continue, check Carey Creek (milepost 23.2) for more riparian species. You can also walk across the Wind River foot-bridge (milepost 23.5) to explore the 1992 Scott Fire Burn, which has been particularly good for woodpeckers.

OTHER:

Maps can be obtained from FS offices in McCall (208/634-0700) or Grangeville (208/983-1950). Food, fuel, and accommodations are available in Riggins. About 1 mile west of Allison Creek is the Riggins Hot Springs Lodge (milepost 9.2), which has an outdoor mineral swimming pool, an indoor spa and sauna, and a stocked trout pond. There are several campgrounds (pit toilets; no showers) along the route.

The Riggins area provides plenty to do besides birding. You can go white-water rafting, jet boating, horseback riding, and fishing, or you can visit the Rapid River Fish Hatchery (which also has birding opportunities). Brundage Mountain, which has excellent downhill skiing, is only about 40 miles south of here.

POLLOCK AREA

Author: Trish Heekin

Site C-4 — Map C-4

Highlights: Mountain Quail
Major Habitats: Deciduous Forest, Dry Conifer Forest
Location: Idaho Co., 7 miles south of Riggins
Spring: *   **Summer:** *   **Fall:** * *   **Winter:** *

The Little Salmon River Canyon in the vicinity of Pollock shelters one of Idaho's last Mountain Quail populations. In fact, the Pollock Area is your best chance of finding this species in the state.

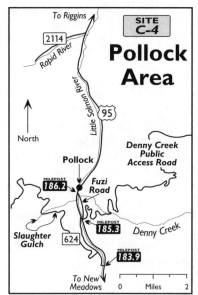

DIRECTIONS:

There are three spots to look for Mountain Quail in the Pollock area: Fuzi Road, Denny Creek Public Access Road, and FR 624. Fuzi Road parallels US 95. Its northern terminus is at US 95 milepost 186.2, while its southern end is at US 95 milepost 185.3. (Watch for handmade wooden signs.) Denny Creek Public Access Road (dirt) heads east from Fuzi Road, about 0.1 mile north of Fuzi Road's southern end. Denny Creek Public Access Road is gated during winter and spring. The road's opening-date varies from year to year. Contact the BLM (208/962-3245) in Cottonwood for more information.

BIRDING:

Idaho's Mountain Quail are extremely difficult to observe, as they tend to stay in or near dense vegetation. If disturbed, they often freeze or move away quietly on foot, rather than flushing. Finding them during winter (when they visit feeders on private land) or in May and June (when they are incubating) is nearly impossible. Your best chance of seeing Mountain Quail is in fall, especially as the light is fading from the day. Watch for coveys foraging along the roadside. Particular spots to be alert for Mountain Quail include the interiors of the draws on FR 624 and the Denny Creek drainage (before and after the cattle-guard) on the Denny Creek Public Access Road. Unfortunately, even under these circumstances your chances of seeing Mountain Quail are not particularly good.

This area offers many other birding attractions. Watch for Common Mergansers, Belted Kingfishers, and American Dippers along the Little Salmon River and Rapid River (see map) year round. While not common, White-headed Woodpeckers have occasionally been seen in the Ponderosa Pine forest near the ridgetop on the west side of the Little Salmon River Canyon. Likely summer species near Pollock include Say's Phoebe, Western and Eastern Kingbirds, Yellow-breasted Chat, Western Tanager, Lazuli Bunting, and Pine Siskin.

Several raptors are also possible. At least two Peregrine Falcon pairs nest nearby, one near US 95 milepost 205, and another in the Rapid River drainage. Golden Eagles often soar above the narrow canyons. Red-tailed Hawks and American Kestrels are common, while Northern Harriers, Northern Goshawks (winter), and Cooper's and Sharp-shinned Hawks are less so. In evenings from March to June, you might hear the calls of a Western Screech-Owl, Northern Pygmy-Owl, Northern Saw-whet Owl, or Great Horned Owl.

Gamebirds are also plentiful. Blue Grouse display (April to June) in Slaughter Gulch along FR 624 (see map). As you drive up Denny Creek Access Road, watch for Wild Turkeys on the first flat past the cattle-guard. Gray Partridge may be flushed from the roadside, while Chukars should be listened for on the surrounding slopes.

During migration you may hear Tundra Swans and Canada and Snow Geese as they fly overhead. In some years Clark's Nutcrackers are seen in the area during late winter or early spring, especially along FR 624.

OTHER:

Food, fuel, and accommodations are available in Riggins. Primitive and undeveloped campsites are abundant on surrounding BLM and FS land. Some developed camping is available in Riggins. Riggins is known as Idaho's Whitewater Capital, for it offers raft and jet-boat excursions on the Salmon River. Note that Western Rattlesnakes, ticks, and Poison-Ivy are common throughout this area. See also Salmon River Route (p. 108).

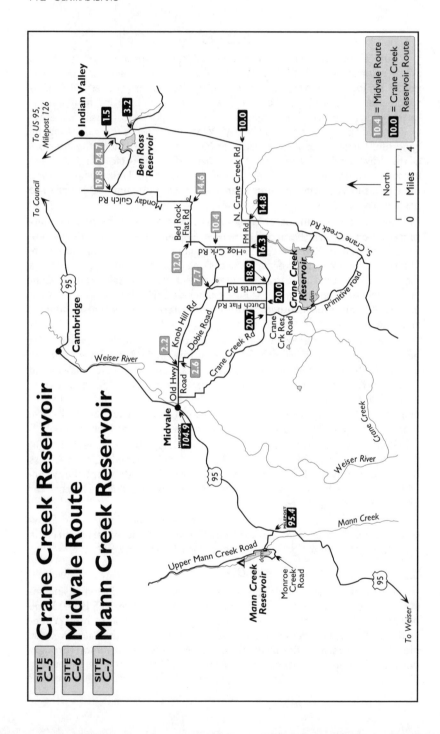

SITE C-5 Crane Creek Reservoir
SITE C-6 Midvale Route
SITE C-7 Mann Creek Reservoir

CRANE CREEK RESERVOIR ROUTE

Authors: John and Marty Hirth
Site C-5 — Map C-5/C-6/C-7

Highlights: Greater Sage-Grouse, Long-billed Curlew, Loggerhead Shrike
Major Habitats: Shrub-steppe, Farmland, Wetland
Location: Washington Co., 24 miles northeast of Weiser
Spring: * *   **Summer:** * *   **Fall:** *   **Winter:** * *

Because of its arid surroundings, Crane Creek Reservoir has the potential to attract lots of interesting birds. Some of the best birding, however, is associated with the surrounding expanses of sagebrush and grasses. This 23-mile-long route begins in Indian Valley and ends near Midvale.

DIRECTIONS:

To reach Indian Valley from US 95, turn south at milepost 126 and follow paved Indian Valley Road for 3.5 miles. Zero your mileage at the store in Indian Valley, and then continue south on Indian Valley Road (a.k.a. Emmett Road). At mile 1.5 stay left. Pavement ends at mile 1.7. At mile 3.2 go right (south), staying on Indian Valley Road. Although there is some public land (BLM) in this area, most of this route passes through private property.

BIRDING:

Watch for Red-tailed, Ferruginous, and Swainson's Hawks, Prairie Falcons, Short-eared Owls, and Brewer's, Vesper, Savannah, and Grasshopper Sparrows along Indian Valley Road. You'll pass in and out of farmland. Near cultivated fields (such as around mile 9.2), look for gallinaceous species, such as Ring-necked Pheasant, California Quail, and Gray Partridge.

After following the road through a curve at mile 10, continue straight (west) onto North Crane Creek Road at mile 10.2. At mile 14.3 turn left (south) on South Crane Creek Road. At mile 14.8 turn right (west) on paved Farm to Market Road.

From February through April, sagebrush and grassland areas along Farm to Market Road are good for displaying Greater Sage-Grouse and Long-billed Curlews. Sharp-tailed Grouse are rare but possible. Side trips on graveled Cutoff Road (mile 14.3), Hog Creek Road (mile 16.3), Curtis (a.k.a. Heinrich) Road (mile 18.9), and Dutch Flat Road (mile 20.0) have revealed Gray Partridge, Burrowing and Short-eared Owls, and lots of Vesper and Savannah Sparrows.

To reach Crane Creek Reservoir itself, turn left (south) at mile 20.7 onto graveled Crane Creek Reservoir Road, and follow it 2.5 miles to the reservoir. Check weedy patches below the dam for sparrows, including American Tree Sparrows (winter). Scope the reservoir for American White Pelicans (summer), Snow and Ross's Geese (migration), and Peregrine Falcons. Be sure to check the periphery for Ferruginous Hawks and Rock and Marsh Wrens. Stilt and Solitary Sandpipers have been found during fall migration.

If you have a high-clearance 4-wheel-drive vehicle, zero your mileage on the dam and continue south on the primitive road. This remote region contains a substantial Loggerhead Shrike population, as well as Rock Wrens, Sage Thrashers, and an occasional Sage Sparrow. The primitive road ends on South Crane Creek Road, 5.2 miles southeast of the dam. Turn left (north) here, and follow South Crane Creek Road to view the east side of the reservoir from afar. Continuing north on South Crane Creek Road, you'll eventually return to Farm to Market Road, 12.4 miles from your starting point at the dam.

OTHER:

For additional maps and information, contact the BLM in Boise (208/384-3300). Undeveloped camping, fishing, and a boat dock are available at Crane Creek Reservoir. Fuel, food, and lodging are available in Council, Cambridge, and Weiser. For other services, try Boise. See also Mann Creek Reservoir (p. 116) and Midvale, the next site.

MIDVALE ROUTE
Author: John F. Gatchet
Site C-6 — Map C-5/C-6/C-7

Highlights: Greater Sage-Grouse, Short-eared Owl, Grasshopper Sparrow
Major Habitats: Shrub-steppe, Grassland, Farmland
Location: Washington Co., Midvale
Spring: **** **Summer:** *** **Fall:** ** **Winter:** *

This 26-mile route takes you from Midvale to Indian Valley. Spring is the best time to bird here, since it is then that dancing Greater Sage-Grouse, calling Long-billed Curlews, and courting Short-eared Owls are particularly prominent. As if all this action weren't enough, Midvale also provides some of Idaho's best birding for Swainson's and Ferruginous Hawks, Burrowing Owls, and Grasshopper Sparrows.

DIRECTIONS:

Zero your mileage at the junction of US 95 and Old Highway Road (unsigned) in Midvale (US 95 milepost 104.9), then go east on Old Highway Road. At mile 2.2, the road forks—stay right (straight) on Knob Hill Road. At mile 2.6 continue straight as the pavement ends. All land along this route should be considered private.

BIRDING:

At mile 3.4 is a feedlot below a small knoll. Just beyond the feedlot (at mile 3.6) is a Greater Sage-Grouse lek which hosts about 40 birds. Most of the dancing is on the right (south) side of the road. Another Greater Sage-Grouse lek should be looked for at mile 7.0.

At mile 7.7, continue straight as Knob Hill Road merges into Dobie Road. Burrowing and Short-eared Owls and Grasshopper Sparrows can be found anywhere in this area, so keep an eye (and an ear) out. In winter, look for Northern Shrikes and Snow Buntings, and check the Horned Lark flocks for stray Lapland Longspurs.

At mile 8.1 scan the small pond on the right (south) for waterfowl, including Eurasian Wigeons (spring). At mile 8.5 look for Sharp-tailed Grouse (uncommon to rare), Burrowing Owls, and Grasshopper Sparrows. To date, there are no Sharp-tailed Grouse leks visible from the road, but keep searching since lek locations change year to year.

At mile 10.4 turn left (north) on Hog Creek Road, which is particularly good for Rough-legged Hawks in winter and spring. At mile 12 turn right (east) on Bed Rock Flat Road. At mile 14.6 go straight, staying on Bed Rock Flat Road (which will turn into Monday Gulch Road). There's a small pond on the right (east) side of the road at mile 14.7, which should be scanned for waterfowl and shorebirds. Monday Gulch Road is good for Greater Sage-Grouse, Long-billed Curlews, and Short-eared Owls. Additional Greater Sage-Grouse leks can be found at miles 15.1 and 16.2.

At mile 19.8 turn right (east) onto Ben Ross (a.k.a. Swisher) Road, watching and listening for Gray Partridge and California Quail. At mile 21.6 look for a Bank Swallow colony in the cutbank to the left (north). You reach Ben Ross Reservoir at mile 22.6, where a variety of water birds may be found in migration, including Tundra and Trumpeter Swans, Snow and Ross's Geese, Wood Ducks, Canvasbacks, Greater Scaup, and Barrow's Goldeneyes. Western Grebes are present in summer. Ben Ross Road meets paved Indian Valley Road at mile 24.7. Merge and go north here, following Indian Valley Road into Indian Valley at mile 26.3, where you can look for migrating hawks and Say's Phoebes. To rejoin US 95, follow Indian Valley Road north another 3.5 miles.

If you're still searching for Sharp-tailed Grouse or Grasshopper Sparrow, consider backtracking and driving Dobie Road (see map).

OTHER:

Food, gas, and lodging are available in Cambridge, Council, and Weiser. Ben Ross Reservoir has undeveloped campsites, a boat ramp, and fishing. See also Crane Creek Reservoir Route (p.113) and Mann Creek Reservoir, the next site.

MANN CREEK RESERVOIR
Author: John F. Gatchet
Site C-7 — Map C-5/C-6/C-7
Highlights: Shorebirds, Veery, Red-eyed Vireo
Major Habitats: Wetland, Deciduous Forest, Shrub-steppe
Location: Washington Co., 12 miles northwest of Weiser
Spring: * *   **Summer:** * *   **Fall:** * * *   **Winter:** *

This 280-acre reservoir has great birding potential as a fall migrant trap, but it has been little explored. Hopefully, this situation will soon change, since the area can be easily and quickly birded. Be sure to swing in if you're passing by!

DIRECTIONS:
From Weiser follow US 95 north to milepost 95.4, then turn left (west) on Upper Mann Creek Road, following it 1.3 miles to the dam. Mann Creek Reservoir is managed by the BOR, but some private land does occur—watch for posted signs.

BIRDING:
To scan the entire length of the reservoir, turn left at the dam and follow Monroe Creek Road to the parking areas on the right (north and west) in 0.3 and 1.7 miles, respectively. Migrating Eurasian Wigeons (rare), Barrow's Goldeneyes, and an occasional Wood Duck use Mann Creek Reservoir as a resting area, as do Bonaparte's Gulls and Forster's Terns. Unexpected species, such as Horned Grebes in June or Pacific Loons in fall, have also been found.

To bird the east side of the reservoir, zero your mileage at the east end of the dam and continue north on Upper Mann Creek Road. Watch the shrub-steppe habitat to the right (east) for Say's Phoebes, Eastern Kingbirds, Sage Thrashers, and Loggerhead Shrikes. In winter look for Northern Goshawks, Merlins, and Northern Shrikes. Parking areas on the left (west) at miles 0.8 and 1.4 are good vantage points.

At mile 1.6 turn left (west) onto the 0.3-mile-long, graveled entrance road to the campground, where Mann Creek enters the reservoir. There is a short road/trail which follows Mann Creek upstream. It begins behind the camp host's site at the north end of the campground. Wading and bushwhacking are required to bird this riparian forest, which shelters a rich variety of breeding passerines, including Warbling and Red-eyed Vireos, Yellow and MacGillivray's Warblers, Common Yellowthroats, Yellow-breasted Chats, Western Tanagers, Black-headed Grosbeaks, Lazuli Buntings, Spotted Towhees, Song Sparrows, Dark-eyed Juncos, Bullock's Orioles, and American Goldfinches.

The north end of the reservoir is excellent for shorebirds, especially in late fall when water levels are low. In addition to more common species, look for American Golden-Plover, Black-necked Stilt, American Avocet, and Long-billed Curlew.

Mann Creek's riparian habitat can also be birded by following Upper Mann Creek Road 2 miles north of the campground entrance road (see map). The road parallels the creek for about 4 miles. Watch for Prairie Falcons, Western Screech-Owls, Lewis's Woodpeckers, Black-chinned Hummingbirds, Western Wood-Pewees, Veeries, and previously mentioned species.

OTHER:

Food, fuel, and lodging are available in Weiser. Boat ramps, fishing, and a primitive campground (pit toilet; water) are available at Mann Creek Reservoir. For additional maps and information, contact the FS (208/549-4200) in Weiser, or BLM (208/384-3300) in Boise.

GOOSE LAKE
Author: Mark Collie
Site C-8 — Map C-8/C-9/C-10/C-11

Highlights: Red-necked Grebe, American Three-toed Woodpecker
Major Habitats: Mixed Conifer Forest, Wetland
Location: Adams Co., 13 miles northwest of McCall
Spring: N/A   **Summer:** * *   **Fall:** *   **Winter:** N/A

In 1994 over 300,000 acres of woodland burned in central Idaho. A portion of those burns occurred near Goose Lake, a 2-mile-long, high-elevation reservoir. Because of salvage logging, expect heavy logging traffic. Check with the Payette NF for more information (see below). Be aware that access into this area is limited to June through early December.

DIRECTIONS:

From McCall, follow ID 55 northwest 5 miles. At milepost 149.6 turn right (north) onto paved FR 257 (a.k.a. Brundage Mountain Road) and zero your mileage. Continue north 4 miles to the Brundage Mountain Ski Resort, where FR 257 becomes gravel of varying quality (including some rough washboard). At mile 6.8 stay left (northwest) on FR 257 (now called Goose Lake Road). Drive past Brundage Reservoir at mile 7.5. At mile 10.9 (past the entrance to Grouse Creek Campground), turn left (southwest) onto an unmarked dirt road and go 0.2 mile to Goose Lake Dam.

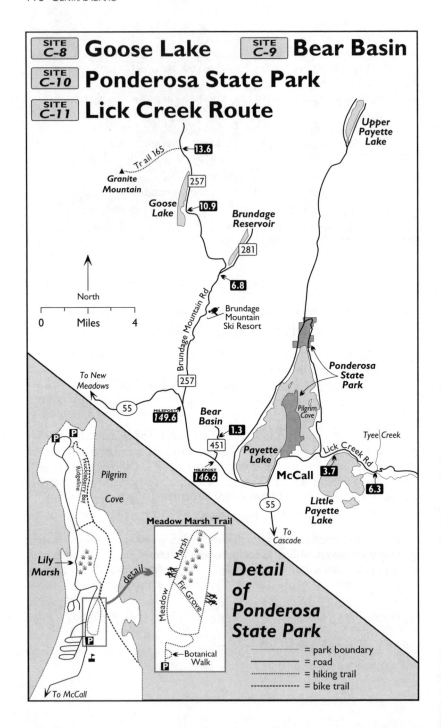

SITE **C-8** **Goose Lake**   SITE **C-9** **Bear Basin**

SITE **C-10** **Ponderosa State Park**

SITE **C-11** **Lick Creek Route**

Upper Payette Lake

Trail 165   **13.6**

Granite Mountain

257

Goose Lake   **10.9**

Brundage Reservoir

281

6.8

North

0   Miles   4

Brundage Mountain Rd

Brundage Mountain Ski Resort

Ponderosa State Park

257

To New Meadows

Pilgrim Cove

55

MILEPOST **149.6**

Bear Basin   **1.3**

Tyee Creek

451

MILEPOST **146.6**

Payette Lake

McCall

Lick Creek Rd   **3.7**

6.3

Little Payette Lake

Pilgrim Cove

Huckleberry Bay Ridgeline

P   P

55

To Cascade

Meadow Marsh Trail

Lily Marsh

Marsh

Meadow

Fir Grove

detail

Detail
of
Ponderosa
State Park

P

P

Botanical Walk

= park boundary
= road
= hiking trail
= bike trail

To McCall

BIRDING:

On the road to Goose Lake watch for Golden Eagles, Northern Goshawks, Cooper's and Sharp-shinned Hawks, and Ruffed, Blue, and Spruce Grouse. At the lake look for Common Loons (migrant), Red-necked Grebes, Common Goldeneyes, Ospreys, and Bald Eagles.

Along the shoreline, watch for Vaux's Swifts, as well as for Calliope, Broad-tailed, and Rufous Hummingbirds. Woodpeckers are the real treat, with nearly all of Idaho's species possible (except White-headed and Lewis's). American Three-toed and Hairy Woodpeckers are the most common ones here. Corvids include Gray and Steller's Jays, Clark's Nutcrackers (most likely on the west slope above the lake), and Common Ravens. All three of our nuthatches are present, as well as Yellow-rumped and MacGillivray's Warblers. Pine Grosbeaks, Cassin's Finches, Red Crossbills, and Pine Siskins are likely breeders. At night listen for Great Horned, Northern Pygmy-, Barred, Great Gray, Boreal, and Northern Saw-whet Owls.

For additional birding continue north on FR 257 to mile 13.6 (3 miles north of Grouse Creek Campground), turn left (west), and go 0.2 mile to the obscure Granite Mountain Trailhead. This trail fords Twin Lakes Creek and heads up into a partially harvested burned forest. This area can be very birdy. You'll reach a fire look-out atop 8,500-foot-high Granite Mountain in about 4 miles (signed mileages vary).

OTHER:

Area maps can be purchased from the FS (208/634-0700) in McCall. Camping is available at Grouse Creek Campground (pit toilets) and at undeveloped sites around the lake. Goose Lake is a popular fishing destination as well. McCall is a full-service community.

BEAR BASIN

Author: Dave Trochlell

Site C-9 — Map C-8/C-9/C-10/C-11

Highlights: Great Gray Owl, Williamson's Sapsucker
Major Habitats: Mixed Conifer Forest, Meadow
Location: Valley Co., 4 miles northwest of McCall
Spring: * *   **Summer:** * *   **Fall:** * *   **Winter:** * *

Bear Basin is just a few minutes outside the resort town of McCall, and is a good place to see a number of interesting owls and woodpeckers. This is probably Idaho's best site for Williamson's Sapsucker. Another specialty is Great Gray Owl, which has been studied here by the Forest Service.

DIRECTIONS:

Follow ID 55 west from downtown McCall about 2.5 miles. At milepost 146.6 turn right (north) on FR 451 (Bear Basin Road) and zero your mileage. At mile 0.8 stay right (straight) and enter public land (FS).

BIRDING:

As you start up Bear Basin Road, stop and listen for Western Screech-Owls, White-breasted Nuthatches, Swainson's Thrushes, and American Redstarts in the open forest. At mile 1.3 park in the pull-out on the left (west), by the large meadow. Walk the old two-track road that leads 0.3 mile northwest to an old corral. Scan the meadow's periphery for Great Gray Owl, which may be present year round. In summer watch for Wilson's Snipe, Red-naped and Williamson's Sapsuckers, Hairy Woodpeckers, Mountain Bluebirds, and Lincoln's Sparrows. Pileated Woodpeckers, Clark's Nutcrackers, and Red Crossbills can often be detected flying overhead. Enter the woods behind the corral and walk the forest/meadow margin. Carefully scan any small forest openings for Great Grays. In spring and summer you may also find Olive-sided Flycatchers, Mountain Chickadees, Golden-crowned and Ruby-crowned Kinglets, Swainson's and Hermit Thrushes, Cassin's Vireos, Yellow-rumped and Townsend's Warblers, and Western Tanagers.

If you continue driving north on FR 451, watch all forest openings for Great Gray Owls. Be sure to stop occasionally to listen for woodpeckers. Though rare, Spruce Grouse, American Three-toed, and Black-backed Woodpeckers, and Pine Grosbeaks are possible. More common species include Dusky Flycatcher, Golden-crowned Kinglet, Hermit and Varied Thrushes, and Wilson's Warbler. An evening's owling could yield Flammulated, Northern Pygmy-, Barred, Boreal, and Northern Saw-whet Owls.

OTHER:

McCall is a full-service community. Area maps and more information are available from the FS (208/634-0700) in McCall. See also Ponderosa SP (the next site), Goose Lake (the previous site) and Lick Creek Road Route (p. 122).

PONDEROSA STATE PARK
Author: Diane Evans
Site C-10 — Map C-8/C-9/C-10/C-11

Highlights: Vaux's Swift, Olive-sided Flycatcher
Major Habitats: Mixed Conifer Forest, Wetland
Location: Valley Co., 2 miles northeast of McCall
Spring: *   **Summer:** * * *   **Fall:** *   **Winter:** *

Towering conifers bordering beautiful Payette Lake are the dominant feature of Ponderosa State Park. This forest packs high densities of Mountain Chickadees, Swainson's Thrushes, Townsend's Warblers, and Western Tanagers.

The best birding at Ponderosa SP is along the trail maze within the Day Use Area. Early mornings are the most productive time, particularly after mid-summer, when nesting activity slows and the number of human visitors increases. Be aware that during winter and early spring, you'll be limited to cross-country ski access.

DIRECTIONS:

The park entrance is 1.8 miles from downtown McCall. Signs to the park are posted at every major intersection in town.

From the intersection of ID 55 and East Lake Street, head east on East Lake Street. Follow the main drag as it turns into Pine Street/Roosevelt Avenue/Hemlock Street. After 0.6 mile turn left on Davis Avenue, then go straight to the park entrance in another 1.2 miles.

Zero your mileage at the park entrance station. The narrow road that leads through the park is paved for 1.5 miles and gravel for the remaining 1.7 miles.

BIRDING:

A good place to begin exploring Ponderosa SP is along Meadow Marsh Trail, which forms a short loop close to the campground. To get there, turn right (east) into the large dirt parking lot at mile 0.3, just before the large wooden gate marking the entrance into the Day Use Area. The trailhead is by the road. Follow the trail northeast, bypassing the Botanical Walk Loop. At the first major junction turn left onto Meadow Marsh Trail. Dusky Flycatchers, Black-headed Grosbeaks, and MacGillivray's Warblers frequent the Quaking Aspens here. Mountain Chickadees, Red-breasted Nuthatches, Swainson's Thrushes, and Yellow-rumped Warblers are common as you continue north. Listen for Steller's Jays as well. For a short loop, turn right onto Fir Grove Trail and continue eastward. Pileated Woodpeckers are often heard along this section. Pick up the Meadow Marsh Trail to follow the loop back to the gravel parking lot. After retrieving your vehicle, continue north on the park's main road. At mile 1.3 stay right.

Lily Marsh parking lot is on the right (east) at mile 2.0. In spring, Lily Marsh supports Wood Ducks, Buffleheads, Common Goldeneyes, Ring-necked Ducks, Lesser Scaup, Mallards, and Hooded Mergansers. A short walk to the bridge (visible from the parking lot at the north end of the marsh) provides easy viewing. There are several Osprey nests around the marsh, including one directly over the bridge. In June listen for Soras, Willow and Olive-sided Flycatchers, Varied Thrushes, Yellow-rumped, Townsend's, and Nashville Warblers, and Cassin's Vireos. Lily Marsh Trail continues to the east, with several hiking options (e.g., south along the east side of the marsh or northeast toward Pilgrim Cove), all of which access good birding territory. Northern Pygmy-Owls and Barred Owls are possible in this general area.

After investigating the Lily Marsh area, drive to the north end of the park. The stupendous overlook at road's end is worth the extra time. *This portion of the road is not suitable for trailers or motorhomes.* At mile 3.0 is the Huckleberry Bay Trailhead, but you cannot park there, so continue 100 yards or so and use the pull-out at the Lake Overlook, then walk back down the road to access the trailhead. Follow Huckleberry Bay Trail east and turn north (left) at the trail junction in 50 yards, and loop down into the woods. Follow the trail south past a small wetland; Pileated Woodpeckers nest here. Listen also for Vaux's Swifts. Hiking options include completing a loop by continuing downhill and returning on the Ridgeline Trail, or backtracking to the road (see map).

OTHER:

A checklist and a trail map can be obtained at the visitors center (mile 0.1). Ponderosa SP supports a popular full-service campground (reservations advised), boat launch, beaches, and picnic pavilions. McCall is a full-service community. For more information, contact the park (208/634-2164). See also Lick Creek Road Route, the next site.

LICK CREEK ROAD ROUTE
Author: Marilyn C. Smith
Site C-11 — Map C-8/C-9/C-10/C-11

Highlights: Townsend's Warbler, Spring migrants
Major Habitats: Dry Conifer Forest, Mixed Conifer Forest, Wetland
Location: Valley Co., McCall
Spring: * * *   **Summer:** * * *   **Fall:** *   **Winter:** *

This short route ascends into the Payette NF near McCall. It is one of central Idaho's best spots for spring migrants, and it also attracts lots of typical conifer forest nesters. Best birding is from mid-May to early July.

DIRECTIONS:

Zero your mileage at the intersection of ID 55 and East Lake Street in downtown McCall, then head east on East Lake Street toward Ponderosa SP. Follow the main drag through the curves as it changes to Pine Street, Roosevelt Avenue, and Hemlock Street. At mile 0.6 turn left (north) on Davis Avenue. At mile 1.1 turn right (east) onto Lick Creek Road at the flashing signal light. At mile 3.2 stay right. From this point on, Lick Creek Road is a graveled road of variable quality.

BIRDING:

Little Payette Lake is on the right (south) at mile 3.8. It can be scoped from the wooden dock. Look for Red-necked Grebes and various waterfowl, including nesting Common Goldeneyes. One or two Common Loons often spend the entire summer. Keep an eye out for Rufous and Calliope Hummingbirds (June to September) in the roadside bushes, and for Ospreys over the lake.

At mile 3.9 park in the pull-off on the right (south). A narrow dirt road on the left (north) side of Lick Creek Road leads into the woods. Walk this road and the maze of trails along its edge for common forest birds, including Cooper's and Sharp-shinned Hawks, Ruffed Grouse, Red-naped and (possibly) Williamson's Sapsuckers, Gray and Steller's Jays, and Golden-crowned and Ruby-crowned Kinglets.

The best birding is around mile 5.7. Park at the road spur on the left (north), next to the large rock. The small clearing allows excellent views of the boggy area to the south, and the high cliff to the north. Bird songs come from every direction! Thick willows beside the road hide warblers, while kinglets sing from the tree-tops and Common Ravens and Clark's Nutcrackers call from the cliff. Other species to watch for include Turkey Vulture, Red-naped Sapsucker, Downy, Hairy, and Pileated Woodpeckers, Cordilleran Flycatcher, Rock Wren, Western Tanager, and Nashville, Yellow, Townsend's, MacGillivray's, and Wilson's Warblers.

At mile 5.9 pull into the large parking lot on the right (south), which borders Scouts Pond. A series of paths radiates around and beyond the pond for additional birding.

There is a good place to turn around by Tyee Creek (mile 6.5). Beyond Tyee Creek, Lick Creek Road has more tantalizing spots for the adventuresome birder, but the road becomes a bit rough.

OTHER:

A Payette NF map is suggested for anyone going beyond Tyee Creek; it is available from the FS office (208/634-0700) in McCall. McCall is a full-service community.

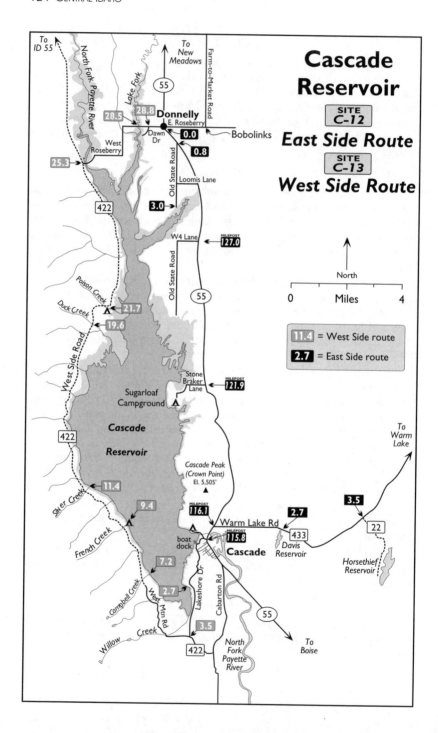

Cascade Reservoir

SITE
C-12
East Side Route

SITE
C-13
West Side Route

North

0   Miles   4

11.4 = West Side route
2.7 = East Side route

To ID 55

To New Meadows

North Fork Payette River

Lake Fork

Farm-to-Market Road

28.5   28.8 **Donnelly**
E. Roseberry
Dawn Dr
0.0   → Bobolinks
0.8

West Roseberry

25.3

Old State Road

Loomis Lane

3.0

422

W4 Lane   MILEPOST **127.0**

Old State Road

55

Poison Creek

Duck Creek

21.7
19.6

West Side Road

Stone Braker Lane   MILEPOST **121.9**

Sugarloaf Campground

Cascade Reservoir

422

Cascade Peak (Crown Point) El. 5,505'

Silver Creek

11.4

9.4

French Creek

MILEPOST **116.1**

Warm Lake Rd   **2.7**

3.5

To Warm Lake

433
Davis Reservoir

22

Horsethief Reservoir

boat dock

MILEPOST **115.8**   **Cascade**

Campbell Creek

7.2

West Mtn Rd

Lakeshore Dr

Cabarton Rd

2.7

55

To Boise

3.5

Willow Creek

422

North Fork Payette River

CASCADE RESERVOIR — EAST SIDE ROUTE
Author: Marilyn C. Smith
Site C-12 — Map C-12/C-13

Highlights: Pacific Loon, Bald Eagle
Major Habitats: Wetland, Grassland
Location: Valley Co., 12 miles south of McCall
Spring: * * *   **Summer:** * *   **Fall:** * * *   **Winter:** *

This site is viewed against a background of conifer-forested mountains, presenting spectacular scenery anywhere along the shore. This 16-mile-long route follows the eastern edge of Cascade Reservoir (managed by the BOR for over 40 years), from Donnelly to Cascade.

DIRECTIONS:

The starting point is the junction of ID 55 and West Roseberry Road in Donnelly (the intersection by the Donnelly store/Sinclair station). Zero your mileage here, then head south on ID 55. At mile 0.8 turn right (south) onto Old State Road at the binoculars sign.

The first few stops discussed are on Old State Road. Most of Old State Road was flooded when the reservoir was built, but those portions which escaped inundation offer excellent view-points; *watch out for broken pavement.* Be aware that much of the shoreline is closed to public use from February 1 to July 1.

BIRDING:

Between mile 0.8 and 2.8 check fences, tree-tops, and power poles for hawks and Great Gray Owls (most likely from August to December). At mile 3.0 stop at the "Road Closed—Water Over Road" sign, and scan the lake for migrant Pacific Loons (October and November), Common Loons, Tundra and Trumpeter Swans, and various waterfowl.

The next birding stop is 4 miles south of the "Road Closed" sign, but you'll usually have to make a loop to get around the flooded portion of Old State Road. To do this, backtrack north along Old State Road 0.7 mile and go right (east) on graveled Loomis Lane 0.7 mile to ID 55, then turn right (south) for 2 miles. At ID 55 milepost 127, turn right (west) on W 4 Lane and continue 0.8 mile to rejoin Old State Road. At the intersection of W 4 Lane and Old State Road, turn left (south) and go to road's end. Old State Road is gated 2.6 miles south of its junction with W 4 Lane. Between February 1 and July 1 you'll have to be content with *long*-distance scoping, but during the rest of the year, you can explore on foot. Old State Road is good for Swainson's Hawks and Northern Harriers in summer, Rough-legged and Red-tailed Hawks in winter, and Bald Eagles anytime. In spring the swan count at the end of Old State Road can reach a hundred. American White Pelicans, Great Blue Herons, and Sandhill Cranes are all regular during summer, while Peregrine Falcons and Soras are more irregular. Snow Buntings are possible, October to April.

To reach the next lake access, backtrack to ID 55 and continue south 5.2 miles. Watch the fence-lines in this general area for Wilson's Snipe and Mountain Bluebirds in summer, and power poles for hawks all year. At milepost 121.9 turn right (west) onto Stone Braker Lane. A quarter-mile down the road, stop to scope the lone pine tree in the south field for a Bald Eagle and its nest, one of about seven found around Cascade Reservoir. Farther along, two good pull-outs allow scoping of the reservoir for loons, grebes, and ducks. The second pull-out also gives foot access to the reservoir. In spring you may see 100 Yellow-headed Blackbirds polka-dotting the hillsides. In summer Horned Larks and Savannah and Vesper Sparrows will be flushed as you continue to the road's end at Sugarloaf Campground (1.8 miles from ID 55). Check the bays for migrating Pacific, Red-throated, and Common Loons, Buffleheads, Barrow's Goldeneyes, Greater and Lesser Scaup, and Long-tailed Ducks. The Bald Eagle nest tree is clearly visible from the Sugarloaf Campground parking lot.

After backtracking to ID 55, continue south toward Cascade. At milepost 116.1 turn left (east) onto Warm Lake Road and continue 2.7 miles to Davis Reservoir (on the south side of the weigh station), where Western and Red-necked Grebes and assorted waterfowl may be scoped from the road.

The 2-mile-long gravel entrance road into Horsethief Reservoir is another 3.5 miles east on Warm Lake Road. Several hours of birding around the reservoir in spring and summer will reveal nesting ducks (including Common Goldeneyes) and birds common to meadows and mixed conifer forest.

When you've finished with Horsethief Reservoir, return to ID 55 and turn left (south). At milepost 115.9 you cross the North Fork Payette River below Cascade Dam. Both flow and water-level affect the number of birds found here, but it's a rare occasion when none is in view. Long-tailed Ducks have been present during winter, while Hooded Mergansers and Barrow's Goldeneyes are common from November to March. Common Mergansers and Ospreys take their turn in summer.

At ID 55 milepost 115.8, Lake Way (a.k.a. Crown Point Road) is on the right (west). Follow this road 0.7 mile to the Crown Point Campground and scan the deep water behind the dam for loons and mergansers, and look on both ends of the dam for Rock Wrens.

OTHER:

For more information call the BOR (208/382-4258) or FS (208/382-4271) offices in Cascade. Also see Cascade Reservoir—West Side Route, the next site.

CASCADE RESERVOIR — WEST SIDE ROUTE

Author: Marilyn C. Smith

Site C-13 — Map C-12/C-13

Highlights: Greater Scaup, Bobolink
Major Habitats: Wetland, Dry Conifer Forest
Location: Valley Co., Cascade
Spring: * * *   **Summer:** * *   **Fall:** * * *   **Winter:** *

Starting in Cascade and ending in Donnelly, this 30-mile-long route takes you between Cascade Reservoir and West Mountain. Although birding is often less productive on this side of the reservoir, the possibility of several unusual species makes this beautiful drive worthwhile any time of the year.

DIRECTIONS:

The route begins at the municipal boat dock in Cascade, at the intersection of Old State Highway and Lakeshore Drive. To find the starting point, go to the Texaco Station at the north end of town and follow Old State Highway northwest 0.6 mile.

At the municipal boat area, zero out your mileage, scan the water for loons and waterfowl, and then head southwest on Lakeshore Drive past the golf course.

BIRDING:

Several dirt roads, campgrounds, and the Cabarton Boat Launch allow lake access along Lakeshore Drive. Use these points to scope the reservoir for waterbirds. The best birding is at mile 2.7, just before you cross a cattle-guard. A short rutted road on the right (west) leads to a small parking area, where you can scan for Western and Clark's Grebes, American White Pelicans, dabbling ducks, and shorebirds.

Return to Lakeshore Drive and continue south. Just past the second cattle-guard, turn right (west) at mile 3.5, onto West Mountain Road (a.k.a. West Side Road). Follow West Mountain Road as it passes through meadow and pine-forest habitat. Varied Thrushes may be heard from March to July along this stretch of road. At mile 7.0 the pavement ends. Lake access is available at Campbell Creek Boat Launch at mile 7.2 (just past the cattle-guard), one of the best places to look for Greater Scaup in fall. Red-naped Sapsuckers and other woodpecker species should be expected in the Quaking Aspens. More Quaking Aspen groves line the road at mile 8.4, where Hairy Woodpeckers, Western Wood-Pewees, Dusky Flycatchers, Eastern Kingbirds, House Wrens, Yellow Warblers, American Redstarts, and Warbling Vireos may be present. At mile 9.4 is French Creek Campground. Bird the campground along both sides of the road for Winter Wrens, MacGillivray's Warblers, and other common conifer-forest birds. You may also want to wander through the forest above the upper campground for American Three-toed Wood-peckers and Townsend's Warblers.

At mile 11.4 check berry bushes at Silver Creek for Warbling Vireos, Ce-dar Waxwings, and Western Tanagers. Another Quaking Aspen patch is on the right (east) side of the road at mile 14.2.

Duck Creek WMA begins at mile 19.6 and continues to the Poison Creek Campground at mile 21.7. The shoreline, grassland, woodland, and riparian areas in the WMA have been little explored for birding potential, but it's known that this is one of the best spots for loons in November. Foot access is allowed from July 2 to January 31.

At mile 25.3 turn right (east) onto West Roseberry Drive (a.k.a. Tamarack Falls) toward Donnelly. The bridge at mile 25.4 has a small parking lot, a fish-ing-bridge, and access to woods and shoreline. Scoping waterfowl from the bridge and carefully perusing the shoreline are frequently productive. River Otters may be found anywhere along the North Fork Payette River.

Continuing east on West Roseberry, you will reach another bridge at mile 28.5. Foot access to the shoreline is at the bridge's west end. Anything from eagles to shorebirds is possible. At mile 28.8 turn right (south) onto Dawn Drive. Good lake views appear immediately on the right (west) with a camp-ground nearby for safe parking. After scanning the lake, continue south on Dawn Drive. About 0.2 mile south of the "Donnelly Public Camping" sign, turn right (west) on the dirt road which leads to a beach and picnic area. From here, grebes, American White Pelicans, mergansers, and gulls can be seen from April to August. Farther south along Dawn Drive, look for Mountain Bluebirds, Cedar Waxwings, and Red Crossbills. In fall hundreds of Canada Geese, American Wigeons, and American Coots stage here. Eurasian Wigeons are possible during migration.

To get to Donnelly, backtrack to West Roseberry Road, and turn right (east) for 0.7 mile. Bobolinks can be found on a short side trip, 1.6 miles east of Donnelly at the intersection of East Roseberry Road and Farm-to-Market Road (see map).

OTHER:

Fuel is available in Donnelly. Fuel, motels, camping, and groceries are avail-able in Cascade and McCall. There are several developed BOR and FS camp-grounds around Cascade Lake and in the nearby mountains. See also Cascade Reservoir—East Side Route, the previous site.

CHAMBERLAIN BASIN

Background by: Pat and Greg Hayward

Site C-14 — See Central map, page 102

Highlights: Spruce Grouse, Boreal Owl, Black-backed Woodpecker
Major Habitats: Mixed and Dry Conifer Forests, Deciduous Forest
Location: Idaho Co., 56 miles northeast of McCall
Spring: * *   **Summer:** * *   **Fall:** * *   **Winter:** N/A

Deep inside the huge Frank Church River of No Return Wilderness, Chamberlain Basin takes a little effort to get to. This inaccessibility, however, provides a unique opportunity to observe large-scale natural processes at work. And the birds are great! Spruce Grouse are easy to find; you can hardly take a spring hike without hearing one. In summer hens and broods can often be found dust-bathing in the trails. Especially intriguing, though, is the well-studied owl community, which includes most of the state's species. Boreals are common nesters in old-growth Ponderosa Pine, Douglas-fir, and Quaking Aspen forests, hunting in the subalpine forest on the ridgelines above the Basin.

DIRECTIONS:

Birding Chamberlain Basin requires good physical condition and practiced map and compass skills. Being able to identify Idaho's conifers is also helpful. You can get to Chamberlain Basin by horseback, hiking, or flying. Riding and hiking are usually possible from mid-June to mid-October. Access via air taxi can begin in mid-May.

To ride or hike to Chamberlain, use a Payette NF forest map (McCall Ranger District portion) to navigate the tortuous 94-mile journey from McCall to Yellow Pine to Edwardburg to the Smith Creek-Big Creek Trailhead. From the trailhead, follow Big Creek Trail east 3 miles, then go north on Chamberlain Trail (# 001). Chamberlain Trail will take you up Beaver and Hand Creeks before heading down into Chamberlain Basin. Most backpackers should plan on two days for this 25-mile jaunt, but a one-day hike is possible for those in excellent shape. If you ride in, bring an ax; you'll need it to clear trails.

Several air charter companies regularly service Chamberlain Basin. Take your pick among Arnold Aviation (208/382-4844) in Cascade, Pioneer Aviation (208/634-7127) in McCall, or Mountain Air (208/383-3325) in Boise.

BIRDING:

The best birding strategy is to sample each of the three main habitats: old-growth dry conifer forest; old-growth mixed conifer forest; and old-growth Quaking Aspen forest. Also investigate the wetlands, riparian areas, meadows, and burns. (The latter is the preferred habitat of American Three-toed and Black-backed Woodpeckers.)

To reach accessible old-growth dry conifer forest, use the north end of the north-south airstrip as your starting point. Follow Trail 024 up Ranch Creek approximately 0.75 mile. After passing a sagebrush slope and cutting through a section of Lodgepole Pine, you'll arrive at the foot of an open bunchgrass slope. Go up the grass slope to the large Ponderosa Pine/Douglas-fir stand visible from the trail. At the grass-forest interface is the cut-off trail used by Stonebraker Ranch to access the Flossie Lake Trail. This is the type of habitat that both Flammulated and Boreal Owls nest in at Chamberlain; in fact, Idaho's first Boreal Owl nest was found in this very stand.

To find old-growth mixed conifer forest, head to the west end of the east-west airstrip. Immediately north of the airstrip is an old wagon road. Follow the wagon road westward less than 0.5 mile to its terminus in dense Lodgepole Pine. Head north and climb to the band of old-growth along the upper half of the hill. Look here for Boreal Owls, Northern Saw-whet Owls, and Pileated Woodpeckers, and listen for the evening songs of Swainson's and Hermit Thrushes.

Boreal Owls also nest in the old-growth Quaking Aspen patches scattered throughout the basin. Two good patches can be reached by heading southwest on Trail 003 from the south side of the east-west air strip. In approximately 2.5 miles Trail 003 traverses the edge of the first good patch. About a mile farther west, go south on Trail 017 toward Moose Jaw Meadows. About a half to three-quarters of a mile farther along, the trail crosses the second aspen stand, which is particularly good for Western Screech-Owls and Pileated Woodpeckers.

To investigate more Quaking Aspen, follow Trail 024 north from the north end of the north-south airstrip for approximately 1.5 miles. At the crossing with Ranch Creek, leave the trail and continue upstream along the creek. In approximately 0.25 mile a small draw comes in from the right (north). Follow this draw up over a small rise into the wet, boggy, aspen.

OTHER:

Topographic maps for the area include: Sheepeater Mountain, Meadow of Doubt, Mosquito Peak, and Lodgepole Creek. Trail numbers are from the Frank Church–River of No Return Wilderness North Half map. This map and additional information are available from the McCall Ranger District (208/634-0400) or Middle Fork Ranger District (208/879-4101).

Chamberlain Basin Outfitters (208/756-3715) can provide more civilized housing and food at their base camp, as well as horse trips for fishing, sightseeing, etc.

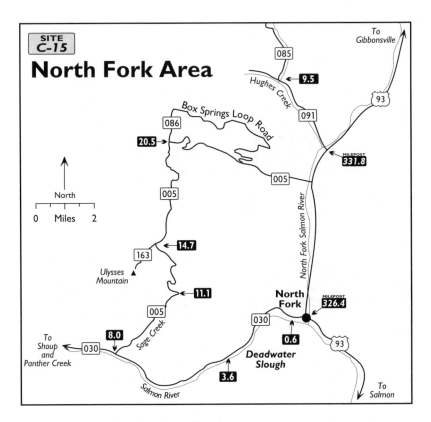

SITE C-15

North Fork Area

085

9.5

Hughes Creek

091

93

Box Springs Loop Road

086

20.5

005

005

MILEPOST **331.8**

North Fork Salmon River

North

0 Miles 2

14.7

163

Ulysses Mountain ▲

11.1

005

North Fork

MILEPOST **326.4**

030

Sage Creek

8.0

To Shoup and Panther Creek

030

005

0.6

93

Deadwater Slough

3.6

Salmon River

To Salmon

To Gibbonsville

NORTH FORK AREA

Authors: Hadley B. Roberts, Noel Wamer

Site C-15 — Map C-15

Highlights: Chukar, Flammulated Owl, Lewis's Woodpecker
Major Habitats: Dry Conifer Forest, Deciduous Forest, Wetland
Location: Lemhi Co., 21 miles north of Salmon
Spring: * * *   **Summer:** * * *   **Fall:** * *   **Winter:** * *

Remote, rugged, and very scenic, the riparian and upland forests around North Fork provide diverse birding. Three of the best spots are described below, but equally good birding can be had almost anywhere in this area. You just have to go exploring to find it!

DIRECTIONS:

The starting point for all three sites is the junction of US 93 and FR 030 in North Fork (US 93 milepost 326.4). Zero your mileage here.

BIRDING:

DEADWATER SLOUGH

Deadwater Slough is one of Lemhi County's best birding spots. Over 60 bird species have been recorded on this 250-acre tract of riparian floodplain. To reach Deadwater Slough from the starting point, turn left (west) on paved FR 030 and follow it 0.6 mile to the FS recreation site on the left (south), at the upstream end of Deadwater Slough.

One of the first birds that you'll probably find is the omnipresent Lewis's Woodpecker, usually seen flycatching over the Salmon River. Pileated Woodpeckers also nest in this area but are less common. Bald and Golden Eagles are frequently seen flying along the river year round. This is also one of the few local nesting areas for Wood Ducks.

The slough (a backwater area of the Salmon River) is best birded by canoe or inflatable raft. A boat ramp is available at the picnic area at mile 3.6. To do additional land-based birding, continue west on FR 030 and use any suitable pull-out that allows investigation of the cottonwood forest. Be aware that some land here is private. In dense cover along the river, look for Eastern Kingbirds, Gray Catbirds, Red-eyed Vireos (uncommon), MacGillivray's Warblers, Yellow-breasted Chats, Black-headed Grosbeaks, Lazuli Buntings, and Bullock's Orioles.

To look for Chukars, search steep, brushy slopes all along FR 030, which extends 45 miles east of Deadwater Slough. Particularly good are the areas near Deadwater, Shoup, and the mouth of Panther Creek (mile 28).

FOREST ROAD 005

This loop will take you on a good half-day drive through a variety of habitats. From the starting point, go west on FR 030 to mile 8, then turn right (north) onto FR 005, a narrow, rocky, steep road. The first few miles of this route follow Sage Creek upstream. This is a good area to look for Northern Saw-whet Owls, Ruffed Grouse, American Dippers, and Nashville Warblers. You should be able to find Mountain Bluebirds and Chipping Sparrows on slopes above the creek.

At mile 11.1 FR 005 crosses Sage Creek and rises quickly through a series of switchbacks into Ponderosa Pine/Douglas-fir forest. Look here for Williamson's Sapsuckers (rare), Olive-sided and Hammond's Flycatchers, Steller's Jays, Clark's Nutcrackers, Common Ravens, Mountain Chickadees, Red-breasted Nuthatches, Ruby-crowned Kinglets, Townsend's Solitaires, Swainson's and Hermit Thrushes, Yellow-rumped Warblers, Western Tanagers, Pine Siskins, and Evening Grosbeaks. At mile 14.7 FR 005 reaches the ridgetop. You may want to park here and walk along FR 163 to the left (southwest) to see more of the species listed above.

From the junction of FR 005 and FR 163, continue driving north on FR 005 along the ridgetop. At mile 20.5 turn sharp left (north) onto FR 086 (a.k.a. Box

Springs Loop Road). This will take you through mature Ponderosa Pine habitat good for Flammulated Owls. At about mile 28.5, FR 086 rejoins FR 005. From here, continue east (downhill) to US 95 at mile 32 or so.

HUGHES CREEK ROAD

To investigate more Flammulated Owl habitat, go 5.4 miles north of the starting point on US 93 to milepost 331.8, then turn left (west) onto FR 091 (a.k.a. Hughes Creek Road). At mile 9.5, turn right (north) on FR 085. This roads leads into the open mature Ponderosa Pine forest favored by Flammulated Owls and away from the noisy waters of Hughes Creek. Start owling from about mile 10 on up.

OTHER:

Deadwater Picnic Area has a boat ramp, pit toilet, and water. Accommodations in North Fork are limited to two motel/campground combinations (fuel available). Other services are available in Salmon. Stop in at the FS (208/865-2700) in North Fork or the North Fork Store (208/865-2412) for maps, checklists, and more information.

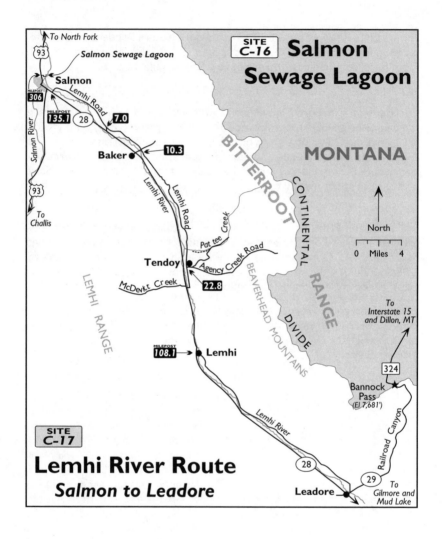

SITE
C-16
Salmon
Sewage Lagoon

To North Fork

Salmon Sewage Lagoon

93

Salmon

Lemhi Road

MILEPOST 306

Salmon River

MILEPOST 135.1

28

7.0

Baker

10.3

Lemhi River

Lemhi Road

93

To Challis

Pat tee Creek

BITTERROOT

CONTINENTAL RANGE

MONTANA

North

0   Miles   4

Tendoy

Agency Creek Road

22.8

McDevitt Creek

LEMHI RANGE

BEAVERHEAD MOUNTAINS

DIVIDE

To Interstate 15 and Dillon, MT

MILEPOST 108.1

Lemhi

324

Bannock Pass (El 7,681')

Railroad Canyon

SITE
C-17
Lemhi River Route
Salmon to Leadore

Lemhi River

28

29

Leadore

To Gilmore and Mud Lake

SALMON SEWAGE LAGOON
Author: Hadley B. Roberts
Site 16 — Map C-16/C-17
Highlights: Grebes, Waterfowl, Shorebirds
Major Habitats: Wetland
Location: Lemhi Co., Salmon
Spring: * * *   **Summer:** * *   **Fall:** *   **Winter:** *

For spring concentrations of waterfowl, shorebirds, and wading birds, no place in the Salmon River drainage can beat the Salmon Sewage Lagoon. Over 100 species have been recorded here in April and May. For reasons unknown, fall migration does not offer the same viewing opportunities.

DIRECTIONS:

To reach the lagoon, drive north from Salmon on US 93 for about a mile to milepost 306. Turn right (east) at the sign marked "Sportsman Access–Lemhi Hole" onto a good dirt road that leads to the lagoon in 0.4 mile. Pull up to the lagoon's perimeter fence and park. Unfortunately, you'll have to view the birds through the chain-link fence; just walk all the way around to get various viewing angles.

BIRDING:

The lagoon is a major stop-over for large flocks of Snow Geese, with occasional sightings of Ross's Geese as well. Barrow's Goldeneyes and Cinnamon Teal are often present, and even a Harlequin Duck was seen here once. Large flocks of Canada Geese can be found on the adjacent stock pond and in the surrounding pasture. Wood Ducks nest in tree cavities along the river. Six species of grebes have been recorded at the lagoon—Pied-billed, Red-necked, Western, Clark's, Horned, and Eared. The latter two are most common. The list of wading and shorebird species includes Great Egret, American Avocet, Marbled Godwit, Long-billed Dowitcher, Wilson's and Red-necked Phalaropes, and Least and Solitary Sandpipers. Franklin's and Bonaparte's Gulls and Black and Forster's Terns are occasional visitors. Ospreys and Bald and Golden Eagles are often sighted as they fly along the river. A small stand of cottonwoods adjacent to the lagoon contains Lewis's Woodpeckers and Western Wood-Pewees.

OTHER:

Salmon is a full-service community.

LEMHI RIVER ROUTE

Authors: Hadley B. Roberts, Helen Ulmschneider

Site C-17 — Map C-16/C-17

Highlights: Gambel's Quail, Cordilleran Flycatcher
Major Habitats: Deciduous Forest, Shrub-steppe, Meadow
Location: Lemhi Co., Salmon
Spring: * * *   **Summer:** * * *   **Fall:** *   **Winter:** *

This route follows the Lemhi River upstream from Salmon to Bannock Pass, a 60-mile drive one-way. During late May and early June you may see over 125 bird species, one of the most diverse bird-assemblages in the state. Among the critters to look for are Gambel's Quail, which were introduced in 1921. This is the only place in Idaho where the species occurs.

DIRECTIONS:

From the junction of ID 28 and US 93 in Salmon, go south on ID 28 for 6 miles to milepost 135.1, then turn left (east) on Lemhi Road, zeroing your mileage. This paved/graveled county road (a.k.a. Old Highway 28) is unsigned for much of the route. *Most of the trip passes through private property, but portions are public (BLM and FS).*

BIRDING:

The best birding strategy here is simply to pull over and investigate wherever you see birds or likely-looking habitat. A few of the more dependable spots are noted below.

Throughout your drive watch riparian habitat for Veeries, Gray Catbirds, MacGillivray's and Wilson's Warblers, Yellow-breasted Chats, and Black-headed Grosbeaks. Where cottonwoods are present, Lewis's and Pileated Woodpeckers, Red-naped Sapsuckers, Western Wood-Pewees, and Bullock's Orioles may be found.

Several ponds and cattail marshes are scattered throughout the lower valley. Watch this habitat for Cinnamon Teal, Soras, Common Yellowthroats, and Yellow-headed Blackbirds. Greater Sage-Grouse, Gray Partridge, Chukars, Rock Wrens, Sage Thrashers, and Brewer's and Vesper Sparrows can be observed in sagebrush areas. In meadows Sandhill Cranes, Long-billed Curlews, Willets, Northern Harriers, Short-eared Owls, and Bobolinks (rare) may be seen. Between Salmon and Baker, listen for the distinctive call of Gambel's Quail.

At mile 7.0 turn left at the T intersection to stay on Lemhi Road. At mile 10.3 is a 4-way intersection. Go straight (east)—do not cross the river.

At mile 22.8 (Tendoy) turn left (east) onto Agency Creek Road. After 0.6 mile, turn left (north) onto a rough, steep, dirt road, and drive 3.2 miles to

Pattee Creek. *Do not attempt this road if it's muddy, or if you have any doubts about your vehicle's suitability. (A high-clearance vehicle is recommended.)* At Pattee Creek one can wander on public land for about 2 miles upstream or 1 mile downstream. Pattee Creek is great for riparian birds, and it is one of the few local spots for Cordilleran Flycatchers. In fall migration Sharp-shinned and Cooper's Hawks and Wilson's Warblers are frequently present. In late fall look for Pine Grosbeaks, Common Redpolls, and Gray-crowned Rosy-Finches.

After birding Pattee Creek, backtrack to Lemhi Road and turn left (south), go 1.8 miles, and cross the Lemhi River. At the junction with ID 28, turn right (north) on ID 28 for 0.1 mile, then turn left (west) on McDevitt Creek Road. Good riparian birding is found along this entire creek, *but the lower portion is private, so please stay on the road.* After 4 miles you'll cross a cattle-guard onto public land (BLM). Many of the previously mentioned riparian birds are also found along this portion of McDevitt Creek. A vagrant Black-and-white Warbler summered here in 1994, 1995, and 1996!

Return to ID 28, turn right (south), and go 7.6 miles. At milepost 108.1 turn left (east) by the Lemhi Mercantile and proceed south on the county road to Leadore. In Leadore, turn left (east) on ID 29 and follow it 14 miles through Railroad Canyon to the Montana boundary at Bannock Pass (elevation 7,681 feet). ID 29 is paved for 4 miles, then turns into a well-maintained gravel road. In the scattered timber of Railroad Canyon, Golden Eagles, Clark's Nutcrackers, Hammond's and Dusky Flycatchers, Hermit Thrushes, Western Tanagers, and Green-tailed Towhees are often found. Bald Eagles, Rough-legged Hawks, Bohemian Waxwings, and Snow Buntings can be seen along this route during winter.

OTHER:

All services are available in Salmon. There are two BLM campgrounds along the route: McFarland Recreation Site (ID 28 milepost 103.6) and Smokey's Cub Recreation Site (ID 29 milepost 3.7). Both have tables and pit toilets. Fuel, telephone, and some groceries are available at Tendoy, Lemhi, and Leadore.

Maps, checklists, and information can be obtained in Salmon at the FS (208/756-5100) or BLM (208/756-5400) offices. In Leadore, try the Leadore Ranger District (208/768-2500).

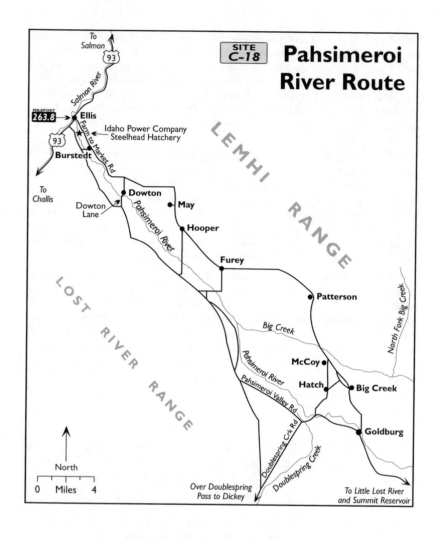

PAHSIMEROI RIVER ROUTE

Author: Hadley B. Roberts

Site C-18 — Map C-18

Highlights: Chukar, Greater Sage-Grouse
Major Habitats: Shrub-steppe, Deciduous Forest, Meadow
Location: Lemhi Co., 17 miles north of Challis
Spring: **   **Summer:** *** **Fall:** **   **Winter:** **

This 70-mile-long loop up the Pahsimeroi (pah-SIM-er-oy) River Valley is a great day-trip during May and June. The main loop starts and ends in Ellis, going upriver as far as Goldburg, an abandoned townsite. Much of this trip passes through public land (BLM). The best birding however, is at the river crossings on private land. Please bird from the road in such areas.

If you don't have enough time to complete the entire loop, you can make "mini-loops" by using one of the several cross lanes which connect the main roads on each side of the valley (see map).

DIRECTIONS:
From Challis follow US 93 north to milepost 263.8, then turn right (southeast) onto paved Farm to Market Road along the north side of the Pahsimeroi River. There are no mileposts along this route.

BIRDING:
The best way to bird is simply to stop wherever you see good habitat or hear birds. The most productive habitat is the riparian zone, accessed by the cross-lanes. Typical riparian species include Western Kingbird, Orange-crowned and Wilson's Warblers, Yellow-breasted Chat, Lazuli Bunting, White-crowned Sparrow, Bullock's Oriole, and American Goldfinch. During winter, Pine Grosbeaks are occasionally found in such habitat.

In sagebrush areas look for Gray Partridge, Chukars, Greater Sage-Grouse, Burrowing Owls, Horned Larks, Rock Wrens, Sage Thrashers, and Brewer's and Vesper Sparrows, as well as Pronghorn. Sandhill Cranes, Long-billed Curlews, Bobolinks, and Savannah Sparrows are occasionally seen in meadows and pastures. Check the infrequent cattail patches for Soras, Common Yellowthroats, and Yellow-headed Blackbirds.

Several waterfowl species can be found in the Pahsimeroi Valley, but the most common is Canada Goose. Lewis's Woodpeckers can sometimes be found in the lower valley's cottonwoods. Of the raptors, Golden Eagles, Red-tailed Hawks, and American Kestrels are common throughout the year. Bald Eagles and Rough-legged Hawks are present in winter. Look for American Dippers year round along the river.

One mile up the Pahsimeroi River is an Idaho Power Company Steelhead Hatchery. In season, these large ocean-going trout can be seen at close range. The riparian zone around the hatchery contains good numbers of several songbird species.

The midpoint of this route is Goldburg, 32 miles up the Pahsimeroi River. If you have time, continue southeast toward Little Lost River through more Chukar habitat. In about ten miles you'll reach Summit Reservoir, which can be alive with migrant waterfowl. The area around the reservoir can also be good for wintering Snow Buntings.

To return to US 93 from Goldburg, follow the Doublespring Road west for about 5 miles to the major intersection, then stay right (northwest). You reach pavement in about 10 miles, and can then follow it all the way to US 93, via Dowton Lane (see map).

OTHER:

A full range of services is available in Challis. Maps can be obtained from the FS (208/879-4321) in Challis. The only service available along this route is a small cafe in May, located on a side road about 11 miles up the Pahsimeroi. The more adventuresome explorers with high-clearance vehicles may also want to wander up the numerous side canyons (use a FS map) for additional riparian birding.

MORGAN CREEK TO PANTHER CREEK ROUTE

Author: Hadley B. Roberts

Site C-19 — Map C-19

Highlights: Blue Grouse, Green-tailed Towhee
Major Habitats: Dry Conifer Forest, Deciduous Forest
Location: Custer Co., 8 miles northwest of Challis
Spring: * *   **Summer:** * * *   **Fall:** *   **Winter:** N/A

Some of east-central Idaho's best birding is along Morgan and Panther Creeks. This very scenic route is 66 miles long (one-way) and is best done over two days. In addition to birds, Mule Deer, Elk, Pronghorn, Mountain Goat, and Bighorn Sheep are often seen. If you're extremely lucky, you may also see a Gray Wolf; two pairs now frequent this area.

DIRECTIONS:

From Challis follow US 93 north 8.3 miles, then turn left (west) up Morgan Creek Road at milepost 254.8. Zero your odometer here. Morgan Creek Road (a.k.a. FR 055) is paved for 2 miles, then turns to good gravel for most of the remainder. The road ascends Morgan Creek to the 7,578-foot-high summit (mile 20), then descends along Panther Creek to the Salmon River (mile 66). The first 8 miles of the route weave in and out of private land, but the rest of it is mostly public (FS).

BIRDING:

The first 5 miles follow a tight canyon along a narrow riparian area. Look in the cottonwoods for Lewis's Woodpeckers and Western Wood-Pewees, on the rocky slopes for Chukars, and in the surrounding cliffs for Canyon Wrens. After mile 5 the canyon opens up into a wide valley surrounded by rolling sagebrush hills and scattered patches of timber, with a shrubby riparian strip along Morgan Creek. *Most of the riparian habitat is on posted private land, so please bird from the road.* Look for Veeries, MacGillivray's and Wilson's

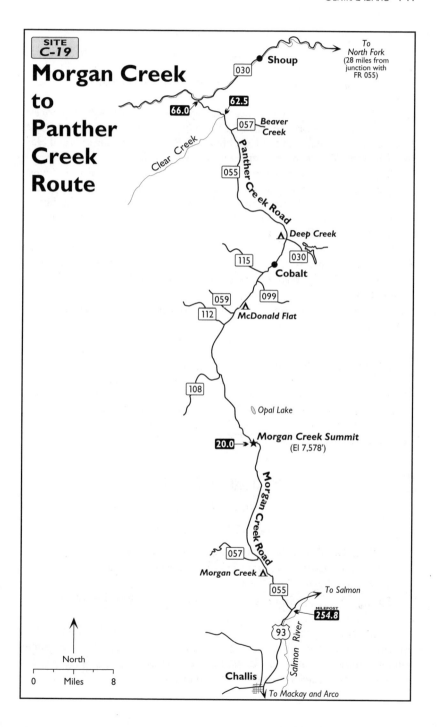

SITE C-19

Morgan Creek to Panther Creek Route

030 — Shoup

To North Fork (28 miles from junction with FR 055)

66.0

62.5

057 — Beaver Creek

Clear Creek

Panther Creek Road

055

Deep Creek

115

030

Cobalt

059

099

112

McDonald Flat

108

Opal Lake

20.0 — Morgan Creek Summit (El 7,578')

Morgan Creek Road

057

Morgan Creek

To Salmon

055

MILEPOST 254.8

93 — Salmon River

North

0   Miles   8

Challis

To Mackay and Arco

Warblers, Yellow-breasted Chats, Black-headed Grosbeaks, and Fox Sparrows. In small ponds along the creek you may see Cinnamon Teal, Soras, and Wilson's Phalaropes. Greater Sage-Grouse, Rock Wrens, Sage Thrashers, Lazuli Buntings, and Green-tailed Towhees should be watched for in sagebrush.

At about mile 17 the road enters Douglas-fir and Lodgepole Pine forest. Look here for Blue Grouse, Pileated Woodpeckers, Hammond's and Dusky Flycatchers, Mountain Chickadees, Mountain Bluebirds, Swainson's and Hermit Thrushes, Western Tanagers, and Red Crossbills.

As you descend Panther Creek, the road passes in and out of more forest. Many of the species found in Morgan Creek can also be found here. In addition, you may find an elusive American Redstart in Quaking Aspen patches, or a vagrant Indigo Bunting in riparian shrubs. Be sure to check the skies for Golden Eagles and Prairie Falcons.

Chukars are often seen or heard near the mouth of Clear Creek (mile 62.5), while White-throated Swifts can be seen flying near the mouth of Panther Creek (mile 66). Bighorn Sheep are common near the mouth of Panther Creek, as well.

When you arrive at the Salmon River, turn right (east) on FR 030 and follow it 28 miles to North Fork.

OTHER:

Salmon and Challis are full-service communities. There are no services along the route. Camping facilities are available at Morgan Creek Recreation Site (mile 5.1, no water), McDonald Flat Campground (mile 37), Deep Creek Campground (mile 43), and Clear Creek Trailhead (mile 62, no water). There are many undeveloped sites, too. Maps are available from the FS in Challis (208/879-4321) or Salmon (208/756-5204).

CHALLIS AREA

Author: Elise Faike

Site C-20 — Map C-20

Highlights: White-throated Swift, Least Flycatcher
Major Habitats: Deciduous Forest, Wetland, Farmland
Location: Custer Co., Challis
Spring: * *   **Summer:** * *   **Fall:** * *   **Winter:** N/A

Challis is a good staging-spot for exploring east-central Idaho. The Salmon River Mountains and Lemhi Mountains offer extensive birding opportunities. Varied birding is also available right around town, in riparian areas, wetlands, and grasslands. Four such sites are highlighted below.

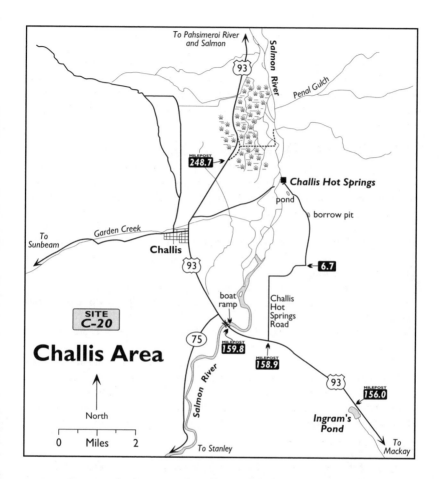

Salmon River
To Pahsimeroi River
and Salmon
93
Penal Gulch
MILEPOST
248.7
Challis Hot Springs
pond
borrow pit
To
Sunbeam
Garden Creek
Challis
93
6.7
boat
ramp
Challis
Hot
Springs
Road
SITE
C-20
75
MILEPOST
159.8
Challis Area
MILEPOST
158.9
93
MILEPOST
156.0
North
Salmon River
Ingram's
Pond
0   Miles   2
To Stanley
To
Mackay

DIRECTIONS:

The starting point for all four sites is the intersection of Main Street and U.S. 93 (signed "City Center") in Challis. Zero your mileage here. Be aware that milepost markers along US 93 change sequence at the junction with ID 75. *Unless otherwise noted, all land here is private.*

BIRDING:

INGRAM'S POND

Ingram's Pond is a small, easily overlooked area that can be full of nice surprises. To reach the pond, follow US 93 south 6.9 miles. Just south of the small hill (at milepost 156), look for a small, steep, turn-out on the right (west) that overlooks the pond (you may need to find a larger parking spot if you're driving an RV).

Birding here is best in the morning. A scope is handy for viewing water-fowl and shorebirds that use the pond. Possible species include Eared Grebe, Tundra and Trumpeter (late fall) Swans, Cinnamon Teal, Canvasback, Bar-row's Goldeneye, Virginia Rail, American Avocet, Solitary, Western, Least, and Baird's Sandpipers, Red-necked and Wilson's Phalaropes, and Black Tern. Eurasian Wigeon are also possible (spring/fall). *Use caution when returning to the highway.*

CHALLIS HOT SPRINGS ROAD

From the starting point follow US 93 south for 3.9 miles, turn left (north) onto paved Hot Springs Road at milepost 158.9, and bird the open meadows and fields for Long-billed Curlews (spring/early summer), Ring-necked Pheas-ants, and an occasional Northern Harrier or Merlin (rare). At mile 6.7 turn left (north) at the Hot Springs sign. On the right (east) at mile 7.8 is a borrow pit housing a large Bank Swallow colony, late May to August. In late summer or fall watch for Chukars from here to the Hot Springs and on the rock slopes above the Hot Springs area.

At mile 8.8 slowly approach the pond on the left (west). Park along the narrow road and look for Cinnamon Teal, Solitary Sandpipers, and other mi-grants. After you've figured out the birds on the pond, check the cliffs on the right (northeast) for perched Red-tailed Hawks and Golden Eagles, soaring White-throated Swifts, and foraging Barn and Tree Swallows.

The parking area for Challis Hot Springs is at mile 9.0. Stop at the office and ask permission to walk through the camping area to bird the riparian habi-tat along the Salmon River. Go slowly along the river bank to the north (downstream) and you may spot Steelhead, River Otter, or Mule Deer, as well as common riparian birds.

SALMON RIVER FLOAT

One of the best ways to bird Challis, from late spring to early fall, is by kayak or canoe. To begin, drive 2.9 miles southeast of the starting point on US 93. At milepost 159.8, turn left (north) onto the short gravel road that leads 0.1 mile to the Junction Bridge boat ramp.

The fairly easy (Class II) 7-mile float from Junction Bridge to Penal Gulch usually takes about 2 hours. Ospreys are frequently encountered within the first few bends of the river. Farther on you're sure to find Great Blue Herons, Mallards, Common Mergansers, Spotted Sandpipers, and Belted Kingfishers, and possibly Sandhill Cranes, American Avocets, and American Dippers. Check trees along the way for thrushes and warblers. Thirty to forty-five min-utes downriver an active Great Blue Heron heronry can be seen along the right channel. As you approach Hot Springs Campground, look for River Ot-ters along the west bank. Past the Hot Springs, watch the cliffs for Red-tailed Hawks, Rock Wrens, White-throated Swifts, and Northern Rough-winged Swallows. Scan the left bank as you get closer to Penal Gulch, and you could be rewarded with a Wild Turkey sighting. Just upriver of the Penal Gulch take-out point, look for American Dippers along the left bank. A Peregrine Falcon hacking-site was located in the cliffs immediately downriver, so watch for returning birds.

PENAL GULCH

From the starting point follow US 93 north 2 miles to milepost 248.7. Turn right (east) onto the gravel road signed "Sportsman Access." At mile 2.5 take the second right to the east. (Skip the first one; it's a drive-way.) Check the small creeks in this general area for waterfowl and the ranchlands for raptors (including Merlins or Prairie Falcons) and Sandhill Cranes. Cliff, Barn, Bank, and Tree Swallows are commonly found on the utility lines along the road. At mile 3.1 you'll see some cattails on the right. Look for Soras, Virginia Rails, Marsh Wrens, and Yellow-headed and Red-winged Blackbirds.

At about mile 3.2 turn left (north) onto "Public Access Road." Scan the fields on the right (east) for Wild Turkeys. At mile 3.5 check the ponds on both sides for Cinnamon Teal and Wood Ducks and the surrounding trees for Western Wood-Pewees. Between miles 3.7 and 3.8 check the roadside trees for Red-naped Sapsuckers and Least Flycatchers (a very rare and local nester in Idaho), and listen for Veeries and Northern Waterthrushes. *Be careful not to trespass on private land.* You'll reach the river at mile 4.0. (This is the take-out point for the Salmon River Float.) Park and scan the cliffs for White-throated Swifts, and keep an eye out for Peregrine Falcons.

OTHER:

Area maps and more information can be obtained from the FS (208/879-4321) or Chamber of Commerce (208/879-2771) in Challis. Camping is available at both Challis Hot Springs (208/879-4442) and Buffalo Jump (kayak rentals, too; 208/879-5454). Bed and Breakfasts include Cottage B&B (208/879-4563) and Darling Creek B&B (208/879-5222), which has Chukars year round and an occasional Wild Turkey. Challis is a full-service community.

The Land of the Yankee Fork Visitors Center (208/879-5244) is located at the junction of US 93 and ID 75, interpreting the mining history of Custer County. Wilson's Warblers, Willow Flycatchers, and other riparian birds frequent the willows near the visitors center's pedestrian bridge.

SOUTHWESTERN IDAHO BIRDING SITES

SW-1 New Plymouth Area
SW-2 Fort Boise Wildlife Mgt Area
SW-3 Boise Foothills
SW-4 Boise Area
SW-5 Pleasant Valley Road Route
SW-6 Hubbard Reservoir
SW-7 Deer Flat Nat'l Wildlife Refuge
SW-8 Dry Lakes
SW-9 Marsing Area
SW-10 Jump Creek
SW-11 North Fork Owyhee River
SW-12 Blacks Creek Reservoir Route
SW-13 Indian Creek Reservoir
SW-14 Mayfield Route

SW-15 Snake River Birds of Prey Area
SW-16 Silver City Area
SW-17 Ted Trueblood Wildlife Mgt Area
SW-18 C.J. Strike Wildlife Mgt Area
SW-19 Bruneau Dunes State Park
SW-20 Trinity Recreation Area
SW-21 Camas Prairie Centennial Marsh
SW-22 Silver Creek Preserve
SW-23 Ketchum/Sun Valley Area
SW-24 Sawtooth Valley Route
SW-25 Hagerman Wildlife Mgt Area
SW-26 Thousand Springs Preserve
SW-27 Twin Falls Area
SW-28 Niagara Springs Wildlife Mgt

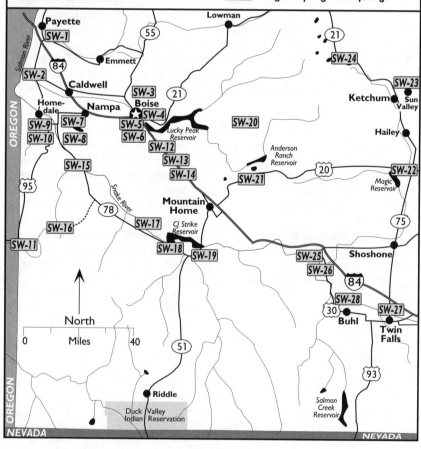

SOUTHWESTERN IDAHO

Dry, open, forbidding landscape characterizes Southwestern Idaho, yet this region also supports the bulk of the state's population. Half of Idaho's large towns are here, including Boise, the state capital. Before venturing too far however, be aware that most of the Southwest's towns and associated services are concentrated along the I-84 corridor. It can be a long walk to a gas station from the Owyhee Uplands!

Two ecoregions, Middle Rocky Mountain and Intermountain Semidesert, meet along the Boise Front Range, providing unique opportunities for avian study. Cassin's and Plumbeous Vireos breed within a few miles of each other, one in the Middle Rocky Mountain's coniferous forest, the other in the Intermountain Semidesert's riparian zones. Lucky Peak is also worthy of attention. More than 5,000 raptors, mostly accipters, fly by Lucky Peak each fall. Extensive, long-term study of Prairie Falcons, Golden Eagles, Long-eared and Burrowing Owls, Ferruginous Hawks, and shrub-steppe passerines and small mammals is carried out at the nearby Snake River Birds of Prey Area. The World Center for Birds of Prey, home to captive California Condors and The Peregrine Fund, may also be of interest to birders.

Additional habitat diversity is provided by the varied nature of the Intermountain Semidesert, from low-elevation agricultural lands to high-elevation shrub-steppe. The moderating effects of the Semidesert in winter make the Southwest the mildest area in the state. Fabulous winter birding is often the result. Trips can be started near the relatively balmy Snake River to witness the massing of hundreds of thousands of waterfowl at Deer Flat National Wildlife Refuge and Hagerman Wildlife Management Area, and then head to world famous Sun Valley to search for Gyrfalcon, Snow Bunting, and Black Rosy-Finch, and perhaps find an outstanding rarity such as the Siberian Accentor that wintered over in 1996-1997.

Sage Thrasher
Mike Denny

147

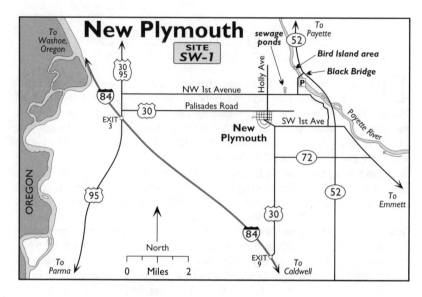

NEW PLYMOUTH AREA

Author: Dan Stephens

Site SW-1 — Map SW-1

Highlights: Ross's Goose, Wood Duck, Red-breasted Merganser
Major Habitats: Wetland, Deciduous Forest
Location: Payette Co., New Plymouth
Spring: * * *   **Summer:** * *   **Fall:** * *   **Winter:** *

A quick stop off I-84 can add several unusual species to a trip list, especially if you're visiting during February to May. The two most productive sites are the sewage ponds, where over 21 waterfowl species have been recorded, and Bird Island.

DIRECTIONS:

At I-84 Exit 9 zero your mileage and follow US 30 north 4.7 miles into New Plymouth. At mile 4.8 turn right (east) for one block, then turn left (north) on Holly Avenue. At mile 5.5 turn right (east) on NW 1st Avenue. At mile 6.1 you'll see the two sewage ponds on your left (north). *All land here is private.*

BIRDING:

You'll have to scope the sewage ponds and surrounding fields from the road, since both are currently posted "No Trespassing." On the ponds look for Tundra Swans in mid-March and for Snow, Ross's, and Canada Geese in late March to early April. Red-breasted Mergansers are likely in March, while

Barrow's Goldeneyes and Common and Hooded Mergansers can be expected throughout spring. Watch for shorebirds, including American Avocets, Marbled Godwits, and Spotted Sandpipers. Fields west of the sewage ponds attract Sandhill Cranes in March and early April and a variety of raptors year round, including Northern Harriers, Red-tailed, Swainson's, and Rough-legged Hawks, and Short-eared Owls.

To investigate Bird Island, continue east on NW 1st Avenue (a.k.a. Black Bridge Road) to mile 7.1, then park in the lot on the right (southeast), just before the bridge. Walk across the road and bird the extensive riparian area downstream from the bridge. *Note that this area is private, but the public is currently allowed to roam.* Birding is best during May and June. Expect common riparian birds, such as Downy Woodpeckers, Western Wood-Pewees, Yellow Warblers, Spotted Towhees, and American Goldfinches. In migration more unusual species, such as Nashville, Townsend's, and Wilson's Warblers, can be expected. This section of the Payette River also supports one of Idaho's largest Wood Duck populations.

OTHER:

New Plymouth offers food, fuel, and lodging. Camping is available in Payette and Caldwell. The closest full-service communities are Caldwell, Idaho, and Ontario, Oregon.

FORT BOISE WILDLIFE MANAGEMENT AREA
Author: John F. Gatchet
Site SW-2 — Map SW-2

Highlights: Greater White-fronted and Ross's Geese
Major Habitats: Wetland, Deciduous Forest, Farmland
Location: Canyon Co., 4 miles northwest of Parma
Spring: ✳✳✳✳   **Summer:** ✳✳✳   **Fall:** ✳✳✳✳ **Winter:** ✳✳✳

Fort Boise WMA covers the confluence of the Snake, Boise, and Owyhee Rivers. The riparian forest is very birdy, and numerous ponds attract hordes of waterfowl and shorebirds. Neighboring farmfields and grasslands add to habitat diversity. This is Idaho's most dependable location for Greater White-fronted Geese. Most birding is done on foot along the maze of trails and gated roads. Be aware that much of the WMA is closed from February to July, and that hunting pressure is intense from October through January.

DIRECTIONS:

From Parma follow US 95 north 3.5 miles. At milepost 50, turn left (west) onto paved Old Fort Boise Road and zero your mileage. As you drive toward

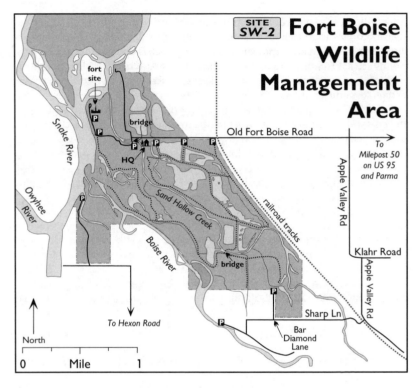

SITE SW-2 **Fort Boise Wildlife Management Area**

the WMA, watch the privately-owned farm fields for migrating Greater White-fronted, Snow, and Ross's Geese, especially from March 15 to April 15.

BIRDING:

You'll enter the WMA after crossing the railroad tracks at about mile 2.6. There are three small parking lots on the left (south) between miles 2.6 and 2.8. From August 1 to January 31, use the stiles at these lots to cross the fence to the south, then wander the 20 miles of roads which snake back-and-forth among brush, wetlands, grasslands, and trees. During the rest of the year you'll be limited to scanning from Old Fort Boise Road. Great and Snowy Egrets, Green Herons (very rare), Black-crowned Night-Herons, Wood Ducks, Cinnamon and Blue-winged Teals, Sharp-shinned and Cooper's Hawks, Northern Goshawks, Merlins, Peregrine Falcons, Virginia Rails, and Soras should all be looked for. Red-tailed and Swainson's Hawks are common nesters. Ponds on the north side of the road are closed to entry year round, but a scope can often find shorebirds and Caspian, Common, Forster's, and Black Terns. (You may have to stand on your car's bumper to see them well, though.) Black-bellied Plovers, American Golden-Plovers, Black-necked Stilts, American Avocets, Baird's, Pectoral, and Solitary Sandpipers, Marbled Godwits, Long-billed Curlews, and Dunlins have all been seen here.

Continuing west on Old Fort Boise Road, drive past headquarters (mile 2.9) and then follow the left road-fork over the bridge, and drive or walk to the Snake River in another 0.5 mile or so. This area is open to foot traffic year round. Dense riparian cover along the river attracts wintering Northern Shrikes and hordes of White-crowned Sparrows, as well as a few White-throated, Harris's, and Swamp (rare) Sparrows. Other winter birds include Mountain Chickadees, Varied Thrushes, Orange-crowned Warblers, and Fox and Golden-crowned (rare) Sparrows. This is a great spot for spring and fall warblers, including Nashville, Black-throated Gray, Townsend's, MacGillivray's, and Wilson's. In the thickest cover, look for Western Screech-Owls, Barn, Long-eared, and Northern Saw-whet Owls, Yellow-breasted Chats, Hermit Thrushes, and Black-headed Grosbeaks. Vagrants have included a Yellow-billed Cuckoo and several Lesser Goldfinches.

OTHER:

Parma offers food, fuel, and accommodations. The WMA is closed at night. The closest developed campgrounds are in Caldwell, Idaho, and in Succor Creek State Recreation Area (southwest of Homedale, Oregon). All services are available in Caldwell/Nampa. For a map and more information, contact the WMA (208/722-5888).

*Long-billed
Curlew*

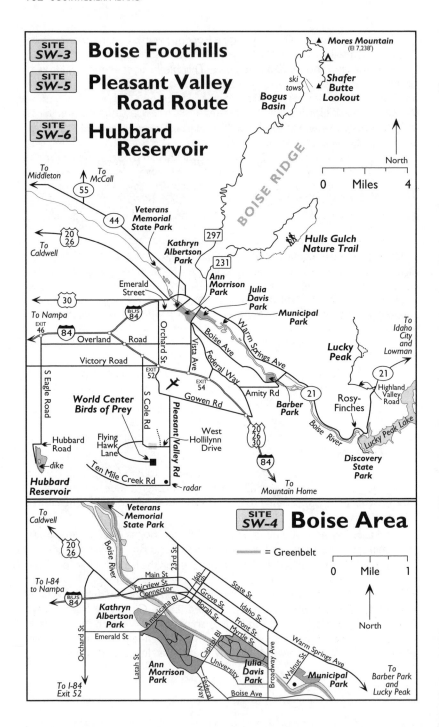

SITE SW-3 Boise Foothills

SITE SW-5 Pleasant Valley Road Route

SITE SW-6 Hubbard Reservoir

Mores Mountain (El 7,238')

Shafer Butte Lookout

ski tows

Bogus Basin

BOISE RIDGE

North

0 Miles 4

To Middleton

To McCall

55

44

Veterans Memorial State Park

297

To Caldwell

20 26

Kathryn Albertson Park

231

Ann Morrison Park

Hulls Gulch Nature Trail

Emerald Street

BUS 84

Julia Davis Park

Municipal Park

To Nampa

EXIT 46

84

Orchard St

Vista Ave

Boise Ave

Warm Springs Ave

Lucky Peak

To Idaho City and Lowman

30

Overland Road

Federal Way

21

Highland Valley Road

Victory Road

EXIT 52

EXIT 54

Amity Rd

Rosy-Finches

S Eagle Road

World Center Birds of Prey

S Cole Rd

Gowen Rd

West Hollilynn Drive

Barber Park

Boise River

Lucky Peak Lake

Hubbard Road

Flying Hawk Lane

Pleasant Valley Rd

20 26 30

Discovery State Park

dike

Ten Mile Creek Rd

84

Hubbard Reservoir

radar

To Mountain Home

To Caldwell

Veterans Memorial State Park

SITE SW-4 Boise Area

20 26

Boise River

= Greenbelt

0 Mile 1

To I-84 to Nampa

BUS 84

Main St

23rd St

16th

State St

North

Fairview St Connector

Grove St

Idaho St

Kathryn Albertson Park

Americana Bl

Borah St

Front St

Orchard St

Emerald St

Capitol Bl

Myrtle St

Broadway Ave

Warm Springs Ave

To Barber Park and Lucky Peak

Latah St

Ann Morrison Park

University

Julia Davis Park

Walnut St

Municipal Park

To I-84 Exit 52

Federal Way

Boise Ave

BOISE FOOTHILLS

Author: Dave Trochlell

Site SW-3 — Map SW-3/SW-4/SW-5/SW-6

Highlights: Raptors, Sparrows
Major Habitats: Shrub-steppe, Deciduous Forest, Farmland
Location: Ada Co., Boise
Spring: * *   **Summer:** * *   **Fall:** * *   **Winter:** * *

The Boise Foothills cover 65 square miles of rolling uplands. As defined here, they are bounded by Boise Valley and Boise Ridge and run from ID 55 to ID 21. More than 175 bird species have been recorded, including 26 raptors and 14 sparrows! This species list will undoubtedly change, however, since a great range fire consumed huge chunks of shrub-steppe habitat in the fall of 1996.

DIRECTIONS:

Because of the Foothill's large size, two routes and a site are recommended to sample the habitat variety. There are different starting points for each. You'll need a Boise city map, available at most convenience stores in Boise, or from "King of the Road Map Service" (800/223-8852). A DeLorme Atlas will also be useful.

Most land along this route is public (state, BLM, FS). The majority of private land is unposted and is generally open to public use. You should have no problem if you respect posted signs.

BIRDING:

BOGUS BASIN ROUTE

Bogus Basin Road climbs from the Boise Valley to Bogus Basin Ski Resort. Along the way this 14-mile paved route passes through a wide variety of habitats, providing the opportunity to inventory several "life zones" in the course of a single day.

The tour begins at the intersection of Hill and Bogus Basin Roads. Zero your mileage here, then head north on Bogus Basin Road (a.k.a. FR 297).

At mile 2.7 stop and park in the pull-out area on the left (west) across from an old road. Walk the old road northeast toward Boise Ridge. In summer species here include Northern Harrier, Red-tailed Hawk, Golden Eagle, Gray Partridge, Chukar, Blue Grouse, Horned Lark, Common Raven, Sage Thrasher, Brewer's, Vesper, and Lark Sparrows, and Western Meadowlark. In winter watch for Sharp-shinned Hawk, Rough-legged Hawk, Merlin, Horned Lark, White-crowned Sparrow, Dark-eyed Junco, and Snow Bunting (rare).

Bogus Basin Road crosses Dry Creek at mile 4.8. Park in the small pull-out on the right (north) and hike uphill along the canyon for riparian birds. (A trail at mile 5.0 follows the creek uphill, making for easier walking.) Spring and summer species include California Quail, Great Horned Owl, Black-chinned and Calliope Hummingbirds, Downy Woodpecker, Western Wood-Pewee, House Wren, Black-capped Chickadee, Warbling Vireo, Red-eyed Vireo (uncommon), Orange-crowned and Yellow Warblers, Yellow-breasted Chat, and Song Sparrow. Broad-tailed Hummingbird, Bushtit, and Blue-gray Gnatcatcher are rare migrants. Winter species might include Sharp-shinned and Cooper's Hawks, Northern Goshawk, Merlin, Great Horned Owl, Brown Creeper, Winter Wren, Ruby-crowned Kinglet, Northern Shrike, and White-crowned Sparrow. Northern Pygmy-Owl, Long-eared and Northern Saw-whet Owls, and Bohemian Waxwings are rare but possible. You can also access Dry Creek at mile 6.9. Park along the tree-belt and hike the old gulch trail down to the creek bottom.

Bogus Basin Road enters mountain brush habitat at mile 10.6. Stop anywhere where you can safely park. This ecotone hosts birds of both shrub-steppe and conifer forest habitats. Likely summer species include Red-tailed Hawk, Golden Eagle, American Kestrel, Blue Grouse, Wild Turkey, Common Poorwill, Calliope Hummingbird, Lewis's and Hairy Woodpeckers, Red-breasted Nuthatch, Mountain Bluebird, Chipping Sparrow, Dark-eyed Junco, Cassin's Finch, and Pine Siskin. Elk and Mule Deer are likely to be seen, as well.

At mile 12 you transition into the conifer forest zone. Typical birds here include Sharp-shinned and Cooper's Hawks, Northern Goshawks, Blue Grouse, Wild Turkeys, Flammulated Owls, Northern Pygmy-Owls, Hairy Woodpeckers, White-headed Woodpeckers (uncommon to rare), Dusky Flycatchers, Steller's Jays, Clark's Nutcrackers, Mountain Chickadees, Red-breasted Nuthatches, Townsend's Solitaires, Golden-crowned and Ruby-crowned Kinglets, Swainson's and Hermit Thrushes, Varied Thrushes (uncommon migrant), Cassin's Vireos, Nashville and Yellow-rumped Warblers, Western Tanagers, Chipping Sparrows, Dark-eyed Juncos, Pine Grosbeaks, Cassin's Finches, Red Crossbills, and Pine Siskins. In riparian zones within the conifer forest, look for Northern Saw-whet Owls, Calliope and Rufous Hummingbirds, Downy Woodpeckers, Olive-sided Flycatchers (uncommon), Winter Wrens, Warbling Vireos, Orange-crowned and Wilson's Warblers, Black-headed Grosbeaks, and Fox Sparrows.

At mile 14.2 you pass the junction with Boise Ridge Road (stay left); you will reach the end of pavement at Bogus Basin Ski Resort at mile 16.3. At mile 19.8 go right (east) to Shafer Butte Campground, which is open July to September. Look for Clark's Nutcrackers, White-crowned Sparrows, and migrating accipiters.

HULLS GULCH ROUTE

The Hulls Gulch tour begins at the intersection of West Fort and 8th Streets in Boise. Zero your mileage here, then go north on 8th Street (a.k.a.

Hulls Gulch Road, a.k.a. Mile High Road, a.k.a. Sunset Peak Road)...watch out for speed bumps!

You enter the Boise Front Recreation Area at mile 1.1. At mile 1.3 park on the left (west) and walk the graveled road southwest 0.25 mile to a small pond. Bird the maze of trails that head up the gulch. The summer bird list is similar to that for the Bogus Basin riparian area, but it can also include wetland species such as Great Blue Heron, Wood Duck, Mallard, Cinnamon Teal, Virginia Rail (uncommon), Wilson's Snipe, Great Horned Owl, Marsh Wren, and Common Yellowthroat.

In fall and winter this site attracts lots of sparrows because of its wet, brushy habitat. Look for Lincoln's, White-throated, Golden-crowned, and Harris's Sparrows among the more common species. Swamp Sparrow may also be possible. Great Horned Owls have nested across the road from the wetland in the small grove of trees. Barred Owls (rare) have been found in winter. This is a very popular recreation area, so it is best birded early in the day or on weekdays.

To monitor the impact of wildfire on shrub-steppe, riparian, and mountain brush habitats, drive up Hulls Gulch Road (pavement ends at mile 1.5) to the BLM's Hulls Gulch Interpretive Trail parking lot and trailhead at mile 4.6. Before the 1996 range fire, this 3-mile (one-way) interpretive trail was one of the best birding areas in the Boise Foothills, full of nesting Plumbeous Vireos, Yellow-breasted Chats, and Lazuli Buntings, as well as hosting Great Basin Gopher Snakes, racers, Western Toads, and Western Fence Lizards.

LUCKY PEAK

A hawk-watch was recently established on top of Lucky Peak. Approximately 3,000 raptors fly by each fall, August–October. Interestingly, these

Harris's Sparrow
Mike Denny

flights have included a few Broad-winged Hawks during the last two weeks of September. Flammulated Owls, Northern Pygmy-Owls, and Northern Saw-whet Owls have been trapped here, as well.

To get to Lucky Peak from Boise, go east from the intersection of Broadway and Warm Springs Avenue for 13.1 miles on Warm Springs Avenue (Warm Springs Avenue becomes ID 21) to Highland Valley Road (signed). Turn left (west) and head up Highland Valley Road. After 2 miles turn right at the intersection. Continue climbing toward Boise Ridge on this main road. (You will pass other, unsigned intersections.) You can see Lucky Peak's radio towers and forested ridgeline from quite a distance. *Do not attempt this steep, rutted dirt/rock road without a high-clearance 4-wheel-drive vehicle.*

OTHER:

Boise is a full-service community. Maps and information can be obtained from the FS (208/373-4100) or BLM (208/384-3300) in Boise. For more information on Lucky Peak, contact the IDFG Southwest Volunteer Coordinator (208/327-7099).

BOISE AREA

Author: Dave Trochlell

Site SW-4 — Map SW-3/SW-4/SW-5/SW-6

Highlights: Eurasian Wigeon, Western Screech-Owl, Black Rosy-Finch
Major Habitats: Deciduous Forest, Wetland
Location: Ada Co., Boise
Spring: * *   **Summer:** * *   **Fall:** * *   **Winter:** * * *

Boise, Idaho's capital and largest city, boasts a remarkable 19-mile public parkway known as the Greenbelt. Running along the Boise River, the Greenbelt is a mostly-paved bicycle/pedestrian path connecting various parks and natural areas. Several common birds can be found in the parks, including Great Blue Herons, Canada Geese, Wood Ducks, Mallards, Common Mergansers, Western Screech-Owls, American Kestrels, Downy Woodpeckers, Northern Flickers, Black-capped Chickadees, and Song Sparrows. Some of the best birding, however, is in the riparian wetlands and vegetation along the pathway itself. Two of the "birdiest" sections are highlighted below.

DIRECTIONS:

The starting point for both sites is I-84. A city map can be very useful and is sold in most convenience stores. A Boise Park and Greenbelt map can be picked-up at the Boise Parks and Recreation administration office (208/384-4240), at 1104 Royal Boulevard (the east end of Ann Morrison Park).

BIRDING:

KATHRYN ALBERTSON and ANN MORRISON PARKS

Boise's most popular parks are neighboring Kathryn Albertson and Ann Morrison. To find this area from I-84, take Exit 52, zero your mileage, and head north on Orchard Street. At mile 2.5 turn right (east) onto Emerald Street and continue straight at mile 3.2 as Emerald Street becomes Americana Boulevard. At mile 3.5 turn left (west) into Kathryn Albertson Park or right (east) into Ann Morrison Park, just before crossing the Boise River bridge.

Ann Morrison Park is 153 acres of exotic trees, lawns, ballfields, tennis courts, picnic areas, and parking lots, but it still produces good birding. In spring or fall check the shrubby hillside along the park's entire south end. It can be good for flycatchers, thrushes, vireos, warblers, towhees, and sparrows.

In winter check the bird flocks near the large pond at the park's west entrance on Americana Boulevard. This is a popular bird-feeding location, so several dozen geese, ducks, and gulls are usually present. Search the American Wigeon flocks carefully; this is Idaho's most reliable spot for Eurasian Wigeons. Keep an eye out for Herring Gulls among abundant Ring-billed and California Gulls. Possible rarities include Thayer's, Glaucous, and Glaucous-winged Gulls.

In Kathryn Albertson Park, walk the entire perimeter path through different man-made wildlife habitats. Scan the park's west-side trees and shrubs for migrant flycatchers, vireos, and warblers. Look and listen for an occasional Yellow-headed Blackbird among the nesting Red-wings during spring. In winter watch for Sharp-shinned Hawks, American Kestrels, Merlins, Golden-crowned and Ruby-crowned Kinglets, Cedar and Bohemian Waxwings, and Yellow-rumped Warblers. The pond attracts wintering Gadwalls, Hooded Mergansers, and Virginia Rails and has even hosted a rare Green Heron.

From Kathyrn Albertson Park, you can walk the Greenbelt about 1.5 miles downstream to Veterans Memorial State Park. The Greenbelt section between the parks passes by cottonwoods, ponds, and urban areas. Watch and listen for migrating flycatchers, vireos, warblers, and tanagers in the cottonwoods. Check the ponds on the east side of Veterans Memorial State Park for migrating loons, grebes, geese, ducks, gulls, and terns.

BARBER PARK

Barber Park is the farthest east of the Greenbelt parks. It is open to vehicular traffic from 8 am to sunset. Foot traffic is welcome anytime.

To reach Barber Park from I-84, take Exit 54, zero your mileage, and follow Broadway Avenue north toward Boise State University. At mile 0.4 exit right (southeast) on Federal Way. At mile 2.1 turn left (east) on Amity Road (a.k.a. ID 21). At mile 4 keep left as Amity runs into Healey Road, curves, crosses a canal, and goes downhill to become Eckert Road. Just before crossing the Boise River at mile 4.4, turn left (west) into Barber Park.

Barber Park is particularly good for Western Screech-Owls. To try for these birds, park outside the park at dusk and walk the park's drive to the park's western border, where the Greenbelt connects. Western Screech-Owls may be found anywhere in this area.

For additional daylight birding follow the Greenbelt downstream 1.5 miles to River Run Subdivision (or even farther, if you prefer). Between Barber Park and River Run, the Greenbelt harbors old-growth cottonwoods, native riparian shrubs, ponds, and a marsh. Nesters include Wood Ducks, Western Screech-Owls, Lewis's Woodpeckers, Western Wood-Pewees, and Black-headed Grosbeaks. These species are supplemented in season with migrant Ospreys, Dusky Flycatchers, Swainson's and Hermit Thrushes, Plumbeous Vireos, Nashville, MacGillivray's, and Wilson's Warblers, Western Tanagers, and Lazuli Buntings. In spring look for Cinnamon Teal and Red-breasted Mergansers. Rare late-summer or early-fall visitors have included Green Herons, Caspian Terns, and Blue-gray Gnatcatchers. Late fall and winter is the best time to walk this section for waterfowl and raptors, including Wood Ducks and Bald Eagles. American Dippers are rare but regular during these seasons. Migrant or winter sparrow flocks occasionally yield Lincoln's Sparrows and may even include a few White-throated or Harris's Sparrows. In recent winters, species such as Green Heron, Barn Owl, Northern Saw-whet Owl, Blue Jay, Varied Thrush, and Northern Mockingbird have also been found here.

To bird the Greenbelt upstream of Barber Park, return to the east end of Barber Park and drive north on Eckert Road for 0.6 mile. Park here to access the paved bike-trail, and walk 3.5 miles upstream to Lucky Peak Park (Discovery Unit). The first 1.2-mile section of the trail parallels the highway before dropping down to riverside cottonwoods, where Wood Ducks and Yellow-breasted Chats can be found. (NOTE: There are other access points along this section of Greenbelt, but they are limited because most neighboring land is private and posted.) While on the Greenbelt, be sure to look and listen for locally rare Red-eyed Vireos in cottonwoods and for Lesser Goldfinches in shrubs. In winter this area is good for Bald Eagles, Western Screech-Owls, and (possibly) Northern Pygmy-Owls. Townsend's Solitaires and Northern Shrikes are occasionally present. One of the great winter treats is to walk or drive (see map) to Lucky Peak Park (Discovery Unit) and watch Gray-crowned and Black Rosy-Finches come to roost in Cliff Swallow nests, right before dusk. The swallow nests are on the basalt cliff, across the road (ID 21) from the park.

OTHER:

Boise is a full-service community. Accommodations, food, and fuel are abundant. Campgrounds, however, are limited. For more information contact the Boise Chamber of Commerce (208/472-5200) or the Boise Convention and Visitors Bureau (208/344-7777).

A unique natural-history experience can be had at the IDFG's Morrison Knudson Nature Center. The "MK" Nature Center, located at the west end of Municipal Park, offers a close-up look at a variety of simulated Idaho wildlife habitats, including an outdoor stroll along a mountain stream complete with underwater-viewing windows! Western Screech-Owls can often be heard calling near the center. The nature trail is free and is open sunrise to sunset. The center is open Tuesday through Sunday, but the hours change seasonally. There is an admission fee. Call the center (208/368-6060) for more information.

PLEASANT VALLEY ROAD ROUTE
Author: Dave Trochlell
Site SW-5 — Map SW-3/SW-4/SW-5/SW-6

Highlights: Long-billed Curlew, Chukar, Gray Partridge
Major Habitats: Shrub-steppe, Farmland
Location: Ada Co., Boise
Spring: * *   **Summer:** * *   **Fall:** * * *   **Winter:** * *

Located just a few miles south of the Boise Airport, this 12-mile route accesses the single most dependable spot for Chukars and Gray Partridge in Idaho.

DIRECTIONS:
Zero your mileage at I-84 Exit 52, then head south on Orchard Street, following it as it curves around the airport and merges with Gowen Road. *Most land here is private.*

BIRDING:
Scope the large waste-water pond on your right (west) at mile 1.3 for grebes, ducks, and swallows. At mile 2 turn right (south) on Pleasant Valley Road and start looking for soaring Northern Harriers, Swainson's, Red-tailed, and Rough-legged Hawks, and American Kestrels. At mile 4.3 turn right (west) on West Hollilynn (a.k.a. Hollylynn) Drive. At mile 4.8 a dirt trail takes off to the right (northwest). Walk here to find Burrowing and Short-eared Owls amid sagebrush and annual grasses; nesting Long-billed Curlews are very conspicuous here in spring and summer.

Continue west on West Hollilynn Drive and enter a small subdivison. Drive slowly, scanning the large house lots, plantings, and grass-covered hillside. This subdivison is the easiest and most consistent spot in Idaho for Gray Partridge and Chukars. The birds often feed in the yards like chickens! At mile 6.4 West Hollilynn ends at South Cole Road near the intersection with

Flying Hawk Lane, which is the entrance road to the Peregrine Fund/World Center for Birds of Prey.

The center (fee) is full of information on birds of the area and on raptors of the world. The center's facilities include live raptors, multi-media presentations, interactive displays and exhibits, a gift shop, and more. The center boasts a history of raptor breeding projects including years of Peregrine Falcon experience as well as recent Harpy Eagle and California Condor work. The center grounds are also good for Chukar and Gray Partridge; these species often water here. After you finish your visit to the center, turn around and backtrack east on West Hollilynn Drive. At the intersection with Pleasant Valley Road, re-zero your mileage and turn right (south) on Pleasant Valley Road.

At mile 2.4 turn right (west) on a graveled road that leads to a globe-shaped National Weather Service radar tower. At the BLM hayshed/corral, park and walk around to search for Gray Partridge and Chukars. You may also see Barn Owls in the open-sided hayshed; the birds have even nested here.

Return to Pleasant Valley Road and continue south. In 0.2 mile turn right (west) on Ten Mile Creek Road. Stop often along this road to scan for Northern Harriers, Swainson's and Red-tailed Hawks, American Kestrels, and Ring-necked Pheasants. Ferruginous Hawks are possible. If you drive this road at dawn or dusk, watch for hunting Barn, Great Horned, Long-eared, and Short-eared Owls.

OTHER:

For maps and more information, contact the BLM (208/384-3300) in Boise. Boise is a full-service community. See also Blacks Creek Reservoir Route (p. 173) and Snake River Birds of Prey Area (p. 178). The World Center Birds of Prey (208/362-8687) is open Tuesday-Sunday, 9 am to 5 pm.

HUBBARD RESERVOIR

Author: John F. Gatchet

Site SW-6 — Map SW-3/SW-4/SW-5/SW-6

Highlights: Shorebirds, Burrowing Owl
Major Habitat: Wetland
Location: Ada Co., 7 miles south of Meridian
Spring: * * *   **Summer:** * * * * **Fall:** * * *   **Winter:** * *

This small irrigation reservoir offers waterbirds an isolated sanctuary amid miles of agricultural fields. Birding is particularly productive when mudflats attract hundreds of shorebirds. This spot is also good for Burrowing Owl, which can be found on 9 out of 10 visits from late spring through summer.

DIRECTIONS:

From I-84 Exit 46 (between Nampa and Boise), head south on S. Eagle Road for about 5 miles, then turn right (west) on Hubbard Road and follow it southwest for 0.9 mile. Park at the narrow dirt pull-out on the left (east), just before the wooden fence. Walk up the steep slope on the narrow footpath and then hike south to the wetland along the top of the dike. *The public is currently allowed to use this private reservoir, but do not trespass on the neighboring agricultural land (posted).*

BIRDING:

Watch for Burrowing Owls along the dike top. One or two families usually nest in the soft dirt along the dike's fill-slope.

From July to October, regular shorebird species include Semipalmated Plover, Black-necked Stilt, American Avocet, Greater and Lesser Yellowlegs, Solitary Sandpiper, Long-billed Curlew, Semipalmated, Western, Least, Baird's, and Pectoral Sandpipers, Dunlin, Stilt Sandpiper, Long-billed and Short-billed (rare) Dowitchers, Wilson's Snipe, and Wilson's and Red-necked Phalaropes. In late summer you may also find Great and Snowy Egrets, White-faced Ibis, Black-crowned Night-Heron, and Forster's and Black Terns. During migration Franklin's, Bonaparte's, and Herring Gulls can be found among the more-common Ring-billed and California Gulls. If you're lucky, you may also see the small group of feral Ruddy Shelducks that have used the reservoir during recent falls, adding a splash of color among the more-expected Green-winged, Cinnamon, and Blue-winged Teals.

OTHER:

Food, fuel, and lodging are available in Meridian. Boise is the closest full-service community.

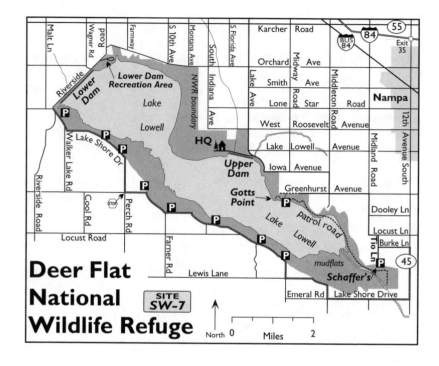

DEER FLAT NATIONAL WILDLIFE REFUGE

Author: John F. Gatchet

Site SW-7 — Map SW-7

Highlights: Peregrine Falcon, Shorebirds, Warblers
Major Habitats: Wetland, Deciduous Forest
Location: Canyon Co., 4 miles west of Nampa
Spring: ****　**Summer:** ***　**Fall:** ****　**Winter:** ****

*Deer Flat NWR is southwest Idaho's best birding spot. An impressive 230 bird
species have been recorded. In years when the refuge's mudflats are exposed,
thousands of shorebirds stop to feed. Winter months find over 10,000 geese
and 100,000 ducks present, attracting both Bald and Golden Eagles. Deer Flat
is also the state's most dependable spot for vagrant passerines, having attracted
rarities such as Palm, Black-and-white, Tennessee, Hooded, and Magnolia
Warblers!*

DIRECTIONS:

From I-84 Exit 35 near Nampa, turn north on Northside Boulevard and go 0.3 mile to the 4-way stop-sign. Turn left (west) on ID 55 (a.k.a. Karcher Road) and find a safe place to park. Look for Idaho's most dependable Peregrine Falcon pair atop the adjacent Amalgamated Sugar Company's towers and buildings, then continue west 4.2 miles on ID 55 and turn left (south) on Lake Avenue. After 3.4 miles the road curves to the left below the refuge's "Upper Dam." Turn sharp right (northwest) onto Upper Embankment Road and pull into the parking lot at the east end of the dam.

BIRDING:

From the parking lot scan Lake Lowell, which is the reservoir encompassed by Deer Flat NWR. Among the rare or unusual migrant species possible are Pacific Loon, Great Egret, Greater Scaup, Barrow's Goldeneye, Red-breasted Merganser, Franklin's, Bonaparte's, Herring, and Sabine's Gulls, and Common and Black Terns. If the gate on Upper Embankment Road is open, drive west across the dam 1.1 miles to refuge headquarters. The interpretive center has maps, information, and a checklist. There is also a short nature trail, where Clark's Grebes, Trumpeter Swans, Bald Eagles, and a variety of ducks and other waterfowl can be seen for much of the year.

After visiting headquarters, backtrack east across the dam to Lake Avenue, re-zero your mileage, and turn right (east). At mile 0.3 park in the second parking area on the left (east). Bird the brush and trees for wintering Northern Saw-whet Owls, Varied Thrushes, Orange-crowned Warblers, and White-throated Sparrows, but be aware that the adjacent area is closed to public access (watch for warning signs).

Continue east on what is now Iowa Avenue. At mile 2.0 turn right (south) onto Middleton Road. At mile 2.5 turn right (west) onto Greenhurst Avenue. The sagebrush, Russian-olives, and willows in the public hunting area on the left (south) at mile 3.3 attract a wide variety of birds, including Gray Partridge. Migrant or summer species include Common Poorwill, Lewis's Woodpecker, Red-naped Sapsucker, "Western," Dusky, and Gray Flycatchers, Hermit Thrush, Sage Thrasher, Loggerhead Shrike, Plumbeous Vireo, Townsend's, MacGillivray's, and Wilson's Warblers, Western Tanager, Black-headed Grosbeak, Lazuli Bunting, and White-throated Sparrow (rare).

At mile 3.5 is a great birding area, but public use is prohibited from October 1 to January 31. During the rest of the year, drive or walk the 0.5-mile dead-end dirt road to Gott's Point, passing Greenhurst Access parking lot along the way. Investigate both the excellent riparian cover and the great lake views for additional birds, then backtrack to Greenhurst Access parking lot. From here a gated patrol road heads southeast along the lakeshore all the way to Schaffer's Access. Walk or bicycle this 4-mile-long road to experience the refuge's best birding. Scan any mudflats along the patrol road for White-faced Ibises, Black-bellied Plovers, American Golden-Plovers (rare), Snowy Plovers (rare), Black-necked Stilts, American Avocets, Solitary Sandpipers, Marbled

Godwits, Sanderlings, Semipalmated, Western, Baird's, and Pectoral Sand-pipers, Dunlins, Stilt Sandpipers, Short-billed Dowitchers (rare), and Parasitic Jaegers (rare). In the woodland bordering the patrol road, watch for more va-grants such as Black Swifts, Blue Jays, and Black-and-white and Hooded War-blers.

To continue birding, drive east on Greenhurst Avenue 2 miles, then turn right (south) on Midland Road. At the L intersection in 1 mile, turn left (east) onto Locust Lane and go only 0.3 mile before turning right (south) onto paved/graveled Tio Lane and driving 1 mile to Schaffer's Access parking lot at the end of the road. Walk the two gated roads which come into the parking lot. The east road accesses excellent woodland and marsh habitats. Both Blue Jays and White-throated Sparrows have been seen here several times. In winter Western Screech-Owls and Northern Saw-whet Owls can be found in Wood Duck boxes. Listen for vagrant Swamp Sparrows (winter) in marsh habitat. (The west road is the patrol road mentioned above.)

Backtrack 0.5 mile north on Tio Lane and turn right (east) on Burke Lane. After 0.8 mile turn right (south) on ID 45, then turn right (west) on Lake Shore Drive after 1.3 miles. Lake Shore Drive parallels the southwest shore of Lake Lowell for 11.2 miles to Lower Dam. Along the way you'll pass eight "Ac-cess Point" parking lots which allow additional lake-scoping and investigation of the shoreline's deciduous forest, which might harbor wintering Barn Owls. Be aware that Lake Shore Drive makes a 90-degree turn to the north at the stop-sign, which is 8.2 miles west of the Lake Shore Drive/ID 45 junction. At the end of Lake Shore Drive, turn right (northeast) onto Riverside Road and cross the Lower Dam. "Good" birds seen from the dam include Pacific Loons, Clark's Grebes (nests), Great and Cattle Egrets, Greater White-fronted and Ross's Geese, Barrow's Goldeneyes, Red-breasted Mergansers, Merlins, Gyr-falcons, and even an Ancient Murrelet! In winter look for Rough-legged Hawks and Northern Shrikes.

At the northeast end of Lower Dam, turn right into the recreation area. This is one of the refuge's most productive birding areas. There are trees and hedge-rows at the end of the park road. In fall there is usually a mudflat, too. Among the more unusual migrants have been Northern Goshawks, Lewis's Woodpeckers, Olive-sided and Least Flycatchers, Hermit Thrushes, Plumbeous Vireos, Tennessee, Nashville, Palm, and Townsend's Warblers, American Redstarts, Clay-colored and White-throated Sparrows, and Com-mon Grackles.

OTHER:

For more information call the refuge (208/467-9278). Nampa is a full-ser-vice community. The refuge is open during daylight hours only. The visitors center is generally open from 7:30 am to 4:00 am on weekdays.

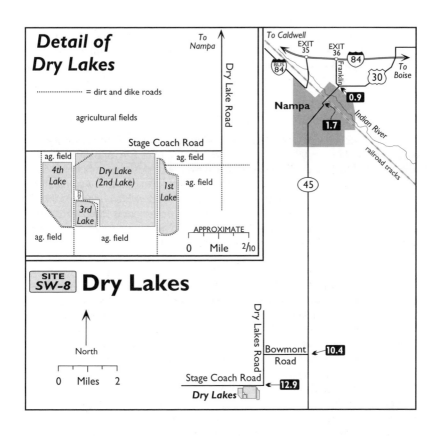

DRY LAKES

Author: John F. Gatchet

Site SW-8 — Map SW-8

Highlights: Shorebirds
Major Habitat: Wetland
Location: Canyon Co., 10 miles southwest of Nampa
Spring: * * * **Summer:** * * **Fall:** * * * **Winter:** * *

Dry Lakes is one of those tiny, out-of-the-way, easily-overlooked spots that provides great birding. The "lakes" are actually four small pools used to hold irrigation water; but that doesn't prevent them from acting as an oasis amid miles of potato, bean, and mint fields!

Dry Lakes is privately owned. Although public use is currently allowed, that could change at any time. The dried lake beds are very popular with ultra-light-aircraft users, model-airplane enthusiasts, and ORV owners. The one hard and fast etiquette rule is: Do not drive or walk across the lake bed until it is completely dried out.

DIRECTIONS:

Zero your mileage at I-84 Exit 36 and head south on Franklin Boulevard into Nampa. At mile 0.9 turn right (southwest) onto 11th Avenue North. Follow signs to Murphy and ID 45 as you weave through downtown Nampa. Specifically, at mile 1.7 turn left (southeast) on Third Street South. After 1 block turn right (southwest) on 12th Avenue. Stay on 12th, which becomes ID 45, headed south. At mile 10.4 turn right (west) on Bowmont Road. At mile 11.9 turn left (south) onto Dry Lake Road. At mile 12.9 turn right (west) on Stage Coach Road. The lakes are on the left (south), at mile 13.1.

BIRDING:

The eastern-most pool has water year round, and it occasionally attracts migrating Red-necked and Clark's Grebes. Other migrant species include Great Egret, White-faced Ibis, Tundra and Trumpeter Swans, Cinnamon Teal, Greater Scaup (also present in winter), and Bonaparte's Gull. Franklin's and Herring Gulls and Caspian, Forster's, and Black Terns are possible.

The second pool is the largest and is the one referred to as "Dry Lake." It is here that most of the migrant shorebirds have been seen, including Black-bellied Plovers, Black-necked Stilts, American Avocets, Solitary Sandpipers, Long-billed Curlews, Marbled Godwits, and Semipalmated, Western, Least, Baird's, and Pectoral Sandpipers. You may also see large numbers of Willets and Wilson's and Red-necked Phalaropes. Rarities have included American Golden-Plovers, Snowy Plovers, Dunlins, Stilt Sandpipers, and Short-billed Dowitchers. In fact, this spot has produced most of Idaho's winter shorebird records.

There are two more pools on the west side of Dry Lake. Dike roads encircling these pools are usually navigable, but you may want to walk to avoid driving in ruts and mud. Ducks favor these two wetlands year round.

OTHER:

Nampa is a full-service community.

MARSING AREA

Author: John F. Gatchet

Site SW-9 — Map SW-9/SW-10

Highlights: Eurasian Wigeon, Long-tailed Duck, Great-tailed Grackle
Major Habitats: Wetland, Farmland
Location: Owyhee Co., Marsing
Spring: * * *   **Summer:** *   **Fall:** * * *   **Winter:** * * * *

Winter birding is excellent in Marsing, but good birding is also available during migration. Most birds are concentrated in a few miles of riverfront, so checking out this potential hotspot requires little time.

DIRECTIONS:

To reach Marsing from Nampa, take I-84 Exit 35, turn north on Northside Boulevard, and go 0.3 mile to the 4-way stop-sign. Turn left (west) on ID 55 (a.k.a. Karcher Road) and find a safe place to park. Look for Idaho's most dependable Peregrine Falcon pair atop the adjacent Amalgamated Sugar Company's towers and buildings, then continue west on ID 55 for 11.1 miles, follow the road as it curves left (south), and enter Marsing in another 4.3 miles. As soon as you cross the Snake River on the edge of town, turn left (east) and visit the small city park along the river's south bank.

BIRDING:

The city park's fishing-pond attracts over a dozen wintering waterfowl species, including Wood Duck, Canvasback, Ring-necked Duck, Long-tailed Duck, Hooded Merganser, and Eurasian Wigeon. Along the riverbank look for Wilson's Snipe and for Great-tailed and Common Grackles, the latter two being irregular but increasing vagrants. Other possible winter birds include American White Pelicans, Black-crowned Night-Herons, Trumpeter Swans, and Merlins. The park road passes beneath the bridge to access more ponds and a wooded area to the west. These ponds attract Great and Snowy Egrets, and (perhaps) a Green Heron in fall, while the woods often support wintering Yellow-rumped and Orange-crowned Warblers.

After birding the park, follow ID 55 southwest another 0.1 mile. Before crossing the railroad tracks, turn left (southeast) onto Bruneau Highway. This road follows the Snake River upstream, offering more opportunities to find wintering waterfowl and passerines. *All land here should be considered private.* After about one mile you'll reach a large feedlot area where Red-winged, Yellow-headed, and Brewer's Blackbirds and Brown-headed Cowbirds can be found, November to April. Along the road search flocks of wintering White-crowned Sparrows for the odd American Tree, Fox, White-throated, or Harris's Sparrow. More river views and patches of brush and trees can be investigated by continuing along this road. Watch for wintering and migrating Common Loons, Western Grebes, Double-crested Cormorants, Great Blue Herons, Canada Geese, Wood Ducks, Green-winged Teal, Mallards, Northern Pintails, Gadwalls, American Wigeons, Canvasbacks, Redheads, Ring-necked Ducks, Greater and Lesser Scaup, Long-tailed Ducks (rare), Common and Barrow's Goldeneyes, Hooded and Common Mergansers, Bald Eagles, Sharp-shinned, Cooper's, and Rough-legged Hawks, and Merlins. Enjoy!

OTHER:

Marsing offers food, fuel, and accommodations. For other services try Nampa. See also Deer Flat NWR (p.162) and Jump Creek, the next site.

JUMP CREEK

Author: John F. Gatchet

Site SW-10 — Map SW-9/SW-10

Highlights: Short-eared Owl, White-throated Swift
Major Habitats: Shrub-steppe, Deciduous Forest
Location: Owyhee Co., 12 miles southwest of Marsing
Spring: * * *   **Summer:** * * *   **Fall:** * *   **Winter:** *

The Jump Creek birding site is a remote, beautiful canyon sheltering a small riparian zone. Unfortunately, one of the most common riparian plants is Poison-Ivy; be careful. For the hardy rock scrambler, a short climb up the canyon reveals a pretty waterfall.

DIRECTIONS:

From Marsing head west 5.4 miles on ID 55/US 95. At milepost 29.7 turn left (south) onto South Jump Creek Road and zero your mileage. Pavement ends at mile 4. Most of the land along the way is private, although Jump Creek Canyon itself is public (BLM).

BIRDING:

As you drive Jump Creek Road, watch for Long-billed Curlews and Short-eared Owls in grasslands and for Loggerhead Shrikes and Sage Thrashers in sagebrush areas. In winter look for White-throated and Harris's Sparrows in both habitats, as well as for Northern Shrikes. At mile 4.5 turn right (west), cross the creek, and head uphill, passing several road intersections. Stay on the main road until you reach the major road fork at mile 5.5, then stay left and proceed down to Jump Creek Canyon parking lot at mile 6.0. The constantly changing and mostly unsigned road system may mislead you, so be aware and remember that you're headed for a canyon, not up into the mountains.

At the Jump Creek Canyon parking lot, walk up the stream 400 yards to view the waterfall, watching for White-throated Swifts, Calliope Humming-birds, Downy Woodpeckers, Western Wood-Pewees, Canyon and House Wrens, Black-capped Chickadees, Blue-gray Gnatcatchers, Warbling Vireos, Orange-crowned Warblers, Yellow-breasted Chats, and Lazuli Buntings. You may also see Golden Eagles, Prairie Falcons, Chukars, Say's Phoebes, Dusky Flycatchers, Rock Wrens, Plumbeous Vireos, Western Tanagers, Black-headed Grosbeaks, and Green-tailed Towhees. During migration Gray Flycatchers and Townsend's, MacGillivray's, and Wilson's Warblers may also be present. Wintering birds include Golden Eagles, Mountain Chickadees, Canyon Wrens, Mountain Bluebirds (rare), Northern Shrikes, Snow Buntings (rare), and Gray-crowned Rosy-Finches. The trail ends at the waterfall.

OTHER:

Marsing offers food, fuel, and accommodations. The primitive BLM camp-ground at Jump Creek parking lot has a few picnic tables but no toilets or wa-ter. Nampa/Caldwell is the closest full-service community. For maps and more information, contact the BLM (208/384-3300) in Boise. See also Marsing, the previous site.

NORTH FORK OF THE OWYHEE RIVER

Author: John F. Gatchet

Site SW-11 — Map SW-11

Highlights: Gray and Ash-throated Flycatchers, Bushtit
Major Habitats: Shrub-steppe, Juniper
Location: Owyhee Co., 80 miles southwest of Caldwell
Spring: * * *   **Summer:** * *   **Fall:** * * *   **Winter:** * *

This 32-mile drive provides spectacular scenery, good birding, and an opportunity to see Mule Deer and Pronghorn antelope. The North Fork also provides your best chance for finding Bushtit in Idaho. Owyhee County is arguably the most remote non-wilderness section of this remote state, so be sure that you're well-provisioned before heading out.

DIRECTIONS:

The route begins in Jordan Valley, Oregon. Zero your mileage at the in-tersection of Yuturri Boulevard and US 95 (next to the Chevron Station), then follow Yuturri Boulevard east out of town. At mile 2 you'll reenter Idaho (unmarked). At mile 3 the road forks. Turn right (south) toward South Mountain. Most of this route passes through public land (BLM).

BIRDING:

At mile 3.6 park by the BLM sign reading "Caution" and "North Fk Cross-ing 28." Although this spot looks similar to habitat which you just drove through, it's particularly birdy here. Watch for Gray Flycatchers in the scat-tered trees and large sage, and for Loggerhead Shrikes, Sage Thrashers, Rock Wrens, and Brewer's, Lark, and Vesper Sparrows. Northern Shrikes and Townsend's Solitaires are occasional in winter. In 1994 a vagrant Eastern Phoebe was found immediately behind this sign.

You'll reach another road fork at mile 5.8; stay right (south) on "Owyhee Upland BackCountry Byway" toward South and Juniper Mountains. At mile 6.6 you'll cross Jordan Creek on a single-lane bridge. Pull over to look for MacGillivray's and Wilson's Warblers, Yellow-breasted Chats, and Lazuli Buntings. You may also catch migrating passerines, such as Townsend's War-blers. At mile 7.5 stay right (south) toward Juniper Mountain. Pavement ends

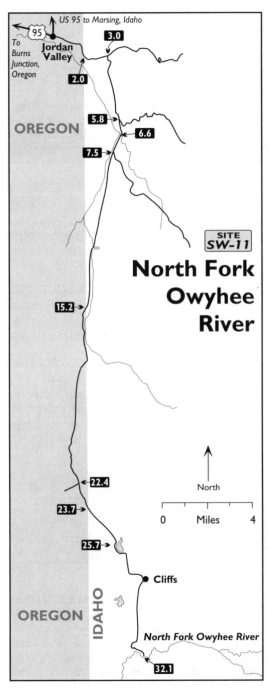

US 95 to Marsing, Idaho

To Burns Junction, Oregon

Jordan Valley

3.0

2.0

OREGON

5.8

6.6

7.5

SITE
SW-11

North Fork Owyhee River

15.2

22.4

23.7

25.7

North

0 Miles 4

Cliffs

OREGON

IDAHO

North Fork Owyhee River

32.1

at mile 7.9, and good gravel begins. *Be aware that this road can get mighty greasy when wet.*

Near mile 10, look in the tall sagebrush for Loggerhead Shrikes and Sage and Brewer's Sparrows. Black-throated Sparrows are a possibility, too. Swainson's Hawks, Golden Eagles, and Common Poorwills frequent this area in summer, as do Rough-legged Hawks in winter. You'll reach another good riparian area at mile 11.7, but the land there is private; *please bird from the road.*

The road sneaks into Oregon at mile 15.2. At the road fork at mile 22.4, stay left (south) toward Cliffs and Juniper Mountain. At mile 23.7 you cross back into Idaho. Dougal Ranch Reservoir at mile 25.7 is excellent for shorebirds and ducks, but you'll likely want to bird from the road because of intermingled private land. Cinnamon Teal, Black-necked Stilt, American Avocet, Marbled Godwit, and Long-billed Curlew are among the species that have been found here. Barrow's Goldeneyes should be looked for in migration.

The real treat is the North Fork of the Owyhee River, which you reach at mile 32.1. As the road descends to the river, listen for Rock Wrens and watch for Mountain Bluebirds (summer) or Townsend's Solitaires (winter). Golden Eagles, Prairie Falcons, Chukars, Western Screech-Owls, Common Poorwills, Gray and Ash-throated Flycatchers, Juniper Titmice, Canyon Wrens, Blue-gray Gnatcatchers, Sage Thrashers, Plumbeous Vireos, Black-throated Gray Warblers, Yellow-breasted Chats, Black-headed Grosbeaks, Lazuli Buntings, and Green-tailed Towhees should be looked for in the junipers, cliffs, and sagebrush that cover this beautiful oasis. Look especially for Bushtits, which are resident but erratic. There is no one spot to bird here; just wander up and down the road and up and down the canyon.

OTHER:

Maps and more information can be obtained from the BLM (208/384-3300) in Boise. There are no services along this route. Jordan Valley offers food, fuel, and lodging. There is a primitive BLM campground (pit toilets, water) at mile 32. The closest full-service community is Nampa/Caldwell.

Black-throated Gray Warbler
Mike Denny

BLACKS CREEK RESERVOIR ROUTE

Authors: Mark Collie, Dave Trochlell

Site SW-12 — Map SW-12/SW-13/SW-14

Highlights: Ferruginous Hawk, Shorebirds, Sage Thrasher
Major Habitats: Shrub-steppe, Wetland
Location: Ada Co., 10 miles southeast of Boise
Spring: * *   **Summer:** * *   **Fall:** * *   **Winter:** *

This 25-mile-long route has two parts: Blacks Creek Reservoir west of the interstate, and Blacks Creek to the east. The entire Blacks Creek area is locally famous for its bird diversity. In spring large numbers of passerines stage here before advancing into the nearby Danskin Mountains. The reservoir itself is popular with waders, waterfowl, and shorebirds.

DIRECTIONS:

From Boise follow I-84 southeast about 10 miles, take Exit 64, and turn right (south) on Blacks Creek Road, zeroing your mileage at this point. Follow Blacks Creek Road (which merges with Kuna-Mora Road) 2.4 miles west/southwest to the reservoir, watching for shy Burrowing Owls along the way. Most land here is public (BLM).

BIRDING:

BLACKS CREEK RESERVOIR

Although usually less than a mile long, Blacks Creek Reservoir varies greatly in size. You can scan most of the water by following Kuna-Mora Road along the south shore. A maze of side roads allows exploration of the north shore, *but drive prudently; even 4-wheel-drives are towed out every year.*

Birds to watch for include migrating Pacific and Common Loons, Tundra and Trumpeter Swans, Greater White-fronted Geese, and Sandhill Cranes. Western, Clark's, and Pied-billed Grebes, Great, Snowy, and Cattle Egrets, Double-crested Cormorants, and a variety of waterfowl summer at the reservoir, while Golden Eagles, Swainson's and Ferruginous Hawks, Short-eared Owls, and Long-billed Curlews nest nearby. In shrub-steppe habitat along the shoreline, look for Sage Thrashers and Brewer's, Vesper, Lark, and Savannah Sparrows. Grasshopper Sparrows are present but very local. Try listening near mile 3.7.

When available, the reservoir's mudflats are visited by shorebirds. Regular species include Black-necked Stilt, American Avocet, Greater and Lesser Yellowlegs, Solitary Sandpiper, Willet, Long-billed Dowitcher, Wilson's Snipe, and Wilson's and Red-necked Phalaropes. American Golden-Plovers (rare) have also been seen. During late fall and winter, watch along

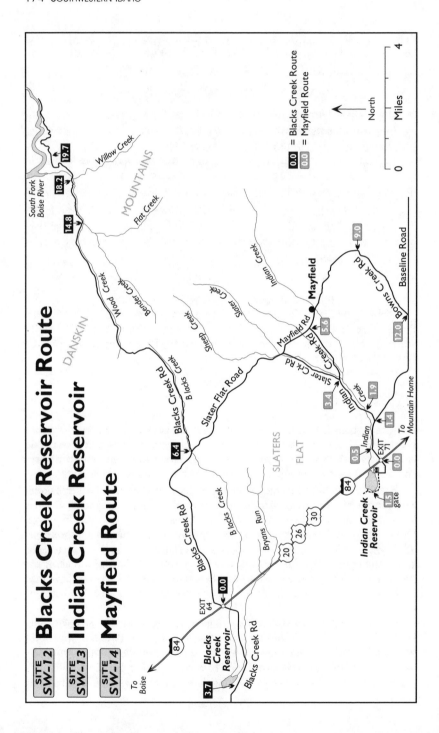

Kuna-Mora Road for Rough-legged Hawks, falcons, Snow Buntings, Lapland Longspurs (rare), and American Tree Sparrows.

BLACKS CREEK

To explore more shrub-steppe and riparian habitat, backtrack to the Interstate and re-zero your mileage. Follow Blacks Creek Road as it passes under I-84 and then heads northeast along Blacks Creek. *Most land along this portion of the route is private.*

From the Interstate to about mile 2.8, watch for Ferruginous Hawks in spring and summer. This is one of the most dependable areas in Idaho for this species. You may also see Gray Partridge, Loggerhead Shrikes, and Sage Thrashers. At mile 5.0 scan the small, private pond on the left (north) for waterfowl, and check the trees for roosting Barn, Great Horned, and Long-eared Owls. Long-eareds have been found nesting in willows on the right (south) side of the road at mile 5.4.

At mile 6.4 turn left (northeast), staying on Blacks Creek Road, which turns to gravel at mile 7.4. Park here and walk up and down the road to investigate this birdy spot.

You may see Mountain Bluebirds in nest boxes around mile 9.8. At miles 10.5 and 11.2 stay left. Around mile 11.4 the grassland gives way to mountain brush. Stop anywhere to look for warblers, Lazuli Buntings, and Spotted Towhees.

At mile 14.0 there is a wide pull-off on the right (south). Stop and bird along the road toward Bender Creek Trailhead (mile 14.8). Look for Bald Eagles (winter), accipiters, Red-tailed Hawks, Golden Eagles, and Blue and Ruffed Grouse. In spring and early summer, watch for woodpeckers, flycatchers, Gray Catbirds, "Solitary" Vireos, Nashville, MacGillivray's, and Wilson's Warblers, Yellow-breasted Chats, Western Tanagers, and Black-headed Grosbeaks. Be sure to listen for Northern Pygmy-Owls and Common Poorwills. You have another shot at all of these species at mile 15.9.

At miles 16.3 and 16.5 check the burned forest patches for woodpeckers. You can explore more burned forest at the Willow Creek Trailhead, which is on the left (north) at mile 18.2. *Beware of falling trees.*

Swallows and Canyon and Rock Wrens are often found along the rocky hillside by mile 19. You will reach the top of the hill and the end of this route at about mile 19.7, where you have a beautiful view into the South Fork Boise River. (Watch for Golden Eagles and Prairie Falcons.)

OTHER:

Fuel and food are available at the truck-stop at I-84 Exit 71. For other services, try Mountain Home or Boise. See also Indian Creek Reservoir (the next site) and Mayfield Route (p. 177). For maps and more information, contact the BLM (208/384-3300) in Boise.

INDIAN CREEK RESERVOIR

Author: Mark Collie

Site SW-13 — Map SW-12/SW-13/SW-14

Highlights: Great Egret, Cinnamon Teal, Shorebirds
Major Habitats: Wetland, Shrub-steppe
Location: Ada Co., 17 miles southeast of Boise
Spring: * *   **Summer:** *   **Fall:** * *   **Winter:** *

Indian Creek Reservoir borders I-84 and is worth a quick stop if unfrozen. The best birding is during migration, since summer activities such as fishing, sailing, and windsurfing scare most birds away. Whenever you visit, be sure to bring a scope.

DIRECTIONS:

From Boise follow I-84 southeast about 17 miles, take Exit 71, and turn right (west), zeroing your mileage here. Drive slowly past the large truck-stop/restaurant complex and turn right (north) onto the single-lane dirt road at mile 0.3, signed for "Indian Creek Reservoir." Continue to the reservoir overlook at mile 1.0. From here the road is strictly "travel-at-your-own-risk." The best spot for shorebirding is along the northwest shoreline. You can access this area by following the single-track dirt road west-northwest to about mile 1.7 and then hoofing it along the shoreline. It's okay to drive through the barbed-wire gate at mile 1.5—just be sure to *leave it as you found it*. Indian Creek Reservoir is public (BLM, IDFG), so feel free to walk around.

BIRDING:

Indian Creek Reservoir attracts few passerines but is often good for loons, grebes, egrets, and waterfowl. Great and Snowy Egrets and Cinnamon Teal are regulars. Migrant Tundra Swans stage here in late fall, and Trumpeters are always a possibility. In spring and again in late fall, watch for wayward scoters or Red-breasted Mergansers.

Shorebirds have a tough time finding reliable habitat in southwest Idaho, making the predictable mudflats at Indian Creek Reservoir important. Although the extent of shorebird use here is poorly understood, rarities like Snowy Plovers, Black-bellied Plovers, American Golden-Plovers, Marbled Godwits, Sanderlings, and Dunlins should be watched for among the more-regular Black-necked Stilts, American Avocets, Greater and Lesser Yellowlegs, and Western, Least, and Baird's Sandpipers.

Species nesting near Indian Creek Reservoir include Swainson's and Ferruginous Hawks, Long-billed Curlew, Sage Thrasher (common), and Savannah, Brewer's, and Lark Sparrows. In winter Snow Buntings, Lapland Longspurs (rare), and American Tree Sparrows may be found in the general area.

OTHER:

Fuel and food are available at the truck-stop. A pit toilet is located at the reservoir overlook. All services are available in Boise. See also Blacks Creek Reservoir (the previous site) and Mayfield Route (the next site).

MAYFIELD ROUTE

Author: Dave Trochlell.

Site SW-14 — Map SW-12/SW-13/SW-14

Highlights: Northern Mockingbird, Loggerhead Shrike
Major Habitats: Shrub-steppe, Deciduous Forest
Location: Elmore Co., 17 miles southeast of Boise
Spring: * * *   **Summer:** *   **Fall:** * *   **Winter:** *

A 16-mile-long loop from I-84 to Mayfield will take you through some of Idaho's most productive shrub-steppe habitat. Loggerhead Shrikes are common here, an increasingly rare situation for this declining species. The tiny "town" of Mayfield has hosted nesting Northern Mockingbirds several times, making it Idaho's hotspot for this erratic visitor.

DIRECTIONS:

From Boise follow I-84 southeast 17 miles, take Exit 71, and turn left (east) onto paved/graveled Indian Creek Road, zeroing your mileage. At mile 0.5 and 1.4 stay left. Private and public (BLM) land is intermingled along this route.

BIRDING:

The road crosses Indian Creek at mile 1.9. Stop for common riparian summer species such as California Quail, Western Wood-Pewee, Warbling Vireo, Yellow Warbler, Black-headed Grosbeak, Lazuli Bunting, and Bullock's Oriole. At mile 2.0 the road parallels basalt-rimrock, where you may find Say's Phoebes, Rock Wrens, Northern Mockingbirds (rare), Loggerhead Shrikes, and Lark Sparrows. In pastures to the right (southeast), watch for waterfowl in spring and for Red-tailed and Swainson's Hawks, Northern Harriers, American Kestrels, and Short-eared Owls in summer. At mile 3.0 look for nesting Swainson's Hawks in willow trees to the right (southeast).

Stay right at mile 3.4, birding along the road for Gray Partridge, Sage Thrashers, Loggerhead Shrikes, and Brewer's, Vesper, Lark, and Grasshopper Sparrows. At mile 5.6 turn right (southeast) on Mayfield Road and follow it into Mayfield at mile 6.1. Stop at the old abandoned buildings in town to look for Barn and Great Horned Owls.

The tall bitterbrush/sagebrush rangeland between mile 7.6 and 9.0 is particularly good for Loggerhead Shrikes, Sage Thrashers, and Brewer's, Vesper, and Lark Sparrows. At mile 9.0 turn right (southwest) on Bowns Creek Road, watching for raptors (including Ferruginous Hawks and Burrowing Owls) and Gray Partridge. Grasshopper Sparrows have been heard between mile 9.5 and 11.1. At mile 12.0 turn right (west) on Baseline Road and return to I-84 in another 5 miles or so.

OTHER:

Fuel and food are available at the truck-stop at Exit 71. For other services try Mountain Home or Boise. See also Indian Creek Reservoir (the previous site) and Blacks Creek Route (p.173). For maps and more information, contact the BLM (208/384-3300) in Boise.

SNAKE RIVER BIRDS OF PREY AREA

Authors: John Doremus, John F. Gatchet, Kas Dumroese

Site SW-15 — See Southwestern map, page 146

Highlights: Swainson's and Ferruginous Hawks, Prairie Falcon
Major Habitats: Shrub-steppe, Deciduous Forest, Wetland
Location: Ada Co., 17 miles south of Kuna
Spring: * * * *   **Summer:** * *   **Fall:** * * *   **Winter:** * * * *

Snake River Birds of Prey National Conservation Area (BLM) encompasses 80 miles of the Snake River. Several hundred Prairie Falcons nest here. Swainson's, Red-tailed, and Ferruginous Hawks, Golden Eagles, American Kestrels, and Barn, Great Horned, Burrowing, and Long-eared Owls are all common. The best time to visit "Birds of Prey" is March into June, before various raptors complete nesting and move on. To fully experience the Conservation Area, you'll have to do lots of hiking, driving, and exploring on your own, since large portions of the reserve have yet to be investigated by birders. A boat trip through the canyon (see below for details) will provide an additional perspective.

DIRECTIONS:

Zero your mileage at the railroad tracks in Kuna, and head south on Swan Falls Road. At mile 16 is Dedication Point Overlook.

BIRDING:

A sample of birding possibilities for the Snake River Birds of Prey National Conservation Area is presented here for two well-known sites. As noted, there are other places for the adventurous birder to explore.

DEDICATION POINT OVERLOOK

As you drive south along Swan Falls Road, look for Swainson's Hawks, April to September. Watch power poles, fence posts, and rocky outcroppings for other raptors, including Northern Harriers, Red-tailed,

Ferruginous, and Rough-legged (November to April) Hawks, Golden Eagles, American Kestrels, Prairie Falcons, and Burrowing and Short-eared Owls. Dedication Point provides a great view of the Snake River Canyon. From the parking lot take the graveled path 0.25 mile to the overlook. During spring Sharp-shinned and Cooper's Hawks and an occasional Northern Goshawk might be glimpsed moving north with migrant songbirds. In early summer one is likely to see Red-tailed Hawks, Golden Eagles, Prairie Falcons, White-throated Swifts, Cliff Swallows, Common Ravens, Say's Phoebes, and Rock Wrens. Look for Sage and Brewer's Sparrows and Western Meadowlarks in shrub-steppe habitats.

SWAN FALLS DAM

From Dedication Point parking lot, continue south on Swan Falls Road. About 0.25 mile south of Dedication Point, watch and listen for Black-throated Sparrows (uncommon to rare) in sagebrush. In winter look for Northern Shrikes, Snow Buntings, and Gray-crowned and Black Rosy-Finches along the road. You'll start to descend into the Snake River Canyon about 4 miles south of Dedication Point. Listen for Rock Wrens in the scree slopes along the road. About 5 miles southeast of Dedication Point, you'll reach Swan Falls Dam. Park and investigate the trees and lawns for Common Nighthawks, Western Wood-Pewees, Say's Phoebes, Common Yellowthroats, Yellow-breasted Chats, Black-headed Grosbeaks, Lazuli Buntings, and Bullock's Orioles. Lesser Goldfinches (rare) have occasionally summered here. In migration look for Olive-sided Flycatchers, "Solitary" Vireos, and numerous warblers including Nashville, Wilson's, MacGillivray's, and American Redstart. In winter Northern Saw-whet Owls, Long-eared Owls, Northern Shrikes, Brown Creepers, and Varied Thrushes are among the species which sometimes visit the area.

On the river look for migrating or wintering loons, grebes, waterfowl, and gulls. The Snake River is a major migration route, and this small treed oasis no doubt attracts many rarities. To see more of the area, follow the dirt road (by car or on foot, depending on whether the gate is closed or not) that follows the river downstream. This area is especially productive during migration and winter, when large flocks of White-crowned Sparrows can be found. Careful searching may reveal White-throated and Harris's Sparrows as well.

OTHER:

For more information contact the BLM (208/384-3300) in Boise. Primitive camping is available at the BLM's Cove Recreation Site on C.J. Strike Reservoir (p. 182). Potable water and restrooms are available at Swan Falls Dam. The closest services are in Kuna. All services are available in Boise. For Snake River float outfitters which cater to birders, try Whitewater Shop River Tours (208/922-5285) in Kuna or for alternatives call the Peregrine Fund/World Center for Birds of Prey (208/362-8687) in Boise.

SILVER CITY AREA

Author: John F. Gatchet

Site SW-16 — See Southwestern map, page 146

Highlights: Green-tailed Towhee, Sage Sparrow
Major Habitats: Shrub-steppe
Location: Owyhee Co., 48 miles south of Caldwell
Spring: * * *   **Summer:** * * * * **Fall:** *   **Winter:** N/A

Silver City is an old mining town full of fascinating history. It also provides excellent spring and summer birding. Tucked away in the remote Owyhee Mountains, this area is well off the beaten path. Be sure to be fully provisioned before leaving civilization.

DIRECTIONS:

From Murphy follow ID 78 southeast 4.7 miles. At milepost 34.1 turn right (south) onto Silver City Road and follow this rough, winding graveled road 23 miles to Silver City. Silver City Road is open from mid-May to October and occasionally into November. Although Silver City can be reached by passenger car, a 4-wheel-drive, high-clearance vehicle makes for a more comfortable trip.

BIRDING:

Along the first half of Silver City Road, watch for nesting Gray Flycatchers, Sage Thrashers, Loggerhead Shrikes, and Sage Sparrows. In evening listen for Common Poorwills in the juniper areas. If you're lucky, you may find Black-throated Sparrows.

The latter half of Silver City Road follows Reynolds Creek. Look for Western Screech-Owls, Northern Saw-whet Owls, Lewis's Woodpeckers (which nest in old cottonwoods along the creek), Red-naped Sapsuckers, Dusky Flycatchers, Western Wood-Pewees, Mountain Bluebirds, MacGillivray's and Wilson's Warblers, Yellow-breasted Chats, Western Tanagers, Black-headed Grosbeaks, and Lazuli Buntings.

When you reach Silver City, walk through town and enjoy the old buildings and the omnipresent history. Although the number of Green-tailed Towhees fluctuates from year-to-year, the species is often common, singing from any bush or running around any corner! A special treat in early and late summer is the presence of four species of hummingbirds: Broad-tailed (common), Calliope, Black-chinned, and Rufous (migrant only).

A particularly productive spot is the old cemetery at the south end of town. You may find nesting Red-naped Sapsuckers, Mountain Chickadees, Ruby-crowned Kinglets, Mountain Bluebirds, Hermit Thrushes, Warbling Vireos, Black-throated Gray, MacGillivray's and Wilson's Warblers, Western

Tanagers, Black-headed Grosbeaks, Green-tailed Towhees, and Fox Sparrows (which nest along the stream).

Fall birding in Silver City has been largely ignored. It seems probable, however, that this "sky island" is a productive migrant trap. Let others know what you find!

OTHER:

Silver City's Idaho Hotel has accommodations, but you must bring your own towel and bedding. A BLM campground is also available. For maps and information, call the BLM (208/384-3300) in Boise.

TED TRUEBLOOD WILDLIFE MANAGEMENT AREA

Author: John F. Gatchet

Site SW-17 — See Southwestern map, page 146

Highlights: Trumpeter Swan, Long-eared Owl, Swamp Sparrow
Major Habitats: Wetland, Shrub-steppe
Location: Elmore Co., 1 mile north of Grandview
Spring: * * *   **Summer:** * * * * **Fall:** * * * * **Winter:** * * *

Ted Trueblood WMA covers only 320 acres, but it still manages to cram in thousands of wintering and migrating waders, waterfowl, and shorebirds. The attraction is three shallow ponds surrounded by dense cattail and brush growth.

DIRECTIONS:

From the intersection of ID 78 and ID 67 in Grandview, follow ID 67 (Roosevelt Avenue) north 1.4 miles, then turn left (west) into the WMA's primary parking lot.

BIRDING:

The ponds just west of the parking lot hold nesting Cinnamon Teal, Black-necked Stilts, and American Avocets and a wide variety of migrant waterfowl. Burrowing and Long-eared Owls are common nesters in open sage and isolated tree groves, respectively. In winter look for Trumpeter Swans and Swamp Sparrows (rare).

Another viewing area can be reached by continuing north on ID 67 another 0.5 mile, then turning left (west) onto graveled Shaw Lane. In 0.6 mile there is a wildlife viewing area on the left (south). The large pond is particularly popular with fall shorebirds. American Golden-Plovers, Black-necked Stilts, American Avocets, Marbled Godwits, Long-billed Curlews, Dunlins, and Solitary, Baird's, and Pectoral Sandpipers have all been found here. American White Pelicans, White-faced Ibises, Great and Snowy Egrets, Franklin's and Herring Gulls, and Caspian, Forster's, and Black Terns may also be present. If you continue down this road, you'll pass additional opportunities to bird wetland, shrub-steppe, and riparian habitats before the road dead-ends in a mile. Watch for Swainson's (summer) and Rough-legged (winter) Hawks, Peregrine and Prairie Falcons, Bald and Golden Eagles, Sage Thrashers, Loggerhead and Northern (winter) Shrikes, Western Tanagers, Black-headed Grosbeaks, Lazuli Buntings, and White-throated Sparrows (rare, winter).

OTHER:

Fuel and food are available in Grandview. For other services, try Mountain Home. For a map and more information, contact IDFG (208/845-2324) in Grandview.

C.J. STRIKE WILDLIFE MANAGEMENT AREA

Authors: John Doremus, John F. Gatchet
Site SW-18 — Map SW-18/SW-19

Highlights: Waterfowl, Wintering and Migrating Songbirds
Major Habitats: Wetland, Deciduous Forest, Shrub-steppe
Location: Owyhee Co., 4 miles west of Bruneau
Spring: ****   **Summer:** ***   **Fall:** **** **Winter:** ***

Huge, convoluted C.J. Strike WMA covers 13,225 acres along the shore of C.J. Strike Reservoir. Access points are abundant at this popular hunting and fishing destination. The best spots for birding are highlighted below. Be aware that much of the WMA is closed from February 1 to July 31.

DIRECTIONS:

This route begins in Bruneau, 21 miles south of Mountain Home along ID 51. At the Sportsman Access sign in Bruneau, zero your mileage and head northwest on Belle Road. At mile 1.6 turn left (west) onto a rough, graveled single-lane road. At mile 2.1 turn left (south) and follow the farm-lane-type road southwest to its end at about mile 2.5.

BIRDING:

Park and walk the access roads into the WMA to investigate the wet brush habitat for migrating and wintering passerines. Regular species include Virginia Rail, Sora, Western Screech-Owl, Marsh Wren, Common Yellowthroat, Lincoln's Sparrow (winter), and Bullock's Oriole. When you have finished exploring, backtrack to Bruneau.

Re-zero your mileage in Bruneau and head west on ID 78. At mile 1.3 turn right (north) into the parking lot signed "Bruneau River Wildlife Area." Use the stile to cross the fence, then follow the road north into riparian and marsh areas, watching for Black-crowned Night-Herons, Virginia Rails, Western

Screech-Owls, Willow Flycatchers, Eastern Kingbirds, Marsh Wrens, Yellow Warblers, Common Yellowthroats, Yellow-breasted Chats, and Black-headed Grosbeaks. In winter search for American Tree Sparrows. There is another parking area, with similar birding, at mile 1.5.

At mile 4.1 (milepost 74), turn right (north) into Jack's Creek Sportsman Access. This is the WMA's single best birding spot. Watch roadside trees between miles 4.1 and 4.4 for huge flocks of wintering sparrows. As you approach the reservoir at mile 4.6, look for waterfowl, coots, and rails in the cove to the left (west). Open water near mile 4.8 is a good place to see both Clark's and Western Grebes in spring and summer.

There is a closed road on the right (south) at mile 5.1 that leads to a Russian-olive thicket. The thicket is a gathering place for wintering songbirds and raptors. Rough-legged Hawks, all three accipiters, Prairie Falcons, and Northern Shrikes are frequently seen in or near the Russian-olives, as are Cedar Waxwings (sometimes with Bohemians mixed in), American Robins, Varied Thrushes, Yellow-rumped and Orange-crowned Warblers, and Fox Sparrows.

From the end of the road at mile 5.4, use a spotting scope to scan the Bruneau River Delta for spring or summer American White Pelicans, Double-crested Cormorants, California and Ring-billed Gulls, Forster's and Caspian Terns, Great Blue Herons, Black-necked Stilts, American Avocets, and Yellow-breasted Chats. Migrant Franklin's, Bonaparte's, and Herring Gulls and Black Terns should also be looked for. Rarer possibilities include Pacific Loons, Great Egrets, Ross's Geese, Red-breasted Mergansers, Eurasian Wigeons, Black-bellied Plovers, American Golden-Plovers, Marbled Godwits, Short-billed Dowitchers, Stilt and Solitary Sandpipers, Parasitic Jaegers, Thayer's, Western, and Sabine's Gulls, and Common and Arctic Terns. After exploring this birdy spot, backtrack to ID 78 and continue west.

At ID 78 milepost 72.3 turn right (north) onto Cottonwood Access. The entrance to Cottonwood Campground is in 1.3 miles. Park here and look for unusual migrant species, such as Lewis's Woodpecker, Olive-sided, Dusky, and Gray Flycatchers, Say's Phoebe, Mountain Chickadee, Hermit and Varied Thrushes, and Townsend's, MacGillivray's, and Wilson's Warblers. For another view of the reservoir, turn right (north) at ID 78 milepost 70.5 and follow Sportsman Access to Bruneau Arm Narrows in about 1.4 miles.

Farther west on ID 78, turn right (north) at milepost 67.9 onto the paved entrance road to Black Sands Bay, and re-zero your mileage. Russian-olive thickets at mile 1 are excellent for wintering passerines, while the small marsh at mile 1.1 held a rare Swamp Sparrow in December 1993. At mile 1.5 stop at the dam and look for loons, grebes, ducks, gulls, and terns. This is an excellent place to see Pacific Loons (rare), Red-breasted Mergansers, and Bonaparte's Gulls in late fall, and Long-tailed Ducks (rare) in winter. At mile 1.7 turn right (north) and cross the wooden bridge below C.J. Strike Dam. At mile 2.5 turn right into the C.J. Strike North Park Recreation Area and look for migrant

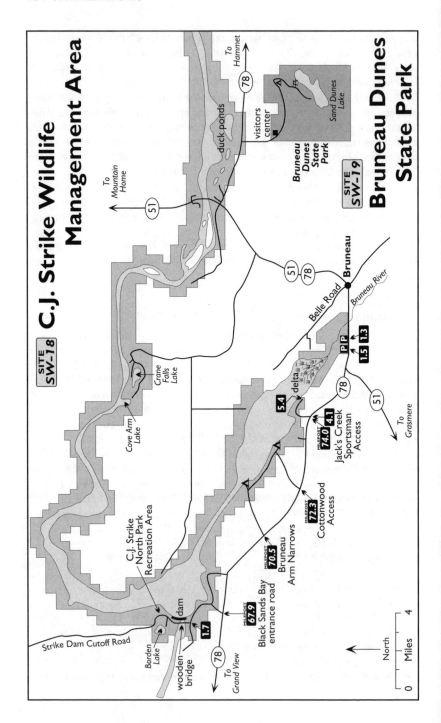

SITE SW-18 C.J. Strike Wildlife Management Area

SITE SW-19 Bruneau Dunes State Park

To Hammet

78

duck ponds

visitors center

Sand Dunes Lake

Bruneau Dunes State Park

To Mountain Home

51

51
78

Bruneau

Belle Road

Bruneau River

P|P

1.5 1.3

78

51

To Grasmere

Crane Falls Lake

delta

5.4

MILEPOST 74.0 4.1

Jack's Creek Sportsman Access

Cove Arm Lake

C.J. Strike North Park Recreation Area

MILEPOST 72.3 Cottonwood Access

MILEPOST 70.5 Bruneau Arm Narrows

dam

Borden Lake

wooden bridge

1.7

Strike Dam Cutoff Road

MILEPOST 67.9 Black Sands Bay entrance road

78

To Grand View

North

0 Miles 4

songbirds, as well as the odd vagrant, such as a Herring Gull or a Common Grackle.

OTHER:

Camping is allowed at the WMA, but there is no electricity. Potable water is available at the Cottonwood Campground Recreation Site and at C.J. Strike North Park Recreation Area. Fuel and food are available in Bruneau. Try Mountain Home for other services. For more information, call IDFG (208/845-2324) in Grandview. A helpful brochure is available. See also Bruneau Dunes State Park, the next site.

BRUNEAU DUNES STATE PARK

Author: John F. Gatchet

Site SW-19 — Map SW-18/SW-19

Highlights: Waterfowl, Black-throated Sparrow
Major Habitats: Wetland, Shrub-steppe
Location: Owyhee Co., 18 miles south of Mountain Home
Spring: ✳✳✳✳   **Summer:** ✳✳   **Fall:** ✳✳✳✳ **Winter:** ✳✳✳

This pretty little park is centered around the continent's highest single sand dune—470 feet tall! The park also encompasses a few small lakes and an expanse of dry sage-desert. Bird-wise the attraction is the park's lure to migrants and vagrants alike.

DIRECTIONS:

From Mountain Home follow US 51 south for 15 miles and cross the Snake River. (Look for waterfowl, shorebirds, and songbirds by the bridge.) At milepost 76.6 turn left (east) on ID 78. After 1.7 miles turn right (south) and follow the road to the park headquarters in 1 mile. Stop for a map, information, and a bird checklist.

BIRDING:

Along the park's entrance road in summer, watch for Sage Thrashers and Lark, Sage, and Black-throated (rare) Sparrows. You can access the 5-mile-long Sand Dunes Hiking Trail behind park headquarters. Even a one-mile walk down this path will bring you additional marsh and shrub-steppe birding.

The campground is along the main park road, 1.7 miles east of headquarters. Look around the campground trees for resident Great Horned Owls and migrant passerines. You may also find roosting Western Screech-Owls or Long-eared Owls.

About 0.8 mile east of the campground the main park road turns to gravel, and there you might hear courting Long-billed Curlews in spring and early summer. The park's two main lakes (actually, it's one big interconnected lake) are to the southeast, encircled by trails. Scan the water for migrating or wintering Pacific Loons, American White Pelicans, Great and Snowy Egrets, White-faced Ibises, Trumpeter Swans, Canvasbacks, Barrow's Goldeneyes, Hooded Mergansers, Bald Eagles, Bonaparte's and Herring Gulls, and Caspian, Forster's, and Black Terns.

In summer check trees around the lakes for Yellow-breasted Chats, Western Tanagers, Black-headed Grosbeaks, Lazuli Buntings, and Yellow-headed Blackbirds. In migration look for Hermit and Varied Thrushes, Townsend's Solitaires, and Nashville, Black-throated Gray, Townsend's, MacGillivray's, and Wilson's Warblers. Vagrant species found here have included Northern Mockingbird, American Redstart, and Northern Waterthrush. During winter look for Rough-legged Hawks, Long-eared Owls (once common but absent for the last several years), Northern Shrikes, and American Tree, White-throated, and Swamp Sparrows (the latter two being rare).

OTHER:

The park has a developed campground and is popular with both fishermen and astronomers. A few supplies (fuel, food) can be found in Bruneau or Hammett, but Mountain Home is the closest full-service community. For more information, call the park (208/366-7919). See also the C.J. Strike WMA, the previous site.

TRINITY RECREATION AREA

Author: Win Shaughnessy

Site SW-20 — Map SW-20

Highlights: Olive-sided Flycatcher, Pine Grosbeak
Major Habitats: Mixed Conifer Forest, Wetland
Location: Elmore Co., 40 miles north of Mountain Home
Spring: N/A   **Summer:** * *   **Fall:** * *   **Winter:** N/A

Trinity Recreation Area is a rugged, remote expanse of high-elevation forest, lakes, and tundra. Because the birding is around 8,000 feet in elevation, the area is accessible by car only between late June (some years late July) and mid-September. It is best to avoid the recreation area during the busy July 4th and Labor Day weekends.

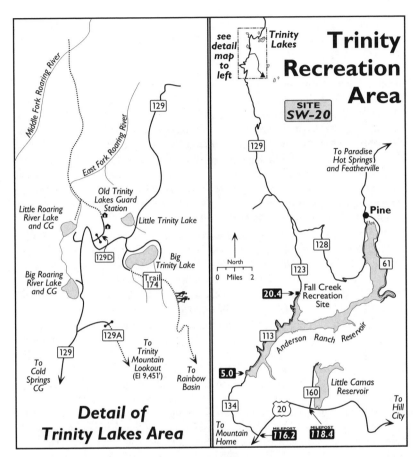

Detail of Trinity Lakes Area

DIRECTIONS:

From Mountain Home head northeast on US 20 for 24 miles. At US 20 milepost 116.2 zero your mileage and turn left (northwest) on FR 134 (toward Anderson Dam and Fall Creek). At mile 5 cross Anderson Reservoir Dam, turn right (northeast) on FR 113, and follow the road along the reservoir. At mile 20.4 turn left (north; by Fall Creek) onto FR 123 and drive another 12 miles to Trinity Recreation Area (FR 123 will turn into FR 129 on the way). *This route is steep and is mostly over unimproved, dusty graveled roads without guard rails. Allow at least 2.5 hours traveling-time from Mountain Home.* Most land here is public (FS).

BIRDING:

On the way to Trinity Recreation Area, you'll pass through a variety of re-warding habitats. Ospreys, Swainson's Hawks, Spruce Grouse (most likely along FR 129), Greater Sage-Grouse, Red-naped Sapsuckers, Western and

Mountain Bluebirds, Western Meadowlarks, and Brewer's Blackbirds should all be looked for in appropriate habitat. Pay particular attention to any water source.

Some of the area's best birding is in campgrounds within the recreation area itself. Look for Ospreys, Spotted Sandpipers, Belted Kingfishers, Red-breasted Nuthatches, Brown Creepers, Ruby-crowned Kinglets, Swainson's and Hermit Thrushes, Warbling and Cassin's Vireos, Western Tanagers, and Pine Grosbeaks. You may also find something out of place, such as the five American Avocets observed swimming in Big Trinity Lake in August 1991.

If you're camping and have enough time, Trail 174 (Rainbow Lakes Basin Trail) is worth investigating. A hike to 12-acre Big Rainbow Lake, the largest of nine lakes within the basin, is 6 miles round trip. Expect few birds along the way but a beautiful, tranquil lake at trail's end. This is a rather strenuous jaunt, about 90% of which is definitely sloped!

In the middle of the recreation area is the old FS Trinity Lakes Guard Station (two cabins and a garage) that is surrounded by good birding. Park in the open area outside the locked gate (FR 129D) and walk in. Just west of the smaller cabin (near the old garage) is a short trail leading north to a large, wet willow thicket. Search along the thicket edges for Yellow and MacGillivray's Warblers, Lazuli Buntings, and Lincoln's, Fox, and White-crowned Sparrows.

The foot trail running north from the smaller cabin is good for Rufous and Calliope Hummingbirds, Olive-sided and Cordilleran Flycatchers, Mountain Chickadees, Cassin's Finches, Red Crossbills, and Pine Siskins. August is the best month for hummers. The trail heads to the ridgetop, where there are scattered clumps of conifers and extensive subalpine meadows. Look for Sharp-shinned and Red-tailed Hawks and Golden Eagles. Northern Goshawks and Prairie Falcons are present in late summer. This is also home to Clark's Nutcrackers, Steller's Jays, Common Ravens, Columbian Ground Squirrels, many wildflowers, sphinx moths, huge bumblebees, and many butterflies.

Towering above Trinity Recreation Area is the fire lookout atop 9,451-foot-high Trinity Mountain. The 1.5-mile, 1,100-foot climb to the lookout from the locked gate on FR 129A is worth the effort (if you take your time). Looking down on soaring Golden Eagles and Violet-green Swallows is an unusual sensation! On the hike up watch for Rock Wrens, Mountain Bluebirds, and Mountain Lion tracks.

OTHER:

For maps and more information, contact the FS (208/587-7961) in Mountain Home. Fuel, food, lodging, and supplies are available at Fall Creek Resort and Marina (at mile 13.7) and at Nester's Mountain Mart in Pine. There are two modest FS cabins (constructed by the Civilian Conservation Corps in the mid-1930s) at the old Trinity Lakes Guard Station that can be rented.

Water and restrooms are available at the primitive campgrounds within the recreation area. *The "warm" weather season is very short at this elevation; a late June snowstorm is not unusual, and frosty nights can occur at any time.*

CAMAS PRAIRIE CENTENNIAL MARSH WMA
Author: Dan Svingen
Site SW-21 — Map SW-21

Highlights: American Avocet, Willet, Wilson's Phalarope
Major Habitats: Wetland, Meadow
Location: Camas Co., 14 miles southwest of Fairfield
Spring: * * *   **Summer:** * * *   **Fall:** *   **Winter:** *

Idaho's largest rush/sedge marsh is protected by the 3,000-acre Camas Prairie Centennial Marsh WMA. This preserve is best known for the Common Camas which bloom in its wet meadows. Hundreds of lily admirers come to drive the loop road in late May. Unfortunately, the area has received little attention from birders.

DIRECTIONS:

From Fairfield follow US 20 southwest to milepost 143.1, turn left (south) onto graveled Wolf Lane, and zero your mileage. At mile 2.8 watch the utility pole nest boxes for American Kestrels and surrounding private land for Long-billed Curlews and Horned Larks. At mile 4.8 turn right (west) onto Stokes Road. At mile 5.8 follow the road curve left (south). At mile 6.0 a road takes off to the right (west). Park here.

BIRDING:

In the WMA's marsh surrounding your vehicle, look for Soras, Black-necked Stilts, American Avocets, Wilson's Phalaropes, and Ring-billed and California Gulls. Sandhill Cranes, Long-billed Curlews, and Short-eared Owls may be present in the meadows.

If the road leading to the west isn't flooded, follow it 0.7 mile to the old farmstead, which provides a good observation point. Deep-water here attracts Eared Grebes, Canada Geese, Redheads, Ruddy Ducks, and other waterfowl. After you're done exploring, return to Stokes Road and turn right (south) to continue the loop.

About 2.9 miles southwest of the turn-off to the old farmstead, Monument Gulch Road leads off to the left (south) into the hills. For a side trip into drier habitat, turn and go 3 miles to the third cattle-guard. A narrow, steep jeep trail climbs the butte to the left (east). A 2-mile drive (or walk) up this road ends at an impressive overlook. Golden Eagles, Swainson's Hawks, Prairie Falcons, Blue Grouse, Greater Sage-Grouse, Rock Wrens, and Sage Thrashers all nest in this general area.

From the junction of Stokes Road and Monument Gulch Road, continue west 0.8 mile, then turn right (north) and follow Swamp Road along the WMA's west side. You'll reach US 20 at Hill City in 3.2 miles. Note that much of this area is inaccessible during winter due to deep snows (*over 100 inches*).

Camas Prairie Centennial Marsh Wildlife Management Area

SITE SW-21

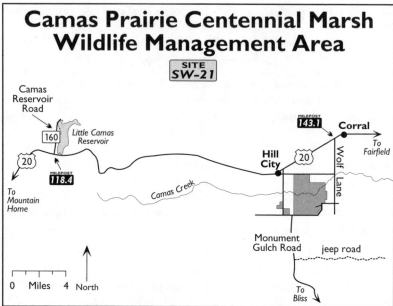

Camas Reservoir Road

160 Little Camas Reservoir

20

MILEPOST 118.4

To Mountain Home

Camas Creek

MILEPOST 143.1 Corral

Hill City 20

To Fairfield

Wolf Lane

Monument Gulch Road   jeep road

To Bliss

0   Miles   4   North

Detail of Camas Prairie Centennial Marsh Wildlife Management Area

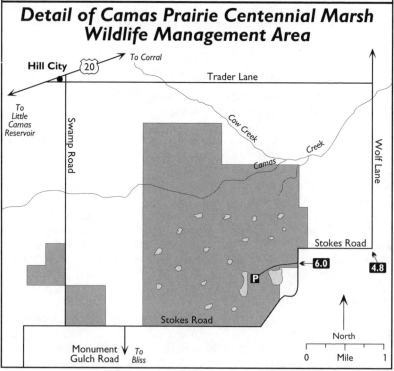

Hill City 20 To Corral

Trader Lane

To Little Camas Reservoir

Swamp Road

Cow Creek

Camas Creek

Wolf Lane

Stokes Road

6.0

4.8

P

Stokes Road

Monument Gulch Road   To Bliss

North

0   Mile   1

You may still be able to find Golden Eagles, Black-billed Magpies, American Crows, Common Ravens, Horned Larks, and Snow Buntings, however.

For additional spring, summer, or fall birding, try Little Camas Reservoir, which is west of Hill City along US 20. At milepost 118.4 listen for Bobolinks on the south side of US 20, then turn north onto graveled FR 160 (a.k.a. Camas Reservoir Road) and follow it 2.4 miles to the dam. Before you reach the dam, you may want to explore along the several dirt 2-track roads leading to the reservoir's west bank. Most land here is public (FS and State). Loggerhead Shrikes, Mountain Bluebirds, Western Meadowlarks, and Brewer's and Vesper Sparrows nest in the dry uplands, while Western Grebes, Trumpeter Swans, various ducks, and Caspian Terns breed on the reservoir itself.

OTHER:

You are currently allowed to walk around both the WMA and Little Camas Reservoir year round. Primitive camping is available at Magic Reservoir, about 18 miles east of Fairfield, and at Morman Reservoir, about 8 miles east of Camas Prairie Centennial Marsh. Food and fuel are available in Fairfield. For other services try Mountain Home or Ketchum. A WMA brochure and a checklist are available from the FS (208/764-2202) in Fairfield. For more information, contact the WMA (208/764-2489).

SILVER CREEK PRESERVE

Author: Dan Svingen

Site SW-22 — Map SW-22

Highlights: American Bittern, Yellow-breasted Chat
Major Habitats: Wetland, Deciduous Forest, Meadow
Location: Blaine Co., 4 miles west of Picabo
Spring: * *   **Summer:** * *   **Fall:** *   **Winter:** *

The Nature Conservancy's Silver Creek Preserve protects a portion of this world-renowned trout stream. Although more than 5,000 acres are included in the preserve, public use is restricted to about 400 acres surrounding the visitors center.

DIRECTIONS;

From the junction of US 20 and US 75, follow US 20 east 7 miles to milepost 185.4, then turn right (south), staying to the left. You'll cross Kilpatrick Bridge in 1 mile. Park here.

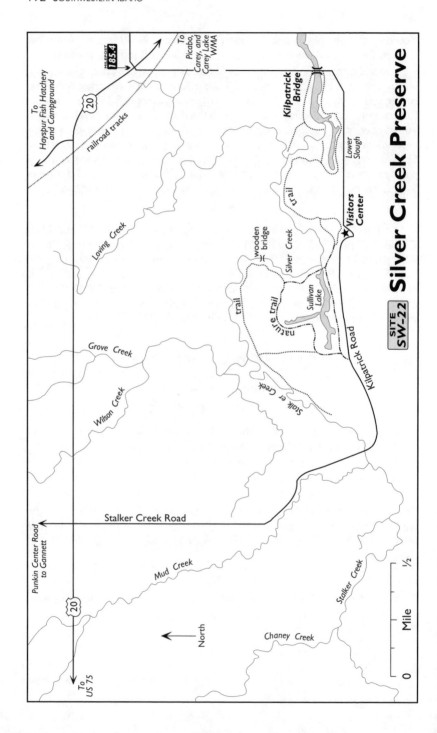

To Ha
Haysur Fish Hatchery
and Campground

MILEPOST 185.4

To
Picabo,
Carey, and
Carey Lake
WMA

20

railroad tracks

Kilpatrick
Bridge

Lower
Slough

Loving Creek

trail

Visitors
Center

wooden
bridge

Silver Creek

Sullivan
Lake

nature trail

trail

Grove Creek

Wilson Creek

Stalker Creek

Kilpatrick Road

SITE
SW-22 Silver Creek Preserve

Stalker Creek Road

Punkin Center Road
to Gannett

Mud Creek

20

North

Stalker Creek

Chaney Creek

To
US 75

0 Mile ½

BIRDING:

At Kilpatrick Bridge scan the marsh and open water for Pied-billed Grebes, American Bitterns, Trumpeter Swans, Virginia Rails, Franklin's Gulls, Short-eared Owls, and Marsh Wrens, then drive the road west 0.7 mile to the Preserve's visitors center on the right (north). Some of the Preserve's best birding is to be had from the visitors center's front porch. Scan the trees to the north for nesting Swainson's Hawks and Bald Eagles. Willow Flycatchers, Gray Catbirds, Warbling Vireos, Yellow and MacGillivray's Warblers, Yellow-breasted Chats, Black-headed Grosbeaks, Bullock's Orioles, and American Goldfinches nest in the riparian shrubs below. The porch's feeder attracts Calliope, Broad-tailed, Rufous, and Black-chinned Hummingbirds in May, and again in July and August.

After enjoying the porch view, pick up a preserve map and explore along the trails. Particularly recommended is the nature trail, where common species include Red-naped Sapsucker, Eastern and Western Kingbirds, Tree and Violet-green Swallows, Yellow-breasted Chat, and Lazuli Bunting.

When you're done hiking, continue driving west along Kilpatrick Road, birding the roadside riparian areas and meadows. Stay on Kilpatrick Road as it curves north, becoming Stalker Creek (a.k.a. Stocker Creek) Road. You'll rejoin US 20, 2.7 miles northeast of the visitors center. From here you can drive straight (north) across the highway onto Punkin Center Road and follow the rough gravel to Gannett in 2 miles. Where Punkin Center Road crosses irrigation canals, stop to look again for American Bitterns.

Because Silver Creek stays open in winter, a relatively diverse avifauna is present at that season. Wintering species include various waterfowl, Golden and Bald Eagles, Northern Harrier, Sharp-shinned Hawk, Northern Goshawk, Rough-legged Hawk, Gyrfalcon (rare but regular during the last few years near Gannett), Prairie Falcon, Belted Kingfisher, Downy and Hairy Woodpeckers, Horned Lark, Marsh Wren, Townsend's Solitaire, Snow Bunting, American Tree Sparrow, Cassin's Finch, and Common Redpoll (rare).

Additional birding is available at Carey Lake WMA, but access into this large, shallow marsh is limited to pull-outs on the north edge of the wetland along US 20. To find the WMA from Carey, follow US 20 northeast for 2 miles. Pull-outs on the right (south) side of the road are available at mileposts 206.5, 206.9, and 207.3. The pull-out at milepost 207.3 is the most developed; it has a primitive boat ramp and pit toilet. Explore along the dike trails that take off from the parking lot for more marsh views. Besides various waterfowl, watch (and listen) for American Bitterns, Black and Caspian Terns, Marsh Wrens, Common Yellowthroats, and Yellow-headed Blackbirds. Migrant shorebirds here have included rare Short-billed Dowitchers.

OTHER:

The closest full-service communities are Twin Falls and Ketchum. Food, fuel, and some accommodations are available in Gannett, Fairfield, Shoshone, Carey, and Hailey. Camping is available at the Hayspur Hatchery, where Idaho's first Fork-tailed Flycatcher was found. For more information, contact the Preserve (208/788-2203).

KETCHUM/SUN VALLEY AREA

Author: Brian Sturges

Site SW-23 — Map SW-23

Highlights: Black and Gray-crowned Rosy-Finches
Major Habitats: Mixed Conifer and Deciduous Forest
Location: Blaine Co., Ketchum
Spring: * *   **Summer:** * * * **Fall:** *   **Winter:** * * *

Known world-wide for its first class sporting facilities, the Sun Valley Area also offers great Idaho birding. Described below are seven nearby sites.

DIRECTIONS:

The common starting point for all seven sites is the intersection of Sun Valley Road (a.k.a. Third Street), and ID 75 in downtown Ketchum. Zero your mileage here.

BIRDING:

TRAIL CREEK WETLAND

The confluence of Trail Creek and Big Wood River creates a productive wetland, attractive to both migrating and nesting birds. To get there, go southwest on Sun Valley Road for 0.3 mile, then follow the sharp left (south) turn onto Third Avenue. Stay on Third Avenue for another 0.6 mile. The road ends near the lower parking lot of Sun Valley Ski Hill's "River Run Entrance."

At the south end of the parking lot is the paved "Wood River Trail." This popular recreation trail runs 16 miles downstream (all the way to Bellevue) and 4 miles upstream. On the south side of the paved trail is an informal dirt path which leads downhill to Trail Creek Wetland.

Common breeding species along Trail Creek include Calliope Hummingbird, Lewis's and Pileated Woodpeckers, Western Wood-Pewee, Cordilleran Flycatcher, American Dipper, Gray Catbird, and Nashville, Yellow, Wilson's, and MacGillivray's Warblers. Also look for Winter Wren, Black-headed Grosbeak, and Fox Sparrow. In winter Bald Eagle, American Dipper, Moose, and Mink may be seen.

TRAIL CREEK CABIN

When Trail Creek Cabin is not rented out for weddings (summer) or used as a supper house (winter), it can be a good place to bird. From the starting point go northeast on Sun Valley Road (a.k.a. Trail Creek Road, a.k.a. FR 408). At mile 2.9, turn right (east) and drive 0.2 mile downhill to Trail Creek Cabin. Park here and walk the various roads and trails to the south and east.

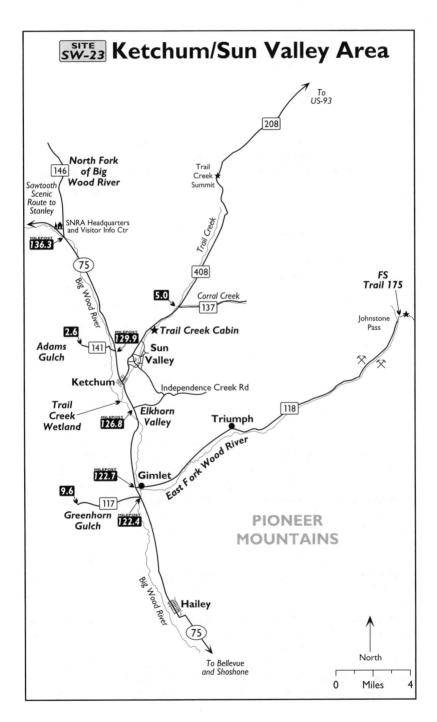

SITE SW-23 **Ketchum/Sun Valley Area**

To US-93

208

North Fork of Big Wood River

146

Trail Creek Summit

Sawtooth Scenic Route to Stanley

SNRA Headquarters and Visitor Info Ctr

MILEPOST **136.3**

Trail Creek

75

Big Wood River

408

5.0

Corral Creek

137

FS Trail 175

Johnstone Pass

MILEPOST **129.9**

2.6

★ Trail Creek Cabin

Adams Gulch

141

Sun Valley

Ketchum

Independence Creek Rd

Trail Creek Wetland

Elkhorn Valley

Triumph

118

MILEPOST **126.8**

East Fork Wood River

MILEPOST **122.7**

Gimlet

9.6

117

Greenhorn Gulch

MILEPOST **122.4**

PIONEER MOUNTAINS

Big Wood River

Hailey

75

North

To Bellevue and Shoshone

0   Miles   4

The mixed deciduous/coniferous woodland along Trail Creek harbors Lewis's Woodpeckers, Red-naped Sapsuckers, Black-headed Grosbeaks, and Lazuli Buntings. Hills on the east side of Trail Creek are covered with conifers and sagebrush. Along the trails in this habitat look for Northern Goshawks, Spruce and Blue Grouse, Northern Saw-whet Owls, and Western Tanagers. Green-tailed Towhees have been heard on the dry, brushy slopes bordering this area.

If you continue driving northeast on Trail Creek Road, look for a Golden Eagle pair by Corral Creek (mile 5). Also keep a lookout for Peregrine Falcon; the species has been hacked just over Trail Creek Summit. Trail Creek Road gets rough after about mile 12. *Use caution if you continue exploring.*

ADAMS GULCH

Adams Gulch is a narrow canyon on the west side of the Wood River Valley. From the starting point go north on ID 75. At mile 1.5 (milepost 129.9) turn left (west) onto Adams Gulch Road (a.k.a. FR 141). At mile 1.7 curve right (north). At mile 1.9 curve left (west). At the stop-sign (mile 2.0) turn left (south) and follow the road as it heads uphill and enters public land (FS) at mile 2.5. The trailhead at mile 2.6 accesses a maze of footpaths, all of which are good for birding.

Riparian habitat along Adams Gulch Creek is home to a variety of species, including Yellow, Yellow-rumped, MacGillivray's, and Wilson's Warblers and Western Tanagers. Spring-time birders might try owling, since Flammulated, Northern Pygmy-, Boreal, and Northern Saw-whet Owls all nest in this general area.

NORTH FORK OF THE BIG WOOD RIVER

The North Fork Valley has some of Idaho's most productive deciduous/coniferous forest. From the starting point go north on ID 75 for 8 miles. At milepost 136.3 (by the Sawtooth National Recreation Area Headquarters), turn right (north) onto FR 146 (a.k.a. North Fork Road), and follow this rough graveled road through North Fork Valley for about 6 miles. Stop often to listen for singing Olive-sided Flycatchers, Swainson's and Hermit Thrushes, Townsend's and MacGillivray's Warblers, and Western Tanagers.

ELKHORN VALLEY

The Elkhorn Valley is full of condo-lined golf courses and subdivisions, but can still provide good birding, particularly at winter feeders. From the starting point head south on ID 75 for 1.5 miles and turn left (east) onto Elkhorn Road at milepost 126.8. At mile 2.1 pull into the parking spot on the right (south) overlooking a tiny pond. When present, exotics such as Black and Black-necked Swans and Bar-headed Geese decoy-in wild waterfowl here.

At mile 2.8 turn right (south) on Juniper Road into the Twin Creek subdivision, which extends for about 1.5 miles. This is one of the best areas to find winter flocks of Black and Gray-crowned Rosy-Finches. Watch for the birds coming to local feeders. Make sure to get permission before peering into someone's yard. The friendly homeowners here have come to tolerate all those "odd" people who look at birds!

To explore backcountry, continue east on Juniper Road. The hills beyond Twin Creek Subdivision are home to Blue, Spruce, and Greater Sage-Grouse in fair numbers. Spring and early summer are the best times to find these species. You may see Gray Partridge in any of the Elkhorn Valley subdivisions, particularly along the roadsides during early morning, November to March.

Another place to explore for grouse and Gray Partridge is along Independence Creek Road, which heads southeast off Elkhorn Road. To get there, follow Elkhorn Road 1.9 miles east from its junction with ID 75 and turn right (east) on Morning Star Road. After 0.2 mile turn right (southeast) on Independence Creek Road and go as far as you like.

EAST FORK ROAD

The East Fork Wood River Valley has a diversity of both habitats and birds. To get there, go south on ID 75 for 5.7 miles. At milepost 122.7 turn left (east) onto East Fork Wood River Road and drive 5.7 miles to Triumph, birding from the road along the way. During summer Black-capped and Mountain Chickadees, Mountain Bluebirds, and Western Tanagers are easy to find.

In winter look for Black and Gray-crowned Rosy-Finches in Triumph. The best time to see the rosy-finches is November to April. The most reliable places are usually feeders or rocky south-facing ledges.

Summertime exploration of the Johnstone Pass area on FS Trail 175 leads into alpine habitat, where the two rosy-finches may nest. The trailhead for Trail 175 is at the end of FR 118, 10 miles northeast of Triumph. (The last 4 road miles are pretty rough.) Trail 175 is typically open from July to September. It's a strenuous 2-mile hike to rosy-finch habitat.

GREENHORN GULCH

Greenhorn Gulch is another of the narrow riparian canyons on the west side of the Wood River Valley. To explore this area, go south on ID 75 for 6 miles. At milepost 122.4 turn right (west) onto FR 117 (unmarked). You enter public land (FS) at mile 9, where the pavement stops. At mile 9.6 the road ends in a parking lot which accesses miles of popular hiking/biking/ORV trails.

Species to watch for in the sagebrush areas include Golden Eagle, Common Poorwill, and Brewer's Sparrow. In the riparian woodland look for Ruffed Grouse, Hermit and Swainson's Thrushes, Veeries, Gray Catbirds, and MacGillivray's Warblers.

OTHER:

Ketchum is a full-service community. The Chamber of Commerce (800/634-3347) runs a helpful visitors center. Other organizations that you may want to contact include Ketchum Ranger District (208/622-5371) and the Sawtooth National Recreation Area (208/727-5000). A Sawtooth National Forest map, available at the Ketchum Ranger District, can be helpful.

SAWTOOTH VALLEY ROUTE

Author: Larry J. Barnes

Site SW-24 — See Southwestern map, page 146

Highlights: Northern Goshawk, American Three-toed Woodpecker
Major Habitats: Mixed Conifer Forest, Shrub-steppe, Wetland
Location: Custer Co., 30 miles northwest of Ketchum
Spring: * *   **Summer:** * * *   **Fall:** *   **Winter:** *

The 754,000-acre Sawtooth National Recreation Area (SNRA) is rich in both cultural and natural history. The 90-mile drive from Galena Summit to Cape Horn follows ID 75 and ID 21 through spectacular scenery. You are likely to see a variety of wildlife right from the highway, but the best birding is along short side trips. Due to the route's length, it is best done over two full days.

The Sawtooth's greatest bird diversity occurs in summer. In winter most of the side roads recommended here are snowblocked. You may still see Bald Eagles, Northern Goshawks, Snow Buntings, Gray-crowned and Black Rosy-Finches, and Common Redpolls along the main highways, however.

DIRECTIONS:

From Ketchum follow ID 75 north 30 miles, passing over Galena Summit.

BIRDING:

At ID 75 milepost 168.5, turn left (west) on paved FR 205. Along the 2.5-mile drive to Alturas Lake, make a few stops and listen for drumming Red-naped and Williamson's Sapsuckers. The rather common Red-napeds are encountered about ten times more frequently than Williamson's are. You may also find Lincoln's and White-crowned Sparrows in wet meadows. At the east end of Alturas Lake, stop at Alturas Lake Picnic Group Area and take a morning walk into the Lodgepole Pine forest along the lake's southeastern shore. There are no established trails, so "bushwhacking" may be required. This is a good place to search for American Three-toed Woodpeckers in April and May. Listen for their drumming. You are most likely to find them in unharvested mature Lodgepole Pine harboring Western Pine Beetles. You'll probably hear Pileated Woodpeckers, Hermit Thrushes, and Western Tanagers. Scan Alturas Lake for waterfowl at various viewpoints along the north shore, then return to the highway.

Back on ID 75, continue north 2.8 miles and turn left (west) on FR 208 at milepost 171.4. This 1.5-mile washboard graveled road leads to Pettit Lake. (Watch for American Dippers along Pettit Creek along the way.) At the lake turn right (north), following signs to Tin Cup Hiker Transfer Camp. Bird the trail/trailhead/campground for Spruce Grouse, sapsuckers, Pileated Woodpeckers, Dusky Flycatchers, and Western Wood-Pewees.

After returning to ID 75, travel north 4.9 miles and turn right (east) at milepost 176.3 onto graveled Fisher Creek Road (a.k.a. FR 132). In spring and summer check the willow riparian habitat for Calliope Hummingbirds, Olive-sided and Willow Flycatchers, Bullock's Orioles, Black-headed Grosbeaks, Lazuli Buntings, Red Crossbills, and Evening Grosbeaks (especially if anyone is feeding birds). In 1993 a Northern Waterthrush was found near the tiny community of Fisher Creek, about 0.7 mile east of ID 75. Follow Fisher Creek Road 1.6 miles east from the highway to the sheep corrals, which mark the start of public land (FS). A male Chestnut-sided Warbler sang in the willows near the corrals through all of June 1995. Dusky Flycatchers are common in the mixed willow/conifer habitat along Fisher Creek Road. Red-naped Sapsuckers, Orange-crowned Warblers, and House Wrens nest in the Quaking Aspens. Keep birding along Fisher Creek Road until the road gets too rough. (About 3 miles is as far as you should push it in a passenger car.)

Continue north on ID 75 for 7.3 miles, then turn left (west) at milepost 183.5 into the Sawtooth Hatchery. Stop here to learn the plight of endangered Chinook and Sockeye Salmon. The hatchery ponds attract a wide variety of ducks. Ospreys and Belted Kingfishers visit the hatchery, as does an occasional Great Blue Heron.

About 1.5 miles north of the hatchery, at ID 75 milepost 185, turn left (southwest) on paved FR 214 and drive toward Redfish Lake, the largest lake in the Sawtooth Valley. If you're visiting in early spring or late fall, stop at Little Redfish Lake and scan for Common Loons and Bald Eagles. American Dippers are common all year on Redfish Creek. After going 2.2 miles, turn right (west) on FR 213 and go another 0.5 mile to Redfish Lake Lodge. Walk east along the beach, where occasional gulls and shorebirds congregate during migration. On the lake itself, look for Western, Clark's, and Red-necked (rare) Grebes. One of Idaho's highest and most productive Peregrine Falcon eyries is at the west end of the lake. With luck, you may see one of the occupants. You should also walk the 0.25-mile path between the lodge and Point Campground, watching for Osprey, Pileated Woodpecker, and Williamson's Sapsucker.

Return to ID 75 and drive north about 1.8 miles to milepost 186.8. Turn left (west) toward Stanley Ranger Station. After 0.1 mile turn right (north) to the RV dump-station and oxidation ponds. Park at the end of the dump-station loop. These humble looking oxidation ponds attract more unusual waterbirds than any other place in the Sawtooth Valley. Most of Idaho's duck species loaf here during some part of the year. In July and August shorebirds refuel on shoreline invertebrates. Among the species attracted are Eared Grebe, Wood Duck, Blue-winged and Cinnamon Teals, Ring-necked Duck, Lesser Scaup, Barrow's Goldeneye, Hooded Merganser, Ruddy Duck, American Avocet, Greater and Lesser Yellowlegs, Wilson's and Red-necked Phalaropes, Western, Least, and Baird's Sandpipers, Bonaparte's Gull, and Black Tern.

Back on ID 75, continue north 2.6 miles to Stanley. Stay on ID 75 another 0.6 mile after it intersects with ID 21. Immediately after you cross Valley Creek, turn left (west) into the Stanley Museum at milepost 190. Continue on this rutted, dirt road 0.2 mile to the Stanley oxidation ponds. It is difficult to see into the ponds because a dike separates the road from the ponds. By standing on your vehicle's bumper or tailgate, however, you can peer into the two ponds without disturbing the birds. Species are similar to those at the Stanley Ranger Station oxidation ponds.

Return to Stanley and take ID 21 through town. About 2.5 miles west of Stanley, at milepost 128.5, turn left (south) on graveled FR 619, which leads 3.2 miles to Iron Creek Trailhead. Look for Northern Goshawks, Spruce Grouse, American Three-toed and Black-backed (rare) Woodpeckers, and Hammond's Flycatchers along the trail to Alpine and Sawtooth Lakes. The trail is steep but well maintained. It takes about 1.5 hours to hike the 3 miles to Alpine Lake.

Return to ID 21 and continue northwest for 2 miles. At ID 21 milepost 126.4 turn left (west) into Elk Mountain Resort. Feeders here sometimes attract large numbers of Cassin's Finches. Unfortunately, a growing number of Brown-headed Cowbirds also use the feeders.

About 0.5 mile north of Elk Mountain Resort, at ID 21 milepost 125.9, turn right (east) on graveled FR 653 and park in the pull-out on the right in 0.1 mile. Bird the willow riparian area for species such as Osprey, Virginia Rail, Sora, Spotted Sandpiper, Wilson's Snipe, Rock Wren, Mountain Bluebird, Common Yellowthroat, and Lincoln's and White-crowned Sparrows. If you continue east along FR 653 for a few miles, you should see Sandhill Crane, Savannah Sparrow, and, in sagebrush country, Vesper and Brewer's Sparrows.

Return to ID 21 and cross over to graveled FR 455. Drive west about 3.5 miles to Stanley Lake. Park at the trailhead at Bridal Veil Falls (4 miles) and bird the mature willow wetland at the upper end of Stanley Lake. Be on the lookout for Northern Goshawks, Peregrine Falcons, Spotted Sandpipers, Wilson's Snipe, Calliope and Rufous Hummingbirds, Olive-sided and Dusky Flycatchers, Gray Jays, Warbling Vireos, Nashville, MacGillivray's, and Wilson's Warblers, Fox and Lincoln's Sparrows, and Cassin's Finches. Great Gray Owls, Northern Pygmy-Owls, Spruce Grouse, and Pine Grosbeaks are uncommon in the conifer forest.

Return to ID 21 and continue north 2.4 miles to the Park Creek Overlook on the left (west) at milepost 123.5. Scan the forest edge at dawn or dusk for Great Gray Owls; one hunted here in June 1994.

About 4 miles north of Park Creek Overlook, at ID 21 milepost 119.5, turn right (north) on graveled Marsh Creek Road (a.k.a. FR 203) and go about 5.5 miles to the Cape Horn Guard Station and the end of this route. Stop periodically along the way to watch for Elk, waterfowl, Northern Goshawks, Swainson's Hawks, Wilson's Snipe, Virginia Rails, Soras, Sandhill Cranes, Great Gray Owls, Mountain Bluebirds, Cassin's and Warbling Vireos, MacGillivray's Warblers, Western Tanagers, and Vesper and Lincoln's Sparrows. In the driest part of the route (near Dry Creek) look for nesting Horned Larks.

OTHER:

Maps and more information are available at the Stanley Ranger Station (2.6 miles south of Stanley at ID 75 milepost 186.8) and at the Sawtooth National Recreation Area Visitors Center (8 miles north of Ketchum at ID 75 milepost 136.3; phone number: 208/726-5018). Camping opportunities are abundant in the SNRA. You can buy lunch at Redfish Lake Lodge and enjoy a breathtaking view of Redfish Lake and the Sawtooth Mountains. Fuel and a few supplies are available in Stanley. For other services, try Ketchum.

HAGERMAN WILDLIFE MANAGEMENT AREA

Author: Jack Trotter

Site SW-25 — Maps SW-25/SW-26 and SW-25

Highlights: Waterfowl
Major Habitats: Wetland, Farmland
Location: Gooding Co., 10 miles west of Wendell
Spring: * *   **Summer:** * *   **Fall:** * * *   **Winter:** * * * *

Hagerman WMA and the entire Hagerman Valley can be productive birding anytime. During winter it can be truly incredible. Over 100,000 ducks loaf in the marshes here. The surrounding fields, pastures, tree groves, and riparian habitat add to the great diversity of birdlife.

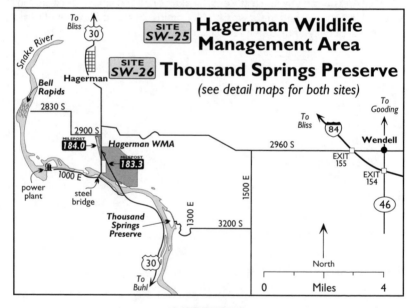

DIRECTIONS:

To bird your way from I-84, zero your mileage at Exit 155 (Hagerman/Wendell) and follow Hagerman Highway (a.k.a. 2960 S) west toward Hagerman. Species to watch for include White-faced Ibis, California Quail, Chukar, Gray Partridge, Long-billed Curlew, and Barn Owl in the farmland and rimrock habitats. In about 9 miles turn left (south) at the T intersection onto US 30. After 0.2 mile turn right (west) on 2900 S (signed "Sportsman Access Bell Rapids"). In 1.0 mile bear right (north) at the Buckeye Ranch sign. In another 0.6 mile take the left (west) turn onto 2830. Stay

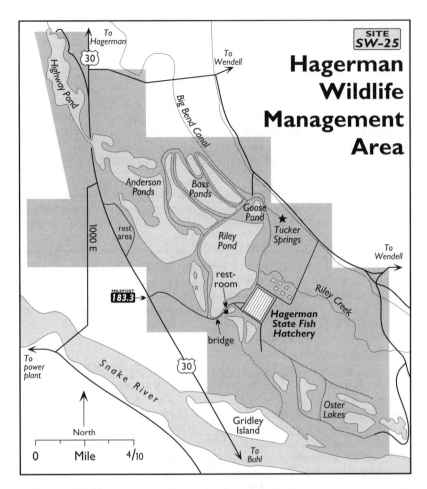

To
Hagerman
30

To
Wendell

Highway Pond

Big Bend Canal

Hagerman
Wildlife
Management
Area

Anderson
Ponds

Bass
Ponds

Goose
Pond

★ Tucker
Springs

1000 E

rest
area

Riley
Pond

To
Wendell

rest-
room

Riley Creek

MILEPOST
183.3

Hagerman
State Fish
Hatchery

bridge

To
power
plant

Snake River

30

Oster
Lakes

North

Gridley
Island

0   Mile   4/10

To
Buhl

straight in 0.5 mile at the intersection of 2830 S and 850 E. The road ends at the Snake River's Bell Rapids boat dock in another mile.

BIRDING:

In summer look around Bell Rapids for Cinnamon Teal, Northern Harriers, Black-necked Stilts, American Avocets, and Wilson's Snipe. In winter and migration you might find Common and Barrow's Goldeneyes, Lesser and Greater Scaup, Long-tailed Ducks (rare), and Bald Eagles.

After investigating Bell Rapids, return to US 30 and continue south another 0.5 mile. At US 30 milepost 184, park on the right (west). Look in the large pond (West Pond) on the west side of the road for various waterfowl. Search the surrounding trees for Great Horned Owls, Western Screech-Owls, Yellow-breasted Chats, Bullock's Orioles, Lazuli Buntings, and more. The wonderful slough on the east side of the highway is full of Marsh Wrens, and it is also good for Virginia Rails and Soras...but highway noise is sometimes a problem.

Continue south on US 30 for another 0.2 mile. At milepost 183.8 turn right (west) on 1000 E and head south toward Upper Salmon Falls Power Plant. After crossing the bridge, turn right (west) and head downstream, sorting through the diving ducks. At mile 2.1 bear right (west) toward Power Plant Substation A in 0.4 mile. Park at the road end and scan for migrating or wintering loons, grebes, and waterfowl.

After returning to US 30, continue south. Be sure to stop at the rest area at milepost 183.6. You can have fabulous birding here. A portion of the WMA's extensive marsh complex borders the rest area's levee. During summer walk this dike to get close views of Pied-billed Grebes, Double-crested Cormorants, Virginia Rails, Common Yellowthroats, and Yellow-headed Blackbirds. Be sure to listen for Warbling and Plumbeous Vireos, and look for vagrants such as Northern Mockingbirds. In winter look for rare Swamp, White-throated, and Harris's Sparrows among the White-crowned Sparrows, and sort through the incredible concentrations of Mallards and Wood Ducks for Eurasian Wigeons. Be sure to watch for American Bitterns, Great Egrets, Black-crowned Night-Herons, Trumpeter Swans, Ross's Geese, scoters, Ospreys, Golden and Bald Eagles, gulls, and Caspian, Forster's, and Black Terns throughout the WMA.

About 0.3 mile south of the rest area, turn left (east) at US 30 milepost 183.3 onto graveled State Fish Hatchery Road and follow it 0.4 mile toward the state fish hatchery. Park on the left (north) just before the bridge. You have a good view of open water here and can walk north on the network of levees for more birding. Idaho's first Tufted Duck wintered here in 1996/1997 amid thousands of Ring-necked Ducks and Lesser Scaup. There's another good viewpoint for this pond just across the bridge. Additional exploration can be very worthwhile. About 0.2 mile east of the bridge is a small rest area (restroom and picnic area) which is a favored Black-crowned Night-Heron roost site. Continue driving around the fish hatchery raceways and walk more of the trail maze for Great Horned Owls, Belted Kingfishers, Ruby-crowned Kinglets, Spotted Towhees, and American Goldfinches. The trails near Oster Lakes (see WMA brochure) are especially recommended.

OTHER:

Hagerman offers fuel, food, accommodations, and an RV park. Contact the WMA (208/324-4359) for additional maps and information. See also Thousand Springs Preserve, the next site.

THOUSAND SPRINGS PRESERVE

Author: Chris O'Brien

Site SW-26 — Maps SW-25/SW-26 and SW-26

Highlights: Clark's Grebe, Waterfowl
Major Habitats: Shrub-steppe, Deciduous Forest
Location: Gooding Co., 22 miles northwest of Twin Falls
Spring: * * *   **Summer:** * *   **Fall:** * *   **Winter:** * * *

Thousand Springs Preserve, owned and operated by The Nature Conservancy, covers 425 acres along 2.5 miles of the Snake River. The preserve is characterized by spectacular waterfalls and transparent spring creeks. It's a lovely place to bird, especially in winter when mist rises off the creeks and giant icicles edge the waterfalls.

DIRECTIONS:

From I-84 Exit 155 follow Hagerman Highway (a.k.a. 2960 S) west. After 3.5 miles turn left (south) on 1500 E and go 2.5 miles. Turn right (west) on 3200 S and drive 2 miles to the T intersection. Turn left (south) on 1300 E for 0.2 mile, then right (west) on Thousand Springs Grade, a mile-long dirt road that descends into the Snake River Canyon and ends in a public park owned by Idaho Power Company. Park here.

The preserve contains mainland and island portions, both accessed from the Idaho Power Company parking lot. The mainland portion (Lower Road, Columbine, and Split Rock trails) is open every day. The island portion (Ritter Island) is open Friday through Monday, Memorial Day to Labor Day. During other times Ritter Island is open only when staff is available; call ahead.

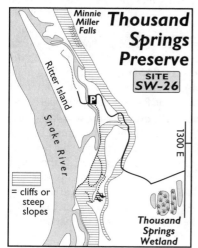

BIRDING:

MAINLAND PORTION

From the parking lot scan Ritter Creek to the west for waterbirds, then hike south along Lower Road Trail (a.k.a. River Road Trail). Check the dirt bank for nesting Northern Rough-winged Swallows. Pass round the "No Vehicle Access" gate, then continue through a small grove of River Birch. Within 100 yards a massive waterfall crashes down on your left (east) and Ritter Creek is again visible to your right (west). Look here for Great and Snowy Egrets, assorted waterfowl,

Belted Kingfishers, and American Dippers. Continue past the second walk-around gate, scanning the cliff to your left (east) for nesting Red-tailed Hawks, Cliff Swallows, and Canyon Wrens, among the resident Rock Pigeons. Rails, Marsh Wrens, and Red-winged and Yellow-headed Blackbirds nest in the sumac and bulrush to your right (west).

Continue south another 100 yards to the half-mile-long Columbine Trail, which is narrow and steep but very pleasant. The trail loops up the sagebrush-covered hillside to your left (east), then enters a surprisingly cool juniper grove fed by underground springs (look for wild columbine by the little bridge) and back down to Lower Road. Great Horned and Barn Owls often roost in the junipers. In winter you may find a Northern Goshawk. From the top of Columbine Trail, the quarter-mile-long Split Rock Trail leads to the cliff top and a stunning vista. Keep your eyes peeled for White-throated Swifts, Rock Wrens, and Lazuli Buntings. From the top of Split Rock look south across the wildlife area, checking creeks below for Great Blue Herons, Black-crowned Night-Herons, Wood Ducks, Mallards, Gadwalls, and Green-winged Teal. Northern Harriers often sky-dance in the fields below you, while Golden Eagles do the same above.

Return to Lower Road Trail and continue south another 0.25 mile to a bend, with the Snake River directly to your right (west). Check again for waterfowl, as well as for Western and Clark's Grebes and American White Pelicans. In fall you may see an occasional Common Loon or Tundra Swan. A few steps farther and you'll encounter a gate which closes off the south part of the reserve.

RITTER ISLAND

If the gates on the bridge are open, you can explore 70-acre Ritter Island. Once across the bridge, stop at the information booth and look for the occasional wintering Mountain and Black-capped Chickadees and Red-breasted Nuthatches in the conifers. Follow the driveway through the historic Minnie Miller Guernsey Farm. Look for nesting American Kestrels in the orchard and check flower beds for visiting hummingbirds. (Please be unobtrusive; staff members live in some of the houses.) Continue through the farmstead on the 0.5-mile trail to Minnie Miller Falls overlook, which is the best place from which to see Wood Ducks (if you sneak). It's also a good spot to look for Great Blue Herons, Belted Kingfishers, Common Ravens, and Song Sparrows.

Russian-olive trees near the Minnie Miller Falls overlook are worth checking for wintering songbirds; accipiters know this, too! During winter it may be productive to hike around the island to look for ducks in the creek and the river. Be careful not to disturb the duck-hunters who often congregate along the river's edge. You will likely put up occasional flocks of Dark-eyed Juncos and White-crowned Sparrows. Watch for Bald Eagles, too, since several of them hunt this area from December to March. At trail's end stop in the huge old dairy barn; a Western Screech-Owl can often be found roosting in the hayloft.

CANOEING

The best way to see the preserve is by canoe. Put in at the Idaho Power Company parking lot's boat ramp and float south down Ritter Creek, then paddle upstream on the Snake River. Virginia Rails and Soras may be spotted in bulrush marshes, and you'll hear many Marsh Wrens. Two miles upstream from the mouth of Ritter Creek is an island heronry (Great Blue Herons, Black-crowned Night-Herons, and Cattle, Snowy, and Great Egrets) which is full of birds year round. Nesting activity is most vigorous during April to June. Please watch from the east bank; *don't approach the island during the nesting season.* Two miles beyond the heronry you will arrive at Blue Heart Springs, which is well worth the trip. You'll see all kinds of herons, raptors, and gulls, and possibly Caspian and Forster's Terns.

THOUSAND SPRINGS WETLAND

As you drive back up the grade to leave the preserve, pull in at the Thousand Springs Wetland sign just before the dirt road reaches the paved county road. When there is water in the ponds (April into October), they are well worth checking for White-faced Ibises, Long-billed Dowitchers, Greater and Lesser Yellowlegs, Long-billed Curlews, Willets, Marbled Godwits, and Wilson's Phalarope. Black-necked Stilts and American Avocets nest here. When the water level is up, look also for ducks. You may walk from the wetland sign along the berm between the sediment basin and filter strip; *please stay away from the rock house (by the deep pond), which is a private residence.*

OTHER:

The nearest fuel is in Wendell or Hagerman. Motels and restaurants are in all surrounding communities. The Idaho Power Company park has picnic tables and restrooms, as well as a boat ramp. Several private campgrounds are nearby. For more information, contact the preserve (208/536-6797). See also the Hagerman WMA, the previous site.

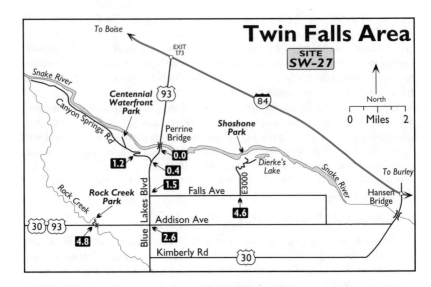

TWIN FALLS AREA

Author: Jack Trotter

Site SW-27 — Map SW-27

Highlights: Rock and Canyon Wrens, Yellow-breasted Chat
Major Habitats: Deciduous Forest, Cliffs
Location: Twin Falls Co., Twin Falls
Spring: * *   **Summer:** * *   **Fall:** *   **Winter:** *

Birding Twin Falls means visiting three beautiful parks. In spring and early summer this trip might yield 50 to 60 species, while in winter 30 to 50 species are more likely.

DIRECTIONS:

From I-84 Exit 173 follow US 93 south toward Twin Falls. At the south end of Perrine Bridge (the one over the Snake River Canyon), zero your mileage and continue south on US 93 (a.k.a. Blue Lakes Boulevard).

BIRDING:

CENTENNIAL WATERFRONT PARK and CANYON SPRINGS ROAD

At mile 0.4 turn right (west) on Canyon Springs Road and follow it into the Snake River Canyon. At the first deep curve (mile 1.2), carefully park and enjoy the waterfall to the west. The power poles or trees on the canyon rim overhead often entice resting Turkey Vultures and Golden Eagles, and the area can be alive with Bullock's Orioles. As you drive farther, you'll see swallow nest-holes in the dirt bank on the right (south). Look here for Bank, Cliff, Northern Rough-winged, Violet-green, and Barn Swallows and listen for Rock and Canyon Wrens. At mile 1.4 park at the switchback and take the uneven trail bearing right (upstream). This shrubby area can be vibrant with spring birdsong! Watch for MacGillivray's and Yellow Warblers, Yellow-breasted Chats, and White-crowned, Song, Lark, and Vesper Sparrows.

After your hike, drive the new road into Centennial Park (the right fork). You'll reach the lower parking lot at mile 1.8. California Quail might be present in the brushy orchard just west of the boat launch. Bald Eagles have nested across the river. The rock bluff overlooking the boat area is good for winter waterfowl-viewing and deserves frequent visits.

ROCK CREEK PARK

From the south end of Perrine Bridge, follow Blue Lakes Boulevard south to mile 2.6, then turn right (west) on Addison Avenue (a.k.a. US 30 and US 93). At mile 4.8 turn right (north) into Rock Creek Park. At the bottom of the short hill (mile 5) is a wet rock wall on the left (west). This area draws migrating warblers in the spring, in addition to the more common Ruby-crowned Kinglets, Cedar Waxwings, American Robins, Yellow and Yellow-rumped Warblers, House Finches, and American Goldfinches. Check the cliff face and nearby areas for Western Kingbirds, Rock Wrens, Red-winged Blackbirds, and Western Meadowlarks. Through the open area you'll find mature trees and pavilions. In the mature trees look for Mourning Doves and Bullock's Orioles. As you walk toward the creek, watch for Mallards, Belted Kingfishers, and Barn and Northern Rough-winged Swallows.

One of the best areas is the path leading downstream (north) which begins at the parking area after you cross Rock Creek. Watch the mature trees and rock bluffs for Western Screech-Owls, Willow Flycatchers, House Wrens, Yellow-breasted Chats, and Western Tanagers.

SHOSHONE PARK and DIERKE'S LAKE

From the south end of Perrine Bridge, follow Blue Lakes Blvd. south to mile 1.5, then turn left (east) on Falls Avenue. At mile 4.6 turn left (north) on E 3000 (signed for Shoshone Falls). Hawks, swallows, and Rock and Canyon Wrens can often be seen on your way to Shoshone Park. Be sure to pick your pull-over spots carefully, and watch out for Sunday race-drivers! Just past the ticket booth (fee), the road forks at mile 6.1. The right fork leads to Dierke's Lake in 0.3 mile. The left fork descends to Shoshone Park. The picnic area and trail around Dierke's Lake offer the best habitat. The complete trail loop has uneven rocky parts requiring some climbing, but the effort is often worthwhile. Birds along this trail are similar to those at Rock Creek Park, except that here one occasionally finds gulls, terns, Bald and Golden Eagles, Downy Woodpeckers, and Townsend's Solitaires. Owls seen or heard here have included Great Horned, Western Screech-, and Northern Saw-whet (rare).

The pond in Shoshone Park may have Pied-billed Grebes. The park's mature trees offer the best spot for Western Kingbirds, "Solitary" and Warbling Vireos, Yellow and Yellow-rumped Warblers, Lazuli Buntings, and Bullock's Orioles. Just behind the snackbar, a poorly formed trail runs west (downriver); it can yield a few more shy species.

OTHER:

Twin Falls is a full-service community. For more information, call the Chamber of Commerce (208/733-3974).

Black-billed Magpie
Mike Denny

NIAGARA SPRINGS
WILDLIFE MANAGEMENT AREA

Author: Chuck Trost

Site SW-28 — Map SW-28

Highlights: Waterfowl, Raptors, Canyon Wren
Major Habitats: Shrub-steppe, Deciduous Forest, Wetland
Location: Gooding Co., 7 miles south of Wendell
Spring: * * *   **Summer:** *   **Fall:** * * *   **Winter:** * * *

With three miles of river frontage protected from development, Niagara Springs WMA provides access to a relatively pristine section of the Snake River. Besides being a good birding spot, this area is also visually impressive—the Snake River Canyon here is 0.5 mile wide and 500 feet deep!

DIRECTIONS:

To reach Niagara Springs WMA from Wendell, take I-84 Exit 157, zero your mileage, and drive south on Rex Leland Highway (a.k.a. Orchard Valley Road, a.k.a. 1950 E). You'll see the rim of the Snake River Canyon at about mile 6. At mile 6.7 follow the road through the sharp left (east) turn and descend into the gorge. Turn into the WMA's main entrance on the right (south) at mile 7.2 to explore the WMA's west side, or continue east another 0.8 mile to the WMA's east entrance.

The main entrance road creates a short loop on an unimproved road. *Be careful not to get stuck in the sand.* There's a (usually) gated road at the west parking lot. From here you can bird either along the river or along the talus slope.

The WMA's east entrance parking lot borders a private fish hatchery. There are several paths that lead down to the river.

IDFG keeps all gates locked except during the fall hunting-season. All roads and paths, however, are open to public hiking year round.

BIRDING:

The best birding is from September to June. Because of its low elevation, the canyon stays relatively warm during winter, attracting Black-crowned Night-Herons and Yellow-rumped Warblers. Gray-crowned Rosy-Finches (watch for Blacks, too) also winter here, roosting in Cliff Swallow nests on the basalt cliffs. Russian-olive patches are good for wintering Cedar Waxwings, American Robins, White-crowned Sparrows, and Evening Grosbeaks, attracting Sharp-shinned and Cooper's Hawks and Northern Shrikes. The abundant Black-billed Magpies don't give the raptors much peace, though! Watch carefully for an occasional Harris's, White-throated, or even Golden-crowned Sparrow in the flocks of White-crowned Sparrows.

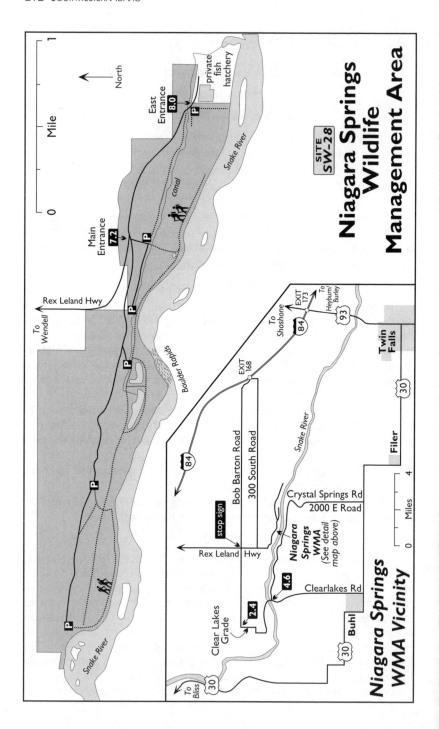

North

Mile

0   1

SITE
SW-28

Niagara Springs
Wildlife
Management Area

East Entrance
8.0

private fish hatchery

P

Snake River

canal

Main Entrance
7.2

P

Rex Leland Hwy

To Wendell

P

Boulder Rapids

P

P

Snake River

Niagara Springs WMA Vicinity

EXIT 173
To Heyburn/Burley
93

84
To Shoshone

EXIT 168

84

Bob Barton Road

300 South Road

Twin Falls

30

Filer

Snake River

Crystal Springs Rd
2000 E Road

stop sign

Rex Leland Hwy

Niagara Springs WMA
(See detail map above)

4.6

Clear Lakes Grade

2.4

Clearlakes Rd

0   4
Miles

Buhl

30

To Bliss
30

In spring and summer check the two ponds about a mile west of the main entrance for waterfowl, Marsh Wrens, and Yellow-headed and Red-winged Blackbirds. Golden Eagles, Red-tailed Hawks, and Prairie Falcons are commonly seen in the WMA during this time of year.

Outside of the nesting season, check scattered nest boxes for Western Screech-Owls and Northern Saw-whet Owls. Throughout the year listen for Canyon Wrens giving their lovely slurring whistle from the talus slopes, and watch for Chukars and Rock Wrens. A few California Quail coveys live in the area (most likely in Russian-olives lining the canal).

The best way to bird the river is from the access road along the south bank. To get there, leave the WMA and backtrack up the hill 2.2 miles to the four-way stop-sign. Re-zero your mileage and take a left (west) on Bob Barton Road (see map). At mile 2.4 bear left (south) on Clear Lakes Grade and follow it across the Snake River. As soon as you reach the south bank (mile 4.6), take a left (east) toward Magic Valley Fish Hatchery. This road overlooks the river along most of its length before climbing out of the canyon at mile 10.6. Along the way watch for wintering species such as Double-crested Cormorant, Canada Goose, American Wigeon, and Mallard, as well as Lesser Scaup, Ring-necked Duck, Bufflehead, Redhead, and Common and Barrow's Goldeneyes.

OTHER:

Wendell offers fuel, food, and lodging. Other services are available in Jerome, Buhl, and Twin Falls. About 0.5 mile east of the WMA's east entrance is Niagara Springs SP, which has a campground, picnic area, and restrooms. For more information and a bird checklist, contact IDFG (208/324-4359) in Jerome.

The geological history here is worthy of a visit in itself. The WMA's basalt was formed from lava originating near Flat Top Butte about 3,500,000 years ago. The Snake River has cut a deep trough through this rock mass, with considerable help from the famous Bonneville Flood, which began near far-off Oxford Slough.

SOUTHEASTERN IDAHO BIRDING SITES

SE-1 Mackay Reservoir and Chilly Slough	**SE-17** Big Canyon to Knox Canyon Route
SE-2 Craters of the Moon Nat'l Mon.	**SE-18** Springfield Ponds
SE-3 Henrys Lake	**SE-19** The Bottoms
SE-4 Black Canyon Road Route	**SE-20** Sterling Wildlife Mgt Area
SE-5 Harriman State Park	**SE-21** Sportsmans Park
SE-6 Mesa Falls Route	**SE-22** American Falls Dam
SE-7 Camas National Wildlife Refuge	**SE-23** Massacre Rocks State Park
SE-8 Mud Lake Wildlife Mgt Area	**SE-24** Minidoka National Wildlife Refuge
SE-9 Market Lake Wildlife Mgt Area	**SE-25** City of Rocks National Reserve
SE-10 Tex Creek Wildlife Mgt Area	**SE-26** Curlew National Grassland
SE-11 Sand Creek Wildlife Mgt Area	**SE-27** Blackfoot Reservoir Route
SE-12 Teton Valley Route	**SE-28** Alexander Reservoir
SE-13 Teton Pass	**SE-29** Grays Lake National Wildlife Refuge
SE-14 Wolverine Canyon Route	**SE-30** Hawkins Reservoir
SE-15 Mink Creek Route	**SE-31** Oxford Slough Area
SE-16 Cedar Ridge Route	**SE-32**

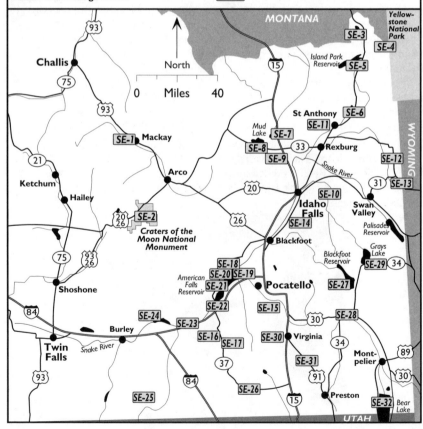

SOUTHEASTERN IDAHO

Southeastern Idaho contains the state's oldest town, most of Idaho's famous potato fields, and the greatest habitat diversity. The Intermountain Semidesert, Middle Rocky Mountain, and Southern Rocky Mountain Ecoregions all meet in southeast Idaho. This fortuitous joining makes Big Days of >160 species possible. Within a few hours drive of Pocatello or Idaho Falls, a birder can watch huge flocks of Snow Geese at Market Lake WMA (spring), listen to Virginia's and Black-throated Gray Warblers along Mink Creek (summer), or sort through hundreds of shorebirds on The Bottoms (fall). Southeast Idaho also contains most of the state's colonial nesters, with thousands of Western and Clark's Grebes, Snowy Egrets, White-faced Ibis, and Franklin's Gulls breeding. Because of the great habitat diversity, most of Idaho's bird species can be found in the Southeast, the exceptions being a few northern species such as Boreal Chickadee, and a few peripheral species such as White-headed Woodpecker.

Great natural beauty also brings visitors to Southeastern Idaho. Recreational options include touring Yellowstone National Park, flyfishing the world famous Henrys Fork, or gawking at the power of Mesa Falls. Services are relatively easy to find, especially in Idaho's second and third largest cities (Pocatello and Idaho Falls).

White-faced Ibis
Mike Denny

MACKAY RESERVOIR AND CHILLY SLOUGH

Authors: Chuck Trost, Eric Lepisto, Jerry Gregson

Site SE-1 — Map SE-1/SE-2

Highlights: Waterfowl, Sandhill Crane, Shorebirds
Major Habitats: Wetland, Shrub-steppe, Deciduous Forest
Location: Custer Co., 5 miles north of Mackay
Spring: * *   **Summer:** * *   **Fall:** * *   **Winter:** *

Mackay Reservoir and Chilly Slough provide precious wetland habitat in an arid environment, attracting a variety of birdlife. Probably the first thing you'll notice, however, is the scenic location. Mackay Reservoir is in the middle of Big Lost River Valley, with majestic 12,230-foot-high Leatherman Peak as a backdrop. Chilly Slough sprawls across Thousand Springs Valley and is ringed by many of the same mountains, including Borah Peak, Idaho's highest at 12,662 feet.

DIRECTIONS:

From Mackay follow US 93 northwest 5 miles to Mackay Reservoir. There are several access places along the east shore, including ones at mileposts 112.9, 113.6, and 114.5. The north-west and southeast ends of the reservoir (by the inlet and out-let) are private land. The rest of the shoreline is public (BLM).

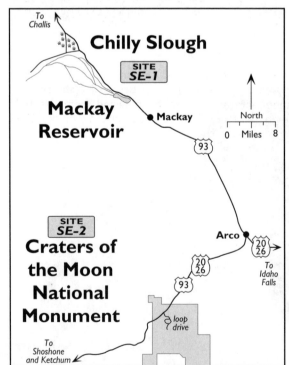

BIRDING:

MACKAY
RESERVOIR

The dam at the south end of Mackay Reservoir overlooks an expansive cotton-wood riparian forest that is mostly pri-vate. Birding oppor-tunities are limited to the Sportsman Access Point. Even with this restriction, however, you should find a variety of nesting birds, including Hairy Wood-peckers, Barn, Cliff, and Violet-green Swallows, Gray Catbirds, Yellow War-blers, Lazuli Buntings, and Bullock's Orioles.

Wading birds can be found at the reservoir's northwest end, but there is no direct land access; you'll have to scope from afar or use a canoe. As the reservoir drops during summer, you may be able to walk around the shoreline to investigate the Western, Least, and Baird's Sandpipers that are regular here.

CHILLY SLOUGH

To visit 400-acre Chilly Slough, continue driving northwest on US 93. During winter watch the roadsides for Snow Buntings and Gray-crowned and Black Rosy-Finches, and an occasional Rough-legged Hawk. At milepost 126, turn into the graveled pull-out on the left (west).

Among the 134 bird species recorded at Chilly Slough are American Bit-tern, Tundra Swan, Sandhill Crane, Long-billed Curlew, Willet, Wilson's Phal-arope, Marsh Wren, and Sage Thrasher. Peregrine Falcons have been reintroduced nearby, so scan the skies carefully. To get additional views of Chilly Slough, walk about 0.75 mile along the edge of the wetland in either di-rection from the highway pull-out (be prepared to get your feet wet.) Bound-ary fences are signed to prevent trespass on adjacent private lands. Putting a canoe in at the highway pull-out is the easiest and most pleasurable way to bird here.

OTHER:

Mackay offers fuel, food, and lodging. Mackay Reservoir provides camping (fee, pit toilets, shelters, water). No developed facilities are available at Chilly Slough. Maps and more information can be obtained from the BLM (208/756-5400) in Salmon, the FS (208/588-2224) in Mackay, or the IDFG (208/525-7290) in Idaho Falls.

CRATERS OF THE MOON NATIONAL MONUMENT

Author: Kit Struthers

Site SE-2 — Map SE-1/SE-2

Highlights: Clark's Nutcracker, Rock Wren, Mountain Bluebird
Major Habitats: Dry Conifer Forest
Location: Butte Co., 18 miles southwest of Arco
Spring: *   **Summer:** *   **Fall:** *   **Winter:** *

Although only a limited number of bird species are found at Craters of the Moon, the monument is still worth a visit; the baked landscape is like no other in the Northwest. The best birding is from April through June. This is also the time to witness the impressive desert wildflowers. Because of the limited moisture, the blooms are so evenly spaced that they look planted!

DIRECTIONS:

From Arco follow US 93 southwest 18 miles. By milepost 230 turn left (south) at the well-signed entrance to the monument. The visitors center is on the left (east) in 0.1 mile. Stop here to pick up a map and a checklist. The park's current biologist is very knowledgeable about birds and may be able to provide additional information.

The monument is most easily birded by following the 7-mile-long main loop road that begins south of the visitors center. This road is open late April until mid-November, depending on snowfall. In winter it's groomed for cross-country skiing.

BIRDING:

Throughout the monument, watch for Golden Eagles, Prairie Falcons, Sage Thrashers, and Brewer's and Vesper Sparrows. Rock Wrens can be found tail-bobbing and singing everywhere! Clark's Nutcrackers, Dusky Fly-catchers, Mountain Bluebirds, and Green-tailed and Spotted Towhees are common in Limber Pine groves, like those along the Wilderness Trail. This trail is accessed from the Tree Mold Trail parking lot. It's about a one-mile walk to good Limber Pine habitat.

OTHER:

Plan your hikes for the coolest parts of the day, since the monument can get very hot. Sturdy hiking-boots are needed to negotiate the sharp lava surfaces.

Full services are available in Idaho Falls and Ketchum; limited services (restaurants, motels, groceries, gas stations) are available in Arco. The monument's developed campground is open from May to October, but it has no showers. For more information, call the monument (208/527-3257).

HENRYS LAKE

Authors: Chuck Trost, Eric Lepisto

Site SE-3 — Map SE-3/SE-4

Highlights: Red-necked Grebe, Boreal Owl, American Pipit
Major Habitats: Shrub-steppe, Mixed Conifer Forest
Location: Fremont Co., 30 miles north of Ashton
Spring: * *   **Summer:** * *   **Fall:** * * *   **Winter:** *

Henrys Lake is nestled in Idaho's northeast corner, just 15 miles from Yellowstone National Park. The 6,200-acre reservoir supports a world-renowned trout fishery, but the best birding is away from the water, in the surrounding plains and mountains.

DIRECTIONS:

The starting point for sites described below is Macks Inn, which is located at US 20 milepost 392.7.

BIRDING:

A good place to begin birding is 5 miles north of Macks Inn along US 20, where meadows and sagebrush flats are favored by staging buteos. From mid-August to mid-September it's possible to see 100 Red-tailed, 40 Ferruginous, and 50 Swainson's Hawks in a single day! Early morning is the best time to look for these birds since they are often off and soaring by 10 am. At US 20 milepost 398.2, zero your mileage and turn left (west) onto Red Rocks Road (a.k.a. FR 053). At mile 5 turn right (north) and follow the rough dirt road 1.1 miles to a boat ramp and overlook. Look for Red-necked Grebes, Trumpeter Swans, and White-crowned Sparrows, then backtrack to FR 053 and turn right, continuing west. Watch for Sandhill Cranes, Long-billed Curlews, Great Gray Owls (at dawn and dusk), and Red Foxes. After 2.5 miles you'll reach a T intersection. Turn right (north) on FR 055. In about 2.9 miles turn right (east) into Bill Frome County Park. The bay on the south side of the park is the best place to look for nesting Red-necked Grebes.

Continuing north on FR 055, look in the area east of Staley Springs for migrant Red-breasted Mergansers or nesting Lesser Scaup and Barrow's Goldeneyes. The small ponds nearby are good sites for Soras. You'll reach ID 87 in about 2.7 miles. Turn right (southeast) here and follow ID 87 as it loops back to US 20.

At the junction of ID 87 and US 20, turn right (south) onto US 20. As you pass through the sagebrush flats, watch for Pronghorn antelope and Sandhill Cranes. Also keep a sharp eye out for Horned Lark flocks in April and May and again in fall, since vagrant McCown's Longspurs have been seen here.

The entrance to Henrys Lake SP (fee) is at US 20 milepost 401. The short nature trail behind campsite #32 may reveal Trumpeter Swans, Soras, Marsh

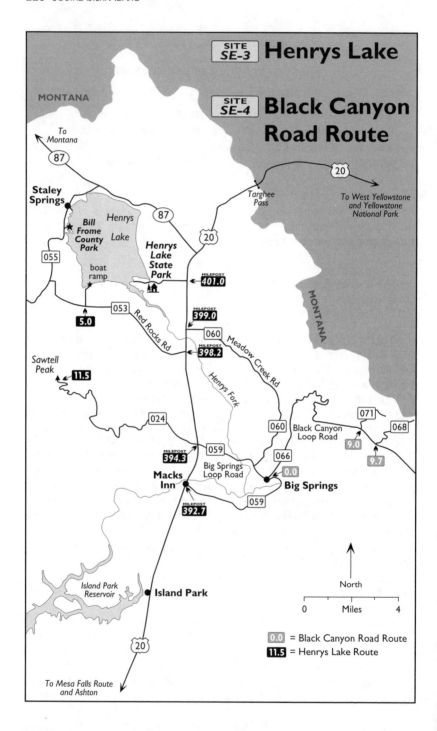

SITE SE-3 **Henrys Lake**

SITE SE-4 **Black Canyon Road Route**

Wrens, and Yellow-headed Blackbirds. At the boat dock look for California, Ring-billed, and Franklin's Gulls. A scan of the lake's eastern shore can produce nesting Bald Eagles. In fall look for migrant loons, Caspian Terns, and vagrant jaegers.

Continuing south on US 20, zero your mileage at milepost 399, turn left (east) onto Meadow Creek Road (a.k.a. FR 060), and follow the road as it loops southeast. After 8.6 miles Meadow Creek Road joins FR 059 near Big Springs. Turn right (west) onto FR 059 and follow it back to US 20 in 3 miles. Stop often to look and listen for birds. Besides common meadow, conifer, and deciduous-forest birds, you may see a Northern Goshawk or a Great Gray Owl. FR 059 crosses the outlet of Henrys Lake 1 mile west of the FR 059/060 junction. Listen here for Ospreys, Willow Flycatchers, MacGillivray's Warblers, and perhaps Northern Waterthrushes.

Boreal Owls nest in the mountains above Henrys Lake, between 7,000 and 8,000 feet in elevation. To reach a representative area, follow US 20 north from Macks Inn about 1.5 miles. At milepost 394.3 zero your mileage and turn left (west) on Sawtell Peak Road (a.k.a. FR 024). This is a good road, but it's closed in winter. At mile 6 you'll reach a maintenance shop on the right (north). In the evening a Boreal Owl tape can sometimes elicit a response from here on up to about mile 10, where the Whitebark Pines begin to thin out. In the whitebark forest look for Clark's Nutcrackers, White-breasted Nuthatches, Cassin's Finches, Red Crossbills, and both Evening and Pine Grosbeaks. In fall this area is hunted regularly by all three accipiters, several buteo species, and Golden Eagles. There's a radar dome at mile 11.5 with an excellent view of the flats, as well as nesting American Pipits.

OTHER:

Henrys Lake SP is open late May to October 31. If you're visiting after September 15, call ahead to check road conditions. The park offers a day-use area, a picnic area and campground, nature trail, restrooms, showers, and a boat ramp. Motels, condos, and private campgrounds are available in Island Park, as are restaurants, fuel, and groceries. Note that the "town" of Island Park is actually a loose conglomeration of houses and businesses stretching for some 30 miles along the highway. For more information call Harriman SP (208/558-7368), which manages Henrys Lake SP, or the Island Park Chamber of Commerce (208/558-7448). See also Black Canyon Road Route, the next site.

BLACK CANYON ROAD ROUTE
Authors: Peder Svingen, Sue Barton
Site SE-4 — Map SE-3/SE-4

Highlights: Clark's Nutcracker, Pine Grosbeak, Red Crossbill
Major Habitat: Mixed Conifer Forest
Location: Fremont Co., 10 miles northeast of Macks Inn
Spring: N/A   **Summer:** * * *   **Fall:** * *   **Winter:** N/A

This 20-mile route offers adventure and exploration along the Continental Divide, but it has received little attention bird-wise. A high clearance, 4-wheel-drive vehicle is required to reach the most interesting habitat.

DIRECTIONS:

From Macks Inn follow US 20 north 1.7 miles. At milepost 394.3 turn right (southeast) on FR 059 (a.k.a. Big Springs Loop Road) and go 4 miles. At the intersection of FR 059 and FR 066, zero your mileage and turn left (northeast) onto FR 066 (a.k.a. Black Canyon Loop Road).

BIRDING:

FR 066 begins by meandering through monotonous Lodgepole Pine forest. As the road climbs past the turn-off to Reas Pass, however, terrain becomes more varied and birdlife more interesting. During a June visit, you might pick up Dusky Flycatchers calling along one side of the road and a Hammond's Flycatcher answering from the other! Stop anywhere for Red-naped Sapsuckers, Mountain Chickadees, Red-breasted Nuthatches, Brown Creepers, Golden-crowned and Ruby-crowned Kinglets, Hermit Thrushes, Red Crossbills, and Pine Siskins. Many side roads in this area are gated, a situation which may actually improve birding on foot or by bicycle. At mile 9.0 you'll reach the intersection of FR 066 and FR 071. Stay right on FR 066.

At mile 9.7 you'll reach a well-marked intersection with FR 068, where you should look for Clark's Nutcrackers and raptors, especially in fall. Turn left (northeast) and follow FR 068 about 2.3 miles to the Continental Divide or to where the road becomes impassable, whichever comes first. This stretch is both scenic and productive, passing through Subalpine Fir and Whitebark Pine forest. Possibilities here include Northern Goshawks, Blue Grouse, Gray and Steller's Jays, Townsend's Solitaires, Pine Grosbeaks, and Cassin's Finches. A tape might solicit a Boreal Owl response during summer or fall evenings.

When you're able to leave this beautiful remote area, backtrack to US 20. The adventuresome birder may want to do additional exploring along FR 071 (a.k.a. Middle Road), as it too climbs to the Continental Divide.

OTHER:

Maps, road conditions, travel restrictions, and other information can be obtained from the FS (208/558-7301) or the Chamber of Commerce (208/558-7448) in Island Park. Full services are available in St. Anthony and in West Yellowstone; fuel, food, and accommodations are abundant in Island Park. See also Henrys Lake Area, the previous site.

HARRIMAN STATE PARK

Author: Kit Struthers

Site SE-5 — Map SE-5

Highlights: Red-necked Grebe, Trumpeter Swan
Major Habitats: Wetland, Mixed Conifer Forest, Meadow
Location: Fremont Co., 18 miles north of Ashton
Spring: * * *   **Summer:** * * *   **Fall:** * *   **Winter:** * *

Harriman SP is well known as a major wintering area for Trumpeter Swans. This 11,700-acre park also offers other birding attractions, as well as turn-of-the-century history. The pristine lakes and river were once the playground of several wealthy families that established the "Railroad Ranch," around which the park is centered. Buildings of that period are now open to the public.

DIRECTIONS:

From Ashton follow US 20 north to milepost 378.9. Turn left (west) onto Green Mountain Road (a.k.a. 3000 N), then immediately right (north) into the actual park entrance. Stop here to pay the $2 entrance fee, and then drive on into the park.

BIRDING:

The best way to bird Harriman is to follow the 1.5-mile-long entrance road to the picnic grounds parking area, and then explore along the 20 miles of trails. Particularly productive are the four-mile-long Silver Lake Trail and the one-mile-long Henrys Fork Trail. The 3.6-mile-long Thurman Creek Loop is recommended for forest birds.

Make sure to scan Silver Lake for Common Loons in spring and for Double-crested Cormorants and American White Pelicans throughout summer and fall. Silver Lake is also one of Idaho's most dependable spots for nesting Red-necked Grebes.

Trumpeter Swans can be found throughout the park year round. You can look for additional nesting Trumpeters at Swan Lake south of the park, at US 20 milepost 376.7. Wintering Trumpeters and Barrow's Goldeneyes are also easily observed along US 20—try Osborne Bridge (milepost 379.2), Last Chance (milepost 382.2), and Buffalo River (milepost 387.2).

Common breeding species at Harriman include Sandhill Crane, Long-billed Curlew, Belted Kingfisher, Northern Flicker, Red-naped Sapsucker, Hairy and Downy Woodpeckers, Eastern Kingbird, Olive-sided Flycatcher, Barn and Cliff Swallows, Steller's Jay, Common Raven, Black-capped and Mountain Chickadees, Red-breasted Nuthatch, Brown Creeper, American Robin, Mountain Bluebird, Ruby-crowned Kinglet, Yellow and Yellow-rumped Warblers, Western Meadowlark, Yellow-headed and Red-winged Blackbirds, Pine Siskin, Dark-eyed Junco, Chipping, White-crowned, Lincoln's, and Song Sparrows, Western Tanager, and Red Crossbill. Moose are often found in the park, especially near the creek flowing out of Silver Lake.

Trails are groomed for cross-country skiing in winter. American Three-toed Woodpeckers are seen irregularly on the Silver Lake Trail during winter, and the Gray Jays are so tame that they may even eat from your hand!

OTHER:

Maps and information are available at park headquarters (208/558-7368), at the picnic area, and at the visitors center. Pets are allowed in parking lots only. There is no camping allowed here.

Fishing, hiking, horseback riding, and mountain biking are popular attractions at the park. Full services are available in St. Anthony and in West Yellowstone; fuel, food, and accommodations are abundant in Island Park. See also Henrys Lake, p. 219.

MESA FALLS ROUTE

Author: Chuck Trost

Site SE-6 — See Southeastern map, page 214

Highlights: Great Gray Owl, American Dipper
Major Habitats: Mixed Conifer Forest, Wetland
Locations: Fremont Co., 10 miles northeast of Ashton
Spring: * *   **Summer:** * *   **Fall:** * *   **Winter:** *

Mesa Falls consists of two spectacular 70-foot waterfalls on Henrys Fork of the Snake River. The falls are contained within the same huge volcanic caldera that houses Yellowstone National Park; they were created by the river slowly cutting through massive basalt layers. The area surrounding the falls is worth exploring for typical southeast Idaho forest birds.

DIRECTIONS:

Zero your mileage in Ashton, then drive east on ID 47 (a.k.a. Mesa Falls Scenic Byway, a.k.a. FR 294) following the highway as it eventually turns northeast and then northwest. Watch for Great Gray Owls throughout this route at dawn and dusk.

At mile 15 turn left (west) at the well-signed entrance to Lower Mesa Falls, and drive 0.1 mile to the overlook. All land here is public (FS).

BIRDING:

The two Mesa Falls are surrounded by Douglas-fir and Lodgepole Pine forest, with scattered Quaking Aspen groves mixed in. Breeding birds here include Ospreys, Hairy Woodpeckers, Red-naped and Williamson's (uncommon) Sapsuckers, Cassin's Vireos, and Western Tanagers. The more extensive forest stands are good nesting habitat for Northern Goshawks. Bald Eagles and Peregrine Falcons should also be watched for, and you may spot Northern Pygmy-Owls in snags along the canyon rim.

If you're willing to do some bushwhacking, park at Lower Mesa Falls parking lot, cross the highway, and hike east through some replanted timber-harvest units. In about a mile you'll come upon a shallow 10-acre pond filled with lily pads. This is a good place to see nesting Ring-necked Ducks, Sandhill Cranes, American Coots, and Black Terns. Olive-sided and Dusky Flycatchers, Yellow-rumped Warblers, and Lincoln's Sparrows also breed here. Be prepared for *lots* of biting flies!

To reach the Upper Mesa Falls overlook, return to ID 47 and drive 0.6 mile farther north to milepost 15.8. Turn left (west) onto FR 295 and proceed 1 mile to the falls. You may want to walk this road, since it provides some of the best birding. From the parking lot at the end of the road, follow the protected walkway down to Upper Mesa Falls, and watch American Dippers at close range. Additional roadside birding is available along FR 294, which continues north 14 miles to rejoin US 20 near Harriman SP.

In winter ID 47 is plowed only to milepost 12.5 (Bear Gulch), so it is popular with snowmobilers and cross-country skiers. From Bear Gulch it is a 3.1-mile ski along the canyon's eastern rim to Lower Falls and about 4.7 miles to Upper Falls. Along the way expect Ruffed Grouse, Clark's Nutcrackers, Common Ravens, Red-breasted Nuthatches, Townsend's Solitaires, Red Crossbills, and Pine Siskins. Look on the river for Mallards, Common Goldeneyes, Common Mergansers, and American Dippers.

OTHER:

Fuel, food, and accommodations are available in Ashton. Grandview Campground (FS) is near the Lower Mesa Falls overlook. There are public restrooms at both falls. Maps and more information can be obtained from the FS stations in Ashton (208/652-7442) or Island Park (208/558-7301).

CAMAS NATIONAL WILDLIFE REFUGE

Author: Kit Struthers

Site SE-7 — Map SE-7

Highlights: Trumpeter Swan, Grasshopper Sparrow
Major Habitats: Wetland, Shrub-steppe, Farmland
Location: Jefferson Co., 36 miles north of Idaho Falls
Spring: * * * *   **Summer:** * * * * **Fall:** * *   **Winter:** * *

Covering 10,500 acres, Camas NWR is part of a large-scale wetland complex encompassing nearby Mud Lake and Market Lake WMAs (see p. 229 and p. 232). Each of these areas has something different. At Camas NWR, the specialties are nesting Trumpeter Swans, Peregrine Falcons, migrant warblers, and grassland birds.

DIRECTIONS:

Camas NWR is accessed from the small town of Hamer. To get there from I-15, take Exit 150 and drive east 0.4 mile, passing through Hamer. At the T intersection, turn left (north) and proceed for 3 miles, then turn left (west) onto 2350 N, crossing I-15 on an overpass and entering Camas NWR in 2 miles. Park at the refuge office, then look in the information board at the rear of the parking lot for a map and a bird list.

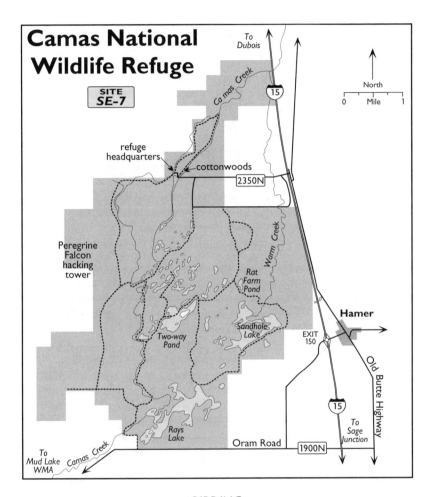

Camas National Wildlife Refuge

SITE
SE-7

To Dubois

Camas Creek

15

North

0   Mile   1

refuge headquarters

cottonwoods

2350N

Peregrine Falcon hacking tower

Warm Creek

Rat Farm Pond

Sandhole Lake

Hamer

EXIT 150

Two-way Pond

Rays Lake

15

Old Butte Highway

To Sage Junction

Oram Road

1900N

To Mud Lake WMA

Camas Creek

BIRDING:

About 100 yards east of the refuge office, on the north side of the entrance road, is a double row of cottonwoods bordering a road and a canal. Leave your car at the refuge office and walk along the cottonwoods, which in spring can be alive with migrants. Olive-sided Flycatchers, Red-breasted Nuthatches, Ruby-crowned Kinglets, Hermit and Swainson's Thrushes, Townsend's Solitaires, most of Idaho's warblers (including Northern Waterthrushes), and Western Tanagers have all been found, as have vagrant Yellow-billed Cuckoos, Least Flycatchers, Yellow-throated Vireos, Black-and-white and Blackpoll Warblers, Northern Parula, Tropical Kingbird, and Baltimore Orioles! During summer look for nesting Red-tailed Hawks, House Wrens, Warbling Vireos, and Bullock's Orioles.

Lilacs and other shrubs surrounding headquarters harbor roosting Common Nighthawks as well as nesting Orange-crowned, Yellow, and Yellow-rumped Warblers, Black-headed Grosbeaks, and Lazuli Buntings. Large trees often have American Kestrels and Great Horned Owls, and attract roosting Bald Eagles in winter. A double row of cottonwoods to the north of headquarters holds nesting Long-eared Owls, various flycatchers, MacGillivray's and Wilson's Warblers, and White-crowned and Song Sparrows. You'll likely see "Unauthorized Entry Prohibited" signs around headquarters. Birding here is an authorized activity—but please avoid disturbing the manager's home.

After birding headquarters, drive the graveled road that heads west from the parking lot. In about a mile you'll reach a hay meadow which sometimes floods in spring, attracting Green-winged Teal and other ducks. The road bends left (south) through sage and grass, 1.2 miles west of headquarters. Watch for Savannah, Grasshopper, Vesper, and Lark Sparrows in spring and summer, and listen for Rock Wrens. A distant hacking tower is visible to the right (southwest). With a scope you may be able to see a pair of nesting Peregrine Falcons there. This road soon becomes rough. It is usually best to turn around here and return to headquarters.

Back at headquarters, turn south at the information board and drive into the heart of the refuge. You'll soon enter a maze of dike roads, allowing you to explore the refuge's interior. Look for Eared, Western, and Pied-billed Grebes, American White Pelicans, Great Blue Herons, Great, Snowy, and Cattle Egrets, Black-crowned Night-Herons, American Bitterns, White-faced Ibises, Trumpeter Swans, Canada, Snow, and Ross's (rare migrant) Geese, Cinnamon Teal, Common and Red-breasted (migration only) Mergansers, Golden Eagles, Sandhill Cranes, Virginia Rails, Soras, American Avocets, Long-billed Curlews, Willets, and Short-eared Owls.

There's also good birding south of Hamer on "Old Butte Highway" (a.k.a. Old Highway 91). Look for Ferruginous Hawks, Loggerhead Shrikes, Sage Thrashers, and Sage and Brewer's Sparrows along this frontage road. Burrowing Owls have been found on the right (west) side of Old Butte Highway. To look for the birds, drive 4.8 miles south of Hamer, then drive or walk the dirt 2-track which leads 0.25 mile west to the interstate. You'll know that you're on the right 2-track if it passes beneath the interstate in a "tunnel" underpass. The owls nest in ground-squirrel mounds on the east side of the interstate. *Please limit your disturbance of these owls.*

OTHER:

The refuge office is often closed, but the refuge itself is open year round, from a half hour before sunrise to a half hour after sunset. Hiking is permitted July 16 to February 28. During nesting season (March 1 to July 15), you'll be restricted to birding from roads only. Hunting is allowed in season, during which period additional access restrictions may apply. For more information call the refuge (208/662-5423).

There's a general store in Hamer. Additional services are available in Dubois, Rexburg, and Idaho Falls. The closest camping is in Roberts. There are no restrooms at Camas NWR. The truck weigh station at Sage Junction has a public restroom, but it's open only when the weigh station is operating.

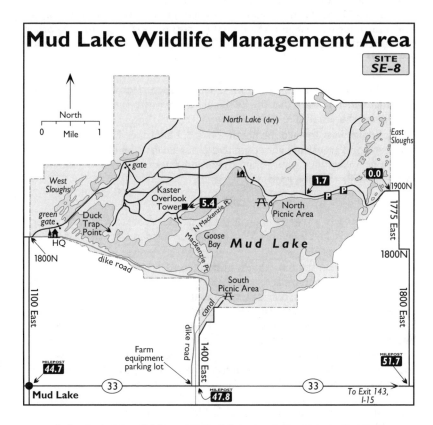

MUD LAKE WILDLIFE MANAGEMENT AREA
Author: Kit Struthers
Site SE-8 — Map SE-8

Highlights: Waders, Snow and Ross's Geese
Major Habitats: Wetland, Shrub-steppe
Location: Jefferson Co., 30 miles northwest of Idaho Falls
Spring: * * * *   **Summer:** * * *   **Fall:** * * *   **Winter:** *

In mid-March even non-birders come to Mud Lake WMA to view the spectacle of 50,000 Snow Geese filling the sky. During summer and fall, concentrations of wading birds and shorebirds can also be very impressive.

DIRECTIONS:

From Sage Junction (I-15 Exit 143) drive 7 miles west on ID 33. At milepost 51.7 turn right (north) on 1800 East. Stay left (straight) at the Y in 2 miles. After crossing Camas Creek (about 3 miles north of ID 33), turn left (west) on 1800 North for 0.2 mile, then turn right (north) on 1775 East. After another mile turn left (west) on 1900 North and follow it to the WMA's east entrance in 0.5 mile. There are small signs indicating the way to the WMA at each intersection.

At the east entrance, stop at the information board for a bird list and zero your mileage. Be aware that the WMA brochure's map can be confusing, especially for the north side of Mud Lake.

Continue west toward the north shore of Mud Lake. Road quality varies between good gravel and very primitive 2-track dirt. The dirt roads may require a high-clearance vehicle, and they can be very muddy and slick after a rain; especially the dike road.

BIRDING:

At mile 0.4 is a tree clump on the right (northwest) where Northern Saw-whet Owls, MacGillivray's Warblers, Black-headed Grosbeaks, and Bullock's Orioles nest.

Parking lots on the left (south) at mile 1 and 1.4 allow you to scan Mud Lake. In mid-March there are usually 300 to 500 Ross's Geese mixed in with the thousands of Snows, but it's often easier to pick 'em out if you can catch the flocks feeding in fields bordering the WMA. There are usually several Bald Eagles watching the geese, as well! Other waterfowl using Mud Lake include Western Grebes (check for Clark's), Tundra and Trumpeter Swans, Canada Geese, Mallards, Gadwalls, Northern Pintails, Green-winged, Blue-winged, and Cinnamon Teals, Eurasian (rare) and American Wigeons, Northern Shovelers, Wood Ducks, Redheads, Canvasbacks, Ring-necked Ducks, Lesser Scaup, Common Goldeneyes, Buffleheads, Ruddy Ducks, and Common, Hooded, and Red-breasted Mergansers. The greatest waterfowl numbers occur in March and April, with smaller numbers in late August and early September.

At mile 1.7 the road forks. Go straight for 0.5 mile, then turn left (south) to the northern picnic-area/primitive-camping spot. The tree groves are good for songbirds, including Black-capped Chickadees, House and Marsh Wrens, Bullock's Orioles, and various warblers and sparrows. Past vagrants on the WMA have included Yellow-billed Cuckoos and Common Grackles. Additional views of Mud Lake and more woodland-type birding can be found along the road between the picnic area turn-off and the "Secondary Headquarters" (see map).

To see the rest of the WMA's north side, backtrack to the road fork (0.5 mile east of the picnic area turn-off) and turn left (north) on a rough dirt road which leads through irrigated farmland. Follow the map and signs to "Kaster Overlook Tower" in 3.7 miles. Look here for nesting Double-crested Cormorants, Great Blue Herons, Great, Snowy, and Cattle Egrets, Black-crowned Night-Herons, and vagrant Green Herons, as well as deer, Elk, and Moose. American Bitterns can sometimes be seen (or more likely heard) in nearby marshes.

Waterfowl, Western Screech-Owls, Northern Saw-whet Owls, and bees all use Wood Duck nest boxes along the north shore of Mud Lake, particularly on MacKenzie Point and Duck Trap Point. You can bird more shrub-steppe habitat by continuing west along the dirt 2-track from the tower, but a high-clearance vehicle is recommended. This road will take you past Duck Trap Point and eventually gets you to a canal where a gate blocks access into the West Slough Area during nesting season. Because of this gate, during most of the year you cannot complete a loop. To bird the WMA's south side, backtrack to ID 33 and turn right (west). At ID 33 milepost 47.8, turn right (north) on 1400 East (on the east side of the canal) and drive 2.3 miles to the WMA's southern boat ramp/picnic-area/primitive-camping spot. After investigating the willow shrubs, the trees, and the wetlands, return to ID 33 and continue west.

In the town of Mud Lake, at ID 33 milepost 44.7, turn right (north) on 1100 East and go 3 miles, then turn right (east) onto 1800 N. Park here and walk the graveled road which parallels the canal northeast on the canal's west bank. In 0.4 mile you'll reach a green metal gate which is locked during nesting season. Go behind the gate and walk the dike northeast to view the West Slough Area. Please stay on the dike when visiting between January 15 and August 30. The West Slough Area hosts White-faced Ibis and Franklin's Gull colonies, and is good for wading birds, shorebirds, and terns. Watch for Peregrine Falcons.

From the junction of 1100 East and 1800 North, continue east on 1800 North. About 1 mile east of the junction, the road swings south on 1200 East. Continue straight on 1800 North as it turns into a graveled 2-track dike road, and follow it 4.1 miles to its terminus on ID 33, in a farm-equipment parking lot. Cattle Egrets, Black-crowned Night-Herons, and shorebirds sometimes feed in large numbers in the field south of the dike road. Listen for Soras in marshy areas.

Most of the common shorebirds, including Killdeer, Black-necked Stilts, American Avocets, Willets, Long-billed Curlews, Spotted, Western, Least, Baird's, and Pectoral Sandpipers, Long-billed Dowitchers, and Wilson's Phalaropes migrate through Mud Lake WMA, with numbers peaking in May. Specific locations used depend on water-level. Some stay to nest.

Watch for Greater Sage-Grouse, Gray Partridge, Sandhill Cranes, Great Horned and Short-eared Owls, Northern Harriers, Eastern and Western Kingbirds, and Sage Thrashers in suitable habitat throughout the WMA. Greater Sage-Grouse are most likely to be seen on the WMA's north side.

In winter bird diversity and abundance decline markedly, but you can still find wintering waterfowl, Northern Goshawks, Rough-legged Hawks, Golden and Bald Eagles, Ring-necked Pheasants, Gray Partridge, and American Tree Sparrows.

OTHER:

Mud Lake WMA is open for visitation year round. It is popular with boaters, fisherman, and hunters. There are no established visiting hours. Limited facilities (fuel, groceries, cafe) are available in Mud Lake; full facilities can be found in Idaho Falls. Pit toilets, grills, and picnic tables are available at the primitive camping spots (no potable water) and at Kaster Overlook Tower. There are restrooms and a pop-and-juice machine at the weigh station at Sage Junction, but the door is locked unless the weigh station is operating. For more information call the WMA (208/663-4664).

MARKET LAKE WILDLIFE MANAGEMENT AREA
Author: Kit Struthers
Site SE-9 — Map SE-9

Highlights: American Bittern, Black-necked Stilt, Long-eared Owl
Major Habitats: Wetland, Farmland, Deciduous Forest
Location: Jefferson Co., 20 miles north of Idaho Falls
Spring: ✳✳✳✳ **Summer:** ✳✳✳ **Fall:** ✳✳✳ **Winter:** ✳

Five-thousand-acre Market Lake WMA is a favorite birding site for local birders, since bird diversity and numbers are high here. Spring and summer evenings are the best time to visit, when light conditions are most favorable and the distant Teton Mountains most impressive.

DIRECTIONS:

From I-15 take Exit 135 and go east 0.3 mile into Roberts. At the stop-sign turn north on ID 48 (a.k.a. 2880 East). Just beyond the north edge of town, stay right at the Y intersection. About 1.6 miles north of town, turn right (east) on 800 N. After 0.5 mile, turn left (north) on 2900 E, then turn right (east) into the WMA headquarters (signed). At the headquarters, pick up a bird list and a brochure. Be aware that graveled and dirt roads in the WMA are sometimes rutty and/or muddy.

BIRDING:

There is no one best way to bird this area; just drive and walk the numerous roads. Local birders spend most of their time at Main Marsh because it's so convenient and has so many birds, but East Springs Marsh often produces unique species, notably Green-winged Teal and shorebirds.

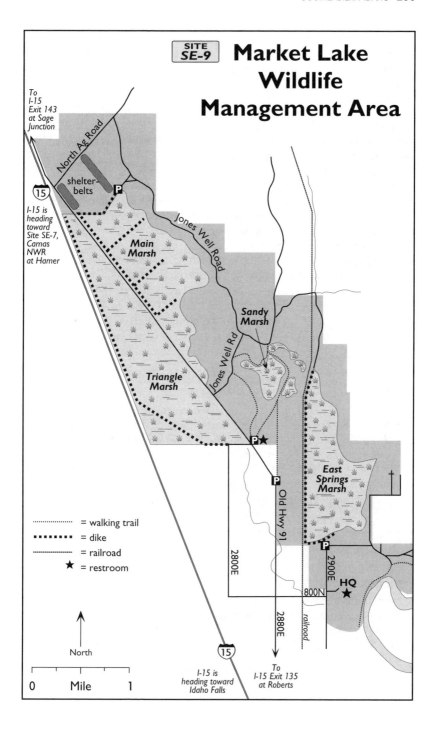

SITE
SE-9

Market Lake
Wildlife
Management Area

To
I-15
Exit 143
at Sage
Junction

North Ag Road

shelter-
belts

P

15

I-15 is
heading
toward
Site SE-7,
Camas
NWR
at Hamer

Jones Well Road

**Main
Marsh**

**Sandy
Marsh**

Jones Well Rd

**Triangle
Marsh**

P ★

P

**East
Springs
Marsh**

P

.... = walking trail

■■■■■■■■ = dike

———————— = railroad

★ = restroom

2800E

Old Hwy 91

2900E

HQ
★

800N

2880E

railroad

↑
North

0   Mile   1

15

I-15 is
heading toward
Idaho Falls

To
I-15 Exit 135
at Roberts

To find East Springs Marsh from headquarters, head north on 2900 E. In 0.4 mile pull into the lot on the left (west) and park. Walk through the gate in the northeast corner of the parking lot, cross the canal, and then follow the main dike to the west and north to view open water and mudflats. Among the possible shorebirds are Red-necked Phalaropes during May and July, Black-necked Stilts and Willets during summer, and Black-bellied Plovers and American Golden-Plovers during fall. You may also find Long-billed Curlews in the tall grass to the east of East Springs Marsh. Rarities have included Marbled Godwits (spring) and Stilt Sandpipers (July).

To explore the rest of the WMA, backtrack all the way to the intersection of 800 N and 2850 E (see map), and follow 2850 E north to Main and Triangle Marshes. Watch the small ponds along the way for Blue-winged Teal, Greater Yellowlegs, and Wilson's and Red-necked Phalaropes. If you have a high-clearance vehicle (and if the road is open), you can bird shrub-steppe habitat by taking the 4.5-mile-long Jones Well/N. Ag Road loop (see map). At Main and Triangle Marshes listen for American Bitterns, Virginia Rails, and Soras at dusk. Keep an eye out for the distinctive, moth-like flight of the Short-eared Owl.

During spring migration (usually late March) search the Snow Goose flocks for Ross's Geese. Later in the year, note the reliable American Coots. It's fun to watch their babies bob around on the water! Other summer species include Eared, Western, Clark's, and Pied-billed Grebes, Great Blue Heron, Great, Snowy, and Cattle (rare) Egrets, Black-crowned Night-Heron, White-faced Ibis, California, Ring-billed, and Franklin's Gulls, and Forster's and Black Terns. Vagrant species have included Tricolored Heron, Eurasian Wigeon, Common Moorhen, and Western Gull.

At the north end of Main Marsh are two shelterbelts. Great Horned Owls nest in the western tree-row; Long-eared Owls, in the eastern. These trees are also great for songbirds. During April a Varied Thrush or two might be present, as may a Plumbeous Vireo. Spring warbler species have included Yellow, Yellow-rumped, MacGillivray's, Virginia's, Black-throated Gray, Townsend's, and American Redstart.

Several raptors hunt Market Lake WMA throughout the year. Northern Harriers and Prairie and Peregrine Falcons may be seen year round, while Bald Eagles, Rough-legged Hawks, and Gyrfalcons (rare) are most likely in winter or early spring.

OTHER:

Market Lake is open all year, but it has no established visiting hours. Portions of the WMA are closed to protect wildlife. Fuel, groceries, and a cafe are available in Roberts. Full facilities can be found in Idaho Falls. The closest camping is in Roberts. There's an outhouse at the headquarters and another at the Sandy Marsh parking lot. For more information, phone the WMA (208/228-3131).

TEX CREEK WILDLIFE MANAGEMENT AREA

Author: Greg Rice

Site SE-10 — Map SE-10

Highlights: Gamebirds, Green-tailed Towhee
Major Habitats: Deciduous Forest, Grassland
Location: Bonneville Co., 16 miles east of Idaho Falls
Spring: N/A   **Summer:** * * *   **Fall:** * *   **Winter:** N/A

Tex Creek WMA is a contorted, meandering preserve encompassing about 28,300 acres. Although the WMA's primary use is as big game winter range, it also provides great habitat for Gray Partridge, Ring-necked Pheasants, and Blue, Ruffed, and Sharp-tailed Grouse.

For explorer-types, Tex Creek's prime allure will be its total obscurity. Almost no one knows about this place, and those who do don't know how to find it! There's a good reason for all this mystique: the WMA's unique shape makes giving directions a full-day affair!

DIRECTIONS:

Before leaving Idaho Falls, stock up on fuel, food, and water, and kiss your loved ones goodbye; you'll be gone a spell. (Actually, if the roads are good, the WMA headquarters are only about an hour from Idaho Falls.) Follow US 26 northeast 14 miles. At milepost 350.7 turn right (south) on paved/graveled Meadow Creek Road (a.k.a. 145th East), and zero your mileage. At the Y at mile 6, stay right (south). You'll immediately begin descending a steep rocky road ("Call Dugway"); watch for Rock Wrens, Green-tailed Towhees, and, in late summer, the beautiful and tenacious yellow Blazing Stars. Be aware that the WMA's graveled/dirt roads can get slick with even slight moisture. Prolonged rains leave some roads impassable for days.

BIRDING:

LOWER MEADOW CREEK and HEADQUARTERS

At mile 7 you'll reach the canyon floor along the lower reaches of Meadow Creek (private land). Park and walk the road to find Calliope and Rufous Hummingbirds, Downy Woodpeckers, Red-naped Sapsuckers, Cordilleran and Willow Flycatchers, Western Wood-Pewees, Common Yellowthroats, Wilson's and Yellow Warblers, Yellow-breasted Chats, Gray Catbirds, Swainson's Thrushes, Green-tailed Towhees, Black-headed Grosbeaks, Lazuli Buntings, and Bullock's Orioles. Look overhead for Turkey Vultures, Bald and Golden Eagles, Red-tailed Hawks, American Kestrels, and Northern Harriers. Keep watch on the hillside for Moose, deer, and Elk.

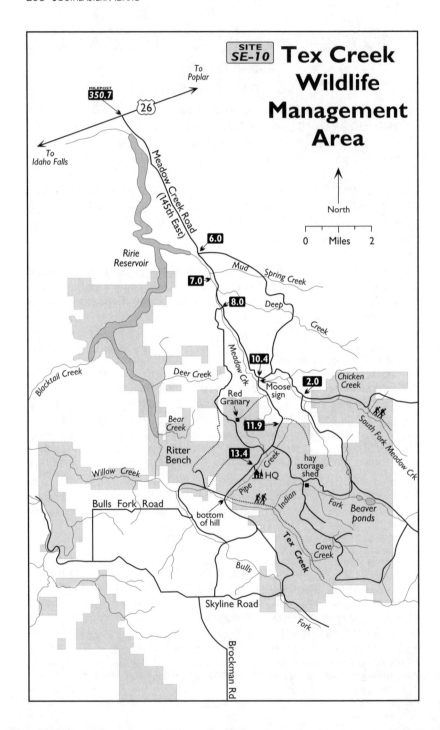

SITE
SE-10

Tex Creek Wildlife Management Area

At mile 8 stay left at the Y. At mile 10.4 is yet another Y. This one is marked with a large sign cautioning hunters to be aware of their target. This "Moose sign" is an important landmark on the road maze; note its location, then go right (south), and start climbing out of the canyon along Blue Creek. Along this stretch you'll pass Quaking Aspen patches, which should be searched for Ruffed Grouse, Mountain and Black-capped Chickadees, Ruby-crowned Kinglets, Yellow-rumped and MacGillivray's Warblers, and Western Tanagers. The road is pretty gnarly, so it's best birded on foot after finding a safe place to park. Be aware that the land off the road is private.

At mile 11.9 you enter Tex Creek WMA and descend along Pipe Creek to the WMA's headquarters at mile 13.4. The H.Q. is centrally located and is a good starting point for further exploration. Before leaving the headquarters, however, consider hiking the surrounding grasslands for Sharp-tailed Grouse and other grassland birds.

RED GRANARY

For additional gamebird opportunities visit Red Granary. From headquarters go back up the road northeast along Pipe Creek about 0.3 mile, then turn left (north) and follow the road 1.5 miles. On the way watch farm fields, mixed grass prairie, and shrub-steppe for Sharp-tailed and Greater Sage-Grouse and Gray Partridge. A closed farm road behind the granary takes off to the northeast. Walk this "trail" and venture into the fields to try to spook something out. Be prepared to do a lot of hoofing!

INDIAN FORK

From headquarters go back up the road northeast along Pipe Creek about 0.6 mile, then turn right (east) and drive the winding road through the low, open valley. After 1.5 miles stay straight (left) at the Y by the hay shed. Two miles beyond the hay shed, turn sharp right and head southeast. In another 0.5 mile you'll reach a beaver pond that's good for waterfowl. Snowy Egrets, White-faced Ibises, and Sandhill Cranes are possible here. The WMA's eastern boundary is about a mile farther down the road. You should turn around somewhere soon, since the road deteriorates quickly once you leave the WMA.

UPPER MEADOW CREEK

Arguably the WMA's best birding is along the upper reaches of Meadow Creek. Certainly one of the nicest hikes to be had is along South Fork Meadow Creek. (By the way, don't be fooled by all of this "South Fork"/"North Fork" business. The creeks are hardly big enough to warrant a name, let alone a pretentious "South Fork"!) To find Upper Meadow Creek from headquarters, follow the road northeast along Pipe Creek and descend down along Blue Creek. At the "Moose sign" turn right (east) and re-zero your mileage. Stay right at the intersection at mile 0.8 and you'll reach a gate. The landowner allows the public to drive through the gate to access Tex

Creek WMA at mile 2.1. *Please leave the gate as you found it.* Stay left at the Y at mile 2.0 (see map). At about mile 3.9 is the South Meadow Creek Trailhead (a semi-cleared area with a small sign) on the right (south). Walk the old farm road "trail" up South Fork Meadow Creek, looking for typical riparian birds. You'll reach Douglas-fir forest on Mount Baldy in a few miles. Search here for Blue Grouse, Northern Goshawks, White-breasted Nuthatches, and Brown Creepers.

TEX CREEK

Tex Creek is yet another mini-canyon. From headquarters go southwest paralleling Pipe Creek downstream about 1.5 miles. At the bottom of the hill you can walk the trail upstream or turn right (west) and continue birding from your car. You'll pass more low riparian willow habitat that harbors high numbers of Rock Wrens, Black-headed Grosbeaks, Green-tailed Towhees, and Lazuli Buntings. You can continue exploring as far upstream or downstream as time and road conditions permit.

OTHER:

There is a developed campground at the Ririe Dam Recreation Area, about 2 miles south of US 26 on Meadow Creek Road. The closest lodging is in Idaho Falls. Fuel and food can be had at the truck stop on US 26, about 1.5 miles west of the Meadow Creek turn-off. For more information and a handy brochure, call the WMA (208/525-7290).

Green-tailed Towhee
Mike Denny

SAND CREEK WILDLIFE MANAGEMENT AREA

Authors: Dan and Ila Svingen

Site SE-11 — Map SE-11

Highlights: Greater Sage-Grouse and Sharp-tailed Grouse
Major Habitats: Shrub-steppe, Wetland
Location: Fremont Co., 9 miles north of St. Anthony
Spring: * *   **Summer:** *   **Fall:** *   **Winter:** N/A

Sand Creek WMA is managed as big-game winter range and is popular with off-road-vehicle enthusiasts, sightseers, hunters, and fishermen. Unfortunately, birders have given the WMA scant attention, so little is known of the site's avian potential. There are at least three productive areas to bird here: White Sands Road, Sand Creek Ponds, and Rick's Pasture Road.

DIRECTIONS:

To access the WMA's main route (Sand Creek Road) from St. Anthony, follow Business US 20 east from the north edge of town 1.5 miles, then turn left (north) onto Sand Creek Road, just before crossing the Del Rio Bridge. Zero your mileage here. At mile 1.4 stay left. You'll enter public land (BLM, IDFG) at mile 9.4.

If you don't have a high-clearance vehicle, you may want to restrict your birding to Sand Creek Road. If the area is particularly dry (and thus sandy), remember that a 4-wheel-drive comes in mighty handy!

BIRDING:

The best way to find the WMA's Greater Sage-Grouse and Sharp-tailed Grouse is to visit March to May. Contact headquarters before visiting to learn the status of active leks. During the rest of the year, Sharp-taileds are closely associated with scattered Chokecherry clumps bordering sand dunes, while Greater Sage-Grouse can be found almost anywhere.

WHITE SANDS ROAD

White Sands Road (a dirt/sand 2-track) heads southwest from Sand Creek Road, 11 miles north of Del Rio Bridge. About 3.7 miles down White Sands Road is Miller's Well, an abandoned farmstead containing relatively luxurious grass. Walk around here for Greater Sage-Grouse, Say's Phoebes, and Savannah and Vesper Sparrows. About 2.0 miles southwest of Miller's Well, you'll reach Black Knoll, a vegetated, low sand ridge on the left (south). This is the type of habitat preferred by Sharp-tailed Grouse, Dusky Flycatchers, Blue-gray Gnatcatchers, Yellow-breasted Chats, Lazuli Buntings, and Bullock's Orioles.

Continuing southwest on White Sands Road, you'll find all kinds of side roads. It is often difficult to determine which is the "main" road, so it helps to

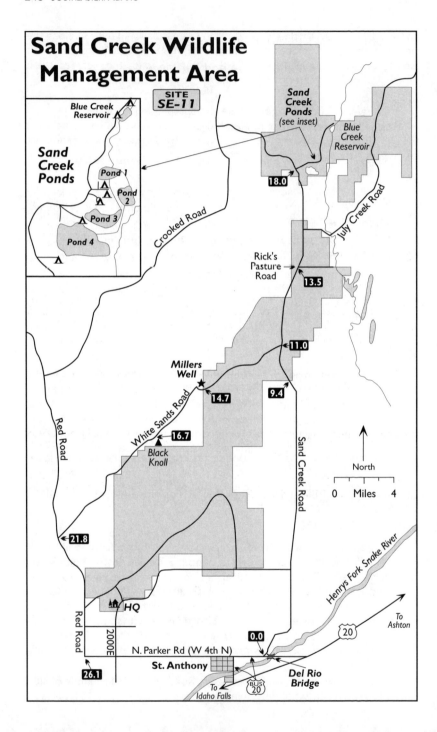

Sand Creek Wildlife Management Area

SITE
SE-11

Sand Creek Ponds (see inset)

Blue Creek Reservoir

Sand Creek Ponds

Blue Creek Reservoir

Pond 1

Pond 2

Pond 3

Pond 4

Crooked Road

18.0

July Creek Road

Rick's Pasture Road

13.5

11.0

Millers Well

14.7

9.4

White Sands Road

16.7

Black Knoll

Red Road

Sand Creek Road

North

0   Miles   4

21.8

Henrys Fork Snake River

HQ

Red Road

2000E

0.0

To Ashton

20

26.1

N. Parker Rd (W 4th N)

St. Anthony

Del Rio Bridge

To Idaho Falls

BUS 20

know that there are cattle-guards along White Sands Road but not along the side roads. Approximately 5.1 miles southwest of Black Knoll, turn left (south) on well-maintained Red Road. After 4.3 miles turn left (east) on North Parker Road and drive 4.5 miles to return to St. Anthony.

RICK'S PASTURE ROAD

Rick's Pasture Road heads east from Sand Creek Road, 13.5 miles north of the Del Rio Bridge. After a mile Rick's Pasture Road forks; stay right and start investigating the Chokecherry habitats for grouse.

SAND CREEK PONDS

Follow Sand Creek Road 18 miles north from Del Rio Bridge to bird the WMA's northernmost segment, which contains Sand Creek Ponds and most of the bird diversity. A portion of this area may be closed during spring and summer to protect nesting Trumpeter Swans. If the road is open, check the four ponds and Blue Creek Reservoir for Western and Pied-billed Grebes, Great Blue Herons, Black-crowned Night-Herons, various waterfowl, Ospreys, Bald Eagles, Marsh Wrens, and Yellow-headed Blackbirds. The road to Blue Creek Reservoir passes by Quaking Aspen clumps containing Swainson's Hawks, Ruffed Grouse, Red-naped Sapsuckers, Warbling Vireos, Yellow Warblers, and Lazuli Buntings.

OTHER:

A brochure and a map are available at WMA headquarters, which is on the southeast corner of the WMA. To get there from St. Anthony, go to the north side of town and turn left (west) on West Fourth North Street (a.k.a. North Parker Road). After 4 miles turn right (north) on 2000 East and follow it 1.5 miles to headquarters. The brochure map is not very detailed, but USGS quadrangle maps can be purchased from the US Geological Survey (888/ASK-USGS). "Black Knoll" map covers White Sands Road.

Much of the WMA is closed to protect wintering big game. Primitive campsites are available at Sand Creek Ponds. For more information, call the WMA (208/624-7065).

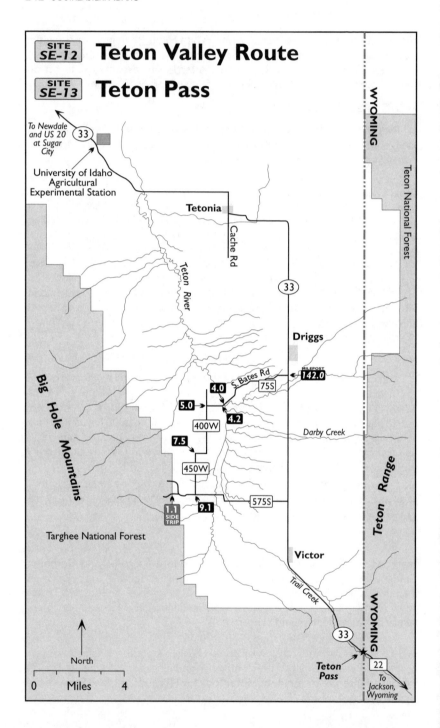

SITE
SE-12 **Teton Valley Route**

SITE
SE-13 **Teton Pass**

To Newdale
and US 20
at Sugar
City

University of Idaho
Agricultural
Experimental Station

WYOMING

Teton National Forest

Tetonia

Cache Rd

Teton River

33

Driggs

S. Bates Rd

MILEPOST
142.0

4.0

75S

5.0

4.2

400W

Darby Creek

7.5

450W

Big Hole Mountains

575S

Teton Range

1.1
SIDE
TRIP

9.1

Targhee National Forest

Victor

Trail Creek

North

33

0   Miles   4

WYOMING

Teton Pass

22

To Jackson, Wyoming

TETON VALLEY ROUTE

Author: Susan Patla

Site SE-12 — Map SE-12/SE-13

Highlights: Trumpeter Swan, Sandhill Crane, Common Grackle
Major Habitats: Meadow, Farmland, Mixed Conifer Forest
Location: Teton Co., Driggs
Spring: ***   **Summer:** **   **Fall:** **** **Winter:** ***

Teton Valley is a high-elevation valley known for its spectacular recreation and scenery. Bordered on three sides by the Teton, Snake River, and Big Hole Mountain Ranges, the valley contains a variety of bird habitats. One of Idaho's most impressive birding events occurs here in mid-September, when thousands of Sandhill Cranes congregate by the river before departing for New Mexico. In most years, a large number of wintering Trumpeter Swans can be observed along the 20-mile loop described below.

DIRECTIONS:

Before you leave Driggs, be sure to look for Common Grackles. A few are usually present in residential areas, April to October. To start this route, zero your odometer at Driggs Key Bank and head south on ID 33. At mile 0.7 (milepost 142) turn right (west) onto graveled S. Bates Road (a.k.a. 75 S). Follow S. Bates Road as it winds toward the river, stopping to scan fields, shrubs, and trees. *All land along this route is privately owned, unless otherwise noted.*

BIRDING:

In spring Swainson's Hawks, Northern Harriers, Long-billed Curlews, Willets, Wilson's Snipe, Short-eared Owls, Sandhill Cranes, and Mountain Bluebirds are often seen in meadows along S. Bates Road. At mile 1.6 listen for Bobolinks. Rough-legged Hawks frequent this stretch of road in winter, as does the occasional Great Horned or Great Gray Owl. Northern Shrikes can often be found foraging from willows or utility wires.

After crossing Teton River (mile 4.0), stay left. A quick stop in spring or summer may yield Cinnamon Teal, Yellow Warblers, and White-crowned Sparrows, while a winter look will likely produce Barrow's and Common Goldeneyes and American Tree Sparrows. At mile 4.2 park in the pull-out on the left (south) and scope the river and marsh for grebes, Tundra and Trumpeter (winter) Swans, various ducks, and Sandhill Cranes (September: spectacular flights at sunrise and sunset).

At mile 5.0 turn left (south) on 400 W. In late summer, migrating Red-tailed, Ferruginous, and Swainson's Hawks, American Kestrels, and an occasional Peregrine Falcon perch on poles and irrigation-rig wheels. Prairie Falcons are seen year round. In winter look for Horned Larks and Snow Buntings along the roadside. Follow the road as it curves right (west) at mile 7.0.

At mile 7.5 turn left (south) on paved 450 W. At mile 8.6 you pass a small pond on the right (west) which should be scoped for swans, ducks, and Wilson's Phalaropes (spring).

At mile 9.1 turn left (east) on 575 S to return to the river and ID 33 or take a side trip into the hills (see below). Driving back over the river, be alert for Golden and Bald Eagles year round, and for Ospreys in summer. Belted Kingfishers, American Tree Sparrows (winter), and Great Blue Herons are common. Check willow patches and scattered cottonwood groves along the road for other surprises such as summering Red-eyed Vireos or wintering Bohemian Waxwings. Back at ID 33, turn left to return to Driggs or right to reach Victor.

If you want to explore the conifer/Quaking Aspen forest on the west side of the valley, zero your mileage at the junction of 450 W and 575 S and turn right (west) on 575 S. This road soon winds through a maze of small ranchettes...telling the difference between the "main" road and driveways can be tough—at mile 0.3 stay left, at mile 0.6 stay right, at mile 0.7 stay left, and at mile 0.8 stay right! If you don't get lost, you'll reach a cattle-guard marking the start of the Targhee NF (signed) at mile 1.1. From here you can walk along the rutted dirt road, looking for Calliope Hummingbirds, Black-headed Grosbeaks, Olive-sided, Hammond's, and Dusky Flycatchers, Mountain Chickadees, Western Tanagers, MacGillivray's Warblers, and Swainson's Thrushes. Be careful crossing electric or barbed-wire fences.

For additional winter birding, return to Driggs, re-zero your mileage, and follow ID 33 north. At mile 8.3 turn left (south) on Cache Road. Great Gray Owls are often seen in roadside trees by the rodeo grounds, between miles 9.2 and 9.5, but numbers vary year-to-year. *All land here is private.* After returning to ID 33, turn left and continue west. Horned Larks, Gray-crowned Rosy-Finches, and Snow Buntings are sometimes seen along the highway, especially near the University of Idaho Experiment Station east of Newdale.

OTHER:

Both Driggs and Victor have accommodations, fuel, and a number of interesting restaurants. The Victor Emporium's huckleberry shakes are of national fame! Area maps and more info can be obtained from the FS (208/354-2312), just south of Driggs. There are several primitive FS campgrounds in the area, as well as a private campground in Victor.

TETON PASS

Authors: Peder Svingen and Sue Barton
Site SE-13 — Map SE-12/SE-13

Highlights: Clark's Nutcracker, Cassin's Finch
Major Habitat: Mixed Conifer Forest
Location: Teton Co., 6 miles southeast of Victor
Spring: * *   **Summer:** * *   **Fall:** *   **Winter:** * *

This is not a major birding area, but it does offer easy access to alpine habitat. Even without birds, stunning wildflowers in late summer and spectacular mountain views makes this a worthwhile stop any time of the year.

DIRECTIONS:

From Victor follow ID 33 southeast 6 miles to the Teton Pass parking area. Park and walk south on the relatively flat graveled road signed "Wildlife Viewing Area." The road ends near a communications station in 0.5 mile. Be aware that ID 33 is subject to periodic closure in winter.

BIRDING:

Teton Pass is good for Clark's Nutcrackers year round. In addition, "winter finches," including Cassin's Finches, Red Crossbills, and Pine Siskins, nest here. Also watch for Red-naped Sapsuckers, Hairy Woodpeckers, Mountain Chickadees, Brown Creepers, Golden-crowned Kinglets, Red-breasted Nuthatches, Hermit Thrushes, Yellow-rumped Warblers, Western Tanagers, White-crowned Sparrows, and Dark-eyed Juncos. Black-chinned, Calliope, and Broad-tailed Hummingbirds should be looked for around wildflowers. In winter any of the finches are possible, although rosy-finches are unlikely. Calling for Boreal Owls may be worthwhile anytime.

OTHER:

Food, fuel, and lodging are available in Victor, Idaho, or Jackson, Wyoming. There is a private campground in Victor, and a primitive FS campground at Mike Harris Trailhead, 4 miles southeast of Victor. The rugged, 4-mile-long Mike Harris Trail leads to more alpine birding on Oliver Peak (elevation 9,004 feet). Maps and additional information can be obtained from the FS (208/354-2312), just south of Driggs. See also Teton Valley Route, the previous site.

WOLVERINE CANYON ROUTE

Author: Kit Struthers

Site SE-14 — Map SE-14

Highlights: Flammulated Owl, Common Poorwill
Major Habitats: Mixed Conifer Forest, Shrub-steppe
Location: Bingham Co., Shelley
Spring: *** **Summer:** *** **Fall:** * **Winter:** N/A

Wolverine Canyon is an unexpectedly rugged and beautiful canyon, about a half hour's drive south of Idaho Falls. This 29-mile route follows Wolverine Creek uphill, through willow, sage/juniper, and cliff habitats and ends in mixed conifer forest on a 7,100-foot summit.

DIRECTIONS:

Zero your mileage at I-15 Exit 113 and drive 4 miles south to Shelley, following "US 91 South" (a.k.a. State Street) through town. At mile 5.3 turn left (east) on Baseline Road (a.k.a. 1200 North). At mile 6.0 turn right (south) on Sugar Factory Road (a.k.a. 900 East). Drive past the Goshen Power Substation to the T intersection at mile 11.9 and turn left (east) on Wolverine Road (a.k.a. 600 N). Bear left at mile 18, staying on Wolverine Road. The entrance to Wolverine Canyon is at mile 20.4. Beyond this point you'll be on a good but narrow graveled road. A spectacular view is found at the top of the "W" (a double switchback near the summit) at mile 28.4. There is ample room to turn around here.

Wolverine Road can be snowy or muddy in spring, and it is closed to automobiles in winter. There is a complex mix of public and private land along this route, but the private stuff is clearly posted.

BIRDING:

Along the willow-lined stream from mile 17.5 to 21, look for Eastern and Western Kingbirds, Gray Catbirds, Blue-gray Gnatcatchers, Plumbeous Vireos, Yellow-breasted Chats, Black-headed Grosbeaks, and Lazuli Buntings. You may also find Green-tailed Towhees on brushy, rocky slopes, Black-throated Gray and Virginia's Warblers in junipers, and Broad-tailed and Calliope Hummingbirds near flowers.

At mile 21 scan cliffs on the left (north) for White-throated Swifts. Prairie Falcons have been seen at about this same spot, and Peregrines should be watched for. An American Dipper pair can usually be found on the rock face above the narrow stream on the right (south) at mile 22.3. Evening Grosbeaks apparently nest at the higher elevations.

Common Poorwills often sit along the road on summer nights, from mile 21 to the summit. Western Screech-Owls, Northern Saw-whet Owls, and Flammulated Owls can be heard on both sides of the summit during June.

OTHER:

Fuel and food are available in Shelley; full services are available in Idaho Falls. Primitive camping is allowed on BLM land. There are rattlesnakes in the lower canyon, but common sense prevents most problems. For a map and more information, contact the BLM (208/524-7500) in Idaho Falls.

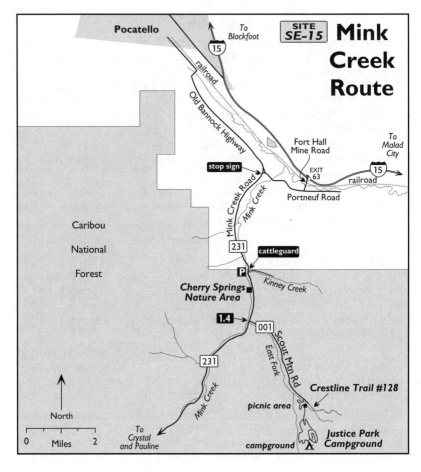

MINK CREEK ROUTE

Authors: Chuck Trost, Matt Radford

Site SE-15 — Map SE-15

Highlights: Western Scrub-Jay, Virginia's Warbler, Lesser Goldfinch
Major Habitats: Juniper, Deciduous Forest, Dry Conifer Forest
Location: Bannock Co., 7 miles south of Pocatello
Spring: **** **Summer:** **** **Fall:** **   **Winter:** ***

A 15-mile drive south of Pocatello will take you from juniper-covered hills at 4,500 feet in elevation to Douglas-fir and Quaking Aspen forest at 7,500 feet. Because of the rapidly changing altitude and southern latitude, this route offers some of Idaho's best birding. Among the regular breeders is Lesser Goldfinch, one of the state's most local species.

DIRECTIONS:

Mink Creek is south of I-15. To get there from Pocatello, follow I-15 south 5 miles and take Exit 63. Turn right (west) on Old Highway 91 for 0.1 mile, then go left (south) over the railroad tracks on Fort Hall Mine Road for 0.3 mile. Turn right (west) on Portneuf Road for 1.4 miles, and then go left (south) at the stop-sign onto Mink Creek Road. Continue south on Mink Creek Road for 3.2 miles until you come to a cattle-guard marking the entrance to the Caribou NF. Pull into unmarked "Kinney Creek" parking area on the right (west), but park out of the way since this is a school-bus turn-around. Zero your mileage here.

BIRDING:

At the Kinney Creek parking area you can find summering Broad-tailed Hummingbirds, Yellow-breasted Chats, Lesser and American Goldfinches, and Fox Sparrows. Even better birding is available across the road in Kinney Creek Canyon. Follow the old 2-track road through the gate and walk east, entering a rich birding habitat of dense juniper and mountain brush. A variety of species breed here, including Western Scrub-Jay, Juniper Titmouse, Blue-gray Gnatcatcher, Plumbeous Vireo, Virginia's, Black-throated Gray, MacGillivray's, and Orange-crowned Warblers, Green-tailed and Spotted Towhees, and Chipping Sparrow. Calliope Hummingbirds are especially common. Look for Dusky Flycatchers in riparian vegetation and for Gray Flycatchers in junipers. After 0.5 mile you will cross a cattle-guard and enter a grazed area. The habitat opens up as junipers drop out. Old magpie nests in hawthorns may be home to nesting Cooper's Hawks or Long-eared Owls. Ruffed Grouse, Mountain Bluebirds, and Warbling Vireos also nest in this area. As you gain elevation, hawthorns give way to Quaking Aspen groves, with sagebrush and bitterbrush on the hillsides. Watch for Downy and Hairy Woodpeckers, Red-naped Sapsuckers, Black-capped Chickadees, and an occasional Northern Saw-whet Owl.

In winter a surprising variety of birds can be found along Kinney Creek. Look for Western Scrub-Jays, Juniper Titmice, Black-capped and Mountain Chickadees, Brown Creepers, Townsend's Solitaires, American Robins, and Spotted Towhees. There's a magpie roost in hawthorns about a mile up the canyon. When snow is deep, look for Sharp-tailed Grouse and Gray Partridge beyond the grazing exclosures, about three miles up.

After walking Kinney Canyon, return to Mink Creek Road and continue south. At mile 0.7 is a pull-off on the right (west) for the Cherry Springs Nature Area. This was formerly a FS campground, but campsites (and trails) have long since become overgrown with thick tangles of willows, hawthorns, Red-oiser Dogwoods, and other riparian vegetation. This spot is handicapped-accessible, and there is a restroom here. The trail forks at the entrance, with each side going for about 0.5 mile to a dead end. A total of 104 species have been seen at Cherry Springs, of which at least 55 nest. Local breeders include Sharp-shinned and Cooper's Hawks, Western Screech-Owl, Great Horned and Northern Saw-whet Owls, Common Poorwills, Calliope and Broad-tailed Hummingbirds, Willow Flycatchers, Rock and House Wrens, Gray Catbirds, Cedar Waxwings, Orange-crowned, Virginia's, Yellow, MacGillivray's, and Black-throated Gray Warblers, Yellow-breasted Chats, Black-headed Grosbeaks, Lazuli Buntings, Green-tailed Towhees, Brewer's, Chipping, Fox, and Song Sparrows, Bullock's Orioles, Cassin's and House Finches, Pine Siskins, and American and Lesser Goldfinches. Several species also winter here, although the area can seem deserted if the wind is blowing. In fall and winter watch for Ruffed Grouse, Golden Eagles, Great Horned Owls, Downy Woodpeckers, American Dippers, Winter Wrens, Black-capped and Mountain Chickadees, Ruby-crowned Kinglets, Song Sparrows, and Dark-eyed Juncos.

Back on Mink Creek Road, continue south to mile 1.4, then take paved Scout Mountain Road (a.k.a. FR 001) to the left (east), and follow it uphill. This road is open from May to November and leads 5.5 miles to Justice Park Campground at the base of Scout Mountain. There are many trails that can be birded in this area, including Crestline Motorcycle Trail, which starts in the picnic area. This trail has produced Flammulated Owls, Northern Pygmy-Owls, and several Common Poorwills on summer evenings. Great Horned Owls frequently call in this general area, and even a Great Gray Owl was heard once. Species that can be seen at the picnic area and campground are Ruffed and Blue Grouse, Northern Goshawk, Hairy Woodpecker, Red-naped Sapsucker, Cordilleran and Hammond's Flycatchers, Common Raven, Clark's Nutcracker, Mountain Chickadee, Brown Creeper, Ruby-crowned and Golden-crowned Kinglets, Red-breasted Nuthatch, Hermit Thrush, Red Crossbill, and Pine Siskin. Lincoln's Sparrows nest at the small marshy area near the campground entrance. Although Scout Mountain Road is closed during winter, snowshoes and cross-country skis can help in finding Northern Goshawks, Sharp-tailed, Blue, and Ruffed Grouse, Steller's Jays, Mountain Chickadees, Red-breasted Nuthatches, Townsend's Solitaires, Northern Shrikes, Red Crossbills, and Pine Siskins.

OTHER:

A checklist, a map, and more information can be obtained from the FS (208/236-7500) in Pocatello. Pocatello is a full-service community.

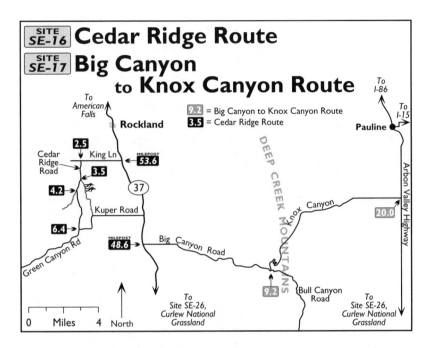

SITE SE-16	**Cedar Ridge Route**
SITE SE-17	**Big Canyon**
	to Knox Canyon Route

9.2 = Big Canyon to Knox Canyon Route
3.5 = Cedar Ridge Route

To American Falls

Rockland

Pauline

To I-86

To I-15

DEEP CREEK MOUNTAINS

Cedar Ridge Road

King Ln

MILEPOST 53.6

2.5

3.5

37

4.2

Kuper Road

Knox Canyon

20.0

Arbon Valley Highway

6.4

MILEPOST 48.6

Big Canyon Road

Green Canyon Rd

Bull Canyon Road

9.2

0   Miles   4   North

To Site SE-26, Curlew National Grassland

To Site SE-26, Curlew National Grassland

CEDAR RIDGE ROUTE

Author: Dave Burrup

Site SE-16 — Map SE-16/SE-17

Highlights: Gray Flycatcher, Blue-gray Gnatcatcher
Major Habitats: Juniper, Farmland
Location: Power Co., 15 miles south of American Falls
Spring: * * *   **Summer:** * * *   **Fall:** *   **Winter:** N/A

Spring and summer birding in this corner of the Sublett Mountains can easily produce 50 to 70 bird species. Birding in late summer and fall is less productive. Most of the birds seen will be various sparrows, which are present throughout the fall period. Whenever you visit, access is a bit tricky! You'll need a high-clearance, 4-wheel-drive vehicle to complete the entire 13-mile-long journey. Luckily, the best birding area is relatively easy to access.

DIRECTIONS:

From Rockland follow ID 37 south 2 miles. At milepost 53.6 zero your mileage and turn right (west) onto graveled King Lane. At mile 2.5 turn left (south) on Cedar Ridge Road. Most land along this route is private, but Cedar Ridge itself is an island of public (BLM) land.

BIRDING:

The best birding is in the first 1.5 miles of Cedar Ridge Road. Stop often to investigate the Utah Juniper habitat for Western Scrub-Jays, Gray and Dusky Flycatchers, Juniper Titmice, Blue-gray Gnatcatchers, Mountain Bluebirds, and Chipping and Brewer's Sparrows. Be sure to scan farmland for Sharp-tailed Grouse, Horned Larks, and Vesper Sparrows.

A very productive hike can be taken at mile 3.5. Walk the primitive side road that heads left (east) to the top of Cedar Ridge, and go as far as you like—*but please leave all gates as you found them.* With luck, you may be able to find Ash-throated Flycatchers, Pinyon Jays, Black-throated Gray Warblers, and Lark Sparrows.

At mile 4.2 stay left (southeast) on Cedar Ridge Road (signed). At mile 6.4 Cedar Ridge Road ends at the junction of Kuper Road and Green Canyon Road. Kuper Road will lead you east to ID 37 in about 4.5 miles.

Good birding is available on Green Canyon Road. *Be aware that Green Canyon Road soon becomes a primitive, narrow mountain trail with few pull-outs. High-clearance vehicles are necessary.* This road is not accessible until late spring, and it becomes impassable with very little rain; beware of thundershowers. If you do go into Green Canyon, look there for Calliope Hummingbirds, Virginia's and MacGillivray's Warblers, and Green-tailed and Spotted Towhees. In stands of Douglas-fir and Quaking Aspen, expect Hairy and Downy Woodpeckers, Red-naped Sapsuckers, and Tree Swallows. Approximately 5.4 miles up Green Canyon Road, you'll pass over a shelf of loose rock requiring a 4-wheel drive. You may want to turn around at the top of Green Canyon (6 miles from Cedar Ridge Road). The rest of Green Canyon Road hangs off the mountain-side with very few pull-outs.

OTHER:

This area is heavily hunted in October and November and is best avoided then. Fuel, lodging, and food are available in American Falls. Undeveloped campsites can be found in Green Canyon. Developed campsites are available in American Falls and in Massacre Rocks SP. Twin Springs Campground has primitive campsites at ID 37 milepost 32.5. For a map and more information, contact the BLM (208/236-6860) in Pocatello. See also Big Canyon to Knox Canyon Route, the next site.

BIG CANYON TO KNOX CANYON ROUTE

Author: Dave Burrup

Site SE-17 — Map SE-16/SE-17

Highlights: Williamson's Sapsucker, Virginia's Warbler
Major Habitats: Farmland, Mixed Conifer Forest, Deciduous Forest
Location: Power Co., 20 miles south of American Falls
Spring: * *   **Summer:** * *   **Fall:** *   **Winter:** N/A

This 20-mile route climbs Big Canyon, crosses the crest of the Deep Creek Mountains, and descends through Knox Canyon. Along the way, the vegetation changes rapidly from sagebrush to Curl-leaf Mountain Mahogany to Quaking Aspen to Subalpine Fir forest. This habitat diversity attracts a great variety of birdlife, as well as supporting a diverse community of wildflowers and butterflies.

DIRECTIONS:

From Rockland follow ID 37 south 7 miles. At milepost 48.6 turn left (east) on graveled Big Canyon Road (signed) and zero your mileage.

The main road along this route is good gravel and is accessible by passenger car. *Don't attempt this journey until the road dries out (mid-June in some years).*

There are several side roads in the canyons, but these can be very rough; some are posted private property. Those that are not posted offer great hiking opportunities.

BIRDING:

At the lower ends of both canyons, look for Mourning Doves, Horned Larks, Vesper, Brewer's, and Lark Sparrows, Western Meadowlarks, and Brewer's Blackbirds in the farmland. In juniper, sagebrush, and Chokecherry communities, watch for Dusky Flycatchers, Juniper Titmice, Blue-gray Gnatcatchers, Mountain Bluebirds, Green-tailed and Spotted Towhees, Virginia's and MacGillivray's Warblers, and Lazuli Buntings. Pay particular attention to the scattered springs and stock ponds, since they are often the birdiest areas.

At mid-elevations you'll be in Quaking Aspen/Douglas-fir forest. Regular nesters include Downy Woodpeckers, Red-naped Sapsuckers, Tree and Violet-green Swallows, Mountain Chickadees, Cedar Waxwings, Hermit and Swainson's Thrushes, Orange-crowned and Yellow-rumped Warblers, Warbling and "Solitary" Vireos, Western Tanagers, and Cassin's Finches.

At the highest elevations search Douglas-fir/Subalpine Fir communities for Hairy Woodpeckers, Williamson's Sapsuckers, Broad-tailed Hummingbirds, Cordilleran Flycatchers, Ruby-crowned Kinglets, and Red Crossbills.

At mile 7 a road heads up a side canyon on the left (north) which is worth hiking. At mile 7.3 a logging-road on the right (south) continues up Big Canyon while the main road begins a steep climb to the top. Stay on the main road. At mile 9.1 is a parking area and logging road on the right (south), where you can hike to the ridgetop. At mile 9.2 Bull Canyon Road goes off to the right (southeast). Stay left along the ridgetop. At mile 9.4, bear right and descend through Knox Canyon. At mile 20 turn left (north) onto paved Arbon Valley Highway and drive 4 miles into Pauline to end this route.

OTHER:

This area is heavily hunted in October and is then best avoided for birding. Fuel, lodging, and food are available in American Falls. Undeveloped campsites are available in both canyons. Developed campsites can be found in American Falls and in Massacre Rocks SP. Additional information and a map can be obtained from the BLM office (208/236-6860) in Pocatello.

SPRINGFIELD PONDS

Author: Chuck Trost

Site SE-18 — Map SE-18/SE-19

Highlights: Waterfowl, Shorebirds
Major Habitats: Wetland
Location: Bingham Co., Springfield
Spring: * * *   **Summer:** *   **Fall:** * * *   **Winter:** * *

Springfield Ponds is a 30-acre bird sanctuary bordering the small town of Springfield. Because no hunting is allowed, waterfowl congregate here during fall and early winter. The ponds still receive a lot of disturbance from fishermen, however. The best time to visit is early morning or during inclement weather. The ponds are spring fed and are usually ice free even during cold snaps.

DIRECTIONS:

Springfield Ponds are on the south and west side of Springfield. The ponds are separated by ID 39 and Chandler Road (a.k.a. 1955 W). Access to the west and south sides of the ponds is limited by private property.

BIRDING:

Hundreds of birds stage on and around the ponds during spring migration. It's not unusual to find nine diving duck species in addition to the occasional rarity such as Long-tailed Duck, White-winged or Surf Scoter, or Harlequin Duck. In April, American Avocets and Black-necked Stilts can be found at the north pond, and migrant Dunlins, Stilt Sandpipers, Long-billed and Short-billed (rare) Dowitchers, and Greater and Lesser Yellowlegs should be looked for, also. Watch for Caspian Terns and Ospreys, especially just after the ponds have been restocked with fish.

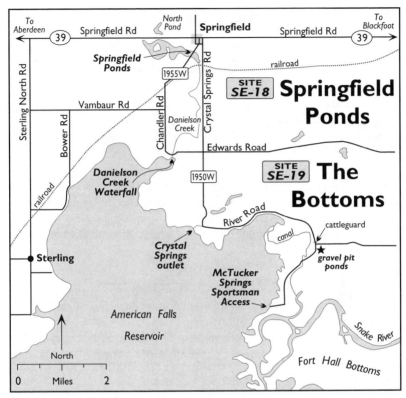

The marsh and Russian-olive patches to the southeast of the ponds offer good birding, but they do take some effort to access. From ID 39 milepost 33.2 turn south onto Crystal Springs Road (a.k.a. 1950 W) and go 0.2 mile. Park as soon as you cross the railroad, then walk to the right (west) along the edge of the railroad embankment.

During winter look for waterfowl (including Trumpeter Swans) and Bald Eagles at the ponds, and for Marsh Wrens and Virginia Rails in the marshy areas. If you're lucky, you may find Hooded Mergansers on Danielson Creek (see map). Northern Shrikes are regular winter residents, and both Northern Mockingbirds and Blue Jays have wintered in Springfield. In good berry years, thousands of Bohemian Waxwings and European Starlings winter in the Russian-olives. When this happens, there is frequently a Sharp-shinned Hawk or a Merlin nearby. You may also find a Varied Thrush mixed in with the American Robin hordes, or a Harris's or White-throated Sparrow among the plentiful White-crowned Sparrows. Roosting Barn Owls are another possibility.

OTHER:

There is a small store in Springfield for picnic needs, but—alas—no beer is sold on Sundays. See also Sportsmans Park (p. 261) and The Bottoms, the next site.

THE BOTTOMS

Author: Chuck Trost

Site SE-19 — Map SE-18/SE-19

Highlights: Cattle Egret, Northern Goshawk, Shorebirds
Major Habitats: Wetland, Deciduous Forest
Location: Bingham Co., 3 miles southeast of Springfield
Spring: * * *   **Summer:** * * *   **Fall:** * * *   **Winter:** * *

The "Bottoms" refers to the northeastern corner of American Falls Reservoir. In spring large expanses of flooded wetland attract migrating waterfowl. From July to late fall there are huge mudflats, with new habitat being exposed daily. Thirty-one shorebird species have been seen here, some in large numbers. Ponds, Russian-olive thickets, and cottonwood forests round out this phenomenal birding site.

DIRECTIONS:

The Bottoms is public land (BOR). Easy access, however, is limited to Danielson Creek Waterfall and McTucker Springs Sportsman Access. Most of the birding is at McTucker Springs.

To find Danielson Creek Waterfall from ID 39, turn south at milepost 33.2 onto Chandler Road (a.k.a. 1955 W) and go southwest 2 miles to the overlook. Note that Chandler and Crystal Springs Road start next to each other but head in slightly different directions (see map).

McTucker Springs Sportsman Access is 4.3 miles southeast of Springfield. To get there from ID 39, turn south at milepost 33.2 onto Crystal Springs Road (a.k.a. 1950 W) for 2.5 miles, then turn left (east) on River Road for 1.8 miles, and cross the cattle-guard. You now have a choice: go straight (east) to bird the gravel-pit ponds, or go right (southwest) for about 1 mile to the boat launch on the Snake River. The road to the boat launch is good gravel. During low water, many birders and fishermen drive beyond the boat launch, out onto the mudflats. *Soft sand and bottomless mud call for very prudent driving! If the mudflats are wet—don't go.* Under any conditions, stay well back from the water's edge. If you insist on being too adventurous, wrecker service is available in Aberdeen, American Falls, and Blackfoot!

BIRDING:

March is the peak of spring waterfowl migration on The Bottoms. Thousands of Northern Pintails court in the shallow bays, as do many other dabblers and both Tundra and Trumpeter Swans. Large flocks of Snow Geese (usually with a handful of Ross's Geese mixed in) can be found feeding in nearby wheat fields.

In summer American White Pelicans dominate The Bottoms' shallows, often pirating fish from unlucky Double-crested Cormorants. Both Clark's and

Western Grebes nest near deeper water, while Eared Grebes can be seen in the shallower portions. Watch also for long lines of Cattle Egrets and White-faced Ibises as they fly overhead. Several Great Egrets nest nearby; Snowies are abundant. In cottonwoods look for Gray Catbirds and Black-headed Grosbeaks.

Thousands of molting ducks congregate at The Bottoms during fall, attracting Peregrine and Prairie Falcons. The real excitement however, begins as mudflats become exposed. By August, there are at least *eight miles* of shorebird habitat exposed. Huge flocks of peep, (mostly Western and Baird's Sandpipers) feed here, and even Whimbrels have been seen. Greater and Lesser Yellowlegs are common to abundant; check these flocks for Stilt Sandpipers. Marbled Godwits number in the hundreds during July and August. Rare species present have included American Golden-Plover, Snowy Plover, Ruddy Turnstone, Red Knot, and Short-billed Dowitcher!

McTucker Springs' brushy habitat harbors fall and winter flocks of American Tree and White-crowned Sparrows. Harris's Sparrows can often be found mixed in, with Spotted Towhees nearby. Russian-olive thickets support Northern Flickers and American Robins all winter (watch for Varied Thrushes) and can attract thousands of Bohemian and Cedar Waxwings. All three accipiters hunt the McTucker Springs area during winter, with Northern Goshawks being particularly prominent. Keep an eye out for Bald Eagles and Merlins.

McTucker Springs' gravel-pit ponds are highly disturbed by fishermen and relatively sterile bird-wise. The ponds may still be worth a quick look, however, since migrating Common Loons do stop over, and both Western and Clark's Grebes sometimes forage there.

Cottonwoods lining the Snake River and McTucker Springs are good for spring owling. Flicker holes are prized by nesting Western Screech-Owls and Northern Saw-whet Owls. Great Horned Owls are also common.

OTHER:

Primitive camping is permitted around the gravel-pit ponds. Fuel, food, and lodging are available in Blackfoot, Springfield, Aberdeen, and American Falls. Pocatello is the closest full-service community. For maps and more information, contact the BOR (208/678-0461) in Burley.

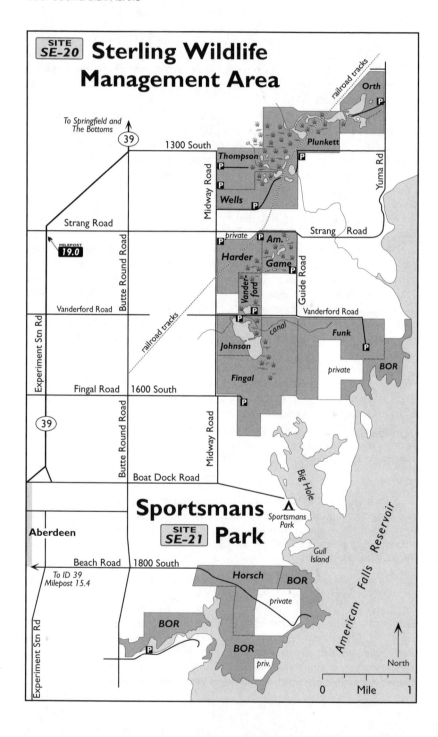

SITE
SE-20 **Sterling Wildlife
Management Area**

railroad tracks

Orth

To Springfield and
The Bottoms

39

1300 South

Plunkett

Thompson

Wells

Midway Road

Yuma Rd

Strang Road

Strang Road

MILEPOST
19.0

Butte Round Road

private

Am.
Game

Harder

Vander-
ford

Guide Road

Vanderford Road

Vanderford Road

Experiment Stn Rd

railroad tracks

canal

Funk

Johnson

private

BOR

Fingal

Fingal Road

1600 South

39

Butte Round Road

Midway Road

Boat Dock Road

Sportsmans

Big Hole

Sportsmans
Park

SITE
SE-21 **Park**

Aberdeen

Gull
Island

American Falls Reservoir

Beach Road

1800 South

To ID 39
Milepost 15.4

Horsch

BOR

private

BOR

BOR

P

priv.

North

Experiment Stn Rd

0   Mile   1

STERLING WILDLIFE MANAGEMENT AREA

Author: Dave Burrup

Site SE-20 — Map SE-20/SE-21

Highlights: Swainson's Hawk, Long-eared and Short-eared Owls
Major Habitats: Wetland, Farmland, Grassland
Location: Bingham Co., 4 miles east of Aberdeen
Spring: * * *   **Summer:** * * *   **Fall:** * * *   **Winter:** * *

Sterling WMA is managed by IDFG and BOR. The WMA covers 3,300 acres; it is broken-up into 11 segments, forming three "blocks." Each segment has at least one public access and parking area. Because of the complexity of land ownership, a good map is essential.

DIRECTIONS:

The starting point for all three "blocks" is Aberdeen. To reach the Horsch block from Aberdeen, turn east onto Beach Road at ID 39 milepost 15.4. The block begins 2.8 miles east of Aberdeen; American Falls Reservoir is 4 miles east of Aberdeen. Loop roads to the north and south of Beach Road are open to the public, but are impassable when wet and are frequently blocked by irrigation equipment. Be aware that there are several private-land inholdings in this area.

The remainder of the WMA is accessed by Strang Road. From Aberdeen go north 3 miles on ID 39. Just past milepost 19, turn right (east) on Strang Road for 2 miles to the intersection with Midway Road (a.k.a. 2500 W). To the northeast of this intersection is the Orth-Plunkett-Thompson-Wells block, and to the south is the Harder-American Game-Vanderford-Johnson-Fingal-Funk block.

BIRDING:

There are three major habitats: wetland/Russian-olive thickets, cultivated farmland, and pasture (which comes in both wet and dry versions). The best birding strategy is simply to sample some of each.

WETLAND HABITAT

Wetland areas offer the most-diverse birding. Common nesting species include Northern Harrier, Sora, Virginia Rail, Short-eared Owl, Marsh Wren, Common Yellowthroat, Song Sparrow, and Red-winged and Yellow-headed Blackbirds. During migration 15 to 20 waterfowl species may be seen. Roosting Barn Owls can sometimes be found in cattail marshes. Extensive wetlands are found on the Orth, Plunkett, Thompson, Wells, American Game, Vanderford, and Johnson segments. The Johnson segment offers a handicapped-accessible observation blind and year-round open water.

FARMLAND AND PASTURE HABITAT

On farmlands and in both dry and irrigated pastures, look for summering Red-tailed and Swainson's Hawks, American Kestrels, Western Meadowlarks, and Brown-headed Cowbirds, and for resident Ring-necked Pheasants and Gray Partridge. During migration be sure to check the tree and shrub windbreaks on the Thompson and Wells segments for a wide assortment of songbirds.

Russian-olive thickets are used as nesting and roosting sites for Great Horned and Long-eared Owls, Black-billed Magpies, and Eastern Kingbirds. In winter, the patches are popular with European Starlings, Bohemian and Cedar Waxwings, and American Robins. American Tree Sparrows are commonly found in brush patches throughout the area in late fall and winter. All of this avian prey attracts Merlins, Prairie Falcons, Sharp-shinned Hawks, Northern Goshawks, and Northern Shrikes. In sagebrush patches look for Loggerhead Shrikes (summer) and Rough-legged Hawks (winter).

Farmland and grassland habitat is most abundant on the Fingal, Funk, Johnson, and Horsch segments.

OTHER:

To obtain a Sterling WMA brochure (which includes a nice map showing the different land ownerships), write or visit Area Manager, Sterling Wildlife Management Area, Idaho Department of Fish and Game, 1345 Barton Road, Pocatello, Idaho 83204-1819; or call 208/232-4703. If you forgot to get a brochure ahead of time, you might look for one at the information station 0.5 mile south on Midway Road from the Strang Road/Midway Road intersection.

Fuel and food are available in Aberdeen. Developed camping is available at Sportsmans Park, 3.5 miles east of Aberdeen. Lodging is available in Blackfoot or American Falls.

Much of the WMA is marshland with difficult walking-conditions; knee-high waterproof footwear is almost a must. From late spring to late summer hordes of mosquitoes are present. Expect lots of hunters during October and November.

SPORTSMANS PARK
Author: Dave Burrup
Site SE-21 — Map SE-20/SE-21
Highlights: Common Tern, Shorebirds
Major Habitats: Wetland
Location: Bingham Co., 3 miles east of Aberdeen
Spring: * * *   **Summer:** * * *   **Fall:** * * *   **Winter:** *

Sportsmans Park is a developed site with camping, boating, and picnic facilities, located on American Falls Reservoir's "Big Hole Bay." This area is often disturbed by boaters and fishermen, but it still yields annual sightings of over 150 species.

DIRECTIONS:
From Aberdeen follow ID 39 north about 1 mile. At milepost 17 turn right (southeast) on Experiment Station Road. After 0.2 mile turn left (east) on East Boat Dock Road (a.k.a. 1700 S) and follow it 2.5 miles to Sportsmans Park.

BIRDING:
The year's birding here begins in late March with the return of Common Loons and some twenty duck species. By early May, the large nesting colony of Ring-billed and California Gulls on nearby "Gull Island" is back in operation. Associated with this colony are Forster's, Caspian, and Common Terns. If Big Hole Bay is flooded, spring migration also brings various grebes, American White Pelicans, Double-crested Cormorants, and diving ducks. Migrating songbirds are found in park trees and brush along the shoreline.

Although shorebird spring migration is generally unimpressive here, vagrant Snowy Plover, Ruddy Turnstone, and Dunlin have been seen near Gull Island. Fall migration is much more spectacular, with up to 30 species attracted to mudflats exposed by the reservoir's drawdown. Drawdown usually begins in July, but it's typically August before extensive habitat is present. In July look for Least and Western Sandpipers. Baird's Sandpipers arrive in large flocks around the first week of August. Watch for Stilt Sandpipers mixed in with Lesser Yellowlegs during August and September. Marbled Godwits are common in July and August, while Black-bellied Plovers and American Golden-Plovers are uncommon in September and October. Great Blue Herons, Great and Snowy Egrets, and Black-crowned Night-Herons are also attracted to mudflats. You may even find a vagrant Arctic Tern in August or September. Winter gulls, including Iceland, Glaucous, Thayer's, and Ross's have been seen feeding on leftovers from the folks ice fishing.

OTHER:
For maps and more information, contact BOR (208/226-2217) in American Falls. Lodging is available in American Falls and Blackfoot. Fuel and food are available in Aberdeen seven days a week. Developed camping can be had at Sportsmans Park.

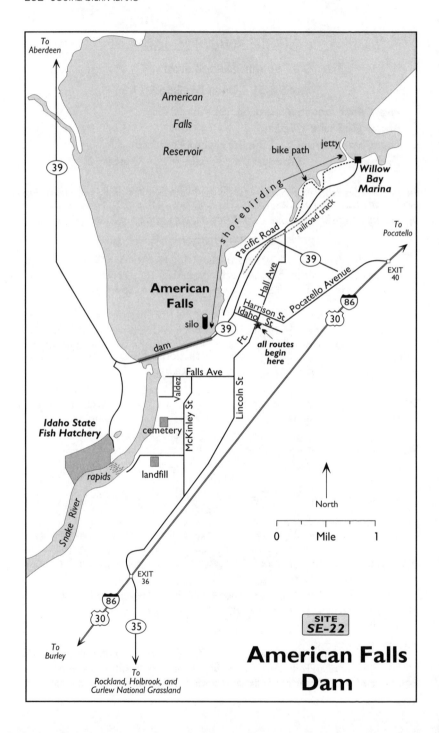

To
Aberdeen

American

Falls

Reservoir

bike path   jetty

Willow
Bay
Marina

39

shorebirding

Pacific Road

railroad track

To
Pocatello

39

Hall Ave

Pocatello Avenue

EXIT
40

**American
Falls**

86

Harrison St

30

silo   39   Idaho St

Ft.

all routes
begin
here

dam

Falls Ave

Valdez

Lincoln St

**Idaho State
Fish Hatchery**

McKinley St

cemetery

rapids   landfill

North

Snake River

0   Mile   1

EXIT
36

86

30

35

To
Burley

To
Rockland, Holbrook, and
Curlew National Grassland

SITE
SE-22

**American Falls
Dam**

AMERICAN FALLS DAM

Author: Chuck Trost

Site SE-22 — Map SE-22

Highlights: Loons, Waterfowl, Shorebirds, Gulls
Major Habitat: Wetland
Location: Power Co., 25 miles west of Pocatello
Spring: * * * *   **Summer:** * * * * **Fall:** * * * * **Winter:** * * * *

American Falls Dam is arguably Idaho's best year-round birding site. In spring migrating loons, ducks, and songbirds congregate in shallow waters and isolated tree groves. During summer huge mudflats are exposed, attracting 30 shorebird species, while fall and winter bring a variety of ducks and gulls to open water below the dam.

DIRECTIONS:

To reach great birding, take I-86 Exit 40 and follow Pocatello Avenue 1.5 miles southwest into American Falls, following the curve to the right (west) onto Harrison Street. Stay on Harrison Street for two blocks, then turn left (south) on Ft. Hall Avenue (a.k.a. Business I-86) and follow it one block to its intersection with Idaho Street. This intersection is the starting point for all four spots described below; zero your mileage here.

BIRDING:

WILLOW BAY MARINA

From the starting point head northeast on Ft. Hall Avenue, crossing over ID 39. The road dead-ends at the marina in 2 miles.

Along the marina's entrance road are seasonally-flooded lagoons surrounded by willows and Russian-olives and bordered by a bike path. Watch for migrating Yellow-rumped and Wilson's Warblers, resident Song Sparrows, and wintering White-crowned, Harris's, and White-throated Sparrows.

The marina's 0.25-mile-long jetty provides good views of the water. During late fall, Long-tailed Duck and Harlequin Duck have been sighted here, along with many other species. When the reservoir is low, spring-fed seeps along the jetty attract foraging shorebirds.

About 0.25 mile east of the jetty is a secluded swampy lagoon and woodland which can be productive for migrating songbirds. You can walk to this area along the shore.

GRAIN ELEVATOR

When American Falls Dam was constructed in the mid-1920s, the entire town site of "old" American Falls was flooded. All buildings were demolished or moved, with the exception of a huge concrete grain-elevator (a.k.a. "the silo") which is still standing near the dam. To reach this area from the starting point, take Ft. Hall Avenue 0.9 mile northeast, crossing ID 39 and the railroad track, then turn left (southwest) on Pacific Road. A half mile down this graveled road, look for some seep ponds on the right (west) that attract herons, shorebirds, and gulls. A few Great and Snowy Egrets and White-faced Ibises often forage here in July and August. Continue driving southwest on the dirt 2-track road to the elevator. *These "roads" are often impassable when wet.*

During low water you can actually watch birds from your car by driving out onto the dried mudflats, along the streets of old American Falls. *The mud away from the old streets can be almost bottomless.*

The best shorebirding is between the elevator and Willow Bay Marina. Disturbance from dirt-bikes can be a factor, so it is best to bird the mudflats in early morning. Western and Baird's Sandpipers can number in the hundreds. Marbled Godwit flocks are common, and a few Black-bellied Plovers and American Golden-Plovers may be found on higher ground. Watch for raptors (including Peregrine Falcons). Rare species seen here have included Snowy Plover, Whimbrel, Hudsonian Godwit, Red Knot, Sanderling, Stilt Sandpiper, and Short-billed Dowitcher.

During some years there's an August/September build-up of hundreds of small terns near the elevator. A few Arctic Terns are possible among the more regular Forster's and Common Terns. All this activity attracts jaegers, which are almost annual. For much of the fall, there are thousands of American Pipits along the beach, with an occasional Merlin or Prairie Falcon thrown in for excitement. In mid-October and November, look for migrating loons. Pacifics can be almost common. Red-throateds are rare but regular, and even a Yellow-billed has shown up! By December the reservoir can be very sterile after freeze-up eliminates habitat.

SNAKE RIVER

From the starting point, follow Ft. Hall Avenue southwest 0.6 mile and turn right (west) on Falls Avenue. After 0.4 mile you'll reach the intersection of Falls Avenue and McKinley Street. From here you have three choices: 1) continue straight (west) 0.3 mile to a river overlook, 2) continue straight (west) 0.2 mile and turn left (south) on Valdez Street and follow the signs to the Sportsman Access Boat Launch at road's end, or 3) turn left (south) on McKinley Street and follow the road 0.5 mile to the cemetery and beyond to the landfill. You will probably want to do all three!

At the river overlook, boat launch, and cemetery, look for hundreds of fall terns foraging in turbulent water below the dam. In April, May, and October you'll likely see Bonaparte's Gulls as well; watch also for vagrant Sabine's Gulls. Several diving ducks winter in this area, including both goldeneyes and all three mergansers.

At the cemetery Northern Flickers and Black-billed Magpies can be found in the junipers, along with Great Horned Owls and Juniper Titmice. During migration, the trees attract Black-capped and Mountain Chickadees,

Red-breasted Nuthatches, Ruby-crowned and Golden-crowned Kinglets, and various warblers. Sharp-shinned and Cooper's Hawks also pass through, but ever-present magpies keep them on the move! Between November and March, Bald Eagles are frequently present. The cemetery is open 8 am to 5 pm except in summer, when it's open 8 am to 8 pm.

About 0.25 mile south of the cemetery, turn right (west) on the paved road. You'll reach the landfill on the left (south) in 0.4 mile. (The landfill is closed on Sundays.) Glaucous, Thayer's, and even Mew Gulls have been spotted here, along with hundreds of Ring-billed and California Gulls. This facility was recently converted to a garbage transfer station, so gull numbers may well decline. If you continue west on the paved road past the landfill, you'll reach another river overlook at road's end. It's okay to walk or drive southwest along the 2-track dirt road to get better views (city property). The small rapids below are used by a variety of wintering waterfowl, including Greater Scaup, Barrow's Goldeneyes, and Red-breasted Mergansers, and have attracted even Harlequin Ducks, Long-tailed Ducks, and Surf, White-winged, and Black Scoters!

FISH HATCHERY

Directly across the river from the landfill is a state-owned fish hatchery which offers good birding in brushy habitats. To get there from the starting point, follow Idaho Street west to ID 39 and take the highway southwest across the dam. At the top of the hill on the west side of the dam, turn left (south), then immediately left again (east), and follow the signs for about a mile to the fish hatchery.

The public is welcome at the hatchery during the day. Trails above and below the workers' houses allow river viewing (bird checklist and nature trail available at hatchery headquarters). Breeding species include Eastern and Western Kingbirds, Yellow Warbler, and Bullock's Oriole. Along the hatchery's effluent you can find summering Blue-winged and Cinnamon Teals and Virginia Rails. Look in dense Russian-olive trees on the north side of the hatchery for either Barn or Great Horned Owls, as well as for roosting Black-crowned Night-Herons. In winter, Northern Flickers, American Robins, Townsend's Solitaires, Cedar and Bohemian Waxwings, Yellow-rumped Warblers, and White-crowned Sparrows can be abundant.

OTHER:

American Falls has motels, fuel, groceries, and camping. Pocatello is a full-service community. For more information, contact the American Falls Parks and Recreation Department (208/226-7055). Other useful contacts are: City Clerk (208/226-2569), Willow Bay Recreation Area (208/226-2688), and BOR (208/226-2217).

MASSACRE ROCKS STATE PARK

Authors: Chuck Trost, Eric Lepisto

Site SE-23 — See Southeastern map, page 214

Highlights: Pacific Loon, Clark's Grebe, Juniper Titmouse
Major Habitats: Wetland, Juniper
Location: Power Co., 10 miles southwest of American Falls
Spring: * *   **Summer:** * *   **Fall:** * *   **Winter:** *

Massacre Rocks SP borders the Snake River at the upper end of Lake Walcott. Although the river freezes in winter, the water offers good birding during the rest of the year. Other park attractions include Oregon Trail history and bizarre lava flows!

DIRECTIONS:

From American Falls follow I-86 southwest for 10 miles, take Exit 28, and turn right (northwest). At the T in 0.1 mile, turn right (northeast) and drive 0.7 mile to headquarters.

BIRDING:

To bird Massacre Rocks SP, wander along the campground loop roads and investigate the narrow riparian zone along the river. Look for resident Juniper Titmice in the juniper. During winter you may also find Black-capped Chickadees, Ruby-crowned Kinglets, and Townsend's Solitaires. Species to watch for at the river include nesting Western and Clark's Grebes, American White Pelican, Double-crested Cormorant, Canada Goose, and Red-tailed Hawk.

The best birding is during spring and fall, since the Snake River serves as a migration corridor for several species. From October to freeze-up, Common and Pacific Loons commonly forage in the calm backwaters of the park. This is also the time to look for Greater Scaup, Long-tailed Ducks (rare), Common and Barrow's Goldeneyes, Common Mergansers, Bald Eagles, and Herring Gulls.

Register Rock Day Use/Group Camping Area is about 1.5 mile downstream from the visitors center. To get there, backtrack to the Interstate and take the overpass to the south side of I-86. Turn right (southwest) on the frontage road and follow it 2 miles to Register Rock. The frontage road is good for Northern Shrikes in fall and winter. Large numbers of Northern Flickers, American Robins, and Cedar and Bohemian Waxwings winter at Register Rock, often attracting the unwelcome attention of Sharp-shinned Hawks and Merlins!

OTHER:

Trails, campgrounds (with solar showers in summer and fall), and a boat launch are available at the park. There is a small interpretive museum at park headquarters (208/548-2672) with many Oregon Trail artifacts. The closest services are in American Falls or Burley.

MINIDOKA NATIONAL WILDLIFE REFUGE
Authors: Jack Trotter, Steve Bouffard
Site SE-24 — Map SE-24

Highlights: Swainson's Hawk, Long-billed Curlew
Major Habitats: Wetland, Shrub-steppe
Location: Minidoka Co., 12 miles northeast of Rupert
Spring: * *   **Summer:** * * *   **Fall:** * *   **Winter:** *

Minidoka Dam is one of many Snake River impoundments. The 12,000-acre reservoir behind the dam ("Lake Walcott") is managed as a NWR. An impressive 200 bird species have been recorded here.

DIRECTIONS:

Zero your mileage in Rupert at the intersection of ID 24 and 25, then go northeast on ID 24. At the north end of Rupert, immediately after crossing the railroad tracks, turn right (north) at the refuge sign, staying on ID 24. This turn is easily missed, so keep alert. At mile 5.9 turn right (east) on Minidoka Dam Road and drive toward refuge headquarters.

BIRDING:

At mile 8 check the small marsh areas for nesting Marsh Wrens, Common Yellowthroats, and Yellow-headed and Red-winged Blackbirds. At mile 11.3, just before reaching refuge headquarters, you'll pass Lake Walcott SP on the right (south). The park (fee) holds nesting Eastern and Western Kingbirds, Western Wood-Pewees, Cedar Waxwings, Yellow and MacGillivray's Warblers, Bullock's Orioles, and more. A short loop road circles the park, allowing easy access to Lake Walcott viewpoints.

Lake Walcott attracts migrating Common Loons, and nesting Western, Clark's, Eared, and Pied-billed Grebes, American White Pelicans, Double-crested Cormorants, Great Blue Herons, California and Ring-billed Gulls, and Caspian, Forster's, and Black Terns.

There are more vantage points for scanning Lake Walcott at refuge headquarters, as well as a paved shoreline trail. The trail is excellent for viewing migrating songbirds. About 0.5 mile northeast of headquarters is a boat launch area. Spend some time listening for warblers here, and again scan the

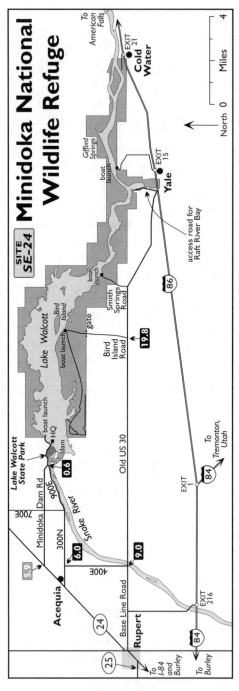

SITE SE-24 Minidoka National Wildlife Refuge

lake. In the shrub-steppe habitat, watch for Sage Thrashers, Western Meadowlarks, and Vesper, Brewer's, and Lark Sparrows.

To further explore the refuge, return to headquarters, re-zero your mileage, and head west on Minidoka Dam Road. At mile 0.6 turn left (south) on 900 E. At mile 0.7 you'll reach a delightful view of the cascading Snake River as it leaves Minidoka Dam. American White Pelicans, Double-crested Cormorants, Common and Red-breasted Mergansers, and Caspian and Forster's Terns are often present. In spring and summer look for Bank Swallows and Yellow-breasted Chats at the river's edge. Follow the road (now called 300 N) downriver, constantly scanning for birds. Check out the marsh on the right (north) at mile 2.7 for more wetland species. At mile 6.0 turn left (south) on 400 E. At mile 9.0 turn left (east) on Old US 30 (a.k.a. Base Line Road), crossing the Snake River. Watch for Swainson's Hawks, Long-billed Curlews, and Burrowing Owls along Old US 30.

At mile 19.8 turn left (north) on an unsigned dirt field road ("Bird Island Road") and follow it 2 miles to the southern border of Minidoka NWR. This road accesses Lake Walcott's south shore, but it is gated until September. If you contact the refuge manager ahead of time, you may receive permission to drive into this area to view nesting American White Pelicans, Great Blue Herons, Snowy Egrets, Black-crowned Night-Herons, Double-crested Cormorants, and California Gulls. When the gate is locked, enter on foot and walk a mile to the nearest water. *If you do drive in, be aware of your vehicle's capability.* (The road can be pretty rough.) Either way, look for Horned Larks, Loggerhead Shrikes, and Vesper, Lark, Brewer's, and Grasshopper Sparrows

You can also access the south shore of Lake Walcott from Smith Springs Road, which is 2.7 miles east of Bird Island Road. If dry, the road is passable to 2-wheel-drive vehicles with good ground clearance. It's about 1.5 miles to the reservoir.

Raft River Bay provides another vantage point. A graveled road follows the bay's western shore. To find the road, follow Old US 30 to I-86 Exit 15, then turn around and backtrack northwest 1.7 miles (see map). Turn right (north) on the graveled road, which is usually passable to at least the large gravel pit, where you can overlook the entire bay for waterbirds, including migrating swans and Bald Eagles.

Other access points along the south shore are best reached from I-86. At Exit 15 go north 0.1 mile, then turn right (east) and follow signs to Gifford Springs in 2 miles, where you can overlook the lake's upper end. Farther east, at Exit 21, follow the graveled road as it heads west on the north side of the interstate. This short road is also gated until September, but you are allowed to walk the short distance to the reservoir year round. This is a good place to see thousands of molting ducks in August and September. In late fall and winter, look for Tundra and Trumpeter Swans. Watch for Juniper Titmice and Blue-gray Gnatcatchers in junipers.

Winter birding at Minidoka NWR can be worthwhile, also. Besides Canada Geese, Mallards, Gadwalls, American Wigeons, Common Goldeneyes, Common Mergansers, Horned Larks, and Snow Buntings, look for rarities such as scoters and Long-tailed Ducks.

OTHER:

Further information, refuge pamphlets, and a checklist are available from the USFWS (208/237-6615) in Pocatello, or from refuge headquarters (208/436-3589). Developed camping is available at Lake Walcott SP. For other services, try Rupert.

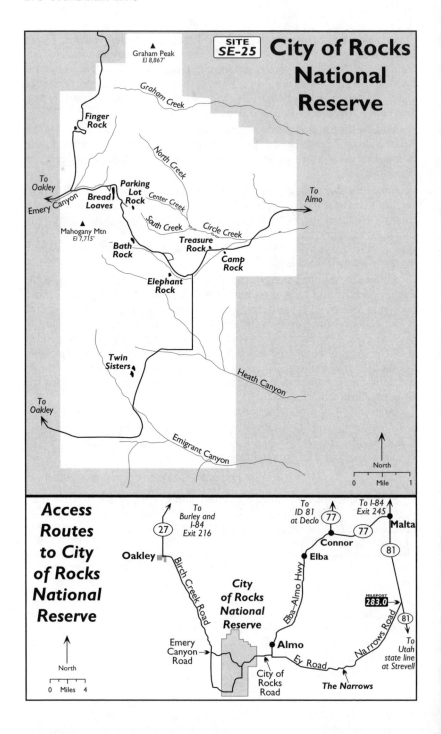

SITE
SE-25

City of Rocks National Reserve

Graham Peak
El 8,867'

Graham Creek

Finger
Rock

North Creek

To
Oakley

Parking
Lot
Rock

Center Creek

To
Almo

Bread
Loaves

Emery Canyon

South Creek

Circle Creek

Mahogany Mtn
El 7,715'

Treasure
Rock

Bath
Rock

Camp
Rock

Elephant
Rock

Twin
Sisters

Heath Canyon

To
Oakley

Emigrant Canyon

North

0   Mile   1

Access Routes to City of Rocks National Reserve

North

0   Miles   4

To
Burley and
I-84
Exit 216

To
ID 81
at Declo

To I-84
Exit 245

27

77

Malta

Connor

77

Oakley

Elba

81

Birch Creek Road

City
of Rocks
National
Reserve

Elba-Almo Hwy

MILEPOST
283.0

Emery
Canyon
Road

Almo

81

To
Utah
state line
at Strevell

City of
Rocks
Road

Ey Road

Narrows Road

The Narrows

CITY OF ROCKS NATIONAL RESERVE

Author: Chuck Trost

Site SE-25 — Map SE-25

Highlights: Prairie Falcon, Pinyon Jay, Juniper Titmouse
Major Habitats: Juniper, Shrub-steppe
Location: Cassia Co., 4 miles west of Almo
Spring: * * *   **Summer:** * * * * **Fall:** * *   **Winter:** * *

City of Rocks National Reserve covers about 14,800 acres and contains a portion of Idaho's only Pinyon Pine forest. Birding is often wonderful here, but most visitors come to marvel at the strange granite monoliths, some over 500 feet high.

DIRECTIONS:

You can access the reserve from the west (through Oakley), east (through Almo), or north (through Albion). All routes are well signed.

To reach the reserve from the west, zero your mileage in Oakley, then go east on Main 2000 S Road. At mile 1.0, turn right (south) on Birch Creek Road. Check out Birch Creek and adjacent cliffs for a variety of birds (including Canyon and Rock Wrens). At mile 13.3 turn left (east) on Emery Canyon Road and drive into City of Rocks National Reserve at mile 14.8.

To access the reserve from the east, zero your mileage in Malta at the junction of ID 77 and ID 81 and drive south on ID 81 to mile 10.2 (milepost 283). Turn right (west) onto graveled Narrows Road and head through the "Narrows" of the Raft River toward Almo. Along this route watch for Turkey Vultures, Ferruginous Hawks, Golden Eagles, and Prairie Falcons. At mile 22.3 Narrows Road goes straight, while Ey Road goes left (southwest). Take Ey Road. (Be aware that the DeLorme Atlas has these road names switched.) When you come to a T intersection at mile 28, turn right (north). The City of Rocks Road goes left (west) in 0.25 mile. Turn here to enter the reserve in 1.6 miles, or go straight for 0.75 mile to visit the reserve office in Almo.

The easiest and most direct route to the reserve is from the north. Take I-84 Exit 216 (east of Burley) and follow ID 77 south for 23.5 miles through Declo and Albion. At the T intersection turn right (west) and drive another 16 miles through Elba to Almo, where you can stop at the reserve office.

Reserve roads can be snow-covered from November to April, and they may be gated if impassable. At other times wet roads may still be too much for a 2-wheel-drive vehicle; 4-wheel drive is advisable during the period of September to May. You can call the park office (208/824-5519) to learn the latest road conditions.

BIRDING:

The best areas for birding are the pinyon/juniper woodlands. This is especially true when the pinyon nut crop is plentiful. The large, meaty pinyon seeds are highly prized by a variety of species. During poor crop years, the woodlands can seem to be almost devoid of birds, particularly in winter. The best example of pinyon/juniper woodland is found at the reserve's east entrance. Most of the habitat is fenced to control grazing. Private and public property is mixed here. Public lands are clearly signed. Among the species to look for are Gray Flycatcher, Juniper Titmouse, Bushtit, Blue-gray Gnatcatcher, Black-throated Gray Warbler (irregular), and Lazuli Bunting. Also keep an eye out for Ash-throated Flycatchers, Loggerhead Shrikes, and Scott's Orioles (only one local record so far). With the exception of Gray Jay, all of Idaho's corvids can be found using the Pinyon Pine habitat. Western Scrub-Jays are present year round, as are Common Ravens, which can be observed doing their mid-air rollovers in spring. During a good mast year, one can watch Pinyon Jays and Clark's Nutcrackers secretly cache pine nuts.

Blue Grouse are year-round residents but are hard to find. Look for them, Hermit Thrushes, and Green-tailed Towhees in the higher forested hills. Listen for Plumbeous and Warbling Vireos in Quaking Aspen groves, such as those near Bread Loaves and Parking Lot Rock. Virginia's and MacGillivray's Warblers can be found in riparian Chokecherry bushes. Good riparian birding can be had along South Circle Creek, east of Bath Rock.

Several raptors nest in the Reserve, including Turkey Vultures, Sharp-shinned, Cooper's, and Red-tailed Hawks, Golden Eagles, American Kestrels, and Prairie Falcons. Western Screech-Owls, Great Horned Owls, and Northern Pygmy-Owls can be heard on spring evenings. In late spring and summer White-throated Swifts often zoom by, sometimes copulating in midair! Wintering birds include Bald Eagles, Rough-legged Hawks, Northern Flickers, American Robins, Spotted Towhees, Dark-eyed Juncos, and Cassin's Finches.

Much remains to be learned about the birdlife at this relatively new park. The helpful and bird-wise staff can be of great assistance in pointing out additional areas for exploration.

OTHER:

Plan to pick up a map and a checklist at the office in Almo, and ask the ranger about recent bird sightings.

This area is decidedly remote, with no repair facilities for many miles. Tray's Store in Almo offers food and showers, but it's not open on Sundays and has no beer (ye gads!).

City of Rocks National Reserve is internationally known for rock climbing. Because of that activity, campgrounds are typically full in spring and summer, so plan on arriving early in the day. There are several camping areas and restroom facilities in the main portion of the rocky outcrops.

CURLEW NATIONAL GRASSLAND

Author: Chuck Trost

Site SE-26 — Map SE-26

Highlights: Ash-throated Flycatcher, Scott's Oriole
Major Habitats: Shrub-steppe, Wetland, Juniper
Location: Oneida Co., 20 miles west of Malad City
Spring: *** **Summer:** *** **Fall:** ** **Winter:** *

Curlew National Grassland encompasses 48,000 acres of Great Basin shrub-steppe in three isolated tracts. Despite its name, there are few curlews here. Instead, this area's birding attraction is Idaho's premier example of Great Basin avifauna.

DIRECTIONS:

Curlew National Grassland surrounds Holbrook, which can be accessed from several directions. From the west follow I-84 south to Snowville, Utah, then turn north on Stone Road and follow it 16 miles to Holbrook. From the east take I-15 south to Malad City (Exit 13) and turn right (west) on ID 38. Follow it 24 miles to Holbrook.

To reach the Grassland's north and west tracts from Holbrook, follow Stone Road (a.k.a. Grassland Road [GR] 080) north 1 mile to the intersection of ID 38 and ID 37. To bird the north tract, follow ID 38 east 0.4 mile, then turn left (north) on Hess Road (a.k.a. GR 029), which bisects the north tract. The west tract lies along ID 37 (a.k.a. North Holbrook Road), from the junction of ID 37/38 to ID 37 milepost 35.5.

The Grassland's south tract is along Stone Road and begins about 3 miles south of Holbrook. Deep Creek Reservoir (a.k.a. Stone Reservoir) is in the center of the south tract. To find the reservoir from Holbrook, head south on Stone Road. After 5 miles, turn right (west) on GR 061 (unsigned), and drive about 2 miles to the reservoir's north end. Another view can be had at the Curlew Campground and boat ramp near the dam. To get there, follow Stone Road 9 miles southwest of Holbrook, then turn right (north) on GR 020 (a.k.a. 22500 West) and follow the road 1 mile to the campground and dam.

BIRDING:

The best way to bird Curlew National Grassland is simply to wander along the various highways and side roads. Be sure to investigate any water in this arid country, particularly Deep Creek Reservoir.

Spring and fall are the most exciting seasons, when a variety of migrants are present. It's in early summer, however, that the sage/grass flats come alive with sky-larking Sage Thrashers and Vesper Sparrows. Summer is also the time to hear the amazing buzzing song of Brewer's Sparrows. If you're lucky, you may also find Black-throated Sparrows in the south tract.

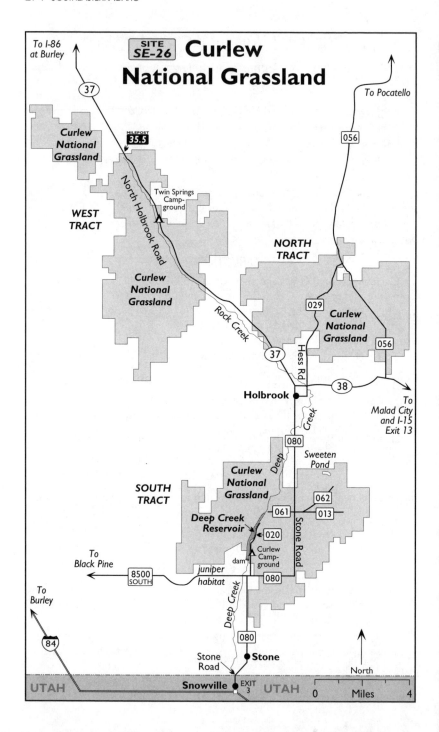

SITE
SE-26 **Curlew National Grassland**

To I-86 at Burley

37

Curlew National Grassland

MILEPOST 35.5

North Holbrook Road

Twin Springs Campground

WEST TRACT

Curlew National Grassland

Rock Creek

37

NORTH TRACT

Curlew National Grassland

029

To Pocatello

056

056

Hess Rd.

38

Holbrook

To Malad City and I-15 Exit 13

Creek

080

Deep

Sweeten Pond

SOUTH TRACT

Curlew National Grassland

061

062

013

Deep Creek Reservoir

020

Stone Road

To Black Pine

8500 SOUTH

juniper habitat

dam

Curlew Campground

080

To Burley

84

Deep Creek

080

Stone Road

Stone

Snowville

EXIT 3

UTAH

UTAH

North

0 Miles 4

Curlew National Grassland has one of the largest Sharp-tailed Grouse populations in the state. Leks are scattered throughout the valley, but their locations often change from year to year. One traditional lek is located about a mile east of West Carter Field. To find this area from Holbrook, follow Stone Road south 5 miles, then turn left (east) on GR 013 (unmarked), go 0.5 mile, then turn left (northeast) on GR 062 for 0.5 mile, and look on the right (east) side of the dike. The grouse dance for only a short time after dawn, and only in late March into April. It would be a good idea to call the IDFG (208/232-4703) in Pocatello, or the FS (208/766-4743) in Malad City, to find out if they can direct you more precisely to an active lek.

Curlew National Grassland is the best place in Idaho to see Ash-throated Flycatchers and Scott's Orioles. To find their preferred juniper habitat, follow Stone Road south from Holbrook for about 7 miles, then follow the road right (west) and stay straight for about 4 miles (road becomes 8500 South, a.k.a. Black Pine Road; do not follow GR 080 to Stone). Juniper habitat can be found from here west, as well as along the numerous side roads. Scott's Orioles have been seen regularly in this area, but they often require a lot of work to encounter. Other nesting species include Ferruginous Hawk, Common Poorwill, Gray Flycatcher, Western Scrub-Jay, Pinyon Jay, Juniper Titmouse, Blue-gray Gnatcatcher, Mountain Bluebird, Loggerhead Shrike, and Chipping Sparrow.

Deep Creek Reservoir attracts many migrating ducks, especially divers. Look for Redheads, Ring-necked Ducks, Canvasbacks, and Lesser Scaup. Common Loons and Western Grebes are regular April visitors, but they do not nest here. In summer look for Yellow-headed and Red-winged Blackbirds in the willows and for Bullock's Orioles in the Russian-olives. Flocks of Canada and Snow Geese stop over in fall.

Deep Creek Reservoir is also a prime focus of winter birding, since it remains open long after nearby wetlands are frozen. Wintering birds include Killdeer and Marsh Wrens at the reservoir outlet and American Tree and Song Sparrows in nearby riparian brush. Look for Sharp-tailed Grouse in shelterbelts near the reservoir. Also watch for Rough-legged Hawks, Common Ravens, and Northern Shrikes on power poles, and for Western Meadowlarks and huge flocks of Horned Larks along snow-covered roads.

OTHER:

Besides Curlew Campground there is a primitive BLM campground ("Twin Springs") 9 miles north of Holbrook along ID 37. Twin Springs campground borders a wet meadow that is worth investigating for Sharp-tailed Grouse, Sage Thrashers, Green-tailed Towhees, and Vesper and Savannah Sparrows.

Food, fuel, and other supplies are available in Malad City, American Falls, and Snowville, Utah. For more information, call the FS (208/766-4743) in Malad City.

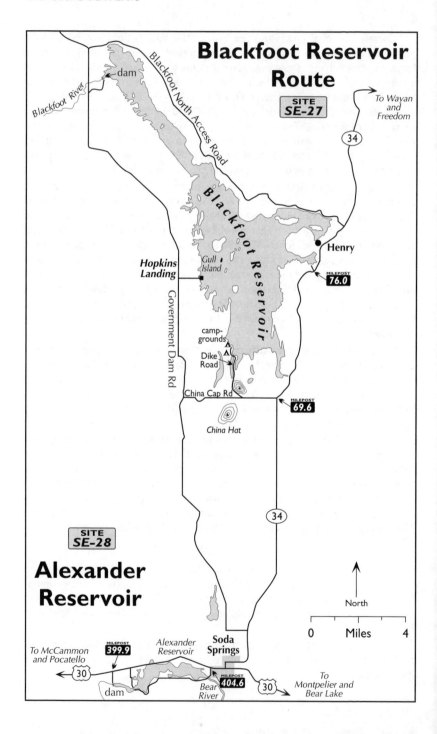

Blackfoot Reservoir Route

SITE SE-27

To Wayan and Freedom

dam

Blackfoot River

Blackfoot North Access Road

Blackfoot Reservoir

Henry

MILEPOST 76.0

Hopkins Landing

Gull Island

Government Dam Rd

camp-grounds

Dike Road

China Cap Rd

MILEPOST 69.6

China Hat

34

SITE SE-28

Alexander Reservoir

North

0   Miles   4

To McCammon and Pocatello

MILEPOST 399.9

30

Alexander Reservoir

Soda Springs

dam

Bear River

MILEPOST 404.6

30

To Montpelier and Bear Lake

BLACKFOOT RESERVOIR ROUTE

Authors: Chuck Trost, Eric Lepisto

Site SE-27 — Map SE-27/SE-28

Highlights: Clark's and Western Grebes, Black Tern
Major Habitats: Wetland, Shrub-steppe, Farmland
Location: Caribou Co., 15 miles north of Soda Springs
Spring: * *   **Summer:** * *   **Fall:** * *   **Winter:** N/A

Blackfoot Reservoir is a large (19,000 acres) impoundment on the Blackfoot River. It shares both water and birds with nearby Grays Lake NWR (p. 279). Although Blackfoot Reservoir is ringed by roads, shore access can be difficult except at designated places. This area is best birded as a 60-mile-long loop.

DIRECTIONS:

From Soda Springs follow ID 34 north 11 miles to milepost 69.6. Turn left (west) on China Cap Road, go 1.5 miles, then turn right (north) on Dike Road (signed for Dike Lake) and follow it 4 miles to the BLM's campground on the southern edge of the reservoir.

BIRDING:

On the way to the campground watch for Black Terns over the small wetlands. At the campground scan the reservoir for Western and Clark's Grebes, various waterfowl, and Caspian Terns, then backtrack to China Cap Road.

Turn right (west) on China Cap Road for 2.7 miles, then turn right (north) at the T intersection onto Government Dam Road. This road follows the west side of the reservoir about 15 miles to the dam. Any road that takes off to the right (east) will lead you to Blackfoot Reservoir. *These side roads can be very muddy.*

Approximately 5.1 miles north of the junction of China Cap Road and Government Dam Road, turn right (east) on a dirt trail and follow it 1 mile to Hopkin's (a.k.a. Hokkin's) Landing. (You may want to hike this road, rather than drive it.) From Hopkins Landing, you can see an island nesting colony of American White Pelicans, California and Ring-billed Gulls, and Caspian Terns. Farther out in the reservoir is a series of low islands with colonies of Black-crowned Night-Herons, Great Blue Herons, Snowy Egrets, and Double-crested Cormorants.

Return to Government Dam Road and continue north. After 10.1 miles stay right at the Y intersection and follow the 1.0-mile-long spur road to view the dam. After looking for additional waterbirds, return to Government Dam Road and follow it northeast across the Blackfoot River. About 1.7 miles after crossing the Blackfoot, stay right at the Y intersection, and explore along unmarked Blackfoot North Access Road as it parallels the reservoir's eastern shoreline for 17 miles. Watch for more waterbirds along this drive, as well as for Sandhill Cranes, Burrowing Owls, Sage Thrashers, and Vesper, Savannah, Lark, and Brewer's Sparrows.

When you reach ID 34, turn right (south) and go 2 miles, passing through Henry, to milepost 76. Either walk or drive the 2-track road to the right (west), which is just before some gravel piles on the left (east) side of ID 34. You'll reach the reservoir in 0.2 mile. Look for shorebirds along the shoreline, especially in summer, when the reservoir is drawn down for irrigation. Greater and Lesser Yellowlegs and Long-billed Dowitcher can be common here, and even a vagrant Ruddy Turnstone has shown up.

OTHER:

The small store in Henry has a few odds and ends. The BLM campgrounds by Dike Lake have a boat ramp, picnic tables, pit toilets, and water. Other services are available in Soda Springs. For a map and more information, contact the FS (208/547-4356) in Soda Springs, or BLM (208/236-6860) in Pocatello.

ALEXANDER RESERVOIR

Authors: Chuck Trost, Eric Lepisto

Site SE-28 — Map SE-27/SE-28

Highlights: Western Grebe, Forster's Tern
Major Habitat: Wetland
Location: Caribou Co., Soda Springs
Spring: * *   **Summer:** * *   **Fall:** * *   **Winter:** *

A dam on the meandering Bear River has created 1,200-acre Alexander Reservoir at the outskirts of Soda Springs. This shallow wetland attracts a variety of waterbirds, particularly waterfowl. It also supports incredible numbers of carp!

DIRECTIONS:

Alexander Reservoir is along ID 34, on the west side of Soda Springs. There are viewpoints all along the northern shore. There is especially good birding at Soda Point Picnic Area and at Betty's Cafe, at ID 34 mileposts 402.4 and 404, respectively.

To explore the dam area, turn south at milepost 399.9 onto Soda Point Power Plant Road and follow it 0.6 mile.

The reservoir's south side is accessed by going into Soda Springs and turning south on West 3rd Street, at ID 34 milepost 404.6. Drive past Caribou County Hospital, then turn right (west) on 4th South Street and cross the Bear River. You can follow this road along the south shore for 3.5 miles until it dead-ends at a turn-around. *Out-of-date maps show a bridge across the reservoir at this point; don't believe it.*

BIRDING:

Common Loons can be seen on the reservoir in April and early May, as can a variety of duck species. Western Grebes and Forster's Terns are fairly common in summer. Look for American White Pelicans loafing at the reservoir's west end. Shorebirds, such as Marbled Godwits and American Avocets, are most often seen near the east end.

In winter the reservoir usually ices up. If the lake's inlet and outlet are still unfrozen, look for Barrow's and Common Goldeneyes, Common Mergansers, and Bald Eagles.

OTHER:

Soda Springs offers food, fuel, and lodging. There are several FS campgrounds within 15 miles of town. For maps and information, contact the FS (208/547-4356) in Soda Springs.

GRAYS LAKE NATIONAL WILDLIFE REFUGE

Author: Dan Svingen

Site SE-29 — Map SE-29

Highlights: Trumpeter Swan, Sandhill Crane
Major Habitats: Wetland, Meadow
Location: Bonneville Co., 27 miles north of Soda Springs
Spring: * *   **Summer:** * *   **Fall:** * *   **Winter:** *

Grays Lake NWR encompasses about 18,300 acres of bulrush/cattail marsh and wet meadow. Because of the large nesting population of (Greater) Sandhill Crane, Grays Lake was chosen for an unique experiment. Beginning in the mid-1970s, Whooping Crane eggs were placed in Sandhill Crane nests on the refuge. The resulting Whooper chicks were then raised by their foster parents. It was hoped that this experiment would result in a second breeding population of Whoopers, but it was not to be. With luck you may still see a Whooping Crane or two on the refuge.

DIRECTIONS:

From Soda Springs follow ID 34 north 33 miles. At milepost 92 turn left (north) onto Grays Lake Road and follow it 3 miles to refuge headquarters on the right (east). Stop here to pick up a bird checklist and a map.

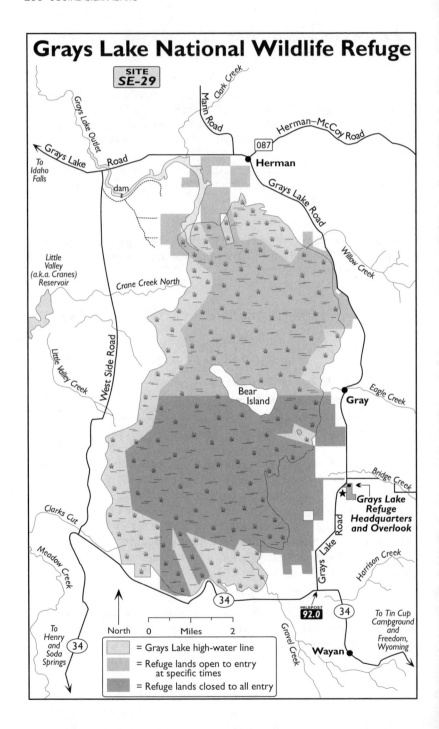

Grays Lake National Wildlife Refuge

SITE
SE-29

BIRDING:

Grays Lake provides great bird habitat but poor birding. From April 1 to October 9 there is no access into the refuge. Birders are then restricted to driving the loop road and using a scope to get distant views of Eared Grebes, American Bitterns, White-faced Ibises, Trumpeter Swans, Cinnamon Teal, Barrow's Goldeneyes, Bald Eagles, Peregrine Falcons, Virginia Rails, Soras, Sandhill Cranes, American Avocets, Willets, Long-billed Curlews, Wilson's Phalaropes, Franklin's Gulls, Forster's and Black Terns, and Short-eared Owls. Many of these species can be seen at closer range in the private meadows that border the loop road. The road gets close to marsh habitat along the south, northeast, and north portions of the loop. An overlook just south of headquarters provides an additional scoping location; look for nesting White-crowned Sparrows in the draw next to the overlook.

Part of the refuge is open to foot exploration from October 10 to March 31, but the area is usually snow-bound from November through April. Portions of the loop road may be impassable in winter. Fall and winter birdlife is greatly affected by open-water availability. Species to look for include various waterfowl, Northern Goshawk, Red-tailed and Rough-legged Hawks, Greater Sage-Grouse, Horned Lark, American Crow, Common Raven, Black-capped Chickadee, and Dark-eyed Junco.

OTHER:

You may be able to get fuel and a few supplies at Henry. Other services are available in Soda Springs. Several FS campgrounds are available in the area. If you stay at Tin Cup Campground, listen for American Redstart. (But watch out for the mosquitoes!) For more information contact the refuge (208/574-2755) or the FS (208/547-4356) in Soda Springs.

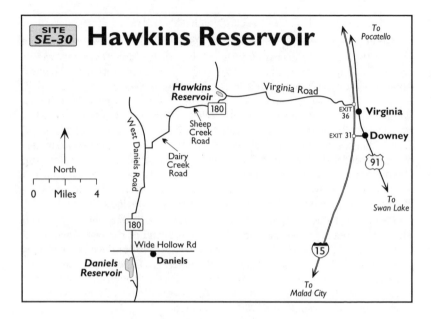

HAWKINS RESERVOIR

Authors: Chuck Trost, Eric Lepisto

Site SE-30 — Map SE-30

Highlights: Sharp-tailed Grouse, Pinyon Jay
Major Habitats: Juniper, Wetland, Farmland
Location: Bannock Co., 9 miles west of Virginia
Spring: * *   **Summer:** * *   **Fall:** * *   **Winter:** *

Fifteen-acre Hawkins Reservoir is a popular fishing and boating area amid scenic mountain views. The BLM has made special efforts to make this area easily accessible for recreationists.

DIRECTIONS:

From I-15 Exit 36 follow Virginia Road west 8.5 miles to Hawkins Reservoir. Watch for Willet and Sandhill Crane along the way. After mile 7.0 most of the land along this route is public (BLM).

BIRDING:

Hawkins Reservoir is surrounded by agricultural fields and rolling juniper hills. In the farmlands look for Northern Harrier and Swainson's and Red-tailed Hawks. The junipers are home to Pinyon Jays, Juniper Titmice, Mountain Bluebirds, and Chipping Sparrows.

The west end of Hawkins Reservoir is shallow and marshy, offering habitat for Great Blue Herons, Great Egrets, and waterfowl. During late summer and early fall, the reservoir is lowered for irrigation, exposing mudflats for shorebirds. Western, Baird's, and Least Sandpipers are regular, and Long-billed Dowitchers and Lesser Yellowlegs are frequently present. Dunlins and Sanderlings should be looked for, September to November.

To continue birding, take graveled Sheep Creek Road (a.k.a. FR 180, a.k.a. Dairy Creek Road) southwest from the south side of Hawkins Reservoir for 7.4 miles. At the junction with West Daniels Road, turn left (south) and go 8 miles to Daniels Reservoir. Be aware that Sheep Creek Road is often impassable during winter.

The route to Daniels Reservoir passes through high-elevation agricultural fields. There are several Sharp-tailed Grouse leks in this area, which are best viewed in April and early May. One lek is next to a deserted farmstead (private) on the east side of Sheep Creek Road, just after you crest the hill above Hawkins Reservoir. Another potential site is in a winter-wheat field (private) on the southeast side of Wide Hollow Road (a.k.a. 10200 West, a.k.a. White Hollow Road), about a half mile north of Daniels Reservoir. Other leks have been seen in fields between Hawkins and Daniels Reservoirs, but they seem to change location year to year.

Daniels Reservoir has a small Great Blue Heron colony in dead trees at the upper end. Search the nests carefully, and you may also find Ospreys and Great Horned Owls. Say's Phoebes can be found at several deserted homesteads south of Daniels Reservoir.

OTHER:

There are a boat ramp, picnic shelters, and restrooms at Hawkins Reservoir. Pocatello is the closest full-service community. Fuel, food, and motels are available in Malad City. For a map and more information, contact the BLM (208/766-4766) in Malad City.

OXFORD SLOUGH AREA

Authors: Chuck Trost, Eric Lepisto

Site SE-31 — Map SE-31

Highlights: Snowy and Cattle Egrets, White-faced Ibis
Major Habitats: Wetland, Farmland, Meadow
Location: Franklin Co., 11 miles northwest of Preston
Spring: ***   **Summer:** ***   **Fall:** **   **Winter:** *

There are three great birding spots in this area: Swan Lake, Oxford Slough, and Twin Lakes. Each offers something different. Swan Lake is a spectacular, shallow, 30-acre wetland which provides close views of waterfowl and wading birds. Oxford Slough is a huge, inaccessible marsh that supports Franklin's Gull and White-faced Ibis colonies. Twin Lakes is a large, deep reservoir used by migrant loons and grebes.

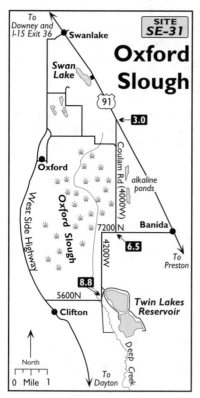

DIRECTIONS:

All three birding sites are within a few miles of US 91 between Swanlake and Preston; all can be easily birded in a loop. To access this area from I-15, take Exit 36 and head south on US 91 through Downey. At milepost 39.1 look on the right (west) side of the highway for Burrowing Owl in a small, bare area surrounded by grass. At milepost 30 watch for nesting Golden Eagles, White-throated Swifts, and Violet-green Swallows on the cliffs of Red Rocks Pass. (This is where the famous "Bonneville Flood" began 15,000 years ago, inundating the Snake River Plain with 380 cubic *miles* of water!) In the tiny town of Swanlake zero your mileage and continue south.

BIRDING:

At mile 1.5 park in the pull-out on the right (west), overlooking Swan Lake (private). From March to April Swan Lake teems with a fantastic concentration of migrant Tundra Swans and Northern Pintails. This wetland is also good for nesting Soras, Virginia

Rails, and Marsh Wrens. Watch for nesting Sandhill Cranes throughout the area, and for flying herons and White-faced Ibises.

Continue south on US 91. At mile 3.0, angle right (south) on Coulam Road (a.k.a. 4000 West). Coulam Road passes through seasonally-flooded agricultural lands and alkaline flats that can harbor tremendous numbers of waterfowl and shorebirds. In spring look for thousands of Northern Pintails and Mallards, with good numbers of Northern Shovelers and both Blue-winged and Cinnamon Teals. Shorebirds include breeding American Avocets, Black-necked Stilts, and Long-billed Curlews. In migration thousands of Wilson's Phalaropes have been present.

At the T intersection at mile 6.5, turn right (west) on paved 7200 North. At mile 7.0 curve left (south) on graveled 4200 West. At mile 8.8 turn left (east) and follow the Sportsman Access signs up a ramp road to Twin Lakes Reservoir.

Twin Lakes is open to the public and is very popular with boaters, campers, and anglers, so plan your birding excursions to avoid summer weekends. There are graveled access roads around most of the two connected lakes, with the exception of the south side of the southern lake. The lakes are surrounded by tall cottonwoods, with sagebrush hillsides above them. It is possible to ride a mountain bike completely around the lakes in about an hour, or to bird most of the area from your car. Look for dancing Western and Clark's Grebes in spring. Eared and Pied-billed Grebes are also common. In April Common Loons stage at Twin Lakes, with as many as 125 having been seen in a single day.

After exploring Twin Lakes, backtrack to 4200 West and turn left (south) for 0.2 mile, then turn right (west) on 5600 N, crossing the railroad tracks. You'll reach West Side Highway in 1.8 miles, where you should turn right (north) and drive 4.2 miles to Oxford. In Oxford, turn right (east) on North Street for 0.2 mile, then left (north) on Harkness Street. After 0.5 mile turn right (east), and follow the road 2.8 miles back to Coulam Road, completing the loop. Watch for Short-eared Owls and Grasshopper Sparrows in this area, as well as Sandhill Cranes.

There are White-faced Ibis and Franklin's Gull colonies in the reeds throughout Oxford Slough. A good number of Black-crowned Night-Herons, Great Blue Herons, and Snowy Egrets nest here, too, while a small colony of Cattle Egrets is mixed in with the Snowies. Black Terns nest at the north end. Waterfowl (especially Redheads) are abundant. The northern portion of Oxford Slough is managed as a Waterfowl Production Area and is open to hiking year round. (Watch for the green-and-white boundary signs.) The remainder of the area is private.

OTHER:

There is a general store in Swanlake with camping and cooking supplies. Additional services are available in Preston. For more information contact the Pocatello offices of the USFWS (208/237-6615) or the IDFG (208/232-4703).

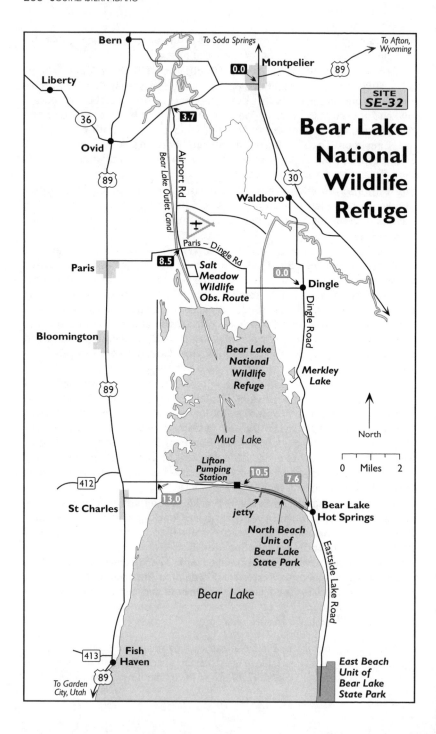

BEAR LAKE NATIONAL WILDLIFE REFUGE

Authors: Peder Svingen, Sue Barton

Site SE-32 — Map SE-32

Highlights: White-faced Ibis, Franklin's Gull, Black Tern
Major Habitats: Wetland, Meadow
Location: Bear Lake Co., 12 miles southwest of Montpelier
Spring: *** **Summer:** *** **Fall:** * **Winter:** N/A

This 18,000-acre refuge is a bird photographer's delight! Waders, waterfowl, and shorebirds can be closely studied right from your car. The 2.5-mile-long Salt Meadow Wildlife Observation Route is particularly productive, especially for some of the 5,000 White-faced Ibises and 13,000 Franklin's Gulls which nest here.

DIRECTIONS:

Zero your mileage at the junction of US 89 and US 30 in Montpelier and head west on US 89. Stop at refuge headquarters along US 89 before leaving town and get a map, a checklist, and information on current travel restrictions. At mile 3.7 turn left (south) onto Airport Road at the refuge sign. Continue straight (south) at the airport turn-off. You'll enter the refuge at mile 8.5.

BIRDING:

Watch flooded meadows and pastures along Airport Road for Snowy and Cattle Egrets, White-faced Ibises, Cinnamon Teal, Black-necked Stilts, American Avocets, and Willets. Check out the scattered willow clumps for migrating passerines.

Airport Road intersects Paris-Dingle Road at the refuge's north boundary. Continue south, following Bear Lake Outlet Canal, watching for Double-crested Cormorants and swallows. The marsh on the left (east) should garner most of your attention. The first half-mile is good for American Bitterns, Virginia Rails, Soras, and Short-eared Owls. The habitat also looks promising for vagrant Yellow Rails.

At mile 10 the road splits; bear left and look for Clark's Grebes. Continue on to the well-marked Salt Meadow Unit's Wildlife Observation Route. Eared Grebes, egrets, White-faced Ibises, Short-eared Owls, and a variety of waterfowl and shorebirds may be seen at close range. Forster's and Black Terns are common, and Marsh Wrens are *abundant.*

When you've completed the Observation Route, return to Paris-Dingle Road, and turn right (east) toward Dingle. Willow thickets and pastures along this road can afford good birding during passerine migration.

In Dingle re-zero your mileage and head south on Dingle Road (a.k.a. Merkley Lake Road). At mile 4.4, begin listening for Sage Thrasher and Brewer's and Sage Sparrows on the left (east) side of the road. Watch the cliffs for Turkey Vultures, Golden Eagles, and Peregrine and Prairie Falcons. At mile 7.6 turn right (west) toward the North Beach Unit of Bear Lake SP. The park's entrance station is at mile 8. The road follows Bear Lake's north shore for several miles. Scan this popular beach for shorebirds, gulls, and terns. This is one of the best local spots for Caspian Terns. If you have a scope, scan Mud Lake on the right (north) side of the road for grebes, American White Pelicans, shorebirds, and terns. Beyond the jetty at mile 9.6 the beach is private property. At mile 10.5 is the Lifton Pumping Station. The small residential area looks good as a migrant trap. You'll reach the intersection with Power Line Road and the end of this route at mile 13.

For additional birding, try the East Beach Unit of Bear Lake SP (see map). Although little is known of the birdlife there, residential areas along Eastside Lake Road on the way to the park look promising for vagrant Purple Martins, while the beach may attract a lost Snowy Plover.

OTHER:

Camping is available at the East Beach Unit of Bear Lake SP (water, pit toilets, no showers), and the Montpelier KOA Campground. Fuel, food, and accommodations are available in Montpelier. For more information contact refuge headquarters (208/847-1757).

MULTI-PURPOSE CHECKLIST

The following Multi-purpose Checklist of 400 Idaho birds should assist the visiting and resident birder in determining the seasonal abundance of our birds statewide and by the four regions as defined in this book. It is an adaptation of the December 1, 2003 list developed by the Idaho Bird Records Committee and follows the 44th Supplement to the AOU Check-list of North American Birds (2003). Not only can you quickly determine the status of these species, but you can also check off the species using the boxes available.

Season:
R — Resident
M — Migrant
W — Winter
S — Summer

Other:
B — Breeder
b — Circumstantial evidence of breeding
End — Threatened or endangered
Int — Introduced
* — Please report and document sightings

Abundance:
1 — Abundant, easily found
2 — Common, but sometimes difficult to find
3 — Uncommon or local
4 — Rare or local
5 — Casual, 3-10 accepted records
6 — Accidental, 1-2 accepted records
7 — Experimental

	BREEDING	Statewide	Panhandle	Central	Southwest	Southeast
☐ Greater White-fronted Goose			M4	M4	M3	M4
☐ Emperor Goose *					M6	
☐ Snow Goose			M3	M3	M2	M2
☐ Ross's Goose		M4	W5		W5	W5
☐ Canada Goose	B	R1				
☐ Brant *			M5		M5	M5
☐ Trumpeter Swan	B		MW4	MW4	MW4	R3
☐ Tundra Swan		M2 W3				
☐ Wood Duck	B		S3 W4	S3 W4	R3	R3
☐ Gadwall	B	R1				
☐ Eurasian Wigeon		MW4				
☐ American Wigeon	B	R1				
☐ American Black Duck *			M5			M5
☐ Mallard	B	R1				
☐ Blue-winged Teal	B	S3				

	BREEDING	Statewide	Panhandle	Central	Southwest	Southeast
☐ Cinnamon Teal	B	S1 W4				
☐ Northern Shoveler	B	S2 W4				
☐ Northern Pintail	B	R2				
☐ Garganey *					M6	
☐ Green-winged Teal	B	S2	W5	W3	W3	W3
☐ Canvasback	B	MW2			R3	R3
☐ Redhead	B	R2				
☐ Ring-necked Duck	B	MW2	S3	S3	S4	S3
☐ Tufted Duck *			W6		W6	
☐ Greater Scaup		MW3				
☐ Lesser Scaup	B	R2				
☐ Harlequin Duck	B		S4	S4		S4
☐ Surf Scoter		MW4				
☐ White-winged Scoter		MW4				
☐ Black Scoter *				M5		M5
☐ Long-tailed Duck		MW4				
☐ Bufflehead	B	R2				
☐ Common Goldeneye	B	W1	S3	S3	S4	S4
☐ Barrow's Goldeneye	B	W3	S4	S3	S4	S3
☐ Hooded Merganser	B	R3				
☐ Common Merganser	B	R2				
☐ Red-breasted Merganser		W4	M4	M4	M2	M2
☐ Ruddy Duck	B	R2				
☐ Chukar (Int)	B			R2	R2	R3
☐ Gray Partridge (Int)	B	R3				
☐ Ring-necked Pheasant (Int)	B	R1				
☐ Ruffed Grouse	B	R2				
☐ Greater Sage-Grouse	B			R3	R3	R3
☐ Spruce Grouse	B		R3	R3	R3	
☐ White-tailed Ptarmigan *			R5			
☐ Blue Grouse	B	R3				
☐ Sharp-tailed Grouse	B				R4	R3
☐ Wild Turkey (Int)	B	R3				
☐ Mountain Quail	B		R4	R4	R4	

	BREEDING	Statewide	Panhandle	Central	Southwest	Southeast
☐ California Quail (Int)	B		R2	R3	R2	
☐ Gambel's Quail (Int)	B			R4		
☐ Northern Bobwhite (Int)	B	R7				
☐ Red-throated Loon		M4				
☐ Pacific Loon		M4				
☐ Common Loon	B	S3 M2 W4				
☐ Yellow-billed Loon *			M5			M5
☐ Pied-billed Grebe	B	S1 W3				
☐ Horned Grebe	B	MW3			S4	S4
☐ Red-necked Grebe	B		R3		S4	S4
☐ Eared Grebe	B	W4	M4	M3	S2	S2
☐ Western Grebe	B	S1	W3		W3	W3
☐ Clark's Grebe	B		S4	S4	S2 W6	S2
☐ American White Pelican	B		S4	S4	S1 W5	S1 W5
☐ Double-crested Cormorant	B		M4	M4	S1 W3	S1
☐ American Bittern	B	S3				
☐ Great Blue Heron	B	R2				
☐ Great Egret	B		S5	S5	S3 W4	S3
☐ Snowy Egret	B		S5	S5	S3	S2
☐ Little Blue Heron *			S6			S6
☐ Tricolored Heron *						S6
☐ Cattle Egret	B		M4	M4	S3	S3
☐ Green Heron	b		R4		R4	R4
☐ Black-crowned Night-Heron	B		M3	M3	S2 W3	S2
☐ White Ibis *					M6	
☐ White-faced Ibis	B		M5	M5	S3	S1
☐ Wood Stork *					S6	
☐ Turkey Vulture	B		S3	S3	S1	S1

	BREEDING	Statewide	Panhandle	Central	Southwest	Southeast
☐ Osprey	B	S2				
☐ White-tailed Kite *			S5		S5	S5
☐ Bald Eagle (End)	B	R3				
☐ Northern Harrier	B	R2				
☐ Sharp-shinned Hawk	B	R2				
☐ Cooper's Hawk	B	R3				
☐ Northern Goshawk	B	R4				
☐ Red-shouldered Hawk *					M5	M5
☐ Broad-winged Hawk			M4		M4	M4
☐ Swainson's Hawk	B		M4	S3	S1	S1
☐ Red-tailed Hawk	B	R1				
☐ Ferruginous Hawk	B	MW4		S3	S3	S3
☐ Rough-legged Hawk		MW2				
☐ Golden Eagle	B		R4	R3	R3	R3
☐ Crested Caracara *						M6
☐ American Kestrel	B	R1				
☐ Merlin	B	S4				
		MW3				
☐ Gyrfalcon		MW4				
☐ Peregrine Falcon (End)	B	SM4				
☐ Prairie Falcon	B	R3				
☐ Yellow Rail *					S6	S6
☐ Virginia Rail	B	W4	S3	S3	S2	S2
☐ Sora	B	S2		W5	W4	W4
☐ Common Moorhen *						S5
☐ American Coot	B	R1				
☐ Sandhill Crane	B		M4		S3	S2
☐ Whooping Crane (Int,End)						S7
☐ Black-bellied Plover		M3				
☐ American Golden-Plover		M4				
☐ Snowy Plover	B	SM4				
☐ Semipalmated Plover		M3				
☐ Killdeer	B	S1				
		W3				
☐ Mountain Plover *		M5				
☐ American Oystercatcher *					M6	

	BREEDING	Statewide	Panhandle	Central	Southwest	Southeast
☐ Black-necked Stilt	B		M5		S3	S3
☐ American Avocet	B		M4	S2	S2	S2
☐ Greater Yellowlegs		M2	W5		W5	W5
☐ Lesser Yellowlegs		M2				W5
☐ Solitary Sandpiper		M3				
☐ Willet	B		M4	S2	S2	S2
☐ Spotted Sandpiper	B	S1		W5	W5	W5
☐ Upland Sandpiper *	b		M4	S4		
☐ Whimbrel *		M4				
☐ Long-billed Curlew	B		S4	S3	S3	S3
☐ Hudsonian Godwit *						M5
☐ Marbled Godwit			M4	M4	M2	M2
☐ Ruddy Turnstone *		M5				
☐ Red Knot *			M5		M5	M5
☐ Sanderling		M3				
☐ Semipalmated Sandpiper		M3				
☐ Western Sandpiper		M1			W5	W5
☐ Least Sandpiper		M1			W5	W5
☐ White-rumped Sandpiper *			M5		M5	M5
☐ Baird's Sandpiper			M3	M3	M3	M2
☐ Pectoral Sandpiper		M3				
☐ Sharp-tailed Sandpiper *					M6	
☐ Dunlin		M4	W5		W5	
☐ Stilt Sandpiper		M4				
☐ Buff-breasted Sandpiper *					M6	M6
☐ Ruff *					M6	M6
☐ Short-billed Dowitcher		M3				
☐ Long-billed Dowitcher		M2				
☐ Wilson's Snipe	B	S2 W4				
☐ Wilson's Phalarope	B		M4	S2	S2	S2
☐ Red-necked Phalarope			M4	M3	M3	M3
☐ Red Phalarope *				M5	M5	M5
☐ Pomarine Jaeger *					M5	M5
☐ Parasitic Jaeger *			M4		M4	M4
☐ Long-tailed Jaeger *					M5	M5

	BREEDING	Statewide	Panhandle	Central	Southwest	Southeast
☐ Franklin's Gull	B		M4	M4	M3	S1
☐ Little Gull *			M5			M5
☐ Bonaparte's Gull		S5 M3				
☐ Mew Gull			MW4		M5	M5
☐ Ring-billed Gull	B	R1				
☐ California Gull	B	MW3			S1	S1
☐ Herring Gull		MW3			S5	
☐ Thayer's Gull			MW4		MW4	MW4
☐ Iceland Gull *			MW5		MW5	MW5
☐ Lesser Black-backed Gull *					MW5	MW5
☐ Slaty-backed Gull *			M6			
☐ Western Gull *			M5		M5	M5
☐ Glaucous-winged Gull			MW4		MW4	MW4
☐ Glaucous Gull			MW4		MW4	MW4
☐ Sabine's Gull *			M4		M4	M4
☐ Black-legged Kittiwake *			M5		M5	M5
☐ Ross's Gull *						W6
☐ Caspian Tern	B		S4		S3	S3
☐ Common Tern			M3		M3	M3
☐ Arctic Tern			M4		M4	M4
☐ Forster's Tern	B		M3	M3	S2	S2
☐ Least Tern *			M6		M6	
☐ Black Tern	B	S3				
☐ Ancient Murrelet *			M5	M5	M5	
☐ Rock Pigeon (Int)	B	R1				
☐ Band-tailed Pigeon	B		M4	M5	M4	M5
☐ Eurasian Collared-Dove	B				R5	R5
☐ White-winged Dove *					S6	S6
☐ Mourning Dove	B	S1 W3				
☐ Black-billed Cuckoo *	B		S5		S5	S5
☐ Yellow-billed Cuckoo	B		S5		S4	S4
☐ Barn Owl	B		R4	R3	R3	R3
☐ Flammulated Owl	B		S4	S3	S3	S3
☐ Western Screech-Owl	B		R3	R2	R2	R2

BREEDING	Statewide	Panhandle	Central	Southwest	Southeast

Species	BREEDING	Statewide	Panhandle	Central	Southwest	Southeast
☐ Great Horned Owl	B	R2				
☐ Snowy Owl		MW4				
☐ Northern Hawk Owl *	B		R5			
☐ Northern Pygmy-Owl	B	R3				
☐ Burrowing Owl	B		S4		S3	S4
☐ Barred Owl	B		R3	R4	R4	R4
☐ Great Gray Owl	B		R4	R3	R3	R3
☐ Long-eared Owl	B	R3				
☐ Short-eared Owl	B	R3				
☐ Boreal Owl	B	R4				
☐ Northern Saw-whet Owl	B	R2				
☐ Common Nighthawk	B	S2				
☐ Common Poorwill	B		S5	S3	S2	S2
☐ Black Swift	B		S4		M6	
☐ Vaux's Swift	B		S2	S2	M4	M4
☐ White-throated Swift	B		S4	S3	S3	S3
☐ Black-chinned Hummingbird	B	S2				
☐ Anna's Hummingbird		M4			W5	
☐ Calliope Hummingbird	B	S2				
☐ Broad-tailed Hummingbird	B		S4	S4	S2	S2
☐ Rufous Hummingbird	B		S2	S2	S2	S4
☐ Belted Kingfisher	B	R2				
☐ Lewis's Woodpecker	B	S3 W5				
☐ Red-headed Woodpecker *		M5				
☐ Red-bellied Woodpecker *			W6			
☐ Williamson's Sapsucker	B		W6	S3		S4
☐ Yellow-bellied Sapsucker *			W6	M6	M6	
☐ Red-naped Sapsucker	B	S2				
☐ Red-breasted Sapsucker *					M6	
☐ Downy Woodpecker	B	R1				
☐ Hairy Woodpecker	B	R1				
☐ White-headed Woodpecker	B		R4	R3	R3	
☐ American Three-toed Woodpecker	B	R3				
☐ Black-backed Woodpecker	B	R4				
☐ Northern Flicker	B	R1				

	BREEDING	Statewide	Panhandle	Central	Southwest	Southeast
☐ Pileated Woodpecker	B		R3	R3	R3	
☐ Olive-sided Flycatcher	B	S3				
☐ Western Wood-Pewee	B	S2				
☐ Willow Flycatcher	B	S3				
☐ Least Flycatcher *	B		S4	S4		S4
☐ Hammond's Flycatcher	B	S3				
☐ Gray Flycatcher	B		M5		S3	S3
☐ Dusky Flycatcher	B	S2				
☐ Cordilleran Flycatcher	B	S3				
☐ Black Phoebe *				S6		S6
☐ Eastern Phoebe *					M6	M6
☐ Say's Phoebe	B	S3	W5		W5	
☐ Ash-throated Flycatcher	B				S4	S4
☐ Tropical Kingbird *						M6
☐ Cassin's Kingbird *					M5	M5
☐ Western Kingbird	B	S2				
☐ Eastern Kingbird	B	S2				
☐ Scissor-tailed Flycatcher *					M5	M5
☐ Fork-tailed Flycatcher *					M6	
☐ Loggerhead Shrike	B	W4	S4	S4	S3	S3
☐ Northern Shrike		MW3				
☐ Bell's Vireo *						M6
☐ Yellow-throated Vireo *					M6	M6
☐ Plumbeous Vireo	B				S2	S2
☐ Cassin's Vireo	B	M2	S2	S2		
☐ Blue-headed Vireo *					M6	M6
☐ Warbling Vireo	B	S1				
☐ Philadelphia Vireo *						M6
☐ Red-eyed Vireo	B		S2	S2	M3	M3
☐ Gray Jay	B		R2	R2	R2	R3
☐ Steller's Jay	B	R2				
☐ Blue Jay		MW4				
☐ Western Scrub-Jay	B				MW5	R3
☐ Pinyon Jay	B				M5	R3
☐ Clark's Nutcracker	B	R3				
☐ Black-billed Magpie	B	R1				

	BREEDING	Statewide	Panhandle	Central	Southwest	Southeast
☐ American Crow	B	R1				
☐ Common Raven	B	R1				
☐ Horned Lark	B		R3	R2	R2	R2
☐ Purple Martin *	b	M5				
☐ Tree Swallow	B	S1				
☐ Violet-green Swallow	B	S2				
☐ Northern Rough-winged Swallow	B	S1				
☐ Bank Swallow	B	S2				
☐ Cliff Swallow	B	S1				
☐ Barn Swallow	B	S1				
☐ Black-capped Chickadee	B	R1				
☐ Mountain Chickadee	B	R1				
☐ Chestnut-backed Chickadee	B			R2	R2	
☐ Boreal Chickadee	B			R4		
☐ Juniper Titmouse	B				MW6	R2
☐ Bushtit	B				R4	R4
☐ Red-breasted Nuthatch	B	R1				
☐ White-breasted Nuthatch	B		R3	R3	R4	R4
☐ Pygmy Nuthatch	B		R3	R3		
☐ Brown Creeper	B	R2				
☐ Rock Wren	B	S2	W4		W4	W4
☐ Canyon Wren	B	S2 W4				
☐ Bewick's Wren	B		R4	R4	R4	R5
☐ House Wren	B	S1			W5	W5
☐ Winter Wren	B		R2	R2	R3	R3
☐ Marsh Wren	B	R1 W4				
☐ American Dipper	B	R3				
☐ Golden-crowned Kinglet	B	R2				
☐ Ruby-crowned Kinglet	B	S1 W3				
☐ Blue-gray Gnatcatcher	B				S3	S3
☐ Western Bluebird	B		S2	S2	S2	M4
☐ Mountain Bluebird	B	S2			W4	W4
☐ Townsend's Solitaire	B	R2				

	BREEDING	Statewide	Panhandle	Central	Southwest	Southeast
☐ Veery	B	S3				
☐ Gray-cheeked Thrush *			M6			M6
☐ Swainson's Thrush	B	S1				
☐ Hermit Thrush	B	S1	W4		W4	W4
☐ American Robin	B	R1				
☐ Varied Thrush	B		R3	R3	R3	MW4
☐ Gray Catbird	B	S3				
☐ Northern Mockingbird	B	S4	MW5		MW5	MW5
☐ Sage Thrasher	B		M5	S3	S1	S1
☐ Brown Thrasher *				M5	M5	M5
☐ Curve-billed Thrasher *					M6	
☐ European Starling (Int)	B	R1				
☐ Siberian Accentor *					W6	
☐ American Pipit	B	S4 M2			W4	W4
☐ Bohemian Waxwing	B	MW2	S4			
☐ Cedar Waxwing	B	R2				
☐ Blue-winged Warbler *				M6		
☐ Golden-winged Warbler *					M6	M6
☐ Tennessee Warbler *		M5				
☐ Orange-crowned Warbler	B	S2	W4		W4	W4
☐ Nashville Warbler	B		S2	S2	S2	M3
☐ Virginia's Warbler	B					S4
☐ Lucy's Warbler *						S6
☐ Northern Parula *					M5	M5
☐ Yellow Warbler	B	S1				
☐ Chestnut-sided Warbler *	b	M3				
☐ Magnolia Warbler *					M4	M4
☐ Cape May Warbler *			M6			M6
☐ Black-throated Blue Warbler *			M5		M5	M5
☐ Yellow-rumped Warbler	B	S1	W4	W4	W3	W3
☐ Black-throated Gray Warbler	B				S3	S3
☐ Black-throated Green Warbler *						M6
☐ Townsend's Warbler	B		S2	S2	S2	M3
☐ Hermit Warbler *					M6	M6
☐ Blackburnian Warbler *					M6	M6

	BREEDING	Statewide	Panhandle	Central	Southwest	Southeast
☐ Yellow-throated Warbler *			W6			M6
☐ Pine Warbler *			W6			
☐ Palm Warbler *			M5		M5	M5
☐ Bay-breasted Warbler *						M5
☐ Blackpoll Warbler *					M4	M4
☐ Black-and-white Warbler *	b	M4		S6		
☐ American Redstart	B	M3	S3	S3	S4	
☐ Prothonotary Warbler *					M6	
☐ Ovenbird		M4				
☐ Northern Waterthrush	B		S3	S3		S3
☐ MacGillivray's Warbler	B	S2				
☐ Common Yellowthroat	B	S1				
☐ Hooded Warbler *					M6	M6
☐ Wilson's Warbler	B	S3 M2				
☐ Yellow-breasted Chat	B		S4	S3	S3	S3
☐ Summer Tanager *					M5	M5
☐ Scarlet Tanager *					M6	M6
☐ Western Tanager	B	S1				
☐ Green-tailed Towhee	B			S4	S2	S2
☐ Spotted Towhee	B	S2	W4		W3	W3
☐ Eastern Towhee *						M6
☐ Cassin's Sparrow *					M6	
☐ American Tree Sparrow		MW3				
☐ Chipping Sparrow	B	S1			W5	W5
☐ Clay-colored Sparrow *	b		M5		M5	M5
☐ Brewer's Sparrow	B		S4	S4	S2	S2
☐ Vesper Sparrow	B	S2				
☐ Lark Sparrow	B		S3	S3	S2	S2
☐ Black-throated Sparrow	B		S5	S5	S3	S4
☐ Sage Sparrow	B				S3	S3
☐ Lark Bunting	B			MS4	MS4	MS4
☐ Savannah Sparrow	B	S2			W5	W5
☐ Grasshopper Sparrow	B	S4				
☐ Le Conte's Sparrow *			M6			
☐ Fox Sparrow	B	S2	W5		W5	

	BREEDING	Statewide	Panhandle	Central	Southwest	Southeast
☐ Song Sparrow	B	R1				
☐ Lincoln's Sparrow	B	S2	W4		W4	W4
☐ Swamp Sparrow *			MW4		MW4	MW4
☐ White-throated Sparrow		MW4				
☐ Harris's Sparrow		MW4				
☐ White-crowned Sparrow	B	R2				
☐ Golden-crowned Sparrow		MW4				
☐ Dark-eyed Junco	B	R1				
☐ McCown's Longspur *						M5
☐ Lapland Longspur		MW4				
☐ Chestnut-collared Longspur *				M6		
☐ Snow Bunting		MW3				
☐ Rose-breasted Grosbeak				M4	M4	M4
☐ Black-headed Grosbeak	B	S2				
☐ Blue Grosbeak	B				S4	S4
☐ Lazuli Bunting	B	S1				
☐ Indigo Bunting				S4	S4	S4
☐ Bobolink	B	S3				
☐ Red-winged Blackbird	B	S1 W3				
☐ Western Meadowlark	B	S1 W3				
☐ Yellow-headed Blackbird	B	S1			W4	W4
☐ Rusty Blackbird *			MW5		MW5	MW5
☐ Brewer's Blackbird	B	S2				
☐ Common Grackle	B	MW4		S3		S3
☐ Great-tailed Grackle *	b				R4	R4
☐ Brown-headed Cowbird	B	S1			W4	W4
☐ Hooded Oriole *					M6	
☐ Bullock's Oriole	B	S1				
☐ Baltimore Oriole *						S6
☐ Scott's Oriole	B					S4
☐ Brambling *			M6			
☐ Gray-crowned Rosy-Finch	B	W3		S4		
☐ Black Rosy-Finch	B			R4	R4	R4
☐ Pine Grosbeak	B	R3				

	BREEDING	Statewide	Panhandle	Central	Southwest	Southeast
☐ Purple Finch		MW4				
☐ Cassin's Finch	B	R2				
☐ House Finch	B	R1				
☐ Red Crossbill	B	R2				
☐ White-winged Crossbill	B		R4	MW4	MW4	MW4
☐ Common Redpoll		MW4				
☐ Hoary Redpoll *		W5				
☐ Pine Siskin	B	R1				
☐ Lesser Goldfinch	B				S4	S4
					W5	W5
☐ American Goldfinch	B	R1				
☐ Evening Grosbeak	B	S3				
		MW2				
☐ House Sparrow (Int)	B	R1				

IDAHO RARITIES AND SPECIALTIES

Authors: Idaho's birders

At least 100 Idaho bird species can be tough to find without additional information. Below are our best estimates on these species' abundance, seasonality, and distribution. Abundance terms follow those of the Multi-purpose Checklist (p. 289). Casual and accidental species are excluded from this treatment.

We have suggested locations in which to look for each species, with the best spots noted by an asterisk (*). Sites are listed geographically, from the northwest to the southeast. They are in the same order as the site descriptions in the previous section. To make cross-referencing easier, we have noted the region of each site (**P** = Panhandle, **C** = Central, **SW** = Southwest, **SE** = Southeast). Regional boundaries are shown on the inside front cover. If a suggested location is not described in the major site treatments in this book, it is referenced by the DeLorme Atlas (DA) map coordinates (DA: page number, coordinates). Additional information can be gleaned from habitat descriptions (pp. 13-15), the Multi-purpose Checklist (p. 289), the full index (pp. 328-339), and Rare Bird Alerts (p. 9). Good bird'n!

Ross's Goose—rare but regular migrant (March–May, October–November) statewide, most dependable around Canyon and Jefferson Counties. Occasionally winters, mostly in southwest. Usually found with large flocks of Snow Geese. **P:** Sandpoint to Beyond Hope Route, Mann Lake. **C:** Midvale Route, Salmon Sewage Lagoon. **SW:** New Plymouth Area, *Fort Boise WMA, *Deer Flat NWR, C.J. Strike WMA, *Hagerman WMA. **SE:** Camas NWR, *Mud Lake WMA, *Market Lake WMA, The Bottoms.

Trumpeter Swan—common resident in southeast, uncommon and local breeder, migrant (April, October–December), and winterer elsewhere, mostly on the Snake River Plain. **SW:** Dry Lakes, Blacks Creek Reservoir Route, Ted Trueblood WMA, Bruneau Dunes SP, Camas Prairie Centennial Marsh, Silver Creek Preserve, Hagerman WMA. **SE:** Henrys Lake, *Harriman SP, *Camas NWR, Mud Lake WMA, Market Lake WMA, Sand Creek WMA, *Teton Valley Route, Springfield Ponds, The Bottoms, Massacre Rocks SP, Minidoka NWR, Grays Lake NWR, Bear Lake NWR.

Eurasian Wigeon—rare but regular migrant (March–May, October–December) and winterer statewide. Should be looked for in any American Wigeon flock. **P:** Sandpoint to Beyond Hope Route, Coeur d'Alene Area, Chain Lakes Route, St. Maries to Harrison Route, *Heyburn SP, St. Joe Route,

302

*Lewiston Area. **C:** Midvale Route, Mann Creek Reservoir, Cascade Reservoir—West Side Route. **SW:** *Boise Area, *Marsing Area, C.J. Strike WMA, Hagerman WMA. **SE:** Mud Lake WMA, Market Lake WMA.

Greater Scaup—rare but regular late fall (October–December) migrant and winterer in deep-water habitats statewide. **P:** *Sandpoint to Beyond Hope Route, Heyburn SP, Lewiston Area. **C:** Whitebird Battlefield, Midvale Route, *Cascade Reservoir—West Side Route. **SW:** Deer Flat NWR, Dry Lakes, Marsing Area, *Hagerman WMA. **SE:** American Falls Dam, Massacre Rocks SP.

Harlequin Duck—rare and very local nester (April–August) in Panhandle, rare migrant (April–October) in central and southeast mountains. Entire Idaho population probably less than 100 birds. Males arrive mid-April, females early May. Most males depart by early June, while females with broods can be seen into mid-August. Most easily found mid-May on undisturbed stretches of favored mountain streams. Look for feeding birds in riffles and for loafing birds on instream rocks, islands, and log jams. One good strategy is to take a float trip down the Moyie River (DA: 63, A-4) in May. Such trips are offered by River Odyssey West (208/765-0841). **P:** Sandpoint to Beyond Hope Route, St. Joe Route, *Wilderness Gateway Campground.

Surf and White-winged Scoters—rare late fall (September–December) migrants and occasional winterers on large lakes and reservoirs statewide, accidental in spring. Almost annual, late October–November at **SE:** *American Falls Dam. Unpredictable elsewhere. **P:** Kootenai NWR, Sandpoint to Beyond Hope Route. **SW:** Indian Creek Reservoir, Sawtooth Valley Route, Hagerman WMA. **SE:** The Bottoms, Minidoka NWR.

Long-tailed Duck—rare late fall (October–January) migrant and occasional winterer on large lakes and reservoirs statewide. **P:** Sandpoint to Beyond Hope Route, Hayden Lake Route. **C:** *Cascade Reservoir—East Side Route. **SW:** Marsing Area, on the Snake River near Grandview (DA: 25, C-4), C.J. Strike WMA, Hagerman WMA. **SE:** Snake River in downtown Idaho Falls (DA: 30, A-2), Springfield Ponds, *American Falls Dam, Massacre Rocks SP.

Barrow's Goldeneye—uncommon and local breeder on central and southeast mountain lakes. Common migrant and winterer on large lakes, reservoirs, and rivers statewide. Look for nesting birds (April–August) at **C:** *Williams Lake (DA: 53, C-6), Jimmy Smith and Sullivan Lakes (DA: 37, A-5). **SE:** *Grays Lake NWR. Migrants (April and October–December) and winterers can be found at **P:** Kootenai NWR, Sandpoint to Beyond Hope Route, Farragut SP, Chain Lakes Route, St. Maries to Harrison Route, St. Joe Route, Spring Valley and Moose Creek Reservoirs, *Lewiston Area. **C:** Mann Creek Reservoir, Cascade Reservoir—East Side Route, Salmon Sewage Lagoon, Challis Area. **SW:** *Snake River at Farewell Bend on the Oregon state line (DA: 50, B-1), Snake River between Swan Falls Dam and C.J. Strike WMA (DA: 25, C-5), Hagerman WMA. **SE:** Harriman SP, American Falls Dam, or on the Snake River in downtown Idaho Falls (DA: 30, A-2).

Red-breasted Merganser—rare migrant (February–April and September–December) on Panhandle and central lakes, common but local migrant and rare winterer on large lakes and rivers across Snake River Plain. **P:** Sandpoint to Beyond Hope Route, St. Maries to Harrison Route. **SW:** New Plymouth Area, Boise Area, Deer Flat NWR, Indian Creek Reservoir, *C.J. Strike WMA, Hagerman WMA. **SE:** Henrys Lake, *downtown Idaho Falls (DA: 30, A-2), *American Falls Dam, Massacre Rocks SP, Minidoka NWR.

Chukar—common resident in broken, rocky, shrub-steppe and juniper habitats from Lewiston southward, but can be hard to find. **P:** Coyote Gulch, Lewiston Area, *Craig Mountain WMA, Graves Creek Route. **C:** Whitebird Battlefield, *Hells Canyon along the Snake River (several raft and jetboat outfitters based in Lewiston and Riggins offer Chukar hunting trips and would likely be good information sources), Salmon River Route, Pollock Area, *North Fork Area, Lemhi River Route, Pahsimeroi River Route, *Morgan Creek to Panther Creek Route, Challis Area, East Fork Salmon River (DA: 37, A-5). **SW:** Boise Foothills, *Pleasant Valley Route, Jump Creek, Jacks Creek Special Recreation Management Area (DA: 17, A-4), North Fork Owyhee River, Niagara Springs WMA. **SE:** City of Rocks National Reserve.

Gray Partridge—common resident in grassland and shrub-steppe surrounding agricultural fields statewide, but local in northern Panhandle. Easiest to find when winter snows concentrate feeding birds at feeders, in winter-wheat fields, or in summer-wheat stubble. Listen for crowing birds at dawn, February–April. **P:** Kootenai NWR, Rathdrum Prairie (DA: 60, A-1, between Post Falls/Coeur d'Alene/Rathdrum), *Palouse Prairie (DA: 58, C-1, south and east of Moscow), Craig Mountain WMA. **C:** Pollock Area, Crane Creek Reservoir Route, *Midvale Route, Lemhi River Route, Pahsimeroi River Route. **SW:** Boise Foothills, *Pleasant Valley Route, Deer Flat NWR, Blacks Creek Reservoir Route, Mayfield Route, Hagerman WMA. **SE:** Mud Lake WMA, Tex Creek WMA, Sterling WMA.

Greater Sage-Grouse—uncommon but widespread resident of shrub-steppe habitats in central and southern Idaho. Look around springs and ponds during dry autumns. Easiest to find while males are on leks during March–May. **C:** Crane Creek Reservoir Route, *Midvale Route, Lemhi River Route, Pahsimeroi River Route. **SW:** Trinity Recreation Area, along Macon Flat Road and in Thorn Creek Special Recreation Management Area (DA: 27, B-4). **SE:** Mud Lake WMA, Tex Creek WMA, *Sand Creek WMA, Blackfoot Reservoir Route, near Atomic City (DA: 29, A-5).

Spruce Grouse—uncommon and local resident throughout Panhandle and central mountains. Most likely in open-canopy Douglas-fir or Lodgepole Pine forest near 5,000-foot elevation, but should also be looked for in both open- and closed-canopy Engelmann Spruce, Subalpine Fir, and Whitebark Pine forests. Watch roadsides June–October. **P:** Smith Creek, *Western Selkirks, Cabinet Mountain Lakes. **C:** Elk City Area, Goose Lake, Bear Basin, *along FR 21 between McCall and Burgdorf (DA: 51, B-5), forest trails near Upper Payette Lake (DA: 51, C-4, see Payette National Forest map), *southwest of Cascade Reservoir along FR 451 (DA: 43, A4), *Chamberlain Basin, Swan Peak (DA: 53, C-6). **SW:** Trinity Recreation Area, Sawtooth Valley Route, sideroads off ID 21 north of Stanley (DA: 44, C-2).

Blue Grouse—uncommon and local resident in Panhandle and central mountains, common resident in southern mountains. Uses high-elevation (>4,000 feet) sagebrush habitats and can sometimes be seen in the same area as Greater Sage-Grouse. Most often found by birders, however, along roadsides on brushy mountain ridgetops with scattered conifer overstory. Pay particular attention to huckleberry and whortleberry patches, July–October. In April and May, listen for the male's quiet, low-frequency hoot along forest edges. Most (if not all) Idaho populations exhibit reverse altitudinal migration, so look for hooting males at mid-elevations, and females with young broods in low-elevation riparian zones. Both males and females move up to mountain ridges in fall to use berry crops, then winter on Douglas-fir needles. **P:** *Western Selkirks, Grandmother Mountain (DA: 59, A-4), Craig Mountain WMA. **C:** Pollock Area, Goose Lake, forested side roads off US 93 between North Fork and Lost Trail Pass (DA: 53, A-6), *Morgan Creek to Panther Creek Route. **SW:** wooded sidedraws on the east side of ID 55 between Banks and Gardena (DA: 35, A-4), Boise Foothills. **SE:** Black Canyon Road Route, Tex Creek WMA, Mink Creek Route.

Sharp-tailed Grouse—rare and local resident in southwest (mostly on private land in western Washington County), uncommon and local in southeast. Recently reintroduced to Shoshone Basin (DA: 19, C-4). Idaho's birds are "Columbian" Sharp-tailed Grouse, which prefer shrub-steppe habitat with intermixed sage, Chokecherry, hawthorn, serviceberry, bitterbrush, and native grasses. Easiest to find while males are on leks March–May. **C:** Midvale Route. **SE:** *Tex Creek WMA, *Sand Creek WMA, Cedar Ridge Route, Curlew National Grassland, Hawkins Reservoir.

Mountain Quail—another of Idaho's extremely local species. Mountain Quail were once resident throughout much of west-central and southwest Idaho, but are now dependably found only in **C:** *Pollock Area, where resident in small numbers.

Gambel's Quail—one of Idaho's most local species, Gambel's are found only along **C:** *Lemhi River Route, where fairly common. The species is most easily found by listening for crowing males in May–July between Kirtley and Geertson Creeks (DA: 57, C-5).

Northern Bobwhite—although repeatedly introduced, no Northern Bobwhite population has persisted long-term in Idaho. Don't be surprised if you find Bobwhite, however, as introductions occur annually (especially in central and southwest Idaho).

Red-throated Loon—rare and irregular fall (October 15–31) migrant with about 30 records statewide. **P:** Sandpoint to Beyond Hope Route, Chain Lakes Route, St. Maries to Harrison Route. **C:** Payette Lake (DA: 43, A-4), Cascade Reservoir—East Side Route. **SW:** Sawtooth Valley Route. **SE:** *American Falls Dam, Massacre Rocks SP.

Pacific Loon—rare but regular fall (October 15–December 30) migrant on large lakes and reservoirs statewide, occasional winterer. **P:** *Sandpoint to Beyond Hope Route, Coeur d'Alene Area, St. Maries to Harrison Route. **C:** Mann Creek Reservoir, Payette Lake (DA: 43, A-4), *Cascade Reservoir—East Side Route, Cascade Reservoir—West Side Route. **SW:** Deer Flat NWR, Blacks Creek Reservoir Route, C.J. Strike WMA, Bruneau Dunes SP, Sawtooth Valley Route. **SE:** *American Falls Dam, Massacre Rocks SP.

Yellow-billed Loon—rare and irregular fall migrant in Panhandle, accidental in southeast (American Falls Dam). Approximately 12 records statewide. **P:** *Sandpoint to Beyond Hope Route, *St. Maries to Harrison Route. Most sightings November 15–January 15, but the species has overwintered at Harrison.

Red-necked Grebe—uncommon breeder (April–October) on large lakes in northern Panhandle, rare and local breeder on large lakes and reservoirs in west-central and southeast Idaho. Occasionally winters. **P:** Kootenai NWR, *McArthur Lake WMA (DA: 62, B-3), *Sandpoint to Beyond Hope Route, Round Lake (DA: 62, C-2), Mirror Lake (DA: 62, C-3), Hoodoo Valley Route, Blanchard Lake, Coeur d'Alene Area, St. Maries to Harrison Route, *Heyburn SP. **C:** *Goose Lake, Lick Creek Route, Cascade Reservoir—East Side Route, Warm Lake (DA: 43, B-6). **SE:** *Henrys Lake, Harriman SP.

Clark's Grebe—common breeder in scattered colonies across Snake River Plain. Occasionally wanders as far north as Lake Pend Oreille. Should be looked for April–September anywhere that Western Grebes are found. **C:** Cascade Reservoir—West Side Route. **SW:** *Deer Flat NWR, C.J. Strike WMA, Mountain View Lake (DA: 17, C-4). **SE:** Mud Lake WMA, Market Lake WMA, The Bottoms, *Minidoka NWR, Blackfoot Reservoir Route, Oxford Slough, *Bear Lake NWR.

American Bittern—uncommon, local, and likely declining nester statewide. Check any extensive cattail or bulrush wetland, April–September. **P:** Kootenai NWR, *Hoodoo Valley Route, Cataldo Area, Chain Lakes Route, St. Joe Route. **SW:** C.J. Strike WMA, *Silver Creek Preserve, Hagerman WMA. **SE:** Mackay Reservoir and Chilly Slough, *Camas NWR, Mud Lake WMA, *Market Lake WMA, Minidoka NWR, Oxford Slough, *Bear Lake NWR.

Great Egret—rare and very local breeder (April–July) on Snake River Plain, rare post-breeding visitor (July–September) elsewhere. Approximately 20 pairs nest in Idaho. **SW:** Hubbard Reservoir, Deer Flat NWR, Marsing Area, Blacks Creek Reservoir Route, Indian Creek Reservoir, Ted Trueblood WMA, C.J. Strike WMA, *Duck Valley Indian Reservation (DA: 17, C-4, along west side of ID 51 about 2 miles north of reservation headquarters), Hagerman WMA, Thousand Springs Preserve. **SE:** *Camas NWR, *Mud Lake WMA, Market Lake WMA, *The Bottoms, American Falls Dam.

Cattle Egret—uncommon and local nester (May–July) on Snake River Plain (mostly on eastern half), rare post-breeding visitor (July–October) elsewhere. Watch for Cattle Egrets where other colonial waders nest or stage. Most often seen feeding in cow pastures. **SW:** Deer Flat NWR, Blacks Creek Reservoir Route. **SE:** *Camas NWR, *Mud Lake WMA, Market Lake WMA, along the Snake River between Blackfoot and American Falls Reservoir (DA: 30, B-1), The Bottoms, Blackfoot Reservoir Route, *Oxford Slough, *Bear Lake NWR.

Green Heron—rare wanderer to south Idaho, usually August–November. **SW:** Fort Boise WMA, *Boise Area, Marsing Area. **SE:** Mud Lake WMA, along the Snake River between Blackfoot and American Falls Reservoir (DA: 30, B-1).

Northern Goshawk—uncommon resident in coniferous forest statewide, but hard to find because of secretive behavior, love of thick cover, and large (5,000-acre) home-range size. Usually nests in old-growth mixed conifer forest. Often detected by adult's alarm call (March–May) or fledgling's begging call (June–August). **P:** Western Selkirks, Snow Peak Trail, *Emerald Creek, McCrosky SP, Moscow Mountain Route, Winchester Lake SP. **C:** Pollock Area. **SW:** Boise Foothills, Trinity Recreation Area, Sawtooth Valley Route, **SE:** *Mesa Falls Route. Specific information may be available from local FS or BLM offices (pp. 17-18), since many conduct goshawk surveys. Regularly migrates past Lucky Peak Hawk-watch (**SW:** Boise Foothills). In winter look for goshawks in coniferous forests, river valleys, and agricultural lands statewide. **SW:** Fort Boise WMA, Boise Foothills, *Deer Flat NWR, Silver Creek Preserve, *Thousand Springs Preserve. **SE:** Mud Lake WMA, Mink Creek Route, *The Bottoms, Sterling WMA, Grays Lake NWR.

Broad-winged Hawk—rare and very local migrant (May, September) on Snake River Plain. Broad-wingeds were recorded only about 5 times in Idaho before 1991, mostly in the first week of May near Pocatello (DA: 30, C-1). Since the hawk-watch was established at Lucky Peak in 1994 (**SW:** *Boise Foothills), however, 5 to 10 Broad-wingeds have been documented annually, September 10-30.

Ferruginous Hawk—uncommon and local nester across most of southern Idaho (i.e., the Intermountain Semidesert portion), rare elsewhere. Easiest to find April–June, but an occasional bird is resident. **SW:** *Pleasant Valley Route, Blacks Creek Reservoir Route, Indian Creek Reservoir, *Mayfield Route, *Snake River Birds of Prey Area, *Raft River Valley (DA: 20, B-3). **SE:** *Big Lost River Valley (DA: 38, C-3), Henrys Lake, Camas NWR, Market Lake WMA, City of Rocks National Reserve, Curlew National Grassland, Grays Lake NWR.

Gyrfalcon—very rare but annual winter visitor, November–April. About 5 to 10 birds are reported annually, statewide. Gyrs should be looked for in any open country. **P:** Rathdrum Prairie (DA: 60, A-1, between Post Falls/Coeur d'Alene/Rathdrum). **C:** Howe (DA: 39, B-4), Gannett (DA: 27, A-6).

Peregrine Falcon—rare breeder (March–July) and uncommon migrant and winterer statewide. Approximately 17 pairs nest in Idaho, some of which are resident. For the most dependable birds in the state, try **SW:** *Deer Flat NWR. Other spots include: **SW:** Fort Boise WMA, Sawtooth Valley Route. **SE:** *Camas NWR, Mud Lake WMA, Market Lake WMA, The Bottoms, American Falls Dam, Grays Lake NWR, Bear Lake NWR.

American Golden-Plover—very rare but annual fall (September–December) migrant statewide, accidental in spring (April–May). **P:** Sandpoint to Beyond Hope Route, *Mann Lake. **C:** Mann Creek Reservoir. **SW:** Fort Boise WMA, *Deer Flat NWR, Dry Lakes, Blacks Creek Reservoir Route, Indian Creek Reservoir, Ted Trueblood WMA, C.J. Strike WMA. **SE:** Market Lake WMA, *The Bottoms, *Sportsmans Park, *American Falls Dam.

Snowy Plover—accidental in Panhandle, rare, irregular migrant in south. Most records are from May–June. **P:** Sandpoint to Beyond Hope Route, Mann Lake. **SW:** Deer Flat NWR, Dry Lakes, Indian Creek Reservoir. **SE:** The Bottoms, Sportsmans Park, American Falls Dam.

Upland Sandpiper—until the early 1990s Upland Sandpiper was a rare and very local breeder in Round Valley, between Cascade and Smiths Ferry (DA: 43, C-4). Birds were found, both east and west of the highway, mostly on fenceposts in ungrazed pastures. One pair was present in 1997 at the intersection of Bacon Creek and Gatfield Roads. All land here is private. Your best chance remains Round Valley in June, but also try Farm to Market Road (DA: 43, A-4) and Big Creek meadows surrounding New Meadows (DA: 43, A-4). Listen for birds in extensive meadow habitat.

Marbled Godwit—rare and local fall (August–September) migrant in Panhandle and central Idaho, common but local fall migrant in south. Large (>100 birds) flocks annual in southeast Idaho at *The Bottoms, *Sportsmans Park, *American Falls Dam. Irregular in small numbers (1 to 20) at **P:** Mann Lake. **SW:** New Plymouth Area, Fort Boise WMA, Deer Flat NWR, Dry Lakes, Indian Creek Reservoir, Ted Trueblood WMA, C.J. Strike WMA, Thousand Springs Preserve. **SE:** Mud Lake WMA, Market Lake WMA, Alexander Reservoir.

Stilt Sandpiper—rare, local but regular fall migrant statewide. Up to 10 birds are annual, August–September, at **P:** *Mann Lake. **SE:** *The Bottoms, *Sportsmans Park, *American Falls Dam. Irregular fall migrant at **P:** Kootenai NWR. **C:** Crane Creek Reservoir Route. **SW:** Hubbard Reservoir, Deer Flat NWR, Dry Lakes, C.J. Strike WMA. **SE:** Market Lake WMA, Springfield Ponds.

Short-billed Dowitcher—rare, local, and irregular fall migrant statewide. One or two immatures have been found at **P:** *Mann Lake and **SE:** *American Falls Dam in recent falls, August and September. Should also be looked for at **P:** Sandpoint to Beyond Hope Route, Chain Lakes Route. **SW:** Hubbard Reservoir, Deer Flat NWR, Dry Lakes, C.J. Strike WMA, Silver Creek Preserve. **SE:** Market Lake WMA, Springfield Ponds, The Bottoms.

Winter Gulls—in Idaho, winter gull habitat is largely limited to **P:** Sandpoint to Beyond Hope Route, *Coeur d'Alene Area, Lewiston Area. **SW:** Boise Area, Deer Flat NWR, Hagerman WMA. **SE:** *American Falls Dam. Mew, Thayer's, Glaucous-winged, and Glaucous are rare but regular (November–March) at **P:** *Coeur d'Alene Area. These species are accidental elsewhere, except for Thayer's, which is annual (November–February) at **SE:** American Falls Dam.

Common Tern—rare and irregular fall (August–September) migrant in Panhandle and central Idaho, uncommon but annual migrant in south Idaho. Has nested in southeast (American Falls Reservoir). **P:** Sandpoint to Beyond Hope Route, Heyburn SP, Mann Lake. **SW:** C.J. Strike WMA. **SE:** The Bottoms, Sportsmans Park, *American Falls Dam.

Arctic Tern—very rare migrant May–June and August–September, mostly at **SE:** *American Falls Dam, where recorded about 15 times. Has also been found at **P:** Sandpoint to Beyond Hope Route and **SW:** C.J. Strike WMA.

Band-tailed Pigeon—very rare irregular visitor statewide, with little geographic pattern evident. Most records April–May, near bird feeders or pigeon coops.

Yellow-billed Cuckoo—rare, irregular visitor (April–September) statewide. Very local nester (May–June) in southeast Idaho. The only place where the species has been repeatedly reported is **SE:** *along the Snake River upstream of Tilden Road bridge (DA: 29, B-6). **SW:** Fort Boise WMA. **SE:** Camas NWR, Mud Lake WMA, along the South Fork Snake River upstream of Heise (DA: 41, C-4).

Barn Owl—rare and local resident in Panhandle, uncommon but widespread resident across Snake River Plain. Frequent winter die-offs and recolonizations make presence/absence hard to predict. Often nests in barns or dirt holes along deeply incised rivers and reservoirs. In winter, roosts in Russian-olives, barns, or even cattails. **P:** Rathdrum Prairie (DA: 60, A-1, between Post Falls/Coeur d'Alene/Rathdrum), Lewiston Area. **SW:** Fort Boise WMA, Boise Area, *Pleasant Valley Route, *Deer Flat NWR, Mayfield Route, C.J. Strike WMA, *Hagerman WMA. **SE:** *Springfield Ponds, *American Falls Dam.

Flammulated Owl—rare and local breeder (May–October) in Panhandle, uncommon and local breeder elsewhere. Prefers dry conifer forest, particularly open-canopied, old-growth Ponderosa Pine and Douglas-fir. Recent surveys by FS and BLM are finding this species to be well distributed, but "clumped." Your best chances of hearing (and with a lot of work, perhaps seeing) one is well after dark in June. Contact local FS and BLM offices for more information. **P:** Craig Mountain WMA. **C:** *Chamberlain Basin, *North Fork Area. **SW:** Boise Foothills, along ridgetop roads on the Fairfield District of the Sawtooth National Forest (DA: 26, A-3, see Sawtooth National Forest map). **SE:** *Wolverine Canyon Route, Mink Creek Route, *Black Pine Mountains (DA: 21, C-4). Call FS or BLM offices (pp. 17-18) for more information.

Snowy Owl—rare, irregular winter (November–March) visitor to open fields, statewide. **P:** Sandpoint to Beyond Hope Route, *Rathdrum Prairie (DA: 60, A-1, between Post Falls/Coeur d'Alene/Rathdrum), *Coyote Gulch.

Northern Pygmy-Owl—uncommon and hard-to-find resident in dry and mixed conifer forest statewide, but rare south of Snake River Plain. Usually heard at dusk, February–June and August–October. Winters in varying numbers in major river valleys, where it frequently perches in deciduous trees. **P:** *Sandpoint to Beyond Hope Route, Farragut SP, Coeur d'Alene Area, Cataldo Area, Chain Lakes Route, St. Maries to Harrison Route, *St. Joe Route, *Emerald Creek, Moscow Mountain Route, Spring Valley and Moose Creek Reservoirs. **C:** Pollock Area, Ponderosa SP. **SW:** Boise Foothills, Boise Area, Blacks Creek Reservoir Route, Sawtooth Valley Route. **SE:** Mesa Falls Route, Mink Creek Route, City of Rocks National Reserve.

Burrowing Owl—uncommon, local, and declining breeder across much of southern Idaho (i.e., the Intermountain Semidesert portion). Present April–September. **C:** Crane Creek Reservoir Route, Midvale Route, Pahsimeroi River Route. **SW:** *Pleasant Valley Route, *Hubbard Reservoir, Blacks Creek Reservoir Route, Mayfield Route, *Snake River Birds of Prey Area, Ted Trueblood WMA. **SE:** Camas NWR, Market Lake WMA, Minidoka NWR, Blackfoot Reservoir Route, Oxford Slough.

Barred Owl—uncommon but widespread resident in Panhandle mixed conifer forest, mostly at mid-elevations (3,000-5,500 feet). Rare or absent elsewhere. **P:** *Western Selkirks, Sandpoint to Beyond Hope Route, St. Maries to Harrison Route, Heyburn SP, St. Joe Route, *Emerald Creek, Willow Creek, McCrosky SP, *Moscow Mountain Route, Craig Mountain WMA, Winchester Lake SP. **C:** Goose Lake, Ponderosa SP, near Sage Hen Reservoir (DA: 43, C-4).

Great Gray Owl—rare and local resident in Panhandle and most of central Idaho, uncommon resident from McCall southeast to Wyoming. **C:** *Bear Basin, Cascade Reservoir—East Side Route. **SE:** Henrys Lake, *Mesa Falls Route, *Teton Valley Route.

Boreal Owl—rare but widespread resident in high-elevation (5,000 feet), mixed conifer forest statewide. Hard to find because of large territory size (5,000 acres) and limited response to tapes, being most reliable February–April. Don't be afraid to at least try a tape during other seasons. **P:** Snow Peak Trail. **C:** Goose Lake, Bear Basin, area surrounding Burgdorf (DA: 51, B-5), *Chamberlain Basin, *Lost Trail Pass (DA: 53, A-6, by the ski area turn-outs). **SE:** Henrys Lake, Black Canyon Road Route, Teton Pass, Kilgore Yale Road (DA: 49, C-4, a.k.a. Clark County Road A2), Green Canyon Pass Road (DA: 49, C-4).

Black Swift—rare and very local nester (May–August) in northern Panhandle. Look for a Black or two among Vaux's in late afternoon over rivers or clearcuts. **P:** *Smith Creek, Cabinet Mountain Lakes, Sandpoint to Beyond Hope Route.

Anna's Hummingbird—rare visitor statewide, with about 25 records to date. Most often seen at Panhandle feeders October–November, but has overwintered at Boise (DA: 35, C-4) feeders.

Williamson's Sapsucker—rare and local nester (May–August) in northern-most Panhandle, uncommon and hard to find in central and southeast mountains. Prefers partially-open, high-elevation coniferous forest (especially Douglas-fir, Engelmann Spruce, Subalpine Fir, and Quaking Aspen). **P:** Eastport (DA: 49, A-4), Craig Mountain WMA. **C:** Elk City Area, *Bear Basin, North Fork Area, mountains near Custer (DA: 45, C-4). **SE:** along Green Canyon Pass Road (DA: 49, C-4), *Mesa Falls Route, West End Campground (DA: 49, C-4, see Island Park Reservoir on Targhee NF map), *Big Canyon to Knox Canyon Route.

White-headed Woodpecker—rare and local resident in west-central and southwest mountains, accidental elsewhere. Prefers open-grown, old-growth Ponderosa Pine and Douglas-fir forest. Occasionally uses burned areas. Most likely to be heard and seen April–mid-May, July–September. Contact southwest birders for current locations, or try **C:** Salmon River Route, *Pollock Area, Sage Hen Reservoir (DA: 43, C-4). **SW:** along ID 21 near Idaho City (DA: 35, B5), Boise Foothills.

American Three-toed Woodpecker—widespread, uncommon resident of high-elevation (4,000 feet) mixed conifer forest statewide, but hard to find. Most regularly found in recent forest burns (less than five years old), but should also be looked for in mature or old-growth Lodgepole Pine. Best located by its loud drumming, similar to that of Hairy Woodpecker. May come to tapes during April–June period. **P:** Smith Creek, *Roman Nose Lakes, *Western Selkirks, Cabinet Mountain Lakes, Willow Creek, Moscow Mountain Route. **C:** *Elk City Area, *Goose Lake, Bear Basin, Cascade Reservoir—West Side Route, Chamberlain Basin, Mosquito Flat Reservoir (DA :45, B-5). **SW:** Sawtooth Valley Route. **SE:** mountains north of Shotgun Valley (DA: 49, C-4), Harriman SP.

Black-backed Woodpecker—similar pattern to American Three-toed, but generally rarer. Black-backeds use low-elevation dry forest as well as high-elevation mixed conifer forest. Try the same spots listed for American Three-toeds. Black-backeds are a "species of special concern" for several land-management agencies, so you might try contacting local IDFG, FS, and BLM offices (pp. 17-18), to learn of recent sightings.

Least Flycatcher—rare and very local breeder in extensive deciduous forest, statewide. Most records from June and July. **P:** *Chain Lakes Route. **C:** *Challis Area. **SE:** *Camas NWR.

Gray Flycatcher—uncommon nester (May–August) in juniper habitats, mostly south of Snake River Plain. **SW:** *North Fork Owyhee River, Mudflat Road (DA: 16, A-2, between Grandview, Idaho, and Jordan Valley, Oregon). **SE:** along Pocatello Creek Road (DA: 30, C-1), *Mink Creek Route, *Cedar Ridge Route, City of Rocks National Reserve, Curlew National Grassland.

"Western" Flycatcher—uncommon but widespread nester (May–August) in Panhandle, uncommon and local in central and southeast mountains. Because it will nest on small ledges on barns, porches, sheds, and bridges, this species should be looked for around undisturbed structures. In 1989 "Western" Flycatcher was split into Cordilleran and Pacific-slope Flycatchers. All Idaho birds are considered Cordillerans. There are no accepted state records of Pacific-slope Flycatcher. Several birders, however, think that Panhandle birds sound like Pacific-slopes. To investigate for yourself, go birding in both portions of the state and compare the males' primary songs.

Listen for Pacific-slope-sounding birds in closed-canopy, moist, mixed conifer forest, such as that at **P:** Sandpoint to Beyond Hope Route, Chain Lakes Route, *St. Maries to Harrison Route, *Heyburn SP, Emerald Creek.

More typical Cordilleran-sounding flycatchers breed in riparian areas within shrub-steppe habitat or in dry conifer forest. **P:** *Moscow Mountain Route, Coyote Gulch, Spalding Site, Graves Creek Route. **C:** *Lemhi River Route. **SE:** Tex Creek WMA, *Mink Creek Route, Big Canyon to Knox Canyon Route.

Ash-throated Flycatcher—rare and local nester (May–July) in junipers to the south of the Snake River Plain. **SW:** North Fork Owyhee River. **SE:** *Cedar Ridge Route, Massacre Rocks SP, *City of Rocks National Reserve, Curlew National Grassland, *Juniper Rest Area (DA: 21, C-5, along I-84, five miles north of the Utah/Idaho boundary).

Cassin's Vireo—Solitary Vireo was split into three species just before this guide was originally published in 1996. Two of these—Cassin's and Plumbeous—nest in Idaho. (When we did not know the identity of either species in the birdfinding section of this book, the form was indicated as simply "Solitary" Vireo.) The third, Blue-headed Vireo, has been reported as an accidental migrant in southern Idaho, April and September.

Cassin's Vireo is a common, widespread nester in Panhandle and west-central mountains, but it is rare in east-central and eastern Idaho. It prefers partially-open, dry and mixed conifer forest. Cassin's Vireos are relatively easy to find at **P:** Cabinet Mountain Lakes, Sandpoint to Beyond Hope Route, *Hoodoo Valley Route, Farragut SP, Hayden Lake Route, Coeur d'Alene Area, Cataldo Area, Emerald Creek, Willow Creek, Craig Mountain WMA, Winchester Lake SP, Graves Creek Route. **C:** Salmon River Route,

Bear Basin, Ponderosa SP. **SW:** Boise Foothills, Trinity Recreation Area, Sawtooth Valley Route. **SE:** Mesa Falls Route.

Plumbeous Vireo—Plumbeous Vireo can be found throughout the Intermountain Semidesert in deciduous riparian strips amidst shrub-steppe habitat. **SW:** *Boise Foothills, Boise Area, Deer Flat NWR, Jump Creek, North Fork Owyhee River, Hagerman WMA. **SE:** Wolverine Canyon Route, *Mink Creek Route, City of Rocks National Reserve.

Blue Jay—rare, erratic winter (November–April) visitor statewide. Has been almost annual recently in deciduous trees in **P:** Coeur d'Alene (DA: 60, B-2), St. Maries (DA: 60, C-2), *Moscow (DA: 58, C-1). **C:** Grangeville (DA: 55, C-4), Salmon (DA: 57, C-5). **SW:** Boise (DA: 35, C-4), Deer Flat NWR. **SE:** Pocatello (DA: 30, C-1), Idaho Falls (DA: 30, A-2).

Western Scrub-Jay—uncommon and local resident in juniper habitat on eastern edge of the Intermountain Semidesert, but has wandered to Panhandle and southwest. **SE:** *Mink Creek Route, Cedar Ridge Route, City of Rocks National Reserve, Curlew National Grassland. In winter sometimes comes to feeders in Pocatello (DA: 30, C-1); contact local birders for more information.

Pinyon Jay—uncommon and local resident in juniper and pinyon/juniper habitats on eastern edge of the Intermountain Semidesert. In irruption years Pinyon Jays might be found in the southwest as well. **SE:** *Pocatello Creek Road (DA: 30, C-1, stop to listen at turn-outs in early morning), Cedar Ridge Route, *City of Rocks National Reserve, Curlew National Grassland, Hawkins Reservoir, Juniper Rest Area (DA: 21, C-5, along I-84, five miles north of the Utah/Idaho boundary). Occasionally visits feeders on the east side of Pocatello (DA: 30, C-1); contact local birders for information.

Chestnut-backed Chickadee—common resident in wet, closed-canopy, mature to old-growth, mixed conifer forest in Panhandle and central Idaho, occurring as far south as Cascade Reservoir. Absent elsewhere. **P:** Cabinet Mountain Lakes, Hoodoo Valley Route, Coeur d'Alene Area, Chain Lakes Route, St. Maries to Harrison Route, *Heyburn SP, *Moscow Mountain Route, Wilderness Gateway Campground, Winchester Lake SP. **C:** Elk City Area.

Boreal Chickadee—rare and very local resident in mixed conifer forests around 5,000-foot elevation in northern-most Panhandle. **P:** *Smith Creek, Trout Creek Road (DA: 48, A-2), north half of Pack River Road (DA: 62, A-2), Western Selkirks.

Juniper Titmouse—common but local resident in junipers in southeast Idaho, rare and local in southwest Idaho. **SW:** North Fork Owyhee River. **SE:** Mink Creek Route, Big Canyon to Knox Canyon Route, *Massacre Rocks SP, Minidoka NWR, City of Rocks National Reserve, Curlew National Grassland, Hawkins Reservoir, *Juniper Rest Area (DA: 21, C-5, along I-84, five miles north of the Utah/Idaho boundary).

Bushtit—rare and local resident in junipers south of Snake River Plain. Populations east of Twin Falls have recently shown sharp decline. Most easily located May–June. Listen for their distinctive calls. **SW:** *North Fork Owyhee River, *along Third Fork Rock Creek (DA: 19, B-5). **SE:** City of Rocks National Reserve.

Pygmy Nuthatch—uncommon and local resident in Panhandle and west-central mountains. Rare and local in east-central mountains. Prefers open-grown, old-growth Ponderosa Pine. Most easily located by its pipping call. **P:** Hayden Lake Route, *Coeur d'Alene Area, *St. Maries to Harrison Route, *Heyburn SP, Winchester Lake SP. **C:** McCall (DA: 43, A-4), near Sage Hen Reservoir (DA: 43, C-4) lower portions of Salmon River side-drainages downstream of North Fork (DA: 53, B-6), Corn Creek Campground (unmarked, but near DA:53, B-4, ask local FS for better directions).

Bewick's Wren—becoming more abundant and widespread throughout the state. Now common in Clearwater and St. Joe river drainages, most often April–June and October–February. Sightings have been increasing in the southwestern and southeastern portions of the state. **P:** St. Maries to Harrison Route, Heyburn SP, *Coyote Gulch, Lewiston Area, *Heart of the Monster.

Blue-gray Gnatcatcher—uncommon and local nester in riparian willows, cottonwoods, or junipers across the Intermountain Semidesert. Present at least April–August. **SW:** Boise Area, Jump Creek, North Fork Owyhee River. **SE:** Craters of the Moon National Monument, Sand Creek WMA, Wolverine Canyon Route, *Mink Creek Route, Cedar Ridge Route, Big Canyon to Knox Canyon Route, Minidoka NWR, City of Rocks National Reserve, Curlew National Grassland.

Varied Thrush—common and widespread nester (March–October) in mixed conifer forest in northern-most Panhandle, decreasing in abundance southward to central mountains. Uncommon to rare migrant (March–April, October–December) and winterer elsewhere. Nesting birds may be resident in some places or in some years. Often found in the same habitat as Chestnut-backed Chickadees. Varied Thrushes can be tough to locate on breeding grounds because of thick cover and shy behavior. Most easily found when birds sing at dawn and dusk, especially in March–June period. **P:** *Smith Creek, Chain Lakes Route, McCrosky SP, *Moscow Mountain Route, Craig Mountain WMA. **C:** *Elk City Area, Bear Basin, Ponderosa SP, Cascade Reservoir—West Side Route. **SW:** Boise Area (winter), Deer Flat NWR (winter), Snake River Birds of Prey Area (winter), C.J. Strike WMA (winter), Bruneau Dunes SP (winter). **SE:** Springfield Ponds (winter), The Bottoms (migration).

Northern Mockingbird—very rare irregular nester, visitor, and winterer statewide. Apparently increasing in the southwest, where it has been almost annual in the 1990s. **SW:** Boise Area (winter), *Mayfield Route (nesting), intersection of Poison Creek Road and Shoofly Road (DA: 25, C-4, nesting), Hagerman WMA (winter).

Migrant Warblers—13 warblers regularly breed in Idaho, with Yellow, Yellow-rumped, MacGillivray's, and Common Yellowthroat being most abundant and widespread. Ten additional warblers have been recorded as rare or casual migrants. A few of these, such as Tennessee, Palm, and Black-and-white, are undoubtedly more regular than currently appreciated. Tennessee and Black-and-white may even turn out to be local nesters. Peak warbler numbers appear in mid-May and late August. Most of this diffuse migration goes unnoticed, however, because of Idaho's paucity of known "migrant traps" and of birders. If you want to work migrant warblers, the best single spot would be **SE:** *Camas NWR.

Virginia's Warbler—uncommon and local nester (May–July) in junipers and Chokecherries in southeast Idaho. **SE:** Wolverine Canyon Route, *Mink Creek Route, Cedar Ridge Route, Big Canyon to Knox Canyon Route, *City of Rocks National Reserve.

Black-throated Gray Warbler—uncommon nester (May–August) in juniper habitat south of Snake River Plain. **SW:** *North Fork Owyhee River. **SE:** *Mink Creek Route, Cedar Ridge Route, *City of Rocks National Reserve.

American Redstart—uncommon nester in Panhandle (May–August), rare and local nester elsewhere. Nests in wet deciduous forest, most often in patches of Quaking Aspen surrounded by conifers. **P:** Kootenai NWR, *Sandpoint to Beyond Hope Route, *Hoodoo Valley Route, *Chain Lakes Route, St. Maries to Harrison Route, Heyburn SP, St. Joe Route, *Wilderness Gateway Campground. **C:** Bear Basin, Cascade Reservoir—West Side Route, Morgan Creek to Panther Creek Route. **SE:** Grays Lake NWR.

Northern Waterthrush—uncommon and local nester (May–July) in Panhandle. May also be a rare nester in east-central and southeast Idaho. Rare migrant elsewhere. Breeds in wet (often flooded) cottonwood forest along large rivers or lakes. **P:** *Sandpoint to Beyond Hope Route, *St. Maries to Harrison Route, *Heyburn SP, St. Joe Route. **C:** Challis Area. **SE:** Henrys Lake, Camas NWR (migration).

Black-throated Sparrow—uncommon to rare (numbers fluctuate year to year) and very local nester, April–July in southern-most Idaho. Found in extensive patches of large sagebrush in very dry shrub-steppe habitat, often on south-facing hillsides. **SW:** along US 95 from French John Hill to Oregon border (DA: 24, A-1), *Triangle Road near Oreana (DA: 24, B-3), North Fork Owyhee River, *Snake River Birds of Prey Area, Tom Draw (DA: 24, B-3, the creek 3 miles south of Swan Falls Dam), Bruneau Dunes SP. **SE:** City of Rocks National Reserve, Curlew National Grassland.

Sage Sparrow—common but local nester in shrub-steppe habitat across Intermountain Semidesert, March–August. Most abundant in extensive tracts of sagebrush. **C:** Crane Creek Reservoir Route. **SW:** North Fork Owyhee River, *Snake River Birds of Prey Area, *Silver City Area, Bruneau Dunes SP. **SE:** *sagebrush along US 20 between Arco and Craters of the Moon National Monument (DA: 38, C-3), Camas NWR, Bear Lake NWR.

Lark Bunting—irregular summer visitor and breeder that irrupts into Idaho once or twice a decade. When present, this species might be found anywhere in southeast shrub-steppe or grassland habitats. Most records are from May–July.

Grasshopper Sparrow—uncommon and local in widely scattered locations statewide, April–July. Most grasslands used have a few scattered shrubs (often sagebrush). **P:** Coyote Gulch, Lewiston Area. **C:** Whitebird Battlefield, Crane Creek Reservoir Route, *Midvale Route. **SW:** Blacks Creek Reservoir Route, *Mayfield Route. **SE:** *Camas NWR, Minidoka NWR, Oxford Slough.

Swamp Sparrow—rare, local, and irregular late-fall migrant and occasional winterer in Panhandle and southwest, recorded about 15 times. All sightings were in flooded brush and cattails near unfrozen water, November 1–April 1. **P:** St. Maries to Harrison Route, *Heyburn SP. **SW:** Deer Flat NWR, *Ted Trueblood WMA, C.J. Strike WMA, Bruneau Dunes SP, Hagerman WMA.

White-throated Sparrow—rare but annual migrant (April, October–December) and occasional winterer statewide, most often found mixed with large flocks of White-crowneds. **P:** Heyburn SP, Moscow Mountain Route, Coyote Gulch. **SW:** Fort Boise WMA, Boise Area, *Deer Flat NWR, *Marsing Area, Jump Creek, Ted Trueblood WMA, Hagerman WMA, Niagara Springs WMA. **SE:** Springfield Ponds.

Harris's Sparrow—rare but annual migrant (April, October–December) and winterer statewide. Should be looked for in the same areas as those listed for White-throated.

Golden-crowned Sparrow—rare and irregular migrant (May, October–December) statewide, most often found in southwest. Should be looked for in the same areas as those listed for White-throated.

Lapland Longspur—rare and local late fall (October–November) migrant in Panhandle and east-central Idaho. Very uncommon, local, and irregular migrant and winterer (November–March) on Snake River Plain. Most often found in Horned Lark flocks. Listen for Lapland's distinct rattle. **P:** Cabinet Mountain Lakes, *Sandpoint to Beyond Hope Route. **SW:** *Blacks Creek Reservoir Route, Indian Creek Reservoir, near Fairfield/Bellevue/Gooding (DA: 27). **SE:** Henrys Lake, *Michaud Flats (DA: 29, C-6).

Snow Bunting—uncommon winter (November–March) visitor statewide. Annual in small numbers (fewer than five) at **P:** Sandpoint to Beyond Hope Route, rare and irregular elsewhere in Panhandle. Regular in larger (30 to 100 birds), widely scattered flocks in east-central and southern Idaho. Almost all records are from October–March. **C:** Cascade Reservoir—East Side Route, *Lemhi River Route, *Pahsimeroi River Route. **SW:** Boise Foothills, Blacks Creek Reservoir Route, Snake River Birds of Prey Area, near Grandview (DA: 25, C-4), near Fairfield (DA: 26, A-3), *Silver Creek Preserve. **SE:** *Teton Valley Route, Minidoka NWR.

Rose-breasted Grosbeak—rare migrant statewide, with about 20 records. Most sightings are in May on the Snake River Plain or at feeders in Ketchum (DA: 37, C-5).

Blue Grosbeak—rare summer visitor and occasional nester in south. Recorded about 12 times, May–August. You might try looking in suitable brushy ravine habitat near Glenns Ferry (DA: 26, C-2), where the species has previously nested.

Indigo Bunting—rare migrant statewide, reported about 15 times, mostly in May in the southern third of Idaho. Overall, however, there is little pattern evident from past sightings.

Bobolink—uncommon and very local in widely scattered colonies statewide. Present late May to early August, but easiest to find mid-June to early July by listening for displaying males in early morning. All Idaho colonies are small (<10 males) and tenuous. Recent housing developments have eliminated several sites in hay meadows, while grain harvest often disrupts colonies in wheatfields. **P:** *Sandpoint to Beyond Hope Route, Chain Lakes Route, St. Maries to Harrison Route. **C:** *Elk City Area, Big Creek Meadows (DA: 43, A-4, approximately 1 mile east of New Meadows), *Cascade Reservoir—West Side Route, Hawthorne Road (DA: 30, B-1, between Sheepskin Road and Marshall Road), Lemhi River Route. **SW:** Camas Prairie Centennial Marsh. **SE:** Teton Valley Route.

Rusty Blackbird—very rare late-fall (October–January) visitor and winterer in Panhandle and southeast, with just over 10 records total. Should be looked for in mixed blackbird flocks. Only spot of repeated records is **P:** *St. Maries to Harrison Route.

Common Grackle—uncommon and local nester (April–August) in east-central and southeast Idaho. Rare visitor elsewhere, mostly April–May and August–September. **C:** *Salmon (DA: 57, C-5, especially in parks and residential areas). **SW:** Deer Flat NWR, Marsing Area, C.J. Strike WMA. **SE:** *St. Anthony (DA: 41, B-4, near the Lutheran church along ID 47 and at the park where Bus. US 20 crosses the Snake River), Rexburg (DA: 40, B-3, residential areas), Mud Lake WMA, *Teton Valley Route.

Great-tailed Grackle—recent Idaho arrival, with scattered records across the Snake River Plain during all times of the year. Still considered very rare, irregular, and local. **SW:** *Marsing Area, Burley (DA: 20, A-1, from I-84 Exit 208 to north side of Snake River, especially in parking lots and garbage dumpsters near Wendy's and Wal-Mart). **SE:** American Falls Dam.

Scott's Oriole—rare, irregular nester in southeast juniper habitat. This is Idaho's most local species, being repeatedly found only at **SE:** *Curlew National Grassland in June.

Gray-crowned Rosy-Finch—irregular, rare winterer (November–March) in Panhandle, increasingly more common and regular winterer to the south. Roosts in Cliff Swallow nests along ID 21 from Lucky Peak Dam to Idaho City (DA: 35, C-5). **P:** Willow Creek, McCrosky SP. **C:** Salmon (DA: 57, C-5),

Lemhi River Route, East Fork Salmon River (DA: 37, A-5). **SW:** *Boise Area, Snake River Birds of Prey Area, *Ketchum/Sun Valley Area, *Thousand Springs Preserve, Niagara Springs WMA. Reportedly nests in alpine areas of Pioneer Mountains east of Ketchum (see **SW**: Ketchum/Sun Valley Area).

Black Rosy-Finch—uncommon and local winterer (November–March) in central and southwest valleys. Occasionally found elsewhere mixed with Gray-crowneds. Roosts in Cliff Swallow nests along ID 21 from Lucky Peak Dam to Idaho City (DA: 35, C-5). **C:** East Fork Salmon River (DA: 37, A-5). **SW:** *Boise Area, *Ketchum/Sun Valley Area, Thousand Springs Preserve, Niagara Springs WMA. Reportedly nests in alpine areas of the Pioneer Mountains east of Ketchum (see **SW:** Ketchum/Sun Valley Area). Rare but regular during summer (June–August) along snow-fields on Borah and Leatherman Peaks (DA: 38, A-1) and at rear of Meadow Lake Campground (DA: 46, C-3).

Pine Grosbeak—uncommon to rare resident statewide. Summers in high-elevation (5,000 feet) mixed conifer forest, particularly Engelmann Spruce, Subalpine Fir, Mountain Hemlock, and Whitebark Pine. Most easily located by call. **P:** Western Selkirks, Snow Peak Trail, Moscow Mountain Route. **C:** *Elk City Area, Goose Lake, Bear Basin, Sage Hen Reservoir (DA: 43, C-4). **SW:** Trinity Recreation Area. **SE:** *Henrys Lake, Black Canyon Road Route. Some birds descend into lower river valleys during winter (November–March), frequenting deciduous trees and feeders. **P:** Bonners Ferry (DA: 62, A-3), *Schweitzer Ski Resort (DA: 62, B-2), Sandpoint to Beyond Hope Route, Silver Mountain Ski Resort (DA: 61, C-4), St. Maries to Harrison Route. **C:** Ponderosa SP, Lemhi River Route, Pahsimeroi River Route. **SE:** Kelly Canyon Ski Area (DA: 41, C-4).

Purple Finch—irregular visitor statewide, most often in southwest. Sightings peak in January and May–June. Most reports are from feeders in **P:** Coeur d'Alene (DA: 60, B-2), Lewiston (DA: 54, A-1). **C:** Salmon (DA: 57, C-5). **SW:** Boise (DA: 35, C-4).

White-winged Crossbill—resident in northern-most Panhandle (Selkirk, Cabinet, and Purcell Mountains), where abundant some years, rare others. Rare irruptive winter visitor to mixed conifer forest elsewhere. **P:** *Smith Creek, Cabinet Mountain Lakes, Sandpoint to Beyond Hope Route.

Common Redpoll—uncommon, annual winterer (November–January) south to Sandpoint, progressively rarer and more irregular to the south. **P:** Kootenai NWR, *Sandpoint to Beyond Hope Route, Moscow Mountain Route. **C:** Lemhi River Route. **SW:** Silver Creek Preserve.

Lesser Goldfinch—rare, irregular nester across Snake River Plain, April–September. A few birds have recently been reported from the Panhandle. A few pairs are annual at **SE:** *Mink Creek Route. Lesser Goldfinches have also been found at **SW:** Fort Boise WMA, *Boise Area, Snake River Birds of Prey Area.

American Birding
A S S O C I A T I O N

Join the American Birding Association

When you become a member of the American Birding Association, you join thousands of birders who are eager to improve their knowledge and skills to get the most out of their birding experiences.

- ✔ Network with friends and share the passion of birding.

- ✔ Learn more about birds and birding.

- ✔ Sharpen and augment your birding skills.

- ✔ Participate in workshops, conferences, and tours.

- ✔ Receive our full-color magazine, *Birding*, and our monthly newsletter, *Winging It*.

- ✔ Use our directory and catalogs to expand your birding horizons.

You don't have to be an expert birder to be a member of the American Birding Association. You're qualified simply by having a desire to learn more about birds, their habitats, and how to protect them.

ABA membership offers you the opportunity to meet and learn from experts and to improve your skills through our internationally attended conferences and conventions, Institute for Field Ornithology workshops, specialized tours, and volunteer opportunities. It is great way to get to know others who share your interests.

Contact ABA at 800/850-2473, or www.americanbirding.org, or PO Box 6599, Colorado Springs, CO 80934

BEST BIRDING SITES

The following chart lists the best local and state-wide birding sites, represented by three stars or four stars. This chart can help you to prioritize your site visits. Because an area may provide great birding during one time of year, but be dull in another, a separate rating is given for each season. The total rating is the cumulative score, which can be used to assess year-round birding potential. Sites not appearing in this chart are also good, but might best be birded in tandem with other locations.

SITE	SPRING	SUMR	FALL	WINTER	TOTAL *'s	PAGE
Smith Creek	N/A	* * *	* *	N/A	5	22
Kootenai Nat'l Wildlife Refuge	* * *	* * *	* * *	*	10	24
Western Selkirks	N/A	* * *	* *	N/A	5	27
Sandpoint	* * * *	* * *	* * * *	* * * *	15	33
Hoodoo Valley	* * *	* * *	*	N/A	7	37
Farragut State Park	* * *	* * *	* *	* *	10	41
Coeur d'Alene	* *	*	* *	* * *	8	46
Cataldo	* * *	* * *	* * *	* *	11	53
St. Maries to Harrison Route	* * *	* * *	* * * *	* * * *	14	59
Heyburn State Park	* * *	* *	* * * *	* * * *	13	63
St. Joe	* * *	* * *	* *	* *	10	65
Snow Peak Trail	N/A	* * *	* *	N/A	5	68
Coyote Gulch	* * *	* *	* * *	*	9	81
Lewiston	* * *	*	* * *	* * * *	11	83
Mann Lake	* * *	* *	* * * *	*	10	88
Wilderness Gateway Campgr'd	* *	* * *	* * *	N/A	8	93
Garden Gulch	* *	* * *	* *	* * *	10	97
Graves Creek	* * *	* * *	* *	*	9	100
Midvale	* * * *	* * *	* *	*	10	114
Mann Creek Reservoir	* *	* *	* * *	*	8	116
Ponderosa State Park	*	* * *	*	*	6	121
Lick Creek Road	* * *	* * *	*	*	8	122
Cascade Reservoir - East	* * *	* *	* * *	*	9	124
Cascade Reservoir - West	* * *	* *	* * *	*	9	127
North Fork Area	* * *	* * *	* *	* *	10	131
Salmon Sewage Lagoon	* * *	* *	*	*	7	134
Lemhi River	* * *	* * *	*	*	8	136
Pahsimeroi River	* *	* * *	* *	* *	9	138
Morgan Creek	* *	* * *	*	N/A	6	140
New Plymouth	* * *	* *	* *	*	8	148
Fort Boise WMA	* * * *	* * *	* * * *	* * *	14	149
Boise Area	* *	* *	* *	* * *	9	156
Pleasant Valley	* *	* *	* * *	* *	9	159
Hubbard Reservoir	* * *	* * * *	* * *	* *	12	161

SITE	SPRING	SUMR	FALL	WINTER	TOTAL *s	PAGE
Deer Flat Nat'l Wildlife Refuge	* * * *	* * *	* * * *	* * * *	15	162
Dry Lakes	* * *	* *	* * *	* *	10	165
Marsing	* * *	*	* * *	* * * *	11	167
Jump Creek	* * *	* * *	* *	*	9	169
North Fork Owyhee River	* * *	* *	* * *	* *	10	170
Mayfield	* * *	*	* *	*	7	177
Snake River Birds of Prey Area	* * * *	* *	* * *	* * * *	13	178
Silver City	* * *	* * * *	*	N/A	8	180
Ted Trueblood WMA	* * *	* * * *	* * * *	* * *	14	181
C.J. Strike WMA	* * * *	* * *	* * * *	* * *	14	182
Bruneau Dunes State Park	* * * *	* *	* * * *	* * *	13	185
Camas WMA	* * *	* * *	*	*	8	189
Ketchum/Sun Valley	* *	* * *	*	* * *	9	194
Sawtooth Valley	* *	* * *	*	*	7	198
Hagerman WMA	* *	* *	* * *	* * * *	11	202
Thousand Springs Preserve	* * *	* *	* *	* * *	10	205
Niagara Springs WMA	* * *	*	* * *	* * *	10	211
Henrys Lake	* *	* *	* * *	*	8	219
Black Canyon	N/A	* * *	* *	N/A	5	222
Harriman State Park	* * *	* * *	* *	* *	10	223
Camas Nat'l Wildlife Refuge	* * * *	* * * *	* *	* *	12	226
Mud Lake WMA	* * * *	* * *	* * *	*	11	229
Market Lake WMA	* * * *	* * *	* * *	*	11	232
Tex Creek WMA	N/A	* * *	* *	N/A	5	235
Teton Valley	* * *	* *	* * * *	* * *	12	242
Wolverine Canyon	* * *	* * *	*	N/A	7	246
Mink Creek	* * * *	* * * *	* *	* * *	13	248
Cedar Ridge	* * *	* * *	*	N/A	7	251
Springfield Ponds	* * *	*	* * *	* *	9	254
The Bottoms	* * *	* * *	* * *	* *	11	256
Sterling WMA	* * *	* * *	* * *	* *	11	258
Sportsmans Park	* * *	* * *	* * *	*	10	261
American Falls Dam	* * * *	* * * *	* * * *	* * * *	16	262
Minidoka Nat'l Wildlife Refuge	* *	* * *	* *	*	8	267
City of Rocks Nat'l Reserve	* * *	* * * *	* *	* *	11	270
Curlew National Grassland	* * *	* * *	* *	*	9	273
Oxford Slough Area	* * *	* * *	* *	*	9	284
Bear Lake Nat'l Wildlife Refuge	* * *	* * *	*	N/A	7	286

OTHER GOOD BOOKS

Birding

Burleigh, Thomas D. *Birds of Idaho.* 467 pp. 1972. Caxton Printers, Caldwell, ID. ISBN: 0-87004-208-4. Note: out-of-print.

Larrison, Earl J., Jerry L. Tucker, and Malcolm T. Jollie. *Guide to Idaho Birds.* 220 pp. 1967. Journal of the Idaho Academy of Science. Vol. V. Note: out-of-print.

Roberts, Hadley B. *Birds of East Central Idaho.* 119 pp. 1992. Northwest Printing, Boise, ID. ISBN: 0-9634903-0-3. Available from ABA Sales and IDFG.

Stephens, Daniel, and Shirley Sturts. *Idaho Bird Distribution.* 76 pp. 1991. Idaho Museum of Natural History, Idaho State University, Pocatello, ID. Available from IDFG.

Sturts, Shirley Horning, and S. Shultz. *Birds and Birding Routes of the Idaho Panhandle.* 63 pp. 1993. Self-published. Copies can be purchased from IDFG or Idaho Panhandle National Forests, PO Box 310, Coeur d'Alene, ID 83544 (telephone 208/667-2561).

Flora and Fauna

(For information about Idaho's mammals, amphibians, reptiles, wildflowers, and butterflies, the National Audubon Society Field Guides and the Peterson Field Guides are your best bets.)

Carpenter, Leslie Benjamin. *Idaho Wildlife Viewing Guide.* 104 pp. 1990. Falcon Press Publishing Co., Helena and Billings, MT. ISBN: 1-56044-021-X. Available from ABA Sales and IDFG.

Johnson, Frederic. *Wild Trees of Idaho.* 212 pp. 1995. University of Idaho Press. ISBN: 0-89301-145-2.

Travel Guides

Alt, David D., and Donald W. Hyndman. *Roadside Geology of Idaho.* 393 pp. 1989. Mountain Press Publishing Company, Missoula, MT. ISBN: 0-87842-219-6.

Conley, Cort. *Idaho for the Curious.* 704 pp. 1982. Backeddy Books, Cambridge, ID. ISBN: 0-903566-3-0.

Derig, Betty. *Roadside History of Idaho.* 362 pp. 1996. Mountain Press Publishing Company, Missoula, MT. ISBN: 0 87842-328-1.

Fanselow, Julie. *Idaho—Off the Beaten Path.* 145 pp. 1995. The Globe Pequot Press, Old Saybrook, CT. ISBN: 1-56440-637-7.

Gottberg, John. *Idaho.* 285 pp. 1996. Compass American Guides, Oakland, CA. ISBN: 1-878-86778-4.

Harris, Richard. *Hidden Idaho: the adventurer's guide.* 292 pp. 1996. Ulysses Press, Berkeley, CA. ISBN: 1-56975-038-6.

Huegel, Tony. *Idaho Off-Road: back-country drives for the whole family.* 96 pp. 1993. The Post Co., Idaho Falls, ID. ISBN: 0-9636560-0-7.

Loftus, Bill. *Idaho Handbook* (2nd Edition). 282 pp. 1994. Moon Publications, Inc., Chico, CA. ISBN: 1-56691-061-7.

London, Bill, and Charlie Powell. *Natural Wonders of Idaho: a guide to parks, preserves, and wild places.* 145 pp. 1994. Country Roads Press, Castine, ME. ISBN: 1-56626-059-0.

London, Bill. *Country Roads of Idaho.* 147 pp. 1995. Country Roads Press, Castine, ME. ISBN: 1-56626-069-8.

Hiking, Fishing, and Rafting

Amaral, Grant. *Idaho—The Whitewater State: a guidebook.* 315 pp. 1990. Bookcrafters, Chelsea, MI. ISBN: 0-9622344-0-0.

Fuller, Margaret. *Trails of Western Idaho* (Revised Edition). 271 pp. 1992. Signpost Books, Edmonds, WA. ISBN: 0-9131140-48-1.

Landers, Rich, and Idaho Rowe Dolphin and the Spokane Mountaineers. *100 Hikes in the Inland Northwest.* 256 pp. 1992. The Mountaineers, Seattle, WA. ISBN: 0-89886-130-6.

Lopez, Tom. *Exploring Idaho's Mountains: a guide for climbers, scramblers, and hikers.* 288 pp. 1990. The Mountaineers, Seattle, WA. ISBN: 0-89886-235-3.

Manghan, Ralph, and Jackie Johnson Manghan. *Hiking Idaho* (formerly *The Hiker's Guide to Idaho*). 342 pp. 1995. Falcon Press Publishing Co., Helena and Billings, MT. ISBN: 1-56044-469-X.

Retallic, Ken, and Rocky Barker. *Fly Fisher's Guide to Idaho.* 368 pp. 1996. Wilderness Adventures Press, Gallatin Gateway, MT. ISBN: 1-885106-30-0.

IDAHO'S NONGAME
WILDLIFE PROGRAM

The Nongame Wildlife Program of the Idaho Department of Fish and Game (IDFG) was launched in July 1982 as a result of legislative action establishing a nongame checkoff connected to the state income tax. Nongame activities are generally grouped into three categories: information and education; research, monitoring, and management; and advertisement and promotion.

The Nongame Wildlife Program depends on public support and voluntary contributions through tax checkoff and wildlife license plate purchase. The program helped in the production of the *Idaho Wildlife Viewing Guide* describing 94 of the best and most easily accessible general wildlife viewing sites in the state. This project has helped to popularize the "binocular logo" placed at the viewing sites. The IDFG Nongame Wildlife Program has prepared a series of "nongame leaflets," several of which are on birds.

Other popular bird-related projects of the Nongame Wildlife Program include the annual Nongame Poster Contest for children from kindergarten through sixth grade; a Backyard for Wildlife Award to acknowledge the efforts of homeowners to enhance their properties; establishment and support of regional raptor rehabilitation centers for sick and injured raptors; and construction and distribution of raptor platforms, bird feeders (e.g., at nursing homes), bluebird nestboxes, American Kestrel nestboxes, and shelters for other wildlife.

The IDFG Nongame Wildlife Program also plays an important role in Idaho's Partners in Flight (PIF). This broad bird conservation network is striving to develop the best management practices for vital habitats in the state, such as riparian and shrub-steppe. Idaho PIF not only focuses on a broad avian conservation and management issues, but also the popularization of bird appreciation.

Each year thousands of Idaho taxpayers and concerned citizens donate to the Nongame Wildlife Program on their tax forms, through direct contributions to the Nongame Trust Fund, or by purchasing a wildlife license plate for their vehicle. This support allows the Program to continue efforts for nongame birds and other wildlife. The Nongame Program needs continued support to work toward protecting and preserving Idaho's wildlife and educating citizens about the natural world around them.

For more information on the Nongame Wildlife Program, visit www2.state.id or write to IDFG, Nongame Wildlife Program, PO Box 25, Boise, ID 83707. Or visit IDFG's home page on the Internet at http://www2.state.id.us/fishgame/fishgame.html.

PLANTS AND ANIMALS

(other than birds) mentioned in this book

Plants

alder . . . . *Alnus* spp.
Big Sagebrush . . . . . *Artemisia tridentata*
bitterbrush . . . . *Purshia* spp.
Black Cottonwood . . . *Populus trichocarpa*
Blazing Star . . . . . . *Mentzelia laevicaulis*
Bluebunch Wheatgrass *Agropyron spicatum*
bulrush . . . . *Scirpus* spp.
cattail . . . . *Typha* spp.
Cheatgrass . . . . *Bromus tectorum*
Chokecherry . . . . . . *Prunus virginiana*
columbine . . . . *Aquilegia* spp.
Common Camas. . . . . *Camassia quamash*
Common Reed Grass. *Phragmites communis*
Common Snowberry. *Symphoricarpos albus*
cottonwood . . . . *Populus* spp.
Douglas-fir. . . . . *Pseudotsuga menziesii*
Engelmann Spruce . . . . *Picea engelmannii*
Grand Fir . . . . *Abies grandis*
Idaho Fescue. . . . . . . *Festuca idahoensis*
hawthorn . . . . *Crataegus* spp.
huckleberry . . . . *Vaccinium* spp.
lilac. . . . . *Syringa* spp.
Limber Pine . . . . *Pinus flexilis*
Lodgepole Pine. . . . . . . *Pinus contorta*
Mallow Ninebark. . *Physocarpus malvaceus*
Medusahead Wildrye *Taeniatherum asperum*
Mountain Hemlock . . . *Tsuga mertensiana*
Curl-leaf Mountain Mahogany . . . .
. . . . *Cercocarpus ledifolius*
Oceanspray. . . . . . . *Holodiscus discolor*
Pinyon Pine. . . . . . . *Pinus monophylla*
Poison-Ivy . . . . *Toxicodendron radicans*
Ponderosa Pine . . . . . *Pinus ponderosa*
Quaking Aspen . . . . . *Populus tremuloides*
rabbitbrush . . . . . . *Chrysothamnus* spp.
Red-oiser Dogwood . . . *Cornus stolonifera*
Rocky Mountain Juniper . . . .
. . . . *Juniperus scopularum*
rose . . . . *Rosa* spp.
rushes . . . . (see bulrush)
Russian-olive . . . . . *Elaeagnus angustifolia*
sagebrush . . . . *Artemisia* spp.
sedge. . . . . *Carex* spp.
Serviceberry . . . . . *Amelanchier alnifolia*
Subalpine Fir . . . . *Abies lasiocarpa*
Subalpine Larch . . . . *Larix lyallii*
sumac. . . . . *Rhus* spp.
Teasel . . . . *Dipsacus sylvestris*
Utah Juniper. . . . . *Juniperus osteosperma*

Western Hemlock. . . . *Tsuga heterophylla*
Western Juniper . . . *Juniperus occidentalis*
Western Larch . . . . . . *Larix occidentalis*
Western Redcedar. . . . . . . *Thuja plicata*
Western White Pine . . . . *Pinus monticola*
Whitebark Pine . . . . *Pinus albicaulis*
whortleberry . . . . *Vaccinium* spp.
Wild Rice . . . . *Zizania aquatica*
willow. . . . . *Salix* spp.

Animals

Bighorn Sheep . . . . *Ovis canadensis*
Black Bear . . . . *Ursus americanus*
bumblebee . . . .
. . . . . *Hymenoptera: Bombinae: Bombini*
butterfly . . . . *Lepidoptera*
carp . . . . *Cyprinus carpio*
Chinook Salmon *Oncorhynchus tshawytscha*
Columbian Ground Squirrel. . . . .
. . . . *Citellus columbianus*
Coyote. . . . . *Canis latrans*
American Elk (Wapiti). . . . *Cervus elaphus*
Gray Wolf . . . . *Canis lupis*
Great Basin Gopher Snake . . . .
. . . . *Pituophis melanoleucus deserticola*
Grizzly Bear . . . . *Ursus arctos*
Kokanee Salmon . . . *Oncorhynchus nerka*
Long-toed Salamander . . . .
. . . . *Ambystoma macrodactylum*
Moose . . . . *Alces alces*
Mountain Goat . . . *Oreamnos americanus*
Mountain Lion . . . . *Felis concolor*
Mule Deer . . . . . . *Odocoileus hemionus*
Pacific Treefrog. . . . . *Hyla regilla*
Pronghorn. . . . . . *Antilocapra americana*
River Otter . . . . *Lutra canadensis*
scorpion . . . . . *Scorpionidae: Vaejovidae*
sphinx moth . . . . *Lepidoptera: Sphingidae*
Spotted Frog . . . . *Rana pretiosa*
Steelhead . . . . . *Oncorhynchus mykiss*
Western Fence Lizard. . . . .
. . . . *Sceloporus occidentalis*
Western Pine Beetle. . . . .
Coleoptera: Scolytidae: Dendroctonus brevicomis
Western Rattlesnake . . . . *Crotalus viridis*
Western Toad. . . . . *Bufo boreas*
White-tailed Deer. . *Odocoileus virginianus*
Woodland Caribou . . . . *Rangifer caribou*

INDEX

A

Aberdeen 259, 261
Accentor
  Siberian 147, 298
Adams Gulch (Ketchum) 196
Alexander Reservoir 278, 308
Alturas Lake 199
American Falls 251, 253-254, 261, 263-266
American Falls Dam 303, 306-309, 317, 321
American Falls Reservoir 259, 261, 307
Ann Morrison Park (Boise) 157
Arco 218
Ashton 223, 225-226
Athol 41
Atomic City 304
Avocet
  American 5, 48, 83, 86, 88-89, 117, 135, 144,
    149-150, 161, 163, 166, 171, 173, 176, 181,
    183, 188-189, 200, 203, 207, 228, 231, 254,
    279, 281, 285, 287, 293

B

Baker 136
Banks 305
Bannock Pass 136-137
Barber Park (Boise) 157
Beach
  Nude 105
Bear Basin 119-120, 304, 310-311, 313-315, 318
Bear Lake National Wildlife Refuge 287, 302,
    306-308, 315, 321
Bear Lake State Park 288
Bell Rapid 203
Ben Ross Reservoir 115
Benewah Lake 64
Big Canyon 253-254, 311-315
Big Creek Meadows 317
Big Lost River Valley 216, 307
Bittern
  American 25, 37, 55-58, 66-67, 191, 193, 204,
    217, 228, 231-232, 234, 281, 287, 291, 306
Black Canyon 222, 305, 311, 318, 321
Black Pine Mountains 310
Blackbird
  Brewer's 14-15, 168, 188, 253, 300
  Red-winged 14-15, 37, 48, 52, 55, 90, 145, 157,
    168, 206, 209, 213, 224, 259, 267, 275, 300
  Rusty 59, 300, 317
  Yellow-headed 3, 14-15, 37, 55, 107, 126, 136,
    139, 145, 157, 168, 186, 193, 204, 206, 213,
    221, 224, 241, 259, 267, 275, 300
Blackfoot 307
Blackfoot Reservoir 277, 304, 306-307, 310
Blacks Creek 175
Blacks Creek Reservoir 173, 177, 302, 304,
    306-308, 310, 316
Blanchard 40
Blanchard Lake 39-40, 306

Bluebird
  Mountain 3, 14, 32, 37, 41-42, 54, 57, 67, 70,
    73, 82, 90-91, 100, 120, 126, 128, 132, 142,
    154, 169, 172, 175, 180, 188, 191, 197,
    200-201, 218, 224, 243, 249, 252-253, 275,
    282, 297
  Western 37, 40-42, 73-75, 77-78, 82, 86,
    90-92, 100, 187, 297
Bobolink 33, 35, 39-40, 54, 105, 127-128, 136, 139,
    243, 300, 317
Bobwhite
  Northern 291, 305
Bogus Basin Ski Resort 153
Boise 156, 159, 170, 173, 175-177, 303, 307,
    309-311, 313-314, 316, 318, 320
Boise Foothills 153, 304-305, 307, 310-311, 313, 316
Boise Front Recreation Area 155
Boise Greenbelt 156-158
Bonners Ferry 23, 25-27, 318
Brambling 300
Brant 85, 289
Brundage Reservoir 117
Bruneau 182
Bruneau Dunes State Park 185-186, 302, 306,
    314-316, 321
Bufflehead 47-48, 50-51, 54, 59, 79, 85, 122, 126,
    213, 230, 290
Bunting
  Indigo 142, 300, 317
  Lark 299, 316
  Lazuli 3-4, 13, 36-37, 54, 68, 77, 82, 101, 107,
    109, 111, 116, 132, 139, 142, 155, 158, 163,
    169-170, 172, 175, 177, 179-180, 182, 186,
    188, 193, 196, 199, 203, 206, 210, 217, 228,
    235, 238-239, 241, 247, 250, 253, 272,
    300
  Snow 33, 55, 115, 126, 137, 139, 147, 153, 169,
    175-176, 179, 191, 193, 198, 217, 243-244,
    269, 300, 316
Bureau of Land Management 2, 9, 16, 18, 47-48, 53,
    90, 101, 110-111, 113-114, 117, 136-137, 139,
    153, 155-156, 160, 169-170, 172-173,
    175-179, 181, 216-217, 239, 247, 251-252,
    254, 275, 277-278, 282-283, 307, 309-311
Bureau of Reclamation 16, 116, 126, 128, 256-257,
    259, 261, 265
Burgdorf 310
Burley 317
Bushtit 14, 154, 170, 272, 297, 314

C

C.J. Strike Wildlife Management Area 182, 186,
    302-303, 306, 308-309, 314, 317, 321
Cabinet Mountain Lakes 31, 304, 311-313, 316, 318
Calder 68
Caldwell 149, 151, 170, 180
Camas National Wildlife Refuge 226, 229, 302,
    306-310, 315, 321
Camas Prairie Centennial Marsh Wildlife Manage-
    ment Area 189, 302, 317, 321
Cambridge 114-115

Abbreviated Table of Contents

Godwit
    Hudsonian 264, 293
    Marbled 33, 54, 89, 135, 149-150, 164, 166, 171,
       176, 181, 183, 207, 234, 257, 261, 264, 279,
       293, 308
Goldburg 139
Goldeneye
    Barrow's 25, 35, 42, 47, 51, 58-59, 66, 80, 85,
       107, 115-116, 126, 135, 144, 149, 163-164,
       168, 171, 186, 200, 203, 213, 219, 224, 243,
       265-266, 279, 281, 290, 303
    Common 37, 47, 50-51, 59, 79, 85, 119,
       122-123, 126, 168, 203, 213, 226, 230, 243,
       266, 269, 279, 290
Golden-Plover
    American 33, 89, 117, 150, 163, 166, 173, 176,
       181, 183, 234, 257, 261, 264, 292, 308
Goldfinch
    American 13, 15, 58, 80, 85-86, 97, 109, 116,
       139, 149, 193, 204, 209, 249-250, 301
    Lesser 5, 151, 158, 179, 248-250, 301, 318
Goose
    Bar-headed 196
    Canada 13-14, 25, 35, 47-48, 55, 62, 71, 79, 85,
       111, 128, 135, 139, 148, 156, 168, 189, 213,
       228, 266, 269, 275, 289
    Emperor 289
    Greater White-fronted 25, 85, 88, 149-150,
       164, 173, 289
    Ross's 35, 88, 113, 115, 135, 148-150, 164, 183,
       204, 228-230, 234, 256, 289, 302
    Snow 88, 105, 111, 113, 115, 135, 148, 150,
       228-229, 234, 256, 275, 289
Goose Lake 117, 119, 304-306, 310-311, 318
Goshawk
    Northern 6, 13, 29, 42, 69-71, 75, 77, 91, 100,
       111, 116, 119, 150, 154, 164, 179, 188, 193,
       196, 198, 200-201, 206, 221-222, 225, 232,
       238, 250, 256, 260, 281, 292, 307
Grackle
    Common 164, 168, 185, 230, 243, 300, 317
    Great-tailed 5, 167-168, 300, 317
Grandmother Mountain 305
Grandview 181-182, 303
Grangeville 101, 105-108, 110, 313
Graves Creek 100-101, 304, 312, 320
Grays Lake National Wildlife Refuge 279, 302-303,
    307-308, 315
Grebe
    Clark's 5, 15, 52, 89, 127, 135, 163-164, 166,
       173, 183, 199, 205-206, 215, 230, 234,
       256-257, 266-267, 277, 285, 287, 291, 306
    Eared 15, 85-86, 89, 135, 144, 189, 200, 228,
       234, 257, 267, 281, 287, 291
    Horned 15, 39, 44, 47, 51, 57, 63, 85-86, 89,
       116, 135, 291
    Pied-billed 15, 37, 48, 54-55, 57, 63, 78, 89, 98,
       135, 173, 193, 204, 210, 228, 234, 241,
       267, 291
    Red-necked 3, 6, 15, 25, 35, 37, 39, 42-45,
       47-48, 51, 63-64, 89, 117, 119, 123, 126,
       135, 166, 199, 219, 223-224, 291, 306
    Western 15, 35, 51, 57, 78, 85-86, 89, 98, 115,
       126-127, 135, 168, 173, 183, 191, 199, 206,
       215, 228, 230, 234, 241, 257, 266-267,
       275, 277-279, 285, 291
Green Canyon Pass Road 311
Grosbeak
    Black-headed 3, 13, 29, 42, 44-45, 52, 57, 59,
       67-68, 73, 77, 82, 86, 89, 96-98, 101, 107,
       116, 121, 132, 136, 142, 151, 154, 158, 163,
       169, 172, 175, 177, 179-183, 186, 193-194,
       196, 199, 228, 230, 235, 238, 244, 247,
       250, 257, 300
    Blue 300, 317
    Evening 15, 37, 40, 51, 75, 132, 199, 211, 221,
       247, 301
    Pine 3, 6, 27, 29, 31-32, 35, 52, 61, 65, 68-69,
       73, 77, 79, 105-106, 119-120, 137, 139, 154,
       186, 188, 200, 221-222, 300, 318
    Rose-breasted 300
Grouse
    Blue 5, 13, 29, 69, 75, 92, 103, 111, 119, 140,
       142, 153-154, 175, 189, 196-197, 222, 235,
       238, 250, 272, 290, 305
    Ruffed 3, 13-14, 41, 47, 62, 70, 74-75, 94, 99,
       119, 123, 132, 175, 197, 226, 235, 237, 241,
       249-250, 290
    Sharp-tailed 5, 14-15, 113, 115, 235, 237, 239,
       249-250, 252, 275, 282-283, 290, 305
    Spruce 5, 13, 21, 23, 27, 29, 32, 106, 119-120,
       129, 187, 196-197, 199-200, 290, 304
Gull
    Bonaparte's 33, 35, 59, 79, 116, 135, 161, 163,
       166, 183, 186, 200, 264, 294
    California 14-15, 50, 157, 161, 183, 189, 221,
       234, 261, 265, 267, 269, 277, 294
    Franklin's 5, 33, 59, 135, 161, 163, 166, 181,
       183, 193, 215, 221, 231, 234, 281, 284-285,
       287, 294
    Glaucous 21, 33, 35, 48, 50, 52, 157, 265, 294,
       309
    Glaucous-winged 21, 50, 52, 157, 294, 309
    Herring 21, 48, 50, 52, 157, 161, 163, 166, 181,
       183, 185-186, 266, 294
    Iceland 33, 85, 294
    Lesser Black-backed 294
    Little 33, 294
    Mew 21, 33, 50, 52, 87, 265, 294, 309
    Ring-billed 14-15, 33, 50, 54, 79, 157, 161, 183,
       189, 221, 234, 261, 265, 267, 277, 294
    Ross's 294
    Sabine's 33, 163, 183, 264, 294
    Slaty-backed 294
    Thayer's 21, 50, 157, 183, 265, 294, 309
    Western 183, 234, 294
Gyrfalcon 147, 164, 193, 234, 292, 308

Pleasant Valley 304, 307, 309-310, 320
Plover
    Black-bellied 89, 150, 163, 166, 176, 183, 234, 261, 264, 292
    Mountain 292
    Semipalmated 54, 89, 161, 292
    Snowy 33, 89, 163, 166, 176, 257, 261, 264, 292, 308
Pocatello 248, 250, 307, 313
Pocatello Creek Road 312-313
Pollock 110-111, 304-305, 307, 310-311
Ponderosa State Park 121, 123, 310, 313-314, 318, 320
Poorwill
    Common 14, 92, 154, 163, 171-172, 175, 180, 197, 246-247, 250, 275, 295
Post Falls 47, 304, 308-309
Potlatch 77
Priest Lake 27, 30
Priest River 27, 30
Ptarmigan
    White-tailed 29, 290
Pygmy-Owl
    Northern 33, 41, 44, 48, 52, 54, 58, 62, 65, 67, 70-71, 76, 79, 111, 119-120, 122, 154, 156, 158, 175, 196, 200, 225, 250, 272, 295, 310

Q

Quail
    California 5, 13-15, 82, 85-86, 95-97, 107, 113, 115, 154, 177, 202, 209, 213, 291
    Gambel's 5, 103, 136, 291, 305
    Mountain 5, 103, 110-111, 290, 305

R

Raft River Valley 307
Rail
    Virginia 5, 15, 35, 37, 48, 78, 80, 85, 144-145, 150, 155, 157, 182, 193, 200-201, 204, 207, 228, 234, 255, 259, 265, 281, 285, 287, 292
    Yellow 292
Ramsey Transfer Station (Coeur d'Alene) 50
Rapid River 111
Rathdrum Prairie 304, 308-310
Raven
    Common 13-15, 32, 71, 119, 123, 132, 153, 179, 188, 191, 206, 224, 226, 250, 272, 275, 281, 297
Red River 106
Red River Wildlife Management Area 106

Redhead 85, 168, 189, 213, 230, 275, 285, 290
Redpoll
    Common 3, 26, 44, 77, 97, 137, 193, 198, 301, 318
    Hoary 301
Redstart
    American 3, 26, 36-37, 58, 62-63, 67, 93-94, 120, 127, 142, 164, 179, 186, 234, 281, 299, 315
Rexburg 317
Riggins 108, 110-111
Robin
    American 13, 15, 183, 209, 211, 224, 249, 255, 257, 260, 265-266, 272, 298
Rock Creek Park (Twin Falls) 209
Roman Nose Lakes 26, 311
Rose Lake 56-57
Rosy-Finch
    Black 5, 13, 147, 156, 158, 179, 194, 196-198, 211, 217, 300, 318
    Gray-crowned 13, 73, 75, 137, 158, 169, 179, 194, 196-198, 211, 217, 244, 300, 317
Round Lake 306
Round Valley 308
Ruff 293

S

Sage Hen Reservoir 311, 314, 318
Sage-Grouse
    Greater 5, 15, 113-115, 136, 138-139, 142, 187, 189, 197, 231, 237, 239, 281, 290, 304
Salmon 131, 133, 136-137, 313, 317-318
Salmon River 90, 101, 108, 111, 132, 140, 142
Salmon River, East Fork 304, 318
Salmon Sewage Lagoon 135, 302-303, 320
Sand Creek Wildlife Management Area 239, 302, 304, 314
Sanderling 89, 164, 176, 264, 283, 293
Sandpiper
    Baird's 89, 144, 150, 161, 164, 166, 176, 181, 200, 217, 231, 257, 261, 283, 293
    Buff-breasted 293
    Least 40, 89, 135, 144, 161, 166, 176, 200, 217, 231, 261, 283, 293
    Pectoral 54, 58, 150, 161, 164, 166, 181, 231, 293
    Semipalmated 40, 54, 89, 161, 164, 166, 293
    Sharp-tailed 293
    Solitary 54-55, 89, 98-100, 114, 135, 144, 150, 161, 163, 166, 173, 181, 183, 293
    Spotted 54, 68, 71, 86, 89, 93, 106, 109, 144, 149, 188, 200, 231, 293
    Stilt 26, 89, 114, 161, 164, 166, 183, 234, 254, 257, 261, 264, 293, 308
    Upland 40, 293, 308
    Western 40, 48, 54, 89, 144, 161, 164, 166, 176, 200, 217, 231, 257, 261, 283, 293
    White-rumped 293
Sandpoint 31-33, 37, 39, 302-304, 306, 308-312, 315-318, 320
Sapsucker
    Red-breasted 295
    Red-naped 3, 13, 32, 36-37, 45, 47, 52, 54, 62-63, 80, 90-91, 99, 120, 123, 127, 136, 145, 163, 180, 187, 193, 196, 198-199, 222, 224-225, 235, 241, 245, 249-250, 252-253, 295

Abbreviated Table of Contents

About the Artist

Mike Denny was born in Klamath Falls, Oregon. Most of his early years were spent in Zambia and Malawi where, with the help of his parents, he developed a passion for natural history in general and birds in particular. This is also where he first started drawing the animals he encountered on his many safaris into the local bush. By his fourteenth birthday he and the family were back in the Pacific Northwest. Mike graduated from high school in Caldwell, Idaho. He entered college in 1978 to work on a major in Biology with an Art minor. It was in college that his artistic interests were boosted by several superb teachers.

Mike and his wife now live to bird in Walla Walla County, Washington. He is past President of the Blue Mountain Audubon Society, founder and compiler of the Two Rivers Christmas Bird Count, and an active member of the Oregon Field Ornithologists and the Washington Ornithological Society. He has illustrated and written numerous articles and notes for Pacific Northwest birding publications.

About the Authors

Dan Svingen (right) grew up birding on the North Dakota prairie. After completing his graduate degree, Dan worked as a wildlife biologist for a number of land management agencies in Idaho and Colorado before accepting a position as a wildlife biologist for the U.S.D.A. Forest Service back in Bismarck, North Dakota. Although Dan's past research efforts focused on waterfowl ecology and shorebird migration, his main research interest is in avian distribution. While living in Idaho, Dan was the Idaho/Western Montana Regional Editor for Field Notes, a member of the Idaho Rare Bird Committee, and chair of Idaho Partners in Flight. Dan and his wife Ila have two daughters, Emily and Elana, to keep them busy, but Dan is still finding time to work on a birder's guide to North Dakota.

Kas Dumroese (left), born and raised in Freeport, Illinois, got his start in birding from his dad and by filling feeders during the winter at Oakdale Nature Preserve. Kas moved to Idaho in 1984 and got serious, or possessed, about birding. He worked 17 years at the University of Idaho Forest Research Nursery and received his doctorate in Forest Resources. Through the university's Enrichment Program, Kas taught courses on bird feeding, landscaping for wildlife, landscaping with native plants, and birdwatching. In 2001 he joined the U.S.D.A. Forest Service as a nursery specialist. Kas has been the voice of the northern Idaho/eastern Washington bird hotline since 1993. Kas, his wife Debbie, and son Niklaas are working to convert 20 acres of the family's Palouse farmland back to native Palouse shrub-steppe.

PANHANDLE

- P-1 Smith Creek
- P-2 Kootenai National Wildlife Refuge
- P-3 Roman Nose Lakes
- P-4 Western Selkirks
- P-5 Cabinet Mountain Lakes
- P-6 Sandpoint to Beyond Hope Route
- P-7 Hoodoo Valley Route
- P-8 Blanchard Lake
- P-9 Farragut State Park
- P-10 Hayden Lake Route
- P-11.1 Coeur d'Alene: Post Falls
- P-11.2 Coeur d'Alene: US 95
- P-11.3 Coeur d'Alene: North Shore
- P-11.4 Coeur d'Alene: Wolf Lodge Bay
- P-12 Cataldo Area
- P-13 Chain Lakes Route
- P-14 St. Maries to Harrison Route
- P-15 Heyburn State Park
- P-16 St. Joe Route
- P-17 Snow Peak Trail
- P-18 Emerald Creek
- P-19 Willow Creek
- P-20 McCrosky State Park
- P-21 Moscow Mountain Route
- P-22 Spring Valley/Moose Creek Res.
- P-23 Coyote Gunch
- P-24 Lewiston Area
- P-25 Mann Lake
- P-26 Craig Mountain Wildlife Mgt Area
- P-27 Heart of the Monster
- P-28 Wilderness Gateway Campground
- P-29 Spalding Site
- P-30 Garden Gulch Route
- P-31 Winchester Lake State Park
- P-32 Graves Creek Route

CENTRAL

- C-1 Elk City Area
- C-2 Whitebird Battlefield
- C-3 Salmon River Route
- C-4 Pollock Area
- C-5 Crane Creek Reservoir Route
- C-6 Midvale Route
- C-7 Mann Creek Reservoir
- C-8 Goose Lake
- C-9 Bear Basin
- C-10 Ponderosa State Park
- C-11 Lick Creek Road Route
- C-12 Cascade Reservoir—East Side
- C-13 Cascade Reservoir—West Side
- C-14 Chamberlain Basin
- C-15 North Fork Area
- C-16 Salmon Sewage Lagoon
- C-17 Lemhi River Route
- C-18 Pahsimeroi River Valley
- C-19 Morgan Creek to Panther Creek
- C-20 Challis Area

SOUTHWESTERN

- SW-1 New Plymouth Area
- SW-2 Fort Boise Wildlife Mgt Area
- SW-3 Boise Foothills
- SW-4 Boise Area
- SW-5 Pleasant Valley Road Route
- SW-6 Hubbard Reservoir
- SW-7 Deer Flat National Wildlife Refuge
- SW-8 Dry Lakes
- SW-9 Marsing Area
- SW-10 Jump Creek
- SW-11 North Fork Owyhee River
- SW-12 Blacks Creek Reservoir Route
- SW-13 Indian Creek Reservoir
- SW-14 Mayfield Route
- SW-15 Snake River Birds of Prey Area
- SW-16 Silver City Area
- SW-17 Ted Trueblood Wildlife Mgt Area
- SW-18 C.J. Strike Wildlife Mgt Area
- SW-19 Bruneau Dunes State Park
- SW-20 Trinity Recreation Area
- SW-21 Camas Prairie Centennial Marsh
- SW-22 Silver Creek Preserve
- SW-23 Ketchum/Sun Valley Area
- SW-24 Sawtooth Valley Route
- SW-25 Hagerman Wildlife Mgt Area
- SW-26 Thousand Springs Preserve
- SW-27 Twin Falls Area
- SW-28 Niagara Springs Wildlife Mgt Area

SOUTHEASTERN

- SE-1 Mackay Reservoir / Chilly Slough
- SE-2 Craters of the Moon Nat'l Mon.
- SE-3 Henrys Lake
- SE-4 Black Canyon Road Route
- SE-5 Harriman State Park
- SE-6 Mesa Falls Route
- SE-7 Camas National Wildlife Refuge
- SE-8 Mud Lake Wildlife Mgt Area
- SE-9 Market Lake Wildlife Mgt Area
- SE-10 Tex Creek Wildlife Mgt Area
- SE-11 Sand Creek Wildlife Mgt Area
- SE-12 Teton Valley Route
- SE-13 Teton Pass
- SE-14 Wolverine Canyon Route
- SE-15 Mink Creek Route
- SE-16 Cedar Ridge Route
- SE-17 Big Canyon to Knox Canyon Route
- SE-18 Springfield Ponds
- SE-19 The Bottoms
- SE-20 Sterling Wildlife Mgt Area
- SE-21 Sportsmans Park
- SE-22 American Falls Dam
- SE-23 Massacre Rocks State Park
- SE-24 Minidoka National Wildlife Refuge
- SE-25 City of Rocks National Reserve
- SE-26 Curlew National Grassland
- SE-27 Blackfoot Reservoir Route
- SE-28 Alexander Reservoir
- SE-29 Grays Lake Nat'l Wildlife Refuge
- SE-30 Hawkins Reservoir
- SE-31 Oxford Slough Area
- SE-32 Bear Lake Nat'l Wildlife Refuge